国家豁免国内立法
和国际法律文件汇编

徐 宏 主编
马新民 副主编

中华人民共和国外交部条约法律司 审定

知识产权出版社
全国百佳图书出版单位

图书在版编目（CIP）数据

国家豁免国内立法和国际法律文件汇编／徐宏主编．
－－北京：知识产权出版社，2019.5
ISBN 978-7-5130-6207-7

Ⅰ.①国… Ⅱ.①徐… Ⅲ.①豁免权—立法—文件—汇编 Ⅳ.①D922.139

中国版本图书馆 CIP 数据核字（2019）第 071432 号

策划编辑：庞从容　　　　　　　　责任校对：谷　洋
责任编辑：薛迎春　　　　　　　　责任印制：刘译文

国家豁免国内立法和国际法律文件汇编

徐　宏　主　编
马新民　副主编

出版发行：知识产权出版社有限责任公司	网　址：http://www.ipph.cn
社　址：北京市海淀区气象路 50 号院	邮　编：100081
责编电话：010-82000860 转 8726	责编邮箱：pangcongrong@163.com
发行电话：010-82000860 转 8101/8102	发行传真：010-82000893/82005070/82000270
印　刷：北京嘉恒彩色印刷有限责任公司	经　销：各大网上书店、新华书店及相关专业书店
开　本：710mm×1000mm　1/16	印　张：23
版　次：2019 年 5 月第 1 版	印　次：2019 年 5 月第 1 次印刷
字　数：386 千字	定　价：98.00 元
ISBN 978-7-5130-6207-7	

出版权专有　侵权必究
如有印装质量问题，本社负责调换。

前　言

国家豁免问题是外交和司法领域的一个重要问题。在司法程序中尊重他国的国家豁免是各国普遍接受的国际法规则，其宗旨在于维护国家主权及其尊严，促进国家间关系的稳定。

在相当长时期内，绝对豁免理论为各国普遍承认和坚持。但是，随着国际经济活动的发展，国家作为民事主体与外国公民或法人从事民商事交往的情形日益增多，纠纷也随之增加。从20世纪后半叶开始，不少国家，特别是欧美发达国家，为保护本国国家利益及本国公民和法人的合法权益，逐步转向采取限制豁免理论，一些国家为此专门制定了国内法。迄今已有13个国家制定了规定限制豁免制度的专门法律，还有一些国家是在一般法律中对国家豁免问题作出专门规定。此外，欧洲委员会于1972年通过了《国家豁免欧洲公约》，联合国于2005年通过了《联合国国家及其财产管辖豁免公约》。上述国内立法和国际公约都将国家享有豁免规定为原则，同时规定豁免的例外情形。但对豁免例外的范围，各国法律、国际条约和司法实践不尽相同。

我国在国家豁免问题上一贯坚持绝对豁免主张。实践中，除有关外国放弃豁免的情形外，我国法院不管辖以外国国家为被告或针对外国国家财产的案件，我国也不接受外国法院对以我国国家为被告或针对我国国家财产的案件享有管辖权。2005年我国制定了《外国中央银行财产司法强制措施豁免法》，但其适用范围有限。目前我国尚未制定全面规定国家豁免问题的专门法律。近年来，随着我国不断扩大对外开放，我国与世界各国交往中的法律保障问题日益突出。在此背景下，国家豁免问题引起了我国外交和法律实务部门以及学术界越来越多的关注，如何进一步完善我国相关法律制度的问题已经提上议事日程。

为给相关工作和研究提供参考，我们编译了这本《国家豁免国内立法和国际法律文件汇编》。本书由外交部条约法律司司长徐宏和副司长马新民分别担任正副主编，参与编辑、翻译、校对和审核工作的条法司工作人员有：胡镔、申钦民、何亮、石午虹、易晨霞、张鹏、杨熙、崔宏宇、纪小雪、曾思琪、徐驰、廖钢强、李久烨等。北京外国语大学法学院姚艳霞副教授和上海国际问题研究院赵隆博士也承担了部分翻译和审校工作。由于水平所限，书中难免有不妥甚至错漏之处，请广大读者批评指正，以便我们今后予以修订和完善。

编者

2019 年 1 月

目　录

第一部分　国内立法　001

1976年美国外国主权豁免法	003
1978年英国国家豁免法	019
1979年新加坡外国国家豁免法	031
1981年巴基斯坦国家豁免条例	039
1981年南非外国国家豁免法	046
1984年马拉维特权与豁免法	054
1985年加拿大国家豁免法	065
1985年澳大利亚外国国家豁免法	074
1995年阿根廷法院对外国国家管辖豁免法	088
2005年中华人民共和国外国中央银行财产司法强制措施豁免法	090
2008年以色列外国国家豁免法	091
2009年日本对外国国家民事管辖法	096
2015年西班牙有关外国政府等享有的特权与豁免的组织法	103
2015年俄罗斯关于外国国家和财产在俄罗斯联邦的管辖豁免法	125

第二部分　国际公约　　　　　　　　　　　　　　　　131

1972年《国家豁免欧洲公约》及其附加议定书　　　　　　133

2004年联合国国家及其财产管辖豁免公约　　　　　　　　149

第三部分　其他国际文件　　　　　　　　　　　　　　　161

1991年联合国国际法委员会国家及其财产的管辖豁免条款草案　　163

1991年国际法研究院关于国家豁免在管辖和执行方面的
　一些现实问题的决议　　　　　　　　　　　　　　　　171

2009年国际法研究院关于国家和代表国家行事的个人犯下
　国际罪行时的管辖豁免的决议　　　　　　　　　　　　175

2013年欧洲委员会国有文化财产管辖豁免声明　　　　　　177

第一部分 国内立法

1976 年美国外国主权豁免法

美国法典第 28 编　司法和审判程序
第四部分　管辖和审判地点
第 85 章　联邦地区法院；管辖权

第 1330 节　以外国国家为被告的诉讼

第一条　联邦地区法院对以本编第 1603 节第一条规定的外国国家为被告的无陪审团审判的民事诉讼，不论案件争议数额多少，均具有原始管辖权，如果该外国国家依本编第 1605 节至第 1607 节之规定或任何可适用之国际协议在该对人诉讼救济请求中不享有豁免。

第二条　联邦地区法院对外国国家具有属人管辖权，如果该法院依第一条对诉讼救济请求具有管辖权，且依本编第 1608 节已进行送达。

第三条　为第二条之目的，在非因交易或本编第 1605 节至第 1607 节列举之情形引起的诉讼救济请求中，外国国家出庭并不赋予法院属人管辖权。

第 1332 节　不同公民身份；争议数额；费用

第一条　联邦地区法院应具有所有民事诉讼的原始管辖权，如果争议事项的金额或价值，不包括利息和费用，超过 75000 美元，并且发生在：

……

二、某州的公民与某外国国家公民或属民之间，除非联邦地区法院不得根据本条对某州公民与居住在同一州的并被法律允许在美国永久居留的某外国国家公民或属民之间的行为行使原始管辖权；

三、不同州的公民之间并且某外国国家公民或属民也作为当事人的案件；以及

四、本编第 1603 节第一条所规定的外国国家作为原告与来自某州或不同州的公民之间。

……

第 1391 节　一般的审判地点

......

第六条　针对外国国家的民事诉讼——本编第 1603 节第一条所规定的针对外国国家的民事诉讼可以在下列地点提出：

一、引起该诉讼请求发生的事件或不作为的主要发生地，或诉讼标的物的主要部分所处的司法管辖区；

二、根据本编第 1605 节第二条提出的诉讼请求所涉的外国国家船只或货物所处的司法管辖区；

三、根据本编第 1603 节第二条被诉的外国国家机构或部门被允许或正在开展业务的司法管辖区；或

四、在哥伦比亚特区联邦的美国地区法院，如果诉讼针对的是某外国国家或其政治分支机构。

......

第 97 章　外国国家管辖豁免

第 1602 节　裁决及目的之声明

国会认为，由美国法院对外国国家提出的司法管辖豁免要求作出决定，将有利于维护公正和保护在美国法院诉讼的外国国家及当事人的权利。根据国际法，国家就其商业活动而言，不能在外国法院享有管辖豁免，且该国商业财产可被扣押以执行与之商业活动有关的判决。因此，外国国家提出的豁免要求应由美国联邦法院或州法院依本章阐明之原则作出决定。

第 1603 节　用语

为本章之目的：

第一条　"外国国家"，包括某一外国的政治分支机构或第二条所指的机构或部门，本编第 1608 节所规定的除外。

第二条　"外国国家机构或部门"是指符合下列条件的实体：

一、独立的法人、公司或其他实体，和

二、外国国家或其政治分支机构的机关，或外国国家或其政治分支机构持有大部分股权或拥有其他所有者权益的实体，和

三、既非本编第 1332 节第三条和第五条所述美国一州之公民，亦非依任何第三国法律建立的实体。

第三条 "美国"包括受美国管辖的所有领土和水域，含陆地和岛屿。

第四条 "商业活动"指常规的商业行为或特定的商业交易或行为。一项活动的商业性质，应根据行为过程或特定交易或行为的性质，而非其目的来确定。

第五条 "外国国家在美国进行的商业活动"指外国国家进行的、与美国有实质性联系的商业活动。

第1604节 外国国家管辖豁免

除依本章第1605节至第1607节之规定外，外国国家在美国联邦法院或州法院享有管辖豁免，但以本法颁布时美国作为当事方的现有国际协议之规定为限。

第1605节 外国国家管辖豁免的一般例外

第一条 在下列任一情况下，外国国家在美国联邦法院或州法院都不享有管辖豁免：

一、外国国家已明示或默示放弃其管辖豁免，尽管该国可能试图撤销放弃豁免，依放弃的条件撤销者除外；

二、诉讼是基于外国国家在美国进行的商业活动提起的；或基于外国国家在美国的行为提起，而该行为与外国国家在美国境外的商业活动相关；或行为虽发生在美国领土外，但与外国国家在美国境外的商业活动相关，且对美国产生直接影响；

三、如果对违反国际法征收的财产发生争议，且该财产或与该财产交换取得的任何财产位于美国境内，并同外国国家在美国进行的商业活动相关；或该财产或与该财产交换取得的任何财产由在美国从事商业活动的外国机构或部门所有或运营；

四、对以遗产继承或捐赠方式在美国获得的财产权，或位于美国境内的不动产权利发生争议；

五、第二款未涵盖的其他情形，如因人身伤害、死亡、外国国家或其官员、雇员在其职权或雇佣范围内的侵权行为或不作为造成的在美国境内的人身伤害或死亡、财产损失或丧失而向外国国家索赔；本款不适用下列情形：

（一）诉讼请求的提出是基于被诉外国国家行使、履行或未能行使、履行自由裁量权，不论该自由裁量权是否被滥用，或

（二）诉讼请求的提出是基于恶意控诉、滥用程序、诬蔑、诽谤、诈称、欺骗或干预合同权利；或

六、诉讼提起之目的在于，请求执行外国国家与私人当事方或为私人当事方之利益订立的协议，该协议将当事方之间就特定的法律关系而言已产生或可能产生的所有或任何相关的争端提交仲裁，不论该争端是否为契约性，所涉诉讼标的根据美国法律可以通过仲裁解决，或者请求确认根据该仲裁协议作出的仲裁裁决，如果

（一）该仲裁在美国或意图在美国进行；

（二）该仲裁协议或仲裁裁决是受或可能受对美国生效的有关要求承认和执行仲裁裁决的一项条约或其他国际协议支配；

（三）若无仲裁协议，私人当事方的主要诉讼请求本可根据本节或第1607节之规定在美国法院提出，或（四）本条第一款应适用的其他情形。

第二条 如果海事诉讼是为了实现外国国家船舶或货物的海事留置权，且该海事留置权是基于该外国国家的商业活动而产生的，则外国国家在美国法院不享有管辖豁免，只要——

一、诉讼通知的发送是通过向占有被留置船舶或货物的人或其代理人送达传唤状和起诉状副本各一份；如果船舶或货物为提起诉讼的原告之利益已被扣押，扣押令的送达将被视为该诉讼通知的有效送达，但如果起诉方确实或推定知悉外国船舶或货物涉及该案，其应对外国因船舶或货物的扣押而造成的损失负责；且

二、依据本编第1608节之规定，应于本条第一款规定的通知送达之日起十日内通知外国国家诉讼开始，如果当事一方不知晓外国船舶或货物涉及该案，该类通知应于该当事方确定涉案外国国家利益存在之日起十日内发出。

第三条 如该船舶已为私人所有和占有，对物诉讼本可继续，则不论诉讼通知根据本节第二条第一款之规定于何时发出，请求执行海事留置权的诉讼应继续进行，且应根据对物诉讼的法律原则和实务规则进行听证和裁决。针对外国国家的判决可包括诉讼费用，如果该判决是以经济赔偿为目的，法院可判决外国国家支付利息，但法院对外国国家赔偿金额的裁决不得超过被海事留置的船舶或货物的价值。船舶或货物的价值在依本节第二条第一款送达通知时决定。与其他海事和海运诉讼案件之规定相同，该司法判决可提起复审和上诉。不得阻止原告在任何适当的情况下在本节规定的执行海事留置权的同一诉讼中寻求对人救济。

第四条 在根据美国法典第 46 编第 31301 节规定的请求执行具有优先权的抵押权的诉讼中，外国国家在美国法院不享有管辖豁免。当该船舶为私人所有和占有，对物诉讼本可继续时，此类诉讼应根据第 46 编第 313 节的规定和对物诉讼的法律原则及实务规则进行起诉、听证和裁决。

（注：第五条、第六条已被修正案删除。）

第七条 开示程序的限制。

一、一般规定。

（一）如非因本编第 1605A 节和第 1605B 节的规定，当某诉讼之提起将被本法第 1604 节禁止时，如果司法部长证实开示请求、开示要求或开示命令将严重干预与引起诉因之事件相关的刑事调查、控诉或国家安全行动，则法院在司法部长的请求下应就开示请求、开示要求或开示命令向美国方面发出延缓令，直至司法部长向法院建议开示请求、开示要求或开示命令将不再干预刑事调查或控诉为止，但以第二款的规定为限。

（二）本款下的延缓令自法院发出开示延缓令之日起十二个月内有效。如果司法部长证实开示请求、开示要求或开示命令将严重干预与引起诉因之事件相关的刑事调查、控诉或国家安全行动，则法院在美国方面的请求下应将延缓令期限延长十二个月。

二、日落条款。

（一）引起诉因之事件发生之日起十年后，法院不得根据第一款第（一）项的规定发出任何延缓令或使延缓令继续有效，但以本款第（二）项的规定为限。

（二）当本款第（一）项规定的期限届满后，法院可在司法部长的请求下就开示请求、开示要求或开示命令向美国方面发出延缓令，如果法院认定极有可能会：

1. 对任何人的生命造成严重威胁或对其人身造成重大伤害；

2. 对美国与外国或国际执法机构就违反美国法律的行为开展合作调查的能力产生不利影响；或

3. 对与引起诉因之事件相关的刑事案件形成阻碍或削弱对此类案件定罪的可能性。

三、审查证据。

法院对司法部长依本条提起的任何延缓请求的审查，将在另一方当事人缺席的情况下不公开进行。

四、禁止驳回诉讼。

如根据本条提起中止开示程序，则不得根据《联邦民事程序规则》第十二条第二款第六项和第五十六条驳回诉讼。

五、解释。

本条任何之规定不得阻止美国方面申请保护令或主张通常具有的特权。

第八条 某些艺术展览活动的管辖豁免。

一、一般规定。应满足：

（一）一件作品是从外国国家进口到美国的作品，且根据拥有或保管该作品的外国国家与美国或位于美国的某个或多个文化或教育机构签订的协议用于临时展览或展出；

（二）总统或总统指定的人已根据公法第89—259号第一条（《美国法典》第22编第2459节第一条）确定该作品具有文化意义且临时展览或展出该作品符合国家利益；且

（三）有关这方面的通知已根据《美国法典》第22编第2459节第一条予以发布，此类外国国家或其任何承运人在美国与该作品临时展览或展出有关的任何活动不得视为为施行本节第一条第三款的此类外国国家的商业活动。

二、例外规定。

（一）纳粹时期诉求。本条第一款在任何情况下都不能确立对本节第一条第三款所指的对违反国际法征收的财产的争议的管辖权，且：

1. 争议的财产是第一款所指的作品；

2. 诉讼是基于此类作品的征收与特定政府在特定时期行为有关的一项主张；

3. 法院认为与展览或展出有关的活动是本编第1603节第四条所定义的商业活动；且

4. 法院根据第3目所作的决定对法院依据本节第一条第三款对外国国家行使管辖权是必要的。

（二）其他具有文化价值的作品。除本款第一项所指的排除豁免权的情形外，本条第一款在任何情形下都不能确立起对本节第一条第三款所指的对违反国际法征收的财产的争议的管辖权，且：

1. 争议的财产是第一款所指的作品；

2. 诉讼是基于主张对该作品的征收与外国国家针对特定弱势群体强行没收或侵占其作品并将此作为一项系统性的工程的一部分的行为有关；

3. 征收发生在 1900 年以后；

4. 法院认为与展览或展出有关的活动是本编第 1603 节第四条所定义的商业活动；且

5. 法院根据第 4 目所作的决定对法院依据本节第一条第三款对外国国家行使管辖权是必要的。

三、定义。为本条之目的：

（一）"作品"指的是艺术品或其他具有文化价值的物品；

（二）"特定政府"指的是：

1. 特定时期的德国政府；

2. 特定时期被德国政府军队占领的欧洲任何地区的政府；

3. 特定时期在德国政府的帮助下或与之合作下建立的位于欧洲的政府；和

4. 特定时期与德国政府同盟的位于欧洲的政府；和

（三）"特定时期"指的是从 1933 年 1 月 30 日开始到 1945 年 5 月 8 日为止的时期。

第 1605A 节　外国管辖豁免的恐怖主义例外

第一条　一般规定。

一、不享有豁免。

向外国国家寻求由酷刑、法外处决、破坏航空器、劫持人质或为此类行为提供物质支持或资源造成的人身伤害或死亡的金钱赔偿时，如果此类行为或物质支持或资源的提供是由外国国家的官员、雇员或代理人在其职务、雇佣或代理范围内实施的，外国国家不得豁免于美国法院或未被本章所涵盖的各州法院的管辖。

二、申诉受理。法院应根据本节受理以下案件：

（一）

1.

（1）以第二小段的规定为限，外国国家在第一款所指的行为发生时被认定为支持恐怖主义的国家，或由于上述行为的发生被认定为支持恐怖主义的国家，并且在根据本条提出申诉时仍被作出此种认定或在根据本条提出申诉之前的 6 个月内被作出此种认定；或

（2）由于 2008 年度《国防授权法》第 1083 节第三条第二款第一项的规定并根据本节重新提起的诉讼，或由于该法第 1083 节第三条第三款的规

定并根据本条提起的诉讼，且在原始诉讼或有关诉讼已经根据本编第 1605 节第一条第七款（在本节通过前有效）或 1997 年《外国业务、出口融资和相关计划拨款法》第五百八十九条（载于第 104—208 号公法第一部分第 101 节第三条）提起时，外国国家已被认定为支持恐怖主义的国家；

2. 在本条第一款所述的行为发生时，申诉人或受害人是：

（1）美国国民；

（2）美国军队的一员；或

（3）美国政府的雇员或个人作为履行美国政府签发的合同的雇员，并在雇佣范围内行事；且

3. 如该行为发生在诉讼所针对的外国国家，申诉人已向外国国家提供了合理的机会依据该外国国家可接受的国际仲裁规则对申诉进行仲裁；或者

（二）第一款所指的行为与美国哥伦比亚特区联邦地区法院的案件 1：00CV03110（EGS）有关。

第二条 限制条款。可能根据本节提起或继续进行的诉讼，如果已经开始，或有关诉讼已经根据本编第 1605 节第一条第七款（在本节通过前有效）或 1997 年《外国业务、出口融资和相关计划拨款法》第五百八十九条（载于第 104—208 号公法第一部分第 101 节第三条）提起，不迟于：

一、1996 年 4 月 24 日后的十年；或

二、诉因发生之日起十年。

第三条 诉讼中的个人权利。被或曾被认定为本节第一条第二款第一项第一目所称的支持恐怖主义的外国国家，以及该外国国家的在其职务、雇佣或代理范围内行事的官员、雇员或代理人，应对下列人员负责：

一、美国国民；

二、美国军队的一员；

三、美国政府的雇员或个人作为在雇佣范围内履行美国政府签发的合同的雇员；或

四、第一、二、三段所述人员的法定代表人，对由本节第一条第一项所述的外国国家的行为造成的或该外国国家的官员、雇员或代理人造成的人身伤害或死亡的损害赔偿请求，美国法院可以根据本条保留对此损害金钱赔偿的管辖权。在任何此类诉讼中，损害赔偿可包括经济赔偿、精神赔偿、身体和精神伤害以及惩罚性赔偿。在任何此类行为中，外国国家对其官员、雇员或代理人的行为负有代位责任。

第四条 附加损害赔偿。

根据本节第三条提出诉讼后，也可基于该诉讼所针对的同一行为并以同样的理由提起诉讼，主张合理可预见的财产损失，不论投保还是未投保，主张第三者责任，并可根据人身和财产保险条款就损失索赔。

第五条 特别专家。

一、一般规定。

美国法院可以任命特别专家审理根据本条提出的损害赔偿请求。

二、资金转移。

司法部长应将根据1984年《犯罪受害人法》（42 U. S. C. 10603c）第1404节第三条规定的可用资金向美国联邦地区法院的行政事务官转移，用于支付已在该法院被提起或继续进行的案件中根据第一款任命的特别专家的费用。任何向该等特别专家支付的报酬，均构成法院费用项目。

第六条 上诉。

在根据本节提出的诉讼中，就不是最终终止诉讼的命令提起上诉，只能根据本编第1292节第二条提起。

第七条 财产处置。

一、一般规定。

在根据本节规定主张管辖权的美国联邦地区法院提起的每一项诉讼中，依据本节发出的、附有起诉状副本的中止诉讼通知，应具有对未决案件中任何不动产或有形的个人财产设立留置权的功能，该类财产应满足：

（一）根据第1610节的规定，为协助执行而扣押或执行；

（二）位于该司法管辖区内；和

（三）以被告的名义命名的，或以任何被告控制的任何实体的名义为名，如果该通知包含列出此类受控实体的一项声明。

二、通知。

根据本节发出的中止诉讼的通知应由地区法院的书记官以与任何待决诉讼相同的方式签发，并通过列出所有被指名的被告和被告控制的实体的方式建立索引。

三、可执行性。

根据本条确立的留置权应按本编第111章的规定执行。

第八条 定义。为本节的目的：

一、"破坏航空器"一词具有《制止危及民用航空安全非法行为公约》第一条给定的含义；

二、"人质劫持"一词具有《反对劫持人质国际公约》第一条给定的含义；

三、"物资支援或资源"一词具有第 18 编第 2339A 节中给定的含义；

四、"武装力量"一词具有第 10 编第 101 节中给定的含义；

五、"美国国籍"一词具有《移民与国籍法》第 101 节第一条第二十二款［8 U.S.C. 1101（a）（22）］中给定的含义；

六、"支持恐怖主义国家"一词系指国务卿为 1979 年《出口管理法》第六节第十条［50 U.S.C. App. 2405（j）］、1961 年《外国援助法》第 620A 节（22 U.S.C. 2371）、《武器出口管制法》第 40 节（22 U.S.C. 2780）或任何其他有关法律规定的目的所确定的，其政府屡次为国际恐怖主义提供支持的国家；和

七、"酷刑"和"法外处决"一词具有 1991 年《酷刑受害人保护法》第三节中有关条款（28 U.S.C. 1350 note）给定的含义。

第 1605B 节　针对美国的国际恐怖主义外国国家应负的责任

第一条　定义。

在本节中，"国际恐怖主义"一词：

一、具有《美国法典》第 18 编第 2331 节给定的含义；和

二、不包括任何战争行为（如该节所定义）。

第二条　外国国家的责任。

当有关案件中对发生在美国的、由下列行为造成的人身伤害或财产损害或死亡向外国国家主张赔偿时，外国国家不得豁免于美国法院的管辖。

一、发生在美国的国际恐怖主义行为；和

二、外国国家、官员、雇员或代理人在其职务、雇佣或代理范围内实施的侵权行为，不论该外国国家的侵权行为发生在何处。

第三条　美国国民的索赔。

如果外国国家根据本节第二条不能豁免，尽管有第 18 编第 2337 节第二款的规定，美国国民仍可以按照该编第 2333 节向外国国家提出索赔。

第四条　解释规则。

外国国家不应因作为或不作为造成的侵权行为，而根据本节第二条受到美国法院的管辖。

第 1606 节　责任范围

关于外国国家根据本章第 1605 节至第 1607 节之规定不享有豁免的诉讼救济请求，外国国家与私人在同等情况下以同等方式承担同等程度的责任；但外国国家不承担惩罚性赔偿责任，外国国家机构或部门除外；如果案件涉及死亡的情形，该作为或不作为发生地的法律规定或被解释为规定的赔偿实质上只是惩罚性的，则外国国家将偿付实际或补偿性损害赔偿金，赔偿金额根据诉讼所维护利益的人因死亡而造成的金钱损失决定。

第 1607 节　反诉

在外国国家于美国联邦法院或州法院提起或介入的任何诉讼中，如果对方当事人提起反诉，该外国在下列情况下不享有豁免：

第一条　如果该反诉是作为一个单独的诉讼针对外国国家提起的，外国国家根据本章第 1605 节或第 1605A 节之规定不享有豁免；或

第二条　反诉产生于作为外国国家诉讼请求中的诉讼标的的交易或事件；或

第三条　反诉所寻求的救济在金额上没有超出外国国家所寻求的救济，或两者所寻求的救济种类并无不同。

第 1608 节　送达；答辩时间；缺席

第一条　在美国联邦法院或州法院，通过以下方式向外国国家或其政治分支机构送达诉讼文书：

一、根据原告与外国国家或其政治分支机构对于送达的特殊安排，送达传唤状和起诉状副本各一份；或

二、若无特殊安排，依据可适用的关于司法文书送达的国际公约送达传唤状和起诉状副本各一份；或

三、如无法按第一款和第二款之规定进行送达，由法院工作人员注明地址并通过任何挂号签收之邮递方式向相关外国外交部长送达传唤状、起诉状副本各一份和诉讼通知，并附上该国官方语言译本；或

四、如送达无法按第三款之规定在三十日内完成，由法院工作人员注明地址并通过任何挂号签收之邮递方式向华盛顿哥伦比亚特区的美国国务卿送达传唤状、起诉状副本各两份和诉讼通知，并附上该外国国家官方语言译本，抄送特别领事部门。国务卿应通过外交途径向外国国家转交上述

文书副本各一份，并向法院工作人员发回核证无误的外交照会副本，注明文书转交时间。

在本节内，"诉讼通知"是指依照国务卿按法令指定的形式向外国国家发出的通知。

第二条 在美国联邦法院或州法院，应通过以下方式向外国国家机构或部门送达诉讼文书：

一、根据原告与该机构或部门对送达的特殊安排，送达传唤状和起诉状副本各一份；或

二、若无特殊安排，采取向执行官员、常务官员或其他任何根据委托或法律在美国有权接收诉讼文书的代理人送达的方式；或根据一项可适用的关于司法文书送达的国际公约送达传唤状和起诉状副本各一份；或

三、如无法按第一款或第二款之规定进行送达，且如果有合理可能给予实际通知，可通过以下方式送达传唤状、起诉状副本各一份和诉讼通知，并附上该外国国家官方语言译本：

（一）按照外国国家或其政治分支机构当局对域外取证信或询问信的答复中指定的方式送达，或

（二）由法院工作人员注明地址并通过任何挂号签收之邮递方式向相关外国机构或部门送达，或

（三）按照法院的指令并符合送达地法律规定的方式送达。

第三条 下列情形视为送达已完成：

一、在本节第一条第四款的情况下，核证无误的外交照会副本注明的转交日期视为送达日期；且

二、在本节中其他任何情况下，核证无误的外交照会副本、邮局的挂号信件回执或其他与所采用的送达方式相适应的送达回执中注明的签收日期视为送达日期。

第四条 外国国家、政府分支机构、机构或部门应在按本章规定完成送达六十日内，向美国联邦法院或州法院提交答辩状或应答的诉答文书。

第五条 美国联邦法院或州法院不得对外国国家、其政治分支机构、机构或部门作出缺席判决，除非原告的诉讼请求或救济权利得到了令法院信服的证据的支持。缺席判决书副本应依本节规定的送达方式向外国国家或其政府分支机构送达。

第 1609 节　外国国家财产免于扣押和执行的豁免

除本章第 1610 节和第 1611 节之规定外，外国国家在美国联邦法院或州法院享有财产扣押、扣留和执行的豁免，但以本法颁布时美国已参加的现有国际协议之规定为限。

第 1610 节　外国国家财产免于扣押和执行之豁免的例外

第一条　为执行美国联邦法院或州法院自本法施行之日起作出的判决，本章第 1603 节第一条规定的外国国家在美国用于商业活动的财产，不享有为协助执行而进行的扣押的豁免或执行的豁免，如果：

一、外国国家已明示或默示放弃为协助执行而进行的扣押的豁免或执行的豁免，尽管该国可能试图撤销放弃豁免，依放弃条件撤销者除外；或

二、该财产正在或曾经用于商业活动，且诉讼基于该商业活动而提起；或

三、财产的执行与确立财产权的判决相关，该财产属于违反国际法征收的财产或与违反国际法征收的财产交换取得的其他财产；或

四、财产执行与如下确立财产权的判决相关：

（一）通过继承或捐赠所得的财产，或

（二）位于美国境内的不动产，倘若该财产未被用作维系外交或领事使团工作或作为此类使团团长的居住场所，或

五、该财产由外国国家或其雇员投保的车险、其他责任险或事故险产生的赔偿其损失的合同义务或根据该合同义务的任何获益构成，该保险涵盖了判决中的诉讼请求；或

六、判决是基于请求执行针对外国不利的仲裁裁决，如果为协助执行而进行的扣押或执行与仲裁协议中的任何规定均无冲突；或

七、判决与某项诉讼请求相关，且根据第 1605A 节或第 1605 节第一条第七款（该款在 2008 年 1 月 27 日有效）的规定，外国国家对该诉讼请求不享有管辖豁免，不论该财产是否正在或曾经涉及引起诉讼请求的行为。

第二条　除本节第一条的规定外，为执行美国联邦法院或州法院自本法施行之日起作出的判决，外国国家的机构或部门在美国用于商业活动的财产，不享有为协助执行而进行的扣押的豁免或执行的豁免，如果：

一、外国国家机构或部门已明示或默示放弃为协助执行而进行的扣押的豁免或执行的豁免，尽管该国机构或部门可能试图撤销放弃豁免，依放弃的条件撤销者除外；或

二、判决与某项诉讼请求有关，且由于本章第 1605 节第一条第二款、第三款、第五款或第 1605 节第二条的规定，机构或部门对该诉讼请求不享有豁免，不论该财产是否正在或曾经涉及引起诉讼请求的行为；或

三、判决与某项诉讼请求有关，且由于本章第 1605A 节或第 1605 节第一条第七款（该款在 2008 年 1 月 27 日有效）的规定，机构或部门对该诉讼请求不享有豁免，不论该财产是否正在或曾经涉及引起诉讼请求的行为。

第三条 除非法院在认定判决生效，且依本章第 1608 节第五条之规定作出通知后经过合理期限才发出扣押或执行令，否则不得采取本节第一条和第二条规定的任何扣押或执行。

第四条 本章第 1603 节第一条规定的外国国家，在美国境内用于商业活动的财产，于美国联邦法院或州法院判决生效前或本节第三条规定之期限届满前，不得豁免于扣押，如果：

一、外国国家在判决前已明确放弃其财产免于扣押的豁免，尽管该国可能试图撤销放弃豁免，依放弃的条件撤销者除外，且

二、扣押财产之目的是保证已作出或最终可能作出的对外国国家不利的判决得以执行，而非取得管辖权。

第五条 在依第 1605 节第四条规定执行具有优先权的抵押权的诉讼中，外国国家船舶不得豁免于对物扣留、临时销售和执行。

第六条

一、

（一）尽管有本法其他条款的规定，包括但不限于《外国使团法》第 208 节第六条之规定［22 U. S. C. 4308（f）］，除本款第二项的规定外，任何财产，若与《与敌国通商法》第五节第二条［50 U. S. C. App. 5（b）］，1961 年《对外援助法》第 620 节第一条［22 U. S. C. 2370（a）］，《国际紧急状态下经济权力法》第 202 节、第 203 节（50 U. S. C. 1701—1702），或任何其他公告、法令、法规，或据此颁布的许可令所禁止或规定的经济交易有关，为执行有关判决，该财产可被执行或为协助执行被扣押，且该判决与根据第 1605 节第一条第七款（在第 1605A 节颁布之前有效）或第 1605A 节的规定主张声索此类财产的外国国家（包括该外国国家的任何机构或部门）不享有管辖豁免的诉讼请求有关。

（二）如果在该财产被外国国家没收或扣押时，已被划归某自然人名下，或该财产为某自然人或数位自然人之利益被托管，本条第一款不得适用。

二、

（一）如果法院已对根据第 1605 节第一条第七款（在第 1605A 节颁布之前有效）或第 1605A 节的规定主张外国国家不享有管辖豁免的诉讼请求作出判决，在胜诉当事方的请求下，财政部长和国务卿应尽一切所能，充分、迅速、有效地协助胜诉债权人或作出该判决的法院确认、寻找和执行该外国国家或其机构或部门的财产。

（二）在提供此类协助时，财政部长和国务卿：

1. 经加盖公章，可向法院提供此类信息；且

2. 得尽一切所能提供信息，以便法院能指示美国法院地方法律执行官办公室对该财产进行迅速和有效的执行。

三、放弃适用。

总统为国家安全利益，可放弃本条第一款的适用。

第七条 某些诉讼中的财产。

一、一般条款。

以第三款的规定为限，根据第 1605A 节作出的判决所针对的外国国家的财产，以及该外国的机构或部门的财产，包括属于独立法人的财产或由独立法人直接或间接享有利益的财产，为执行根据本节规定作出的判决，可以执行和为执行的目的扣押该类财产，不论：

（一）外国国家政府对该财产的经济控制水平；

（二）财产的收益是否交给该政府；

（三）该国政府官员对该财产的管理或以其他方式控制其日常事务的程度；

（四）该政府是否是该财产收益的唯一获益人；或

（五）将财产确定为独立法人是否使得该外国国家在美国法院受益，同时避免其义务。

二、美国的主权豁免不适用。

适用于本条第一款的外国国家或外国国家机构或部门的任何财产，不得因为根据《与敌国通商法》、《国际紧急状态下经济权力法》对该外国国家提起的诉讼使得该财产由美国政府管理，而豁免基于第 1605A 节作出的判决所进行的执行或为执行的目的所进行的扣押。

三、属于共同财产持有人的第三方

本条任何内容，均不得解释为取代了法院适当防止损害诉讼中不承担责任的人对其财产所持利益之权威，该财产基于此项诉讼作出的判决而为执行之目的被扣押或被执行。

第 1611 节　免于执行的某类财产

第一条　虽有本章第 1610 节的规定，在美国联邦法院或州法院针对外国国家提起的诉讼中，不能为了阻止向该外国国家支付或类似目的而对总统指定的享有《国际组织豁免法》规定的特权、义务免除及豁免的组织的财产予以扣押或执行任何其他司法程序。

第二条　虽有本章第 1610 节的规定，外国国家财产仍应免于扣押和执行，如果：

一、该财产为外国央行或货币主管部门自身账户所有，除非此类银行或主管部门，或其本国政府已明示或暗示放弃免于为协助执行而进行的扣押或执行的豁免，尽管该银行或主管部门或其本国政府可能试图撤销放弃豁免，依放弃的条件撤销者除外；或

二、该财产用于或意图用于与军事活动相关之用途，且

（一）属于军事性质，或

（二）为军事当局或国防机构控制。

三、虽有本章第 1610 节之规定，外国国家财产在依 1996 年《古巴自由和民主团结法》第 302 节提起的诉讼中免于扣押和执行，只要该财产是官方认可的外交使团为公务目的使用的设备和设施。

1978 年英国国家豁免法

本法旨在就英国境内由其他国家提起或针对其他国家提起诉讼的程序作出新规定；规定《国家豁免欧洲公约》缔约国法院针对英国作出的判决之效力；就国家元首的特权与豁免作出新规定；及其他相关事项。

[1978 年 7 月 20 日]

第一部分　在英国境内由其他国家提起或对其他国家提起的诉讼的程序

管辖豁免

第一条　一般管辖豁免

一、除本法第一部分下述条款规定的情形外，一国在英国法院中享有管辖豁免。

二、即便一国没有在所涉案件的诉讼中出庭，法院仍应根据本条规定给予该国豁免。

豁免的例外

第二条　接受管辖

一、一国在其已接受英国法院管辖的诉讼中不享有豁免。

二、一国可以在引发诉讼程序的争议发生之后或事先以书面协议方式接受管辖，但任何协议中有关适用英国法律的规定不应被视为接受管辖。

三、在以下情况下，一国被视为接受管辖：

（一）如果该国提起诉讼；或

（二）在符合本条下述第四款和第五款规定的情况下，如果该国介入该诉讼或在诉讼中采取任何行动。

四、本条第三款第（二）项的规定不适用于仅为以下目的参加诉讼或采取任何行动：

（一）主张豁免；或

（二）在被诉国应有权享有豁免的情况下，对财产主张一项利益。

五、如果一国无法合理地知悉使其享有豁免的事实从而忽视了该事实，并且一旦可合理知悉便即刻主张豁免，则该国在此情形下采取的任何行动，不适用本条第三款第（二）项的规定。

六、一国在任何诉讼中接受管辖，即视为在上诉中接受管辖，但不视为在反诉中接受管辖，除非该反诉是针对与本诉相同的法律关系或事实提起的。

七、一国驻英国的使馆馆长，或暂时代行其职务的人，应被视为有权代表国家接受管辖；任何由国家授权代表该国订立合同的人员，应被视为有权就该合同引发的诉讼代表该国接受管辖。

第三条　商业交易和需在英国境内履行的合同

一、一国在涉及下列事项的诉讼中不享有豁免：

（一）该国参加的商业交易；或

（二）该国根据一项全部或部分在英国履行的合同（不论是否属商业交易）而承担的义务。

二、如果诉讼当事方均为国家，或其另有书面协议，则不适用本条；如果该合同（非商业交易）在有关国家境内缔结且涉及的义务适用该国行政法，则不适用本条第一款第（二）项。

三、本条中的"商业交易"指：

（一）任何提供货物或服务的合同；

（二）任何借贷或其他关于提供金融服务的交易，以及任何关于此类交易或其他涉及金融方面义务的担保或保证；以及

（三）一国参与或从事的任何其他交易或活动（无论属于商业、工业、金融、专业，还是其他类似性质），该国行使其主权权力的行为除外；

但本条第一款各项均不适用于一国与个人之间签订的雇佣合同。

第四条　雇佣合同

一、在一国与个人之间就其签订的雇佣合同所引发的诉讼中，如该合同在英国境内缔结或雇佣工作需全部或部分在英国境内履行，则该国不享有豁免。

二、在符合本条第三款和第四款规定的情况下，本条不适用于以下情形：

（一）当诉讼提起时，该受雇人员为该国国民；或

（二）签订雇佣合同时，该受雇人员既不是英国国民，也不惯常居住在英国；或

（三）合同当事方另有书面协议。

三、当雇主是一国出于商业目的在英国境内经营的办公室、机构或企业时，第二款第（一）项和第（二）项不能排除本条的适用，除非该雇员在签订该合同时在该国惯常居住。

四、如果根据英国法律，诉讼应由英国法院审理，则上述本条第二款第（三）项不能排除本条的适用。

五、上述本条第二款第（二）项所称"英国国民"指：

（一）英国公民，英国属地的公民、英国公民（海外）或英国的海外公民；或

（二）根据1981年《英国国籍法》的规定属于英国国民；或

（三）受英国保护的人员（在该《国籍法》的定义范畴内）。

六、本条中"雇佣合同所引发的诉讼"包括该合同的当事方就其作为雇主或雇员所分别享有的法定权利或义务而提起的诉讼。

第五条　人身伤害和财产损害

一国就其在英国境内的作为或不作为造成下列后果而导致的诉讼中不享有豁免：

（一）死亡或人身伤害；或

（二）有形财产的损失或灭失。

第六条　财产的所有、占有和使用

一、一国在与下列事项有关的诉讼中不享有豁免：

（一）该国对位于英国境内的不动产的任何利益，或该国对该不动产的占有或使用；或者

（二）该国由于对任何此类财产的利益或占有或使用而产生的任何义务。

二、一国在涉及其由于继承、赠予或无主物取得而产生对动产或不动产的任何利益的诉讼中不享有豁免。

三、一国对任何财产享有或主张一项利益时，不应排除任何法院对涉及死者或精神失常者的财产或涉及公司清算、解散或信托财产管理诉讼的管辖权。

四、法院可受理针对人员而非国家的诉讼，即使这些诉讼涉及：

（一）一国占有或控制的财产；或

（二）该国对其主张利益的财产，

如果诉讼针对该国，该国不能享有豁免；或在上述第（二）项所述情形下，该国主张既未被承认，也未得到表面证据的支持。

第七条 专利、商标及其他

一国在与下列事项有关的诉讼中不享有豁免：

（一）该国所有且在英国注册或受保护，或该国已在英国提出申请的任何专利、商标、设计或育种权；

（二）该国被指控在英国境内侵犯了任何专利、商标、设计、育种权或版权；或

（三）在英国境内使用商业名称或企业名称的权利。

第八条 法人团体的成员资格及其他

一、一国在与其在法人团体、非法人团体中的成员资格或合伙人资格有关的诉讼中不享有豁免，如果该法人团体或非法人团体：

（一）有非国家成员；并且

（二）系根据英国法律成立或组建，或由英国控股，或其主要营业地在英国，

且该诉讼发生在该国和该团体之间、该国和该团体的其他成员之间或该国和其他合伙人之间。

二、如果争议当事方之间的书面协议作了相反约定，或其章程或其他建立或管理相关团体或合伙关系的文件有相反规定时，本条不适用。

第九条 仲裁

一、如果一国以书面形式同意将已经发生或可能发生的争议提交仲裁，则该国在有关仲裁事项的诉讼中不能在英国法院享有豁免。

二、仲裁协议中的任何相反规定可以排除本条的适用。本条不适用于国家间的仲裁协议。

第十条 用于商业目的的船舶

一、本条适用于：

（一）海事诉讼；以及

（二）任何有可能成为海事诉讼事项的诉讼。

二、如果诉讼事由发生时，船舶正被用于或意图被用于商业目的，则一国在下列诉讼中不享有豁免：

（一）针对归该国所有船舶的对物诉讼；或

（二）为执行与该船舶有关的诉讼请求的对人诉讼。

三、如果针对一国所有的某一船舶提起的对物诉讼，是为了执行与该国所有的另一船舶有关的诉讼请求，则第二款第（一）项不适用于上述前一船舶，除非当关于另一船舶的诉讼事由发生时，两船正被用于或意图被用于商业目的。

四、下列情况下，一国不享有豁免：

（一）针对属于该国的货物的对物诉讼，条件是诉讼事由发生时，货物和运送货物的船舶正被用于或意图被用于商业目的；或

（二）为执行与该所有的货物有关的诉讼请求而进行的对人诉讼，条件是运送这些货物的船舶正被用于或意图被用于商业目的。

五、前述条款所指归一国所有的船舶或货物包括被该国占有、控制或该国对其主张一项利益的任何船舶或货物；在符合本条第四款规定的前提下，本条第二款如同适用于船舶一样，适用于船舶以外的其他财产。

六、如果涉案国家是《布鲁塞尔公约》缔约国，且其诉讼请求涉及该国所有或运营的船舶的运营，此类船舶上货物或人员的承载，或其他船舶上归该国所有的货物的承载，上述第三条至第五条不适用于本条第一款所规定的诉讼。

第十一条　增值税、关税及其他

一国在与以下责任有关的诉讼中不享有豁免：

（一）增值税、任何关税、消费税或任何农业征税；或

（二）与该国因商业目的占有的房产有关的任何税率。

程　序

第十二条　送达程序和缺席判决

一、与对一国提起诉讼有关的任何传票或其他文书，应通过外交及联邦事务部送达该国外交部，送达应自该国外交部收到传票或文书之日起生效。

二、出庭时限（不论依照法院规则或其他规定）应为按前述方式收到传票或文书之日起两个月。

三、一国在诉讼中出庭后，不能再就该诉讼不符合本条第一款规定为由而提出反对。

四、除非有证据证明本条第一款已获遵守，且本条第二款规定的出庭时限届满，否则不得对一国作出缺席判决。

五、法院对一国作出的任何缺席判决，应通过外交及联邦事务部将判决书副本送交该国外交部，申请撤销缺席判决的时限（不论依照法院规则或其他规定）应为该国外交部收到缺席判决之日起两个月。

六、本条第一款的规定不妨碍以经一国同意的任何其他方式送达；以该方式进行的送达，不适用本条第二款和第四款。

七、本条不得被解释为适用于针对一国提出反诉或对物诉讼的情况；本条第一款不得被解释为影响就向管辖范围之外进行送达要求得到法院许可的任何法院规则。

第十三条　其他程序特权

一、如诉讼当事国或其代表不能或拒绝披露或提供任何与诉讼相关的文件或其他信息，不得对该国处以拘禁或罚金形式的处罚。

二、在符合本条第三款和第四款规定的情况下：

（一）不得以禁制令或命令的方式对一国采取强制履行或要求返还土地或其他财产的救济措施；以及

（二）一国财产不受任何判决或仲裁裁决执行或在对物诉讼中对该财产进行扣留、扣押或变卖的程序的约束。

三、本条第二款的规定不妨碍经相关国家书面同意而采取任何救济措施或启动任何程序；任何此种"同意"（可能包含在事前协议中）可以表明仅在限定范围内适用或者普遍适用；但是仅表示接受法院管辖的条款不能被视为本款中的"同意"。

四、本条第二款第（二）项的规定不妨碍启动关于正被用于或意图被用于商业目的的财产的任何程序；但是除上述第十条规定的情形以外，只有当满足下列条件时，本款才适用于《国家豁免欧洲公约》缔约国的财产：

（一）该程序旨在执行第十八条第一款第（二）项所指的终审判决，且该国根据《国家豁免欧洲公约》第二十四条的规定作出了声明；或

（二）该程序旨在执行仲裁裁决。

五、一国派驻英国的使馆馆长或暂时代行其职务的人，应被视为有权代表该国作出本条第三款所规定的"同意"，并为本条第四款的目的，其代表国家所作的关于任何财产未被用于或意图被用于商业目的的证明应被视为充分证据，除非有相反的事实得到证明。

六、本条适用于苏格兰时：

（一）"禁令"（injunction）一词同"禁令"（interdict）。

（二）本条第二款第（二）项替换为：

"（二）一国财产不受任何执行法院判决、命令或仲裁裁决或在对物诉讼中对该财产进行扣留或变卖的程序（diligence）的约束。"；并且

（三）"程序"（process）一词同"注意"（diligence）；"启动任何程序"（the issue of any process）一词同"给予应有的注意"（the doing of diligence）；第四款第（二）项中的"仲裁裁决"（an arbitration award）同"仲裁判决"（adecree arbitral）。

补充规定

第十四条　享有特权与豁免的国家

一、本法该部分中规定的特权与豁免，适用于英国以外的任何外国或英联邦国家；所提及的"国家"包括：

（一）以其公职身份行事的该国君主或其他元首；

（二）该国政府；以及

（三）该政府的任何部门，

但不包括任何独立于该国政府行政机构之外，且有权起诉和被诉的实体（以下简称"独立实体"）。

二、独立实体只有在满足以下条件时，才能在英国法院享有管辖豁免：

（一）诉讼程序与该实体行使主权权力的任何行为有关；且

（二）一国（或当适用上述第十条时，非《布鲁塞尔公约》缔约方的一国）属于可以享有豁免的情形。

三、如独立实体（一国中央银行或其他金融主管机关除外）在可依本条第二款的规定享有豁免的诉讼程序中接受了法院的管辖，则本法第十三条第一款至第四款中关于国家的规定同样适用于该实体。

四、一国中央银行或其他金融主管机关的财产不应被视为第十三条第四款中规定的"被用于或意图被用于商业目的"；如果一银行或机关是独立实体，则该条第一款至第三款中关于国家的规定同样适用于该银行或机关。

五、本法第十二条适用于对联邦国家的成员领土提起的诉讼；女王陛下可通过枢密令使本法第一部分中的其他条款如同适用于国家一样，适用于此类成员领土。

六、如果根据任何此类枢密令，本法该部分的规定不适用于一成员领土，则该成员领土应被视为一个独立实体，适用本条第二款和第三款。

第十五条　特权与豁免的限制和扩大

一、如果女王陛下认为根据本法该部分的规定所给予一国的特权与豁免：

（一）超出根据该国法律给予英国的特权与豁免；或

（二）少于该国与英国同为缔约国的任何条约、公约或其他国际协定所要求的特权与豁免，

则女王陛下可通过枢密令，将此类特权与豁免限制或扩大至女王陛下认为合适的范围。

二、根据上院或下院的决议，任何根据本条规定包含一项命令的规范文件可归于无效。

第十六条　除外事项

一、本法该部分不影响 1964 年《外交特权法》和 1968 年《领事关系法》中所规定的特权与豁免；并且：

（一）第四条不适用于有关 1964 年法律所列公约中所指外交使团人员的雇佣诉讼和 1968 年法律所列公约中所指领馆人员的雇佣诉讼；

（二）第六条第一款不适用于有关一国命名或占有的用于外交使团目的的财产的诉讼。

二、本法该部分不适用于有关一国军队在英国期间的任何行为或与其相关的诉讼，且其法律效力次于 1952 年《访问部队法案》。

三、在应适用 1965 年《核能设施法》第十七条第六款的情况下，本法该部分不适用。

四、本法该部分不适用于刑事诉讼。

五、本法该部分不适用于除第十一条规定以外的任何与税收有关的诉讼。

第十七条　对第一部分的解释

一、在本法第一部分中

"《布鲁塞尔公约》"指 1926 年 4 月 10 日在布鲁塞尔签订的《统一国有船舶豁免若干规则的公约》；

"商业目的"指第三条第三款中规定的交易或活动的目的；

"船舶"包括气垫船。

二、在第二条第（二）款和第十三条第（三）款中，"协议"一词包括条约、公约或其他国际协议。

三、为上述第三条至第八条的目的，英国领土应视为包括英国作为《国家豁免欧洲公约》缔约国的所有属地。

四、本法第三条第一款、第四条第一款、第五条和第十六条第二款中所指的"英国"包括其领水和1964年《大陆架法》第一条第七款中所规定的任何区域。

五、在本法第一部分有关苏格兰的规定中,"对物诉讼"仅指海事诉讼。

第二部分 《国家豁免欧洲公约》缔约国针对英国作出的判决

第十八条 承认对英国作出的判决

一、本条适用于由《国家豁免欧洲公约》另一缔约国法院对英国做出的任何判决,且该判决是:

(一)在按照相当于本法第二条至第十一条英国不享有豁免的诉讼中作出;并且

(二)是终审判决,即不能或不再能上诉,或在缺席判决的情况下,不能被撤销的。

二、在符合第十九条的情况下,适用本条规定的判决应在英国境内所有法院得到承认,并可被相同案由的所有诉讼中的当事双方当作结论引用进行辩护或反诉。

三、本条第二款(不包括第十九条)同样适用于《国家豁免欧洲公约》的另一缔约国法院作出的任何决定,且根据该国法律,上述决定与判决具有同等效力。

四、本条中所指的公约缔约国法院包括缔约国所有领土上的法院。

第十九条 承认的例外

一、如果一项判决属于以下情况,则不适用第十八条:

(一)如果承认此判决明显违背公共政策,或如果作出判决的诉讼任一方未能有充分的陈述机会;或

(二)如果该判决违反本法第十二条的规定而作出,且英国尚未出庭或申请撤销该判决。

二、如果一项判决属于以下情况,则不适用第十八条:

(一)如果在相同当事人之间、基于相同事实和目的的诉讼:

1. 尚在英国法院审理且首先在英国提起;或

2. 尚在公约另一缔约国法院审理、在该国首先提起,且该判决可能导致本条的适用;或

（二）如果该判决结果与相同当事人之间的另一诉讼的判决结果不一致，且

1. 另一判决由英国法院作出，且或者该诉讼首先被提起，或者该英国法院判决在该判决成为第十八条第一款第（二）项所指的终审判决之前即已作出；或

2. 另一判决由公约另一缔约国法院作出，且有关条款已可适用。

三、在根据相当于本法第六条第二款的规定，英国不享有豁免的诉讼中，法院针对英国作出判决，如果作出相关判决的法院符合以下条件，则不适用第十八条：

（一）如果根据英国国内关于此类案件管辖权的规定，该法院对此案无管辖权；或

（二）如果该法院适用的法律与根据英国相关国际私法规则所指定的法律不同，且如适用该法律将产生不同的结论。

四、本条第二款所指的英国法院包括英国作为《关于国家豁免的欧洲公约》缔约国的所有属地上的法院；所指的公约另一缔约国的法院包括缔约方所有领土上的法院。

第三部分　其他及补充

第二十条　国家元首

一、在符合本条规定并作必要修改的情况下，1964年《外交特权法》应适用于：

（一）一国君主或其他元首；

（二）与其构成同一户口的家庭成员；以及

（三）他的私人仆人，

如同其适用于使馆馆长、与其构成同一户口的家庭成员及其私人仆人的规定一样。

二、根据本条第一款第（一）项和第（二）项赋予的特权和豁免不应受1964年《外交特权法》第三十七条第一款或第三十八条中关于国籍或居住地规定的限制。

三、除非国务大臣作出相反指示，根据本条第一款享有特权与豁免的个人，应免予适用1971年《移民法》第八条第三款的规定。

四、除增值税、关税或消费税外，本条不影响个人是否豁免于与税收相关的诉讼程序的任何问题。

五、本条适用于根据本法第一部分的规定而享有特权与豁免的任何国家的君主或其他元首，且不妨碍该部分对以公职身份行事的任何此类国家的君主或元首的适用。

第二十一条 证明书

由国务大臣或其代表出具的证明书应视为证明以下问题的结论性证据：

（一）任何国家是否属于本法第一部分中所指的国家，任何领土是否属于该部分所指的某一联邦国家的成员领土，任何人或团体是否属于该部分所指的国家元首或政府；

（二）一国是否是本法第一部分中提及的《布鲁塞尔公约》的缔约国；

（三）一国是否是《国家豁免欧洲公约》的缔约国，该国是否就该《公约》第二十四条作过声明，或在对与有关领土的关系上英国或任何其他国家均为该《公约》缔约国。

（四）本法第十二条第一款或第五款提及的文书是否被送达或收到；如果是的话，何时送达或收到。

第二十二条 一般解释

一、本法中的"法院"一词包括任何行使司法职能的法庭或机构；提及英国法院或英国法时包括英国任何地区的法院或法律。

二、本法提及的"出庭"和"缺席判决"包括与之有关的所有程序。

三、本法中的"《国家豁免欧洲公约》"指1972年5月16日在巴塞尔签订的公约。

四、本法中的"属地"指：

（一）英吉利海峡诸岛；

（二）马恩岛；

（三）除其对外关系由英国以外的其他国家负责的殖民地以外的所有殖民地；

（四）不在女王陛下统治之内，但女王陛下根据英国政府的权利对其拥有管辖权的所有国家或领土。

五、本法所赋予的任何颁发枢密院命令的权力，包括修改或废除此前命令的权力。

第二十三条 简称、废除、生效和范围

一、本法可被引用为"1978年《国家豁免法》"。

二、1938 年《司法行政法》第十三条（其他规定）和 1940 年《法律改革法》第七条（其他规定）（苏格兰）（因本法第一部分的规定，上述条款已无必要）特在此废除。

三、在符合本条第四款的情况下，本法第一部分和第二部分不适用于与在本法生效之前发生的事项有关的诉讼程序，特别是

（一）第二条第二款和第十三条第三款不适用于本法生效前的任何协定，并且

（二）第三条、第四条和第九条不适用于本法生效前生效的任何贸易、合同或仲裁协定。

四、第十二条适用于本法生效后提起的任何诉讼。

五、本法于大法官通过规范文件颁布的命令上载明的特定日期生效。

六、本法适用于北爱尔兰。

七、女王陛下可以枢密令的方式，将本法的任何规定或原封不动或加以修改延伸适用于任何属地。

1979 年新加坡外国国家豁免法

(第 313 章)
(初次制定的法律：1979 年第 19 号法)
修改版本 2014 年
(2014 年 12 月 31 日)
本法旨在规定新加坡境内，由其他国家提起或针对其他国家提起的诉讼程序，及其他相关事项。

[1979 年 10 月 26 日]

第一部分　前　　言

第一条　简称与适用

一、本法可被援引为"国家豁免法"。

二、在符合本条第三款规定的情况下，本法第二部分不适用于与本法生效前发生的事项有关的诉讼，特别是：

(一) 第四条第二款和第十五条第三款不适用于本法生效前的任何协议；并且

(二) 第五条、第六条和第十一条不适用于本法生效前已生效的任何交易、合同或仲裁协定。

三、第十四条适用于本法生效后开始的任何诉讼。

第二条　解释

一、本法中：

"商业目的"指第五条第三款提及的交易或活动的目的；

"法院"包括任何行使司法职能的法庭或机构；

"船舶"包括气垫船。

二、本法中：

(一) 第四条第二款和第十五条第三款中提及的"协议"包括条约、公约或其他国际协议；

(二) 提及的"出庭"和"缺席判决"包括与之有关的所有程序。

第二部分　在新加坡境内由其他国家提起
或针对其他国家提起的诉讼

管辖豁免

第三条　一般管辖豁免

一、除本部分下述条款规定的情形外，一国在新加坡法院享有管辖豁免。

二、即便一国没有在所涉案件的诉讼中出庭，法院仍应根据本条规定给予该国豁免。

豁免的例外

第四条　接受管辖

一、一国在其已接受新加坡法院管辖的诉讼中不享有豁免。

二、一国可以在引发诉讼程序的争议发生之后或事先以书面协议方式接受管辖，但任何协议中有关适用新加坡法律的规定不应被视为接受管辖。

三、在以下情况下，一国被视为接受管辖：

（一）如果该国提起诉讼；或

（二）在符合本条第四款和第五款规定的情况下，如果该国介入该诉讼或在诉讼中采取任何行动。

四、本条第三款第（二）项的规定不适用于仅为以下目的参加诉讼或采取任何行动：

（一）主张豁免；或

（二）在被诉国应有权享有豁免的情况下，对财产主张一项利益。

五、如果一国无法合理地知悉使其享有豁免的事实从而忽略了该事实，并且一旦可合理知悉便即刻主张豁免，则该国在此情形下采取的任何行动，不适用本条第三款第（二）项的规定。

六、一国在任何诉讼中接受管辖，即视为在上诉中接受管辖，但不视为在反诉中接受管辖，除非该反诉是针对与本诉相同的法律关系或事实提起的。

七、一国驻新加坡的使馆馆长，或暂时代行其职务的人，应被视为有权代表国家接受管辖；任何由国家授权代表该国订立合同的人员，应被视为有权就该合同引发的诉讼代表该国接受管辖。

第五条　商业交易和在新加坡履行的合同

一、一国在涉及下列事项的诉讼中不享有豁免：

（一）该国参加的商业交易；或

（二）该国根据一项全部或部分在新加坡履行的合同（不论是否属商业交易）而承担的义务；

但本款不适用于一国和个人之间签订的雇佣合同。

二、如果诉讼当事方均为国家，或另有书面协议，则不适用本条；如果合同（非商业交易）在有关国家境内缔结且涉及的义务适用该国行政法，则不适用本条第一款第（二）项。

三、本条中的"商业交易"指：

（一）任何提供货物或服务的合同；

（二）任何借贷或其他关于提供金融服务的交易，以及任何关于此类交易或其他涉及金融方面义务的担保或补偿；以及

（三）一国参与或从事的任何其他交易或活动（无论属于商业、工业、金融、专业，还是其他类似性质），该国行使其主权权力的行为除外。

第六条　雇佣合同

一、在与一国和个人之间签订的雇佣合同有关的诉讼中，如该合同在新加坡缔结或雇佣工作需全部或部分在新加坡履行，则该国不享有豁免。

二、在符合本条第三款和第四款规定的情况下，本条不适用于以下情况：

（一）当诉讼提起时，该受雇个人为雇佣国国民；或

（二）签订雇佣合同时，该受雇个人既非新加坡公民，也不惯常居住在新加坡；或

（三）合同当事方另有书面协议。

三、当雇主是一国出于商业目的在新加坡境内经营的办事处、机构或企业时，第二款第（一）项和第（二）项不能排除本条的适用，除非该受雇个人在签订合同时在该国惯常居住。

四、如果根据新加坡法律，诉讼应由新加坡法院审理，则第二款第（三）项不能排除本条的适用。

五、本条中"与雇佣合同有关的诉讼"包括该合同的当事方就其作为雇主或雇员所分别享有的法定权利或义务而提起的诉讼。

第七条　人身伤害和财产损害

一国就其在新加坡境内的作为或不作为造成下列后果而引发的诉讼中不享有豁免：

（一）死亡或人身伤害；或

（二）有形财产的损失或灭失。

第八条　财产的所有、占有和使用

一、一国在与下列事项有关的诉讼中不享有豁免：

（一）该国对其位于新加坡的不动产的任何利益，或该国对该不动产的占有或使用；或者

（二）该国由于对任何此类财产的利益或占有或使用而产生的任何义务。

二、一国在涉及其由于继承、赠予或无主物取得而产生对动产或不动产的任何利益的诉讼中不享有豁免。

三、一国对任何财产享有或主张一项利益时，不应排除任何法院对涉及死者或精神失常者的财产，或涉及公司清算、解散或信托财产管理诉讼的管辖权。

四、法院可受理针对人员而非国家的诉讼，即使这些诉讼涉及：

（一）一国占有或控制的财产；或

（二）一国对其主张利益的财产，

如果诉讼针对该国，该国不能享有豁免，或在上述第（二）项所述情形下，该国的主张既未被承认，也未得到表面证据的支持。

第九条　专利、商标及其他

一国在与下列事项有关的诉讼中不享有豁免：

（一）该国所有并在新加坡注册或受到保护的，或该国已在新加坡提出申请的任何专利、商标或设计；

（二）该国被指控在新加坡侵犯了任何专利、商标、设计或版权；或

（三）在新加坡境内使用商业名称或企业名称的权利。

第十条　法人团体的成员资格及其他

一、一国在与其在法人团体、非法人团体中的成员资格或合伙人资格有关的诉讼中不享有豁免，如果该法人团体或非法人团体：

（一）有非国家成员；并且

（二）系根据新加坡法律成立或组建，或由新加坡控股，或其主要营业地在新加坡，

且该诉讼发生在该国和该团体之间、该国和该团体其他成员之间或该国和其他合伙人之间。

二、如果争议当事方之间以书面协议方式作出了相反约定，或其章程或其他建立或管理相关团体或合伙关系的文件有相反规定，本条不适用。

第十一条　仲裁

一、如果一国以书面形式同意将已经发生或可能发生的争议提交仲裁，则该国在有关仲裁事项的诉讼中不能在新加坡法院享有豁免。

二、仲裁协议中的任何相反规定可以排除本条的适用。本条不适用于国家间的仲裁协议。

第十二条　用于商业目的的船舶

一、本条适用于：

（一）海事诉讼；以及

（二）任何有可能成为海事诉讼事项的诉讼。

二、如果诉讼事由发生时，船舶正被用于或意图被用于商业目的，则一国在下列诉讼中不享有豁免：

（一）针对归该国所有船舶的对物诉讼；或

（二）为执行与该船舶有关的诉讼请求的对人诉讼。

三、如果针对一国所有的某一船舶提起的对物诉讼，是为了执行与该国所有的另一船舶有关的诉讼请求，则本条第二款第（一）项不适用于上述前一船舶，除非当关于另一船舶的诉讼事由发生时，两船均正被用于或意图被用于商业目的。

四、下列情况下，一国不享有豁免：

（一）针对属于该国的货物的对物诉讼，条件是诉讼事由发生时，货物和运送货物的船舶均正被用于或意图被用于商业目的；或

（二）为执行与该国所有的货物有关的诉讼请求而进行的对人诉讼，条件是运送这些货物的船舶正被用于或意图被用于商业目的。

五、本条第二款至第四款所指为归一国所有的船舶或货物包括该国占有、控制或该国对其主张一项利益的任何船舶或货物；在符合本条第四款规定的情况下，本条第二款与适用于船舶一样，适用于船舶以外的其他财产。

第十三条　关税及其他

一国在与以下责任有关的诉讼中不享有豁免：

（一）任何关税或消费税；

（一）之二　任何商品和服务税；或

（二）与该国因商业目的占有的房产有关的任何税种。

程　序

第十四条　送达程序和缺席判决

一、与对一国提起诉讼有关的任何传票或其他文书，应通过新加坡外交部送达该国外交部，送达应自该国外交部收到传票或文书之日起生效。

二、出庭时限（不论依照法院规则或其他规定）应是按前述方式收到传票或文书之日起两个月。

三、一国在诉讼中出庭后，不能再就该诉讼不符合本条第一款规定为由而提出反对。

四、除非有证据证明本条第一款已获遵守，且本条第二款规定的出庭时限届满，否则不得对一国作出缺席判决。

五、对一国作出的任何缺席判决，应通过新加坡外交部将判决书副本送交该国外交部。申请撤销缺席判决的时限（不论依照法院规则或其他规定）应为该国外交部收到缺席判决副本之日起两个月。

六、本条第一款规定不妨碍以经一国同意的任何其他方式送达；本条第二款和第四款不适用于以该方式进行的送达。

七、本条不应被解释为适用于针对一国提出的反诉或对物诉讼；本条第一款不得被解释为影响就向管辖范围以外进行送达要求得到法院许可的任何法院规则。

第十五条　其他程序性特权

一、如诉讼当事国或其代表不能或拒绝披露或提供任何与诉讼相关的文件或其他信息，不得对该国处以拘禁或罚金形式的处罚。

二、在符合本条第三款和第四款规定的情况下：

（一）不应通过禁令或命令的方式针对一国采取强制履行或将土地或其他财产恢复原状的救济措施；以及

（二）一国财产不受任何判决或仲裁裁决执行或在对物诉讼中对该财产进行扣留、扣押或变卖的程序的约束。

三、本条第二款的规定不妨碍经相关国家书面同意而采取任何救济措施或启动任何程序；任何此种同意（可能包含在事前协议中）可以表明仅在限定范围内适用或普遍适用；但仅表示接受法院管辖的条款不能被视为本条款中的"同意"。

四、本条第二款第（二）项的规定不妨碍启动关于正被用于或意图被用于商业目的的财产的任何程序。

五、一国派驻新加坡的使馆馆长或暂时代行其职务的人，应被视为有权代表国家作出本条第三款所规定的"同意"，并为本条第四款的目的，其代表国家所作的关于任何财产未被用于或意图被用于商业目的的证明应被视为充分证据，除非有相反的事实得到证明。

第三部分　补充规定

第十六条　享有特权与豁免的国家

一、本法第二部分规定的特权与豁免，适用于新加坡以外的任何国家或英联邦国家；所提及的"国家"包括：

（一）以其公职身份行事的该国君主或其他元首；

（二）该国政府；以及

（三）该政府的任何部门，

但不包括任何独立于该国政府行政机构之外，且有权起诉或被诉的实体（本条中称"独立实体"）。

二、独立实体仅在满足下列条件时，才能在新加坡法院享有管辖豁免：

（一）诉讼程序与该实体行使主权权力的任何行为有关；且

（二）如果是国家即可以享有豁免。

三、如独立实体（一国中央银行和其他金融主管机关除外）在可依本条第二款的规定享有豁免的诉讼程序中接受管辖，则第十五条第一款至第四款中关于国家的规定同样适用于该实体。

四、一国中央银行或其他金融主管机关的财产不应被视为第十五条第四款中所指"被用于或意图被用于商业目的"。如果一银行或主管机关是独立实体，则第十五条第一款至第三款中关于国家的规定同样适用于该银行或主管机关。

五、第十四条适用于针对联邦国家成员领土提起的诉讼。总统可颁布命令，使本法该部分其他条款如同适用于国家一样，适用于任何此类成员领土。

六、如根据任何上述命令，本法第二部分的规定不适用于一成员领土，则该成员领土应被视为一个独立实体，适用本条第二款和第三款。

第十七条　特权与豁免的限制和扩大

如果总统认为根据本法第二部分的规定给予一国的特权与豁免：

（一）超出该国法律给予新加坡的特权与豁免；或

（二）少于该国与新加坡同为缔约国的任何条约、公约或其他国际协议的要求，

则总统可颁布命令，将此类特权与豁免限制或扩大至总统认为合适的范围。

第十八条　证明书

由外交部长或其代表出具的证明书应被视为证明下列问题的结论性证据：

（一）任何国家是否属于本法第二部分所指的国家，任何领土是否属于该部分所指的某一联邦国家的成员领土，任何人或团体是否属于该部分所指的国家元首或政府；

（二）本法第十四条第一款或第五款所提及的文书是否被送达或收到；如果是的话，何时送达或被收到。

第十九条　除外事项

一、本法第二部分不影响在新加坡的外交及领事机构所享有的任何特权或豁免。第八条第一款不适用于有关一国命名或占有的用于外交使团目的的财产的诉讼。

二、本法第二部分不适用于：

（一）关于一国军队在新加坡期间的任何行为或与其相关的诉讼，并且该部分规定的法律效力次于《部队访问法案》（第344章）；

（二）刑事诉讼；和

（三）第十三条规定之外的与税收有关的诉讼。

1981年巴基斯坦国家豁免条例

1981年第六号条例

兹以本条例修订及整合有关外国国家司法管辖豁免的法律。

鉴于修订及整合有关国家司法管辖豁免法律的必要性，及

总统认同情势要求对相关法律从速进行修订和整合，

同意依据1977年7月5日公告及1977年《立法法》（C. M. L. A. 1977年第1号）制定并公布本条例。

第一条 简称及时空效力

一、本条例简称为《1981年国家豁免条例》。

二、本条例在巴基斯坦全境有效。

三、本条例即时生效。

第二条 释义

本条例中，"法院"是指行使司法审判权的任何审判组织或机构。

司法管辖豁免

第三条 一般管辖豁免

一、除下文规定外，外国国家免受巴基斯坦法院的司法管辖。

二、对未在诉讼中出庭的国家，法院亦应给予其本条第一款所述豁免。

豁免的例外

第四条 接受管辖

一、外国国家就其已经接受管辖的事项不得享受管辖豁免。

二、外国国家可在争端发生后接受管辖或通过事前协议接受管辖；但任何协议中选择适用巴基斯坦法律的规定不得视为接受管辖。

（解释：本款及第十四条第三款所述"协定"包括条约、公约或其他国际协定。）

三、下列情形视为外国国家接受管辖：

（一）外国国家提起诉讼；或

（二）外国国家参加诉讼或采取步骤参与诉讼，但下述第四款规定除外。

四、本条第三款第（二）项不适用于下列情形：

（一）仅为下列目的参加诉讼或采取步骤参与诉讼：

1. 主张管辖豁免；或

2. 在对享有豁免的外国国家提起诉讼的情况下，该外国国家主张其对财产的权利；

（二）如果一国无法合理地知悉使其享有豁免的事实从而忽略了该事实，并且一旦可合理知悉便即刻主张豁免。

五、接受管辖适用于上诉，但不得适用于反诉，除非反诉依据的法律关系或事实与本诉一致。

六、外国国家驻巴基斯坦的使馆馆长，或暂时代行其职权者，应被视为有权代表国家接受管辖。任何由国家授权代表该国订立合同的缔约者，应被视为有权就该合同引发的诉讼代表国家接受管辖。

第五条 商业交易和在巴基斯坦履行的合同

一、外国国家就下列事项不得主张管辖豁免：

（一）该国参加的商业交易；或

（二）该国承担的合同义务全部或部分在巴基斯坦境内履行，无论该合同是否属商业交易。

二、本条第一款规定不适用于国家与个人之间签订的雇佣合同，或缔约方均为国家，或缔约方另行书面约定；如果非商业交易合同的缔约地在该外国领土内，且有关合同义务受该外国行政法律调整，则第一款第二项不适用。

三、本条中的"商业交易"指：

（一）任何提供货物或服务的合同；

（二）任何借贷或其他关于提供金融服务的交易，及任何关于此类交易或其他涉及金融方面义务的担保或补偿；

（三）国家非因行使主权参与或从事的商业、工业、金融、专业或其他类似性质的交易或活动。

第六条 雇佣合同

一、外国国家对其与个人在巴基斯坦签订的，或合同全部或部分在巴基斯坦履行的雇佣合同引起的诉讼不享有豁免。

（解释：本款中"雇佣合同诉讼"包括雇佣合同缔约方作为雇员或雇主基于合同产生的权利或义务的诉讼。）

二、除第三款和第四款规定外，本条第一款规定不适用于下列情形：

（一）当诉讼提起时该受雇人员为该国国民；或

（二）签订雇佣合同时，该受雇人员既非巴基斯坦公民，亦非巴基斯坦常住居民；或

（三）争议双方另行书面约定的。

三、如雇主为外国国家出于商业目的在巴基斯坦境内经营的办公机构或组织工作，除非缔约时雇员为巴基斯坦常住居民，上述第二款第一项和第二项不排除第一款的适用。

四、根据巴基斯坦法律规定，应由巴基斯坦法院管辖的诉讼，第二款第三项不得排除第一款的适用。

第七条 财产的所有、占有和使用

一、外国国家在与下列事项有关的诉讼中不享有豁免：

（一）外国国家对其在巴基斯坦的不动产的任何利益，或该国对该不动产的占有或使用；或

（二）该外国国家对任何此类财产的利益，或占有或使用而产生的任何义务。

二、外国国家在涉及其因继承、赠予或无主物取得而产生对动产或不动产的任何利益的诉讼中不享有豁免。

三、外国国家对任何财产享有或主张一项利益时，不应排除任何法院对涉及死者或精神失常者的财产或涉及公司清算、解散或信托财产管理诉讼的管辖权。

四、法院可受理针对个人而非国家的诉讼，即使诉讼相关财产由：

（一）外国国家占有；或

（二）外国国家对此主张权益，

如果诉讼针对该外国国家，该国不享有豁免；或在上述第（二）项所述情况下，该外国国家的主张既未获承认，也未得到表面证据的支持。

第八条 专利、商标及其他

外国国家在下列事项有关的诉讼中不享受豁免：

一、外国国家所有，且在巴基斯坦注册、受保护，或其已在巴基斯坦提出申请的专利、商标、工业设计、育种权；

二、外国国家被指控在巴基斯坦境内侵犯了任何专利、商标、工业设计、育种权或著作权；

三、在巴基斯坦境内使用商品名称或企业名称的权利。

第九条　法人团体的成员资格及其他

一、外国国家在与其在法人团体、非法人团体中的成员资格或合伙人资格有关的诉讼中，如该诉讼系外国国家与上述机构或机构成员之间进行，则以下情况不得享有豁免，如该：

（一）有关团体或机构的成员不限于国家；且

（二）有关团体或机构根据巴基斯坦法律注册或设立，或其实际控制人或主要经营地在巴基斯坦境内。

二、若争议方书面约定不适用，或设立团体或合伙机构的章程或其他文件另有规定的，不适用本条第一款的规定。

第十条　仲裁

一、书面约定将已发生或可能产生的争议提交仲裁的外国国家，就仲裁相关争议不得主张巴基斯坦法院的管辖豁免。

二、第一款规定须在仲裁协议有约定的情况下方得适用，且该款规定不适用于国家之间的仲裁协议。

第十一条　商用船舶

一、本条规定适用于：

（一）海事诉讼；及

（二）可能构成海事诉讼事项的诉讼。

二、争议行为发生时，船舶被用于，或意图被用于商业目的，则外国国家就下列事项不得主张管辖豁免：

（一）对归本国所有的船舶主张对物诉讼；

（二）为执行与该船舶有关的诉讼请求而进行对人诉讼。

三、为实施外国国家对其所有船舶的主张，而对其所有的另一船舶进行对物诉讼，除非诉因产生时两船舶皆用于或意图用于商业目的，否则第二款第一项规定不适用于被诉船舶。

四、外国国家对下列事项不得主张管辖豁免：

（一）对归本国所有的货物主张对物诉讼，诉因产生时该船舶及其所载货物均用于或意图用于商业目的；或

（二）为执行与上述货物相关的诉讼请求而进行对人诉讼，诉因产生时载货船舶用于或意图用于商业目的。

五、前款规定的外国所有的船舶或货物，包括外国国家占有或控制，或主张权益的船舶或货物；在本条第四款规定条件下，第二款比照适用于非船舶的其他财产。

六、如有关国家是《布鲁塞尔公约》的缔约国，且诉讼涉及该国所有或经营的船舶的运营，或此类船舶所载货物或乘客的承载，或其他船舶上的归该国所有的货物的承载，则本条第五款和第六款规定不适用于第一款所规定的诉讼。

（解释："《布鲁塞尔公约》"指 1926 年 4 月 10 日于布鲁塞尔签订的《关于统一国有船舶豁免权有关规定的国际公约》；"船舶"包括气垫船。）

第十二条 增值税、海关关税及其他

外国国家就其对下列事项承担的责任，不得主张管辖豁免：

（一）增值税、海关关税、消费税或农业征收税；或

（二）为商业目的而占有房屋的房地产税。

程序性规定

第十三条 送达和缺席判决

一、起诉外国国家的通知或文件应经巴基斯坦外交部转送被诉国外交部门，外国外交部收到通知或文件时视为送达。

二、法院诉讼自文件送达之日起两个月后方得启动。

三、外国国家应诉后，不得因本条第一款规定未获满足而反对管辖。

四、法院不得对外国国家进行缺席审判，除非已履行本条第一款规定，且本条第二款规定的期限已过。

五、缺席判决书副本应经巴基斯坦外交部转送被诉国外交部门；申请撤销判决的期限为判决副本送达外交部门之日起两个月。

六、第一款规定不排除外国国家同意的其他送达方式，此时第二款和第四款不再适用。

七、本条规定不适用于对外国国家提出的反诉或对物诉讼。

第十四条 其他程序性特权

一、不得因外国国家或代表该国家的人员未公开或提供，或拒绝公开或提供诉讼有关的文件或信息，而对相关责任人员处以监禁或罚款。

二、除第三款和第四款另有规定外：

（一）不得以禁制令或命令的方式向外国国家采取强制履行或要求返还土地或其他财产的救济措施；

（二）不得以执行判决或仲裁裁决的名义或在对物诉讼中，对外国国家所有的非用于或意图用于商业目的的财产进行扣押、留置或变卖。

三、如外国国家书面同意，则第二款规定不再适用。上述同意可在此前签订的协议中规定，并可指明系普遍适用或针对特定事项适用。国家仅同意接受管辖权的规定，不得视为本款所述的同意。

四、外国国家驻巴基斯坦的外交使团团长，或代行其职权者有权以国家名义同意第三款、第二款第二项所述事项。除有相反证据，其对国家财产非用于或意图用于商业目的的证明应被视为充分证据。

补充条款

第十五条　可主张豁免和特权的外国国家

一、本法案规定的豁免和特权适用于外国国家，包括：

（一）履行公职时的该国君主或国家元首；

（二）该国政府；及

（三）该国政府部门；

本款不适用于有独立诉讼能力的非政府行政机构实体（以下简称"独立实体"）。

二、当且仅当下列条件成立时，独立实体得主张豁免：

（一）因其行使国家主权的行为引起的诉讼；且

（二）相同情形下，外国国家可主张豁免。

三、除中央银行和其他货币管理机构外的独立实体放弃其依第二款享有的豁免而接受管辖的，第十四条第一款至第三款对外国国家适用的程序性规定得对其比照适用。

四、中央银行或其他货币管理机构的财产不得视为第十四条第三款规定的用于或意图用于商业目的的财产。如该中央银行或货币管理机构为独立实体，第十四条第一款和第二款适用于外国国家的规定得对其比照适用。

五、第十三条适用于对联邦国家组成部分的诉讼。巴基斯坦联邦政府可通过政府公报，通知本条例的其他规定亦比照适用于有关联邦国家的组成部分。

六、如根据本条第五款规定的通知，本条例不适用于联邦国家组成部分，则将联邦国家组成部分视为独立实体而比照适用本条第二款和第三款的规定。

第十六条 豁免和特权的限制与扩展

一、本法案规定的豁免和特权出现下列情况时：

（一）超出外国国家赋予巴基斯坦的豁免和特权；或

（二）低于该国与巴基斯坦同为缔约国的条约、公约或其他国际协定的规定；

联邦政府得通过政府公报，将给予该国的豁免和特权限制或扩展到合适的范围。

第十七条 保留

一、本条例不影响《1972年外交与领事特权法案》（1972年第9号）授予的特权与豁免；且

（一）第六条不适用于1972年法案附表1《公约》所述外交使团人员的雇佣诉讼，及附表2《公约》所述领事机构人员的雇佣诉讼；

（二）第七条第一款不适用于涉及外国国家命名、占有的用于外交使团目的的财产的诉讼。

二、本条例不适用于下列情形：

（一）与驻扎在巴基斯坦的外国武装部队有关的讼诉，或涉及其行为的诉讼；

（二）刑事诉讼；

（三）第十二条规定以外的税收相关诉讼。

第十八条 相关事实的证明

巴基斯坦政府代表出具的证明文件对下列问题具有终局证明力：

一、一国是否构成本条例所述的外国国家；一国领土是否构成本条例所述外国联邦国家的组成部分；某人是否为本法案所述的外国国家元首或政府首脑；

二、第十三条第一款或第五款规定的文件是否及何时已送达或收到。

第十九条 废止

《1908年民事诉讼法典》（1908年第5号法案）第八十六条和第八十七条予以废止。

1981 年南非外国国家豁免法

1981 年 10 月 6 日通过,同年 11 月 20 日实施。

本法经"外国国家豁免法修正案"(1985 年第 48 号和 1988 年第 5 号)修订。

为明确外国国家享受南非司法管辖豁免的范围,并就相关事项作出规定,特制定本法。

第一条 定义

一、本法中除另有规定外:

"商业目的",指第四条第三款规定的任何商业交易的目的;

"领事机构",指总领馆、领馆、领事办公室、贸易办事处或劳工办事处;

"南非共和国"包括南非共和国领水,具体参见《1963 年领水法》(1963 年第 87 号法案)第二条的规定。

"独立实体"指下述第二款第(三)项第一目的任何实体。

二、本法中所指的"外国国家"包括:

(一)国家元首;

(二)外国政府;及

(三)政府部门;但不包括:

1. 独立于该国政府行政部门,且具有诉讼资格的实体;或

2. 联邦国家的领土组成部分。

第二条 一般管辖豁免

一、除根据本法有关规定或依据本法发布的公告规定的情形外,外国国家应免受南非共和国法院的司法管辖。

二、即使外国国家未在诉讼中出庭,法院亦应实施本条所赋予外国国家的豁免。

三、本法案任何规定不得解释为使外国国家受南非共和国法院的刑事司法管辖。

第三条　放弃豁免

一、外国国家明示放弃豁免，或依据本条第三款认定外国国家放弃豁免，南非共和国法院可行使管辖权。

二、在引起诉讼的争议发生后或事前的书面协议中，均可表示放弃豁免，但在协议中关于适用南非共和国法律的约定，不得视为放弃豁免。

三、外国国家有如下情况应认定为已放弃豁免：

（一）如该国已提起诉讼；或

（二）在不违反第四款规定的情形下，该国已介入诉讼或已在诉讼中采取行动。

四、仅以下列目的介入诉讼或在诉讼中采取行动，上述第三款第（二）项不得适用：

（一）主张享有豁免；或

（二）有权享有豁免的国家在被起诉的情况下，主张其财产权益。

五、在诉讼中放弃豁免也适用于上诉，以及就本诉的同一法律关系或事实提出的反诉。

六、驻南非共和国的外交使团团长，或暂时代行其职务的人，应被视为有权代表其国家在诉讼中放弃豁免；任何有权代表国家，以及经国家授权签订合同的人员，在因此等合同产生的诉讼中，应被视为有权代表国家表示放弃豁免。

第四条　商业交易

一、外国国家就下列事项，不得享有南非共和国法院的司法管辖豁免：

（一）该外国国家从事的商业交易；或

（二）该外国国家依合同承担的义务（不论该合同是否涉及商业交易），部分或全部在南非共和国境内履行。

二、如争议双方均为外国国家，或根据书面约定争议由外国法院管辖的，则本条第一款规定不适用。

三、本条第一款规定的"商业交易"指：

（一）任何提供货物或服务的合同；

（二）任何借贷或其他关于提供金融服务的交易，以及任何关于此类交易或其他涉及金融方面义务的担保或补偿；以及

（三）外国国家除行使主权外所参与或从事的任何其他商业的、产业的、金融的、专业性的或其他类似性质的行为或活动；商业交易不包括外国国家与个人签订的雇佣合同。

第五条　雇佣合同

一、外国国家在下列情形下，就其与个人签订的雇佣合同的诉讼，不得享有豁免：

（一）合同缔结地、部分或全部履行地在南非共和国境内；并且

（二）缔结合同时，该个人是南非共和国公民或常住居民；并且

（三）提起诉讼时，该个人不是该外国国家公民。

二、前款规定不适用于：

（一）合同双方书面约定有关争议或与合同相关的任何争议，由外国法院管辖；

（二）诉讼涉及外交使团团长、使团成员或外交、行政、技术或服务人员的雇佣，或领馆馆长、领事、劳工、贸易、行政、技术或服务人员的雇佣。

第六条　人身伤害和财产损害

外国国家对其在南非共和国境内作为或不作为引起的下列诉讼不享有南非法院的管辖豁免：

（一）造成人员伤亡的；或

（二）造成有形财产损害的。

第七条　财产的所有权、占有和使用权

一、外国国家就下列事项的诉讼，不享有南非法院的管辖豁免：

（一）外国国家在南非共和国境内的不动产利益，或其对该不动产的占有或使用；

（二）外国国家因本条第一款第（一）项而产生的义务；

（三）外国国家因继承、赠予或无主物取得而产生的动产或不动产利益。

二、本条第一款规定不适用于与外国国家对外交使团或领事机构财产的所有权、使用权或占有权有关的诉讼。

第八条　专利、商标等权利

外国国家对下列事项有关的诉讼，不享有南非法院的管辖豁免：

（一）外国国家所有，并在南非共和国注册或受保护，或其在南非共和国申请的专利、商标、工业设计或育种权；

（二）外国国家被指控在南非共和国境内侵犯了专利、商标、工业设计、育种权或著作权；

（三）在南非共和国境内使用商业名称或企业名称的权利。

第九条　协会等组织成员

一、外国国家是协会或其他组织（不论是否为法人）成员或合作伙伴，如该协会、其他组织或合作伙伴关系有以下情况：

（一）有非外国国家的成员；且

（二）依南非共和国法律注册或设立，或由南非共和国自然人或法人控制，或主要经营地在南非共和国，则该外国国家就下列诉讼不享受南非共和国法院管辖豁免：

1. 与协会、其他组织或合作伙伴关系成员资格有关的争议；以及

2. 该外国国家与协会、其他组织或其成员，或与其他合作伙伴之间的争议。

二、本条第一款规定不适用于以下情况：

（一）争议双方书面约定不适用；或

（二）设立有关协会、其他组织或合作伙伴关系的章程或其他文件规定不适用；

则上述争议由外国法院管辖。

第十条　仲裁

一、外国国家如书面同意将已发生或可能发生的争议提交仲裁，该国在南非共和国法院涉及该项仲裁的诉讼中不得享有豁免。

二、下列情形不适用本条第一款规定：

（一）仲裁协议规定有关诉讼由外国法院受理的；

（二）仲裁协议的双方均为外国国家。

第十一条　海事诉讼

一、如争端发生时，有关船舶用于或意图用于商业目的，则外国国家对下列事项，不得主张南非共和国法院的海事管辖豁免：

（一）对本国所有船舶主张对物诉讼；

（二）与该船舶有关的主张权益的对人诉讼；

二、对下列事项，外国国家不得主张南非共和国法院的海事管辖豁免：

（一）对归本国所有的货物主张对物诉讼，如争端发生时船舶及其所载货物均用于或意图用于商业目的；

（二）与货物有关的主张权益的对人诉讼，如争端发生时载货船舶用于或意图用于商业目的。

三、本条所指外国国家所有的"船舶"、"货物"包括处于外国国家占有或控制下的船舶或货物，或该国得对其主张权利的船舶或货物；在符合

本条第二款规定的情况下，本条第一款规定得比照适用于船舶以外的其他财产。

第十二条 税收

外国国家不得就其以下税收义务主张南非共和国法院的管辖豁免：

（一）营业税、关税或消费税；或

（二）用于商业目的的不动产房产税。

第十三条 送达和缺席判决

一、起诉外国国家的相关文件应通过南非共和国外交和信息部送达外国外交部，该国外交部收到文件时视为送达完成。

二、法院规则规定的时效或外国国家表明答辩、提出异议或出庭意向通知的期限为根据本条第一款规定的方式送达之日起两个月。

三、已出庭的国家不得在其后以未满足本条第一款规定为由反对管辖。

四、除非证明已按照本条第一款的规定送达了文书，并且根据本条第二款的规定出庭期限已经届满，否则不得对外国国家作出缺席判决。

五、对外国国家的缺席判决书副本应通过南非共和国外交和信息部送达外国国家外交部；法院规则规定的时效或申请撤销判决的期限为自判决书副本送达外国外交部之日起两个月。

六、本条第一款规定不排除外国国家同意的其他送达方式，此时本条第二款和第四款不再适用。

七、本条不得解释为适用于对外国国家提出的反诉或对物诉讼。本条第一款的规定不得解释为影响向法院管辖范围以外的送达需获得同意的法院规则。

第十四条 其他程序性特权

一、在符合本条第二款和第三款规定的情况下：

（一）不得以禁令制令或命令的方式对外国国家采取强制履行或要求返还任何动产或不动产的救济措施；

（二）不得对外国国家财产采取以下行动：

1. 对其扣押以确立管辖；

2. 作为判决或仲裁裁决的执行标的；

3. 对其主张对物诉讼，以进行扣押或变卖。

二、如外国国家书面同意执行，本条第一款规定不适用；此类同意可事前达成，可规定普遍适用或适用于特定事项；外国国家放弃管辖豁免不得视为为本款目的所作的同意。

三、第一款第（二）项不禁止对用于或打算用于商业目的的财产采取措施。

第十五条　独立实体的豁免

一、在下列情况下，独立实体得享受管辖豁免：

（一）独立实体行使国家主权产生的有关争端；且

（二）外国国家在相同的条件下得享受管辖豁免。

二、除外国国家中央银行和其他金融机构以外的独立实体放弃其根据本条第一款规定享有的管辖豁免时，第十四条适用于外国国家的程序性规定同样适用于有关独立实体。

三、外国国家中央银行或其他金融机构的财产，不得认为是上述第十四条第三款所指用于或拟用于商业目的的财产；在此种银行或金融机构为独立实体时，第十四条第一款、第二款适用于国家的规定，亦比照适用于此种银行或金融机构。

第十六条　对特权和豁免的限制与扩大

如根据本法案规定的特权和豁免出现下列情况时：

（一）超出或低于有关外国国家给予南非共和国的特权和豁免；或

（二）低于该国与南非共和国同为缔约国的条约、公约或其他国际协定规定的标准；

南非共和国总统得通过政府公报宣布将给予该国的特权和豁免限制或扩大至合适标准。

第十七条　证明文件的效力

由外交和信息部部长作出或代表该部部长签发的证明文件对下列问题具有最终效力：

（一）外国国家是否为本法案所述的"国家"；

（二）某一领土是否构成本法案所述的联邦国家组成部分；

（三）某人是否为本法案所述的国家元首或政府首脑；

（四）文件是否及何时根据本法案第十三条第一款或第五款规定视为送达。

第十八条　简称和生效

本法案简称《1981年外国国家豁免法》，并于总统确定的在政府公报公布之日起生效。

《外国国家豁免法修正案》

1985 年第 48 号

兹修订《1981 年外国国家豁免法》，以明确规定不得对外国国家财产实施扣押以建立管辖：

第一条 对《1981 年外国国家豁免法》（1981 年第 87 号）第十四条第一款进行修订，并取代第（二）项之规定。

第二条 简称：本法案简称《1985 年外国国家豁免法修正案》。

《外国国家豁免法修正案》

1988 年第 5 号

兹修订《1981 年外国国家豁免法》，以确认外国国家享有的南非共和国法院司法管辖豁免，消除特定歧义，并明确相关事项：

第一条 《1981 年外国国家豁免法》（1981 年第 87 号，以下简称"原法案"）第二条兹加入下述规定：

"四、争议各方均为外国国家的，管辖豁免的例外规定不得适用。"

第二条 对原法案第九条修订如下：

下述规定取代原法案第九条第一款第（一）项规定：

"一、其中包括非国家成员的；且"

第三条 对原法案第十条修订如下：

下述规定取代原法案第十条第二款第（二）项规定：

"二、仲裁协议缔约方均是国家"；

第四条 对原法案第十三条修订如下：

一、下述规定取代原法案第一款规定：

"一、对外国国家起诉的相关文件应经南非共和国外交部转送受诉国外交部门；或依据其他南非共和国与该外国同为缔约国的条约，以使该国能够取得该文件的方式转送；文件到达外国外交部门，或处于该国管控领域时视为送达"；

二、下述规定取代原法案第二款规定：

"二、法院规则和其他文件规定的答辩、异议或出庭期限自上述方式送达之日后两个月"；

三、下述规定取代原法案第五款规定：

"五、缺席判决书副本应经南非共和国外交部转送受诉国外交部门，或依据其他南非共和国和该外国同为缔约国的条约，以使该国能够取得该文件的方式送达；申请确认判决无效之诉的期限自判决副本送达外交部门，或进入该国管控领域之日后两个月；"

第五条 对原法案第十四条修订如下：

下述规定取代第十四条第一款第（二）项规定：

"（二）外国国家财产不成立下列程序的对象：（甲）对其扣押以建立或确认管辖；（乙）作为判决或仲裁裁决的执行标的；（丙）对其主张人之诉以实现扣押或变卖；"

第六条 对原法案第十七条修订如下：

一、对第（一）项作如下修改：

"**第十七条** 外交部或以外交部名义出具的证明文件对下列问题有决定性的证明力："；

二、对第（四）项作如下修改：

"（四）文件是否及何时，依第十三条第（一）款或第（五）款规定视为送达，或视为处于该国管控领域"。

第七条 简称和生效

本法案简称为《1988年外国国家豁免法案》，并于总统确定的在政府公报公布之日起生效。

1984 年马拉维特权与豁免法

本法规定外国在马拉维法院享有的管辖豁免范围。通过本法确认有关国际公约在马拉维的法律效力而给予外交和领事特权与豁免，以及国际组织特权与豁免。

[1984 年 4 月 17 日]

第一部分　序　言

第一条　简称
本法可简称为特权与豁免法。

第二条　定义
一、在本法中：
"商业目的"指第五条第三款规定的任何商业交易；
"领事官员"指包括领馆馆长在内的任何受委托行使领事职能的个人，或任何英联邦国家政府行使此职能的个人；
"领馆"指总领事馆、领事馆、副领事馆或领事机构；
"外交代表"见附录一第一条的规定。
二、附录一及附录二有关条款中：
"接受国代表"或"接受国当局"，指包括警务人员及根据成文法有权进入或处于处所内执行职务的人；
"严重犯罪"指初次犯罪即可被判处五年或五年以上拘禁的罪行；
"接受国国民"指马拉维公民。

第二部分　国家豁免

第三条　一般管辖豁免
一、一国在马拉维法院享有管辖豁免，本法另有规定的除外。

二、即使国家未出庭参加诉讼，法院仍应赋予该国本法规定的管辖豁免。

第四条　接受管辖

一、一国接受马拉维法院的管辖将在接受管辖的案件中不再享有豁免。

二、一国可在争端产生后接受管辖，也可通过此前签订的书面协议接受管辖，但协议中规定适用马拉维法律的条款不视为该国放弃豁免。

三、下列情形视为一国接受管辖：

（一）提起诉讼；

（二）除本条第四款的规定外，介入诉讼或在诉讼中采取行动。

四、如仅限于下述目的，则本条第三款第二项不适用：

（一）主张享有豁免；

（二）有权享有豁免的国家在被起诉的情况下，主张其财产权益。

五、接受管辖适用于上诉，以及就本诉的同一法律关系或事实提出的反诉。

六、一国在马拉维的外交使团团长，其时正执行此等职务的人员，应被视为有权代表其国家在诉讼中接受管辖；任何有权代表国家，以及经国家授权签订合同的人员，在因此等合同产生的诉讼中，应被视为有权代表国家接受管辖。

第五条　商业交易

一、一国在下列诉讼中不享有豁免：

（一）国家从事的商业交易；或

（二）该国依合同承担的义务（不论该合同是否为商业交易）全部或部分在马拉维履行。

二、如争议双方均为国家或有书面协议另行规定，则本条第一款不适用。

三、第一款中"商业交易"指：

（一）提供货物或服务的任何合同；

（二）提供资金的任何贷款或交易，及该交易或其他任何债务的担保或补偿；

（三）国家在任何商业、工业、金融、职业或其他类似领域进行非行使主权权利的活动或交易，但不包括国家与个人签订的雇佣合同。

第六条　雇佣合同

一、在下列情形下，一国在其与个人签订的雇佣合同诉讼中不享有豁免：

（一）合同在马拉维签订，或合同全部或部分在马拉维履行；

（二）合同签订时，该个人是马拉维公民或常住居民；

（三）提起诉讼时，该个人不是该国公民。

二、若合同当事人签订书面协议另有规定，则本条第一款不适用，但马拉维法律规定诉讼应在马拉维提起的除外。

第七条　人身伤害和财物损害

一国在下述诉讼中不享有豁免：

（一）任何人身伤害或死亡；

（二）在马拉维的作为或不作为造成的有形资产的损害或损失。

第八条　财产的所有、占有和使用

一国在下列诉讼中不享有豁免：

（一）一国在马拉维不动产的所有、占有或使用权；

（二）一国对上述不动产的所有、占有或使用所产生的义务；

（三）一国因继承、赠予或无主物取得而产生的动产或不动产利益。

第九条　专利、商标等

一国在下述诉讼中不享有豁免：

（一）一国所有，并在马拉维注册、受保护，或其在马拉维申请的专利、商标、设计、育种权或著作权；

（二）一国被指控在马拉维境内侵犯了专利、商标、工业设计、育种权或著作权；

（三）在马拉维使用商业名称或企业名称的权利。

第十条　法人团体资格

一、下列情形下，一国在涉及其法人团体、非法人团体或合伙人资格的诉讼中，如诉讼系该国与法人团体或其成员，或该国与其他合作伙伴之间的争议，不享有豁免：

（一）该团体成员不限于国家；且

（二）该团体依据马拉维法律注册或成立，或由马拉维控制，或其主要营业地在马拉维。

二、如当事方之间另有书面约定，或设立有关法人团体或合作伙伴关系的章程或其他文件另有规定，则本条不适用。

第十一条　仲裁

一、一国如书面同意将已发生或可能发生的争议提交仲裁，则该国在马拉维法院涉及该项仲裁的诉讼中不得享有豁免。

二、如仲裁协议有相反规定，则本条第一款不适用。本条第一款也不适用于国家之间的仲裁协议。

第十二条 用于商业目的的船舶诉讼

一、如诉讼事由发生时，船舶用于或意图被用于商业用途，则一国在下列情况下不享有豁免：

（一）对该国所有的船舶主张对物诉讼；

（二）为执行与该船舶有关的主张而进行的对人诉讼。

二、一国在下列情况下不享有豁免：

（一）对本国所有的货物主张对物诉讼，如争端发生时船舶及其所载货物均用于或意图用于商业目的；

（二）为执行与货物有关的主张而进行的对人诉讼，如争端发生时载货船舶用于或意图用于商业目的。

三、本条所指一国所有的"船舶"、"货物"包括处于一国占有或控制下的船舶或货物，或该国得对其主张权利的船舶或货物；在符合本条第二款规定的情况下，本条第一款规定得比照适用于船舶以外的其他财产。

第十三条 关税和费率

一国在涉及下列义务的诉讼中不享有豁免：

（一）关税或消费税；

（二）用于商业用途的不动产房产税。

第十四条 送达及缺席判决

一、起诉一国的传票或其他文件应通过马拉维外交部送达该国外交部；该国外交部收到文件时视为送达完成。

二、出庭期限（无论法院规则有无规定）为该国外交部收到传票或其他文件起两个月内。

三、已出庭的国家不得在其后以未满足本条第一款规定为由反对管辖。

四、除非证明已按照本条第一款的规定送达了文书，并且根据本条第二款的规定，出庭期限已经届满，否则不得对一国作出缺席判决。

五、对一国的缺席判决书副本应通过马拉维外交部送达该国外交部；申请撤销判决的期限（无论法院规则有无规定）为自判决书副本送达该国外交部之日起两个月。

六、本条第一款规定不妨碍传票或其他文件以该国同意的任何其他方式送达，凡依此等方式有效送达者，本条第二款及第四款的规定不再适用。

七、本条不得解释为适用于对一国提出的反诉或对物诉讼。本条第一款的规定不得解释为影响向法院管辖范围以外的送达需获得同意的法院规则。

第十五条 其他程序性特权

一、在符合本条第二款和第三款规定的情况下：

（一）不得向一国签发禁令、责令履行令，或返还其土地或其他财产，以作为司法救济。

（二）一国的财产不得作为法院判决或仲裁裁决的标的强制执行，在对物诉讼中，不得扣押、留置或拍卖。

二、本条第一款并不妨碍经有关国家书面同意而采取任何司法救济方法，或开始任何程序；此类同意可事前达成，可规定普遍适用或适用于特定事项；一国接受管辖不得视为为本款目的所作的同意。

三、第一款第（二）项不妨碍对用于或意图用于商业目的的财产采取措施。

第十六条 享有特权与豁免的国家

一、本部分所指的特权与豁免适用于其他国家或除马拉维以外的英联邦成员国。本条所指的国家是：

（一）以其公职身份行事的该国君主或其他元首；

（二）一国政府；以及

（三）一国政府部门，但不包括有别于该国政府行政机构并具有起诉和应诉能力的任何实体（以下称"独立实体"）。

二、在下列情况下，独立实体得享受马拉维法院的管辖豁免：

（一）独立实体行使国家主权产生的有关争端；且

（二）外国国家在相同的条件下得享受管辖豁免。

三、如果独立实体（非一国中央银行或其他货币管理机构）依第二款的规定可享有管辖豁免但自愿接受法院管辖，则应比照适用第十五条关于国家的程序性规定。

四、一国中央银行或其他货币管理机构的财产，不得认为是第十五条第三款所指用于或拟用于商业目的的财产；在该央行或货币管理机构被视为独立实体的情况下，比照适用第十五条第一款和第二款适用于有关国家的规定。

五、本条适用于联邦国家的组成部分，并将其视为独立实体予以适用。

第十七条　国家元首

一、以本条和任何必要的修正为限，第三部分适用于：

（一）君主或其他国家元首；

（二）其家庭成员；以及

（三）其私人仆役。

上述人员的待遇参照外交使团团长、其家庭成员及其私人仆役享有的特权与豁免。

二、本法附录一第三十七条第一款或第三十八条有关国籍或经常住所地的规定不得视为对上述第一款第（一）项和第（二）项所述外交特权与豁免的限制。

三、本条适用于君主或其他国家元首，且不得影响本部分其他条款给予行使公职的君主或其他国家元首的有关特权与豁免。

第十八条　排除适用情形

一、本部分不影响本法案第三部分、第四部分规定的特权与豁免。

（一）第六条不适用于附录一《公约》第一条规定的外交使团成员和附录二《公约》第一条规定的有关领事人员雇佣的诉讼。

（二）第八条第一款不适用于涉及一国所有或占有的用作外交使团目的的财产的诉讼。

二、本部分不适用于刑事诉讼。

第十九条　证明证书

外交部长，或代表外交部长出具的证书对下列问题具有最终效力：

（一）一国是否为本部分所指的国家；

（二）某一领土是否为本部分所指联邦国家的组成部分；

（三）某人是否为本部分所指的国家元首或政府首脑；

（四）根据第十四条第一款或第五款，文件是否及何时被送达或收到。

第三部分　外交特权与豁免

第二十条　外交关系公约的适用

一、根据本法第二十九条第二款，附录一（1961年《维也纳外交关系公约》有关条款）在马拉维具有法律效力，并应对其作出符合本条第二款至第五款的解释。

二、为附录一第三十二条的目的，一国使团团长或行使此项职责的任何人放弃豁免应当视为该国对豁免的放弃。

三、附录一第三十五条、第三十六条、第四十条应当解释为应请求给予特权与豁免的情形。

四、附录一第三十七条、第三十八条所指的接受国承认的特权与豁免及其可能承认的其他特权与豁免的范围，应当解释为由外交部长通过法令确定的特权与豁免。

五、适用附录一第三十七条第二款、第三款、第四款时，第三十八条中的"永久居民"不包括仅为履行外交职能而居住在马拉维的人。

第四部分　领事特权与豁免

第二十一条　领事关系公约的适用

一、根据本法第二十二条第二款和第二十九条第二款的规定，附录二（1963年《维也纳领事关系公约》有关条款）在马拉维具有法律效力，并应对其作出符合本条第二款至第九款的解释。

二、附录一第十七条第二段所述根据习惯国际法或者国际协定给予的特权与豁免应解释为本法第五部分所述特权与豁免。

三、附录一第四十四条中所述领馆人员行使职能的行为应解释为领事官员或领事雇员行使职责的行为。

四、为附录一第四十五条之目的及第五十八条的相关规定，一国使团团长或行使该职责的个人对豁免权的放弃应视为代表国家放弃。若无使馆，则领馆馆长或行使该职责的个人对豁免权的放弃应视为代表国家放弃。

五、附录一第五十条、第五十一条、第五十二条、第五十四条、第六十二条和第六十七条应解释为应豁免请求而给予特权与豁免。

六、附录一第五十七条所述第二章规定的特权与豁免应解释为第二章第二节规定的特权与豁免。

七、附录一第七十条所述关于外交关系的国际法规则应解释为本法第三部分和本法附录一的规定。

八、附录一第七十一条所述接受国给予或者可能给予的额外的特权与豁免应解释为由外长以法令形式明确的特权与豁免。

九、在适用根据附录一第四十九条给予的豁免时，第七十一条中的"永久居民"不包括仅为履行领事职能而居住在马拉维的人。

第二十二条　给予特权与豁免的协议

一、无论在本法生效之前或之后，马拉维与其他国家签订的协议中给予领馆及领事官员本法未规定的特权与豁免，外长可通过法令，给予对方国家领馆及领事官员附录三规定的特权与豁免，以确保协议效力。

二、无论在本法生效之前或之后，马拉维与其他国家签订的协议中给予领馆及领事官员本法规定的部分特权与豁免，外交部长可通过法令，排除协议中未规定的特权与豁免对对方国家领馆及领事官员的适用。

第二十三条　英联邦代表

一、外交部长可通过法令给予以下人员：

（一）实质行使领事官员职责的英联邦国家政府工作人员；

（二）被本国政府承认为首席国家代表或英联邦国家首席省代表的人员（本条称国家代表）；

（三）上述第（一）项、第（二）项中所述人员的团队工作人员，根据本部分规定给予或可能给予的豁免与特权，并且任何上述法令可扩展至根据本项给予或可能给予豁免与特权的上述人员的房产、官方档案、通信、文件及个人财产，以及附录二第三十一条、第三十二条、第三十三条、第三十五条、第三十九条和第五十一条所向其征收的任何费用。

二、第一款所述法令可排除特权与豁免对马拉维公民、永久居民或任何此类人员的适用。

三、尽管有本条规定，

（一）英联邦国家政府承认的其在马拉维的首席代表，可放弃其作为政府工作人员享有的豁免；

（二）一国代表可放弃第一款给予其本人或其工作团队人员的豁免。

第五部分　国际组织等

第二十四条　国际组织及其相关人士的特权与豁免

一、外交部长可发布法令：

（一）给予附录四所列组织（以下简称"组织"）附录五第一部分所述的特权与豁免及法人团体资格，特权与豁免的具体范围由法令明确。

（二）给予以下人员：

1. 组织代表、组织部门代表或组织委员会成员（无论其是否为政府代表）；

2. 组织中较高职位的人员，并可在法令中明确此类人员的数量；以及

3. 代表组织执行任务的人员

享有附录五第二部分所述的特权与豁免，特权与豁免的具体范围由法令明确。

（三）明确其他类别的组织官员和仆役享有附录五第三部分的特权与豁免。特权与豁免的具体范围及享有特权与豁免的人员范围由法令规定。

附录五第四部分适用于本条第二款第（一）项所述代表、成员或官员的特权与豁免应扩展适用于上述代表、成员的工作人员，以及上述官员的家庭成员，除非法令排除该附录第四部分有关特权与豁免的适用。

二、第一款所述法令给予的特权与豁免不应高于当时有关国际协议规定的特权与豁免，也不给予马拉维政府代表或其工作人员特权与豁免。

三、外交部长可以法令修正附录四。

第二十五条 出席国际会议的政府代表

在马拉维召开国际会议且有马维拉政府代表及其他一国或多国参会，若外长对这些国家代表及其公务人员应享有的外交特权与豁免范围有疑问，应在政府公报中以通知形式明确上述人员范围及适用附录一的相关条款。为适用附录一条款，通知中列明的国家代表视为使团团长，公务人员视为外交人员。

第二十六条 提供合作或协助的外部机构

一、无论在本法生效之前或之后，政府与外部机构签订协议同意有关机构或人员因向马拉维提供合作、协助或服务而享有特权与豁免，外交部长可发布法令：

（一）宣布有关机构适用本条规定；

（二）明确有关机构应享有附录五第一部分所述特权与豁免，并明确具体特权与豁免范围；

（三）明确有关机构的官员和仆役享有附录五第三部分所述特权与豁免，并明确具体特权与豁免范围。为执行法令的目的，附录五所述组织应理解为法令所指的外部机构。

二、本条第一款所述法令给予的特权与豁免不应高于当时有关国际协议规定的特权与豁免，也不给予马拉维公民或者永久居民特权或豁免。

三、为本条目的，"外部机构"指：

（一）外国国家政府；

（二）被认可的外国国家政府机构；

（三）获国际承认的基金会或其他团体。

第二十七条 对本法作出相应调整以适用于联合国

本法经下列调整后适用于根据1945年6月25日在旧金山签署的《联合国宪章》而成立的联合国：

（一）主管机构或委员会应理解为联合国大会、理事会或联合国其他机构；以及

（二）根据本法第二十四条第一款，外交部长有权给予根据《联合国宪章》建立的国际法院的法官、书记官长以及起诉人，包括其代理、顾问和律师相应的特权、豁免和便利，以满足联合国大会通过的决议或公约的要求。

第二十八条 对等待遇

虽有本部分规定，如一国未给予马拉维公民或代表相应的特权与豁免，外交部长有权拒绝或撤销给予该国或其代表的特权与豁免。

第六部分　一般规定

第二十九条 特权、豁免或权力的限制与扩展

一、本法第二部分给予外国国家的有关特权与豁免：

（一）高于或低于该国法律给予马拉维的特权与豁免；或

（二）低于马拉维和该国同为缔约方的条约，公约或其他国际协定规定的特权与豁免，

外交部长可以法令形式，根据具体情况，将特权与豁免限制或者扩大到其认为合适的程度。

二、如外国给予马拉维驻外使、领馆及外交人员的特权、豁免或权力低于本法第三部分或第四部分给予该国驻马拉维外交使、领馆及外交人员的特权与豁免，外交部长可以法令形式，将有关特权与豁免调整至合理的程度。

第三十条 高等法院的海事管辖权

高等法院指宣布为有海事管辖权的法院。高等法院对马拉维湖、马拉维与另一国接壤的水域，在人、事件和财物方面与英国高等法院对公海和其有海事管辖权的水域有相同管辖权。

第三十一条 有关关税的特别规定

一、如商品被享有外交特权或豁免或享有本法规定的其他特权与豁免

的人员在未缴纳关税的情况下携带出入境，并向不享有海关特许经营权的人出售或转让，海关可责令出售或转让商品的人员，或购买或接收商品的人员按照出售或转让当日应纳税额缴纳税款。

二、为确定出售或转让的二手货物的应纳税额，海关应考虑商品进口或解除海关监管后的折旧程度；除汽车外，如在进口或解除海关监管两年后出售或转让的商品，应减少税额。

第三十二条　证据

如诉讼中出现某人是否享有本法规定的特权或豁免，或行使有关权力的问题，外交部长出具的有关事实证明将视为决定性证据。除非有相反证据证明，声称系由外交部长签署的证书应推定为由其签署。

第三十三条　誓言及公证行为

如一国法律允许，该国外交代表或领事官员可主持宣誓，录取口供或办理公证，则其：

（一）可应任何人要求从事上述行为，如有关文书仅在该国国内或根据该国法律使用；或

（二）可应该国国民要求从事上述行为，但其出具的文书不能在马拉维使用，除非按照其他国家法律另有规定。

1985年加拿大国家豁免法

一部关于在加拿大法院适用国家豁免的法

第一章 简 称

简称

第一条

本法可简称为"国家豁免法"。

第二章 解 释

定义

第二条

本法中,

"外国国家代理机构"系指任何作为为外国国家机关所组织但又与外国国家有别的法律实体;

"商业活动"系指任何特定的交易、活动或行为,或根据其性质,应认为具有商业特性的任何经常的活动过程。

"外国国家"包括

(一)任何外国国家的君主或其他首脑元首,以及以此种身份行使公权力的外国国家政治组成单元的君主或首脑元首,

(二)外国国家以及任何外国国家的政治组成单元的政府,包括政府各部与外国国家的代理机构,以及

(三)外国国家的任何政治组成单元;

"政治组成单元"系指省、州或联邦制国家中类似的政治组织部分。

"恐怖活动"系指具有与刑法典83.01(1)款相同含义的外国国家有关的恐怖活动,且该在刑法典6.1(2)款的名单上列名的外国国家在1985年1月1日或以后从事了作为或不作为。

支持恐怖主义的含义

第二条之一

为实现本法目的，支持恐怖主义的外国国家为了刑法典 83.01（1）分节确定的名单上列名的实体的利益或在其他情况下与其有关联，而在加拿大从事了作为或不作为，则该外国国家根据刑法典 83.02 条至 83.04 条和 83.18 条至 83.23 条应予处罚。

第三章　国家豁免

国家豁免

第三条

一、除本法另有规定者外，外国国家豁免于加拿大法院的管辖。

给予豁免的法院

二、在任何诉讼中，法院应根据第一款的规定，使给予外国国家的豁免得而实行，即便该国在诉讼中未曾采取任何行动。

放弃豁免

第四条

一、如外国国家依本条第二款、第四款的规定自愿接受法院管辖而放弃第三条第一款给予的豁免，则外国国家不得享有法院管辖的豁免。

接受管辖的国家

二、在诉讼中，凡有下列情况者，应认为外国国家自愿接受法院管辖：

（一）在诉讼开始前或开始后，以书面协议或其他方式明示服从法院管辖的；

（二）首先向法院提起诉讼；或

（三）介入诉讼或采取任何诉讼行为。

例外

三、第二款第（三）项不适用于

（一）外国国家的介入或采取诉讼行为是为了向法院主张自己享有豁免；或

（二）外国国家因未曾注意其有权取得豁免的事实而采取诉讼行为，这种事实虽在其采取诉讼行为之前尚未合理认定，且该外国国家在上述事实确定后在合理可行的时间内尽快主张了豁免，只要此种事实一经认定，豁免一旦提出，即得认为合理可行。

第三方诉讼和反诉

四、首先向法院起诉或介入诉讼,或向法院采取诉讼行为的外国国家,除不适用第二款第(三)项的规定者外,在就该国家首先起诉,或介入诉讼,或采取诉讼行为的诉讼中的标的而发生的与任何第三人有关的诉讼或反诉中,亦应认为其已自愿接受法院管辖。

上诉和复审

五、在任何诉讼中,凡外国国家依第二款、第四款的规定,已自愿服从管辖者,应认为该外国也自愿接受对这些诉讼的全部或一部受理上诉或行使复审管辖权的一个或一个以上法院的管辖。

商业活动

第五条

在涉及外国国家商业活动的诉讼中,该国家不得享有豁免。

死亡和财产损坏

第六条

在下列诉讼中,外国国家不得享有豁免:

(一)发生于加拿大的死亡与人身伤害,或

(二)发生于加拿大的财产损坏与灭失。

支持恐怖主义

第六条之一

一、本条第二款所提及的名单上列明的外国国家就因其在1985年1月1日及之后对恐怖主义的支持而遭受的诉讼不享有豁免。

外国国家名单

二、总督可以命令形式设立一份名单,并可在其有合理理由相信某外国国家曾经或正在支持恐怖主义,且外交部长与公共安全和危机准备部长提出建议的情况下,随时将该外国国家列入该名单。

名单的设立

三、上述名单须在本条规定生效之日起六个月内设立。

申请除名

四、如外国国家书面申请从名单上除名,外交部在与公共安全和危机准备部商议之后,须决定是否有充分理由建议总督将其除名。

将决定通知申请人

五、外交部须无延迟地通知申请人其对申请的决定。

新申请

六、如名单上列明的外国国家的上一份申请没有实质性情势变化，或外交部已根据第七款对申请进行了审查，则该外国国家不能根据第四款提出另一份申请。

名单的审查

七、名单设立两年后及此后每隔两年，外交部须

（一）与公共安全和危机准备部商议，审查名单，决定将某外国国家列入名单是否仍然存在第二款列明的合理理由，并就该外国国家是否仍应列入名单向总督提出建议。

（二）与公共安全和危机准备部商议，审查名单，决定不将某外国国家列入名单是否仍然存在第二款列明的合理理由，并就该外国国家是否应列入名单向总督提出建议。

审查的效果

八、对名单的审查不影响其有效性。

完成审查

九、外交部须在可行的时间内尽快完成对名单的审查，但无论如何自开始审查之日起不应超过一百二十天，审查结束后，外交部长应不延迟地在加拿大公报上宣布其审查已完成。

除名对诉讼的影响

十、如名单上的外国国家因对恐怖主义的支持而涉诉且诉讼程序已开始，随后将该外国国家从名单上除名就该诉讼或任何相关的上诉或执行程序不产生恢复该外国国家管辖豁免的效力。

恐怖活动

十一、如具有有效管辖权的法院已判定某个在第二款所提及名单上的外国国家曾经支持恐怖主义，该外国国家就其恐怖活动引发的诉讼也不享有管辖豁免。

海事法

第七条

一、在下列诉讼中，外国国家不得享有豁免：

（一）对国家拥有或营运的船舶提起的对物之诉，或

（二）与此种船舶有关的要求强制执行某种支付请求的对人之诉，只要此种权利主张提出或诉讼开始之时，有关船舶正用于或拟用于商业活动。

货物

二、在下列诉讼中，外国国家不得享有豁免：

（一）对属于国家所有的船货提起的对物诉讼，只要此种权利主张发生之时，或诉讼开始之时，该船货或载运该船货的船舶，正用于或拟用于商业活动；或

（二）对此种船货要求强制执行某种支付请求的对人诉讼，只要此种支付请求发生时，或诉讼开始时，载运此种船货的船舶正用于或拟用于商业活动。

三、第一款、第二款所指国家拥有的船舶或船货，应包括国家占有与控制的任何船舶或船货，以及国家主张自己有利益的任何船舶或船货。

位于加拿大的财产

第八条

在涉及某项利益或国家在魁北克省通过继承、赠与或无主物取得而产生的财产权利的诉讼中，外国国家不得享有豁免。

第四章　程序与司法救助

对外国国家送达

第九条

一、对外国国家送达起诉文书，除对外国代理机构的送达外，应依以下之方式：

（一）该国所同意的任何方式；

（二）该国为缔约国的任何国际公约所规定的方式；或

（三）下述第二款规定的方式。

二、根据上款第（三）项，凡欲向外国国家送达起诉文书者，也可将该文书的副本亲自或通过挂号信，递交给外交部副部长，或其为此种目的而指定的应将文书转交给该外国国家的某人。

对外国国家的机构送达

三、对外国代理机构送达起诉文书，应依以下之方式：

（一）该代理机构同意的任何方式；

（二）适用于该代理机构的国际公约所规定的任何方式；或

（三）法院任何可适用的规则。

四、在不能依第三款规定的方式向外国国家的代理机构送达时，法院可以裁定指明应采取何种送达方式。

送达日期

五、在按照第二款规定的方式送达起诉文书时，文书的送达日，应认为是外交部副部长，或其依第二款指定的某人向有关法院证明该文件副本已转交给该外国国家之日。

缺席判决

第十条

一、在任何诉讼中，如起诉文书已依第九条第一款、第三款或第四款规定的方式向该国家送达，而该国家未能于法院或法律规定的期限内就诉讼采取被告或答辩人应采取的初步诉讼行为，则除非起诉文书送达后六十日期限届满，得进一步作出判决。

二、外国国家未能采取第一款所指的初步诉讼行为而在诉讼中败诉的，应将经过公证的判决副本送达该外国国家。

（一）如起诉文书系送达给外国代理机构的，照原来法院裁定的方式送达；或

（二）在其他情况下，则按第九条第一款第（三）项规定的方式，依送达一个起诉文书的同一方式送达。

三、如第二款经过公证的判决书副本以第九条第一款第（三）项、第九条第二款和第五款规定的方式送达，则依情况要求，亦可作第二款、第五款所规定的变通处理。

申请撤销或撤回判决

四、外国国家可在经公证的判决书副本根据第二款规定送达后六十日内，申请撤销或撤回判决。

未经同意不得发布禁令、指令等

第十一条

一、除第三款规定者外，不得采取禁止外国国家为某种行为，或要求其为某种行为，或者要求其返还土地或其他财产的司法救助方法，除非该外国国家书面同意采取此救助方法，而在同意采取此种救助方法时，其救助亦不得大于该国家同意的范围。

接受管辖不代表同意

二、外国国家自愿接受法院的管辖，不得认为是第一款所指的同意。

例外

三、本条不适用于外国国家代理机构或列入第六条之一第二款所提及的名单，因对恐怖主义的支持或恐怖主义行为而被诉的外国国家。

执行

第十二条

一、除第二款、第三款规定者外，外国国家位于加拿大的财产，应豁免于扣押与执行，在对物之诉中应豁免于扣留、留置、查封或没收，但属下列情况者除外：

（一）国家已明示或默示放弃扣押、执行、扣留、留置、查封或没收的豁免者，除非在允许撤回此种放弃的情况下已撤回其所表示的放弃；

（二）用于或拟用于商业活动的财产，或列入第六条之一第二款所提及的名单上的外国国家使用或意图使用以支持恐怖主义或从事恐怖活动的财产；

（三）执行判决所确认的权利涉及通过继承或赠与所取得的位于加拿大的财产，或位于加拿大的不动产；或

（四）列入第六部分第一条第二款所提及的名单上的外国国家，如被指控支持恐怖主义或参与恐怖活动，并因此被判决扣押和执行的不具有文化和历史价值的财产。

外国国家机构的财产不享有豁免

二、除第三款规定者外，为了满足在外国国家代理机构未能依本法取得豁免的诉讼中作出的判决的要求，凡属外国国家代理机构的财产，不得豁免于执行，并在对物之诉中，不得豁免于扣留、留置、查封与没收。

军事财产

三、外国国家的财产

（一）用于或拟用于与军事有关的活动，以及

（二）具有军事性质，或处于军事当局或国防机构控制之下的，

应豁免于扣押与执行，在对物之诉中，豁免于扣留、留置、查封与没收。

外国国家中央银行的财产豁免

四、除第五款规定者外，凡外国国家中央银行或财政当局存于自己账号下的财产，并且非用于或不拟用于商业活动者，应豁免于扣押与执行。

放弃豁免

五、依第四款给予外国国家中央银行或财政当局的财产豁免，于此等银行、当局或组成它们的外国政府已明示放弃时，不予适用，除非该银行、当局或政府在允许撤回放弃的情况下，已撤回此种放弃。

对胜诉债权人的协助

第十二条之一

一、对根据第六条之一提起的针对外国国家的诉讼，经判决胜诉的任

何一方要求，金融部长或外交部长可以在其职权范围内，并在合理可行的范围内，协助胜诉方识别和定位下列财产，除非外交部长相信如这样做将损害加拿大的国际关系，或两位部长中任何一位相信这样做会损害加拿大的其他利益。

（一）对于金融部长而言，外国国家在加拿大管辖范围内的金融资产；以及

（二）对于外交部长而言，外国国家位于加拿大的财产。

信息披露

二、在行使本条第一款的权力时，金融部长或外交部长，在一些情况下，可以对下列信息不予披露：

（一）未经政府机构授权，在该政府机构内或为了该政府机构产生的信息，以及

（二）未经首次收到信息的政府机构授权，在第（一）项以外的情况下产生的信息。

政府机构的定义

三、在本条第二款中，政府机构系指任何部长对其管理或事务向议会负责的部门、分支机构、办公室、局、代理机构、委员会、公司或其他机构。

不得对未予提供罚款

第十三条

一、不能因外国国家在诉讼进行中未提供或拒绝提供有关文件与资料而科以罚金。

例外

二、第一款的规定不适用于外国代理机构。

第五章　一般规定

证明书作为决定性的证据

第十四条

一、由外交部长，或由外交部长授权某人签发的证明书，对于

（一）某一国家是否为本法所指意义上的外国国家，

（二）外国国家的某一区域或领土是否为该外国的政治组成单元，或

（三）某人或某些人是否应看作是外国国家或其政治组成单元的首脑元首或政府，

应认为证明书中的陈述乃确定证据,而不再需要对外交部长或外交部长授权的其他人的签名提出证明。

二、由外交部副部长或由他依第九条第二款规定所指定的人所作关于向外国国家送达起诉文书或其他文书的证明书,对于这种送达是确定的证据,并不需要再对外交部副部长或其他人的签字,或外交部副部长对该其他人的授权的签字,提出证明。

总督可以下令限制豁免

第十五条

根据外交部长的建议,如果总督认为依本法向有关外国提供的豁免与特权,超过了该外国法律所提供的豁免与特权,可以命令减缩依本法所应提供的豁免与特权。

冲突条款

第十六条

在诉讼或其他事项上,如本法的某一规定与《引渡法》、《访问部队法案》或《外国使团及国际组织法》的某一规定均可适用而又有相互抵触的情况者,则在其抵触的方面,本法有关规定不适用于该诉讼或其他事项。

法院规程不受影响

第十七条

除为使本法要求承认的效力生效所需外,对本法不能作否定或影响法院规程的解释或适用,这里所讲的法院规程包括向法院管辖范围外送达文书的规则。

适用

第十八条

本法不适用于刑事诉讼或具有刑事诉讼性质的程序。

1985年澳大利亚外国国家豁免法

第一部分　前　言

第一条　简称

本法可被称为"1985年外国国家豁免法"。

第二条　生效

本法中的各项规定于公告中确定的某一日期或分别几个日期生效。

第三条　解释

一、在本法中除有相反的意思表示外：

"协议"指一份书面协议，包括：

1. 条约或其他书面国际协议，以及

2. 合同或其他书面协议。

"澳大利亚"用作地理含义时，包括每一个外部领土；

"汇票"包括本票。

"法院"包括法庭或其他具有司法职能或类似司法职能，行使司法权力或类似司法权力的实体（无论其名称）。

"外交部"是指负责实施1967年《外交特权与豁免法》的部长领导的部门。

"外交财产"是指主要为建立或维持外国派往澳大利亚的外交、领事使团或访问使团，在相应时期使用的财产。

"外国国家"指在澳大利亚领土以外的国家领域，且为：

1. 一个独立的主权国家；或为

2. 非为一独立主权国家组成部分的一个独立地区（无论是否自治）。

"启动传票"指一个使个人或法人成为诉讼一方的文件（包括请求书、申请书、传票、书面文件、命令和第三方通知书）。

"澳大利亚的法律"是指：

1. 在澳大利亚全境有效的法律；或

2. 在澳大利亚部分地区有效的法律；

并包括普通法和衡平法中具有同等效力的原则和规则。

"军事财产"是指：

1. 战舰、政府游艇、巡航舰、警察或海关船只、医院船、防御部队补给船或辅助船，这些船只在相应时期内由相关外国国家控制（无论是由于征用还是基于光船出租或其他原因）；或者

2. 下列财产（非船舶或船只）：

（1）被用于与军事相关的活动；或者

（2）由军事机构或防御机构基于军事或防御目的而控制。

"外交部长"是指负责实施1967年《外交特权与豁免法》的部长。

"诉讼程序"指法院内进行的诉讼，但不包括对犯罪的起诉或上诉以及其他与这种起诉相关的本质上为上诉的诉讼程序。

"财产"包括无形财产。

"独立实体"，相对于外国国家，指一自然人（除澳大利亚公民以外）、法人团体或单独法人（除依据澳大利亚法律成立的法人团体或单独法人以外），且

1. 作为外国国家的代理或分支机构；并且

2. 不是作为外国国家执政政府的一个部门或机关。

二、就第一款对"独立实体"的解释而言，自然人、法人团体或单独法人作为一个以上国家机构的，应被视为是各个国家的独立实体。

三、除有相反的意思表示外，本法中所提及的外国国家包括所提及的：

1. 外国国家的省、州、自治地区或其他政治分支（无论其名称）；

2. 外国国家或外国国家的政治分支的首脑，且他或她拥有公职身份；及

3. 外国国家或外国国家的政治分支的执政政府或执政政府的组成部分，包括该外国国家或政治分支的执政政府的部门或机构；

但不包括所提及的外国国家的独立实体。

四、本法所提及的澳大利亚法院包括所提及的在澳大利亚某部分内或对某部分具有管辖权的法院。

五、本法中所提及的为商业目的，包括所提及的贸易、商业、职业和工业目的。

六、本法所提及的出席或作出缺席判决包括所提及的任何类似程序。

第四条　海外领地

本法适用于各海外领地。

第五条 本法对王室的约束

本法对王室具有约束力。

第六条 其他法律的保留

本法不影响 1972 年的《领事特权与豁免法》、1963 年《防卫（外国驻军）法》、1967 年的《外交特权与豁免法》及任何其他法律规定赋予的豁免与特权。

第七条 适用

一、第二部分（除第十条外）不适用于涉及下列内容的司法程序：

1. 达成的合同或其他协议，或已制作的汇票；

2. 已经发生的交易或事件；

3. 已经完成或已经被遗漏的行为；或者

4. 已经存在的权利、责任或义务；

以上内容均应在本法生效以前发生。

二、第十条不适用于本法生效前该条规定的内容。

三、第三部分和第三十六条不适用于本法生效前提起的诉讼。

四、根据第二部分的规定，第四部分仅适用于外国国家在相关司法程序中不能在澳大利亚法院享有豁免的情形。

第八条 法院的适用

法院适用本法时，本法仅对行使或履行司法权力、职能或类似的权力或职能的法院有效。

第二部分　管辖豁免

第九条 一般管辖豁免

除非本法另有规定，外国国家在诉讼中豁免于澳大利亚法院的管辖。

第十条 接受管辖

一、当外国国家已经依据本条规定接受管辖时，就不能在诉讼中享有豁免。

二、外国国家可以以协议或其他方式在任何时候接受管辖，但不能仅因一国为一项协议的一方，而该协议宜适用澳大利亚法律，就认为其接受了管辖。

三、依据第二款接受管辖可能应符合特殊的限制、条件和除外规定（无论是涉及救济还是其他）。

四、若没有对法院不受理、延缓或拒绝审理并判决某一诉讼的权力进行限制，则当某一诉讼的提起符合接受管辖的限制、条件或除外规定的性质（不是涉及救济的限制、条件或除外规定）时，法院可以此为由不受理、延缓或拒绝审理并判决，且应被视为正当。

五、依据本部分，外国国家放弃豁免的协议具有放弃豁免的效力，且除非协议条款另有规定，该放弃不得撤回。

六、根据第七款、第八款、第九款的规定，外国国家可以通过以下方式接受管辖：

1. 提起诉讼；或

2. 参加，或以当事人身份介入该诉讼。

七、外国国家不能仅因下列行为被认为接受了管辖：

1. 提交了损失申请；或者

2. 为主张豁免权而参加或介入该诉讼。

八、当外国国家不是诉讼一方时，不能仅因其为主张其涉诉的或将受诉讼影响的财产利益而介入诉讼的行为，而认为其接受了管辖。

九、当：

1. 不知道或不能合理地被认为知道豁免权的人参与或介入；并且

2. 豁免权的主张并没有不合理的延迟；

则该外国国家不应仅因该参与或介入行为而被视为接受了管辖。

十、若外国国家在诉讼中接受了管辖，则根据第三款的实施规定，当该诉讼请求是基于与诉讼相关的事务或事件时，其不能在诉讼中其他方对其提出的诉讼请求（无论是以反请求、反诉还是其他方式提起）享有豁免。

十一、除此之外，其他有权代表外国国家接受管辖的人员有：

1. 履行外国国家驻澳大利亚的外交使团团长职能之人在其履职期间；以及

2. 代表并行使国家权力签订合同的人员，有权就该合同引发的诉讼而代表国家接受管辖。

第十一条 商业交易

一、在涉及商业交易的司法程序中外国国家不能主张豁免。

二、第一款的规定不适用于：

1. 如果该诉讼中的当事方均：

（1）是外国国家，或者是联邦与一个或多个外国国家；或者

（2）有其他书面协议的；或者

2. 是涉及赠与、奖学金、养老金以及类似情况的支付的诉讼。

三、在本条中，"商业交易"指外国国家已经进入或从事的商业、贸易、交易、职业、工业或类似交易，但不以上述内容为限，还包括：

1. 提供货物或服务的合同；

2. 贷款或其他提供资金交易的协议；

3. 为金融债务提供的担保或保证；

但不包括雇佣合同或汇票。

第十二条　雇佣合同

一、作为雇主的外国国家，其在澳大利亚签署的、全部或部分在澳大利亚履行的雇佣合同中涉及雇用某人的相关诉讼，不能享有豁免。

二、前款提及的诉讼包括涉及以下情形的诉讼：

1. 澳大利亚法律授予或强制规定的雇主或雇员的权利或义务；或者

2. 基于雇佣合同而产生的支付。

三、雇佣合同签订时，当被雇用人员是：

1. 外国国家的国民且不是澳大利亚的永久居民；或

2. 该外国国家的惯常居民；

则前款不适用。

四、前款在下列情况中不适用：

1. 雇佣合同中前后矛盾的规定，并且

2. 对于该规定，澳大利亚的法律没有避免其实施、禁止其内容或者认定其内容违法。

五、第一款在下列雇佣关系中不适用：

1. 代表团的外交人员，即《维也纳外交关系公约》中界定的代表团的外交人员，该公约的英文复本列在《1967年外交特权与豁免法》的附件中；或者

2. 领事官员，即《维也纳领事关系公约》中界定的领事官员，该公约的英文复本列在《1972年领事特权与豁免法》的附件中。

六、第一款在下列雇佣关系中不适用：

1. 公约中第五款第（一）项中提及的代表团的行政和技术人员；或者

2. 公约中第五款第（二）项中提及的领事雇员；

除非在雇佣合同签订时，该人员或雇员为澳大利亚的永久居民。

七、在本节中，"澳大利亚的永久居民"是指：

1. 澳大利亚公民；或者

2. 居住在澳大利亚的人员，且其在澳大利亚的持续居住不受澳大利亚法律规定的时间限制。

第十三条　人身伤害和财产损害

外国国家在涉及下列内容的诉讼中不享有豁免：

1. 人员的死亡或人身伤害；或

2. 有形财产的灭失或损失；

且是由于发生在澳大利亚的作为或不作为而引起的。

第十四条　财产的所有权、占有权和使用权及其他

一、外国国家在涉及以下事项的司法程序中不能享有司法豁免：

1. 该国利益所在，或该国占有或使用的在澳大利亚境内的不动产；或者

2. 该国因上述利益，或占有或使用上述财产而产生的国家责任。

二、外国国家在涉及因发生在澳大利亚的赠与或继承而产生的国家的财产利益的诉讼中不能享有豁免。

三、外国国家在涉及下列事项的诉讼中不享有豁免：

1. 法人团体的破产、清算或解散；或者

2. 信托财产、死者或精神失常的人的不动产的管理。

第十五条　版权、专利和商标权利及其他

一、外国国家在涉及下列事项的司法程序中不能享有司法豁免：

1. 版权的所有权，或发明、设计或商标在澳大利亚的所有权、注册或保护；

2. 由外国国家导致的对澳大利亚的版权、发明专利、注册商标和注册设计的侵害；或者

3. 在澳大利亚使用商品名或商号名。

二、第一款不适用于进口到澳大利亚或在澳大利亚使用的财产，但不包括第十一条第三款中规定的在商业交易过程中或为商业目的的财产。

第十六条　法人团体的成员资格及其他

一、如外国国家是法人团体、非法人团体或合伙企业等组织的成员，当发生涉及成员资格或与此有关的权利和义务的诉讼，且有关诉讼发生在该外国国家与该组织之间，或与其他成员之间时，外国国家在下列情况中不享有豁免：

1. 法人团体、非法人团体或合伙企业中有一个不是外国国家或英联邦成员；并且

2. 依据澳大利亚法律成立或组建，或由澳大利亚控制，或主要经营地在澳大利亚。

二、包含在：

1. 章程或其他建立或管理团体或合伙的文件中；或者

2. 诉讼双方的协议中

的条款与第一款的规定相反时，该条款优先于第一款适用。

第十七条 仲裁

一、当外国国家作为将争议提交仲裁的协议当事一方时，对于协议中任何不一致的条款，该外国国家不能豁免于法院有关该仲裁的履行监督管辖的程序，包括下列程序：

1. 因法院意见引发的案件；

2. 对有关协议的合法性或有效性，或关于仲裁程序的问题的认定；或

3. 撤销裁决。

二、当：

1. 除第十一条第二款第（一）项第二目、第十二条第四款、第十六条第二款的规定外，外国国家在涉及交易或事件的诉讼中不享有豁免；并且

2. 该外国国家是将关于交易或事件的争议提交仲裁的协议的一方；

对于协议中的任何不一致的条款，若诉讼与对根据仲裁作出的裁决之拘束力的出于任何目的的承认或与对上述裁决的执行有关，则该外国国家不享有豁免，且无论该裁决是在何种情况下作出。

三、本条第一款不适用于协议方为两个或两个以上的：

1. 外国国家；

2. 英联邦；

3. 仅由外国国家或英联邦与一个或一个以上外国国家组成的组织。

第十八条 对物诉讼

一、在以船舶为诉讼请求的对物诉讼中，如果在诉讼事由发生时，该船舶正为商业目的而使用，外国国家不享有豁免。

二、对于针对一船舶提起的对物诉讼，如其与针对另一船舶提起的诉讼请求有关，则外国国家在以下情形下不享有豁免：

1. 当提起诉讼时，对物诉讼针对的船舶正为商业目的而使用；及

2. 当诉讼事由发生时，另一船舶正为商业目的而使用。

三、在针对货物的对物诉讼中，如果在诉讼事由发生时该货物是商业货物，外国国家不享有豁免。

四、本节前述条款不适用于扣押、留置或变卖船舶或货物的情形。

五、本节提及的用于商业目的的船舶或商业货船是指第三十二条第二款所界定的属于商业财产的船舶或货船。

第十九条　汇票

当：

1. 外国国家在交易或事件中开出、制作或签发的汇票；并且

2. 外国国家在涉及该交易或事件的诉讼中不享有豁免；

则外国国家在涉及该汇票的诉讼中不享有豁免。

第二十条　税收

若澳大利亚有关税收法律的条款要求外国国家承担义务，且这些被规定或包括在为本条所规定的一类条款中，则对与此有关的诉讼，外国国家不享有豁免。

第二十一条　相关诉讼

当外国国家，由于本部分前述条款的实施，在有关某一事件的诉讼中不享有豁免，则在任何由上述诉讼引起并涉及上述诉讼的其他有关该事件的诉讼（包括上诉）中，该外国国家不享有豁免。

第二十二条　适用于独立实体的部分

本部分前述条款［除第十一条第二款第（一）项第一目、第十六条第一款第（一）项、第十七条第三款外］，如适用于外国国家，则也适用于外国国家的独立实体。

第三部分　送达和判决

第二十三条　协议启动传票送达

外国国家或独立实体可以与诉讼相对方签订协议（无论在何处签订及在本法生效以前或以后签订），约定向外国国家或外国国家的独立实体发出启动传票可视为有效送达。

第二十四条　外交途径送达

一、对外国国家送达启动传票，可以送交总检察长，由其交外交部送达外国国家与之对口的部门或机关。

二、启动传票应连同以下文件送达：

1. 根据附件中表格一提出的申请；

2. 诉讼中原告或申请者的法定声明，声明遵守法院管辖范围以外关于

送达的法院规定或其他法律（如果有的话）；及

3. 如果英语不是该外国国家的官方语言

（1）传票的该外国国家官方语言译本；及

（2）由翻译者签字的以该官方语言制作的证明书，其中包括翻译人员的翻译资格，并声明该翻译版本是传票的正确译本。

三、若传票和文件被送达在外国国家内的外国国家的相应部门或机关，送达自交付时生效。

四、若传票和文件被送达代表外国国家并拥有职权的其他人，送达自交付时生效。

五、本条一至四款（含本款）不排除任何法院规定或其他法律的适用，该规定或法律对涉及管辖以外启动传票的送达的法院级别作出了要求。

六、根据本条，如果送达确实有效，则启动传票的送达应被视为对管辖以外或外国国家有效。

七、出庭期限自启动传票有效送达之日起两个月期满后开始计算。

八、本节不适用于在对物诉讼中的启动传票的送达。

第二十五条　其他送达方式无效

除第二十三条或第二十四条中允许或规定的方式外，其他在澳大利亚的对外国国家启动传票的送达无效。

第二十六条　放弃对送达的拒绝

如外国国家没有拒绝启动传票的送达，出庭参与诉讼，则本法关于该送达的规定应被遵守。

第二十七条　缺席审判

一、除以下情况外，缺席审判对外国国家不适用：

1. 经证实，依本法进行的启动传票的送达已生效，且出庭期限已过；及

2. 法院认为，在该诉讼中，该外国国家不享有豁免。

二、除非法院认为，在诉讼中，独立实体不享有豁免权，否则缺席判决对该独立实体不适用。

第二十八条　缺席判决的执行

一、根据本条第六款，缺席判决不对外国国家开始执行，直到自以下事件起两个月后：

1. 判决的复本，经法院密封后，或未经密封但经法院官员证实其为判决的真实复本；并且

2. 当英文不是该外国国家的官方语言时：

（1）翻译成该外国国家官方语言的译本；并且

（2）由翻译者签字的以该官方语言制作的证明书，其中包括翻译人员的翻译资格，并声明该翻译是判决的正确译本；

依本条的规定对外国国家相当于外交部的部门或组织生效。

二、当文件按第一款的规定送达时，在判决中受益的人将该文件和以表格二的格式制作的申请书，提交总检察长，由外交部转交外国国家相当于外交部的部门。

三、若文件被送达外国国家相当于外交部的部门或机关，送达自文件到达时生效。

四、若文件被送达代表外国国家，并拥有外国国家权力的其他人，送达自文件到达时生效。

五、撤销判决的申请至少应在文件被送达外国国家相应的机关或部门，或由代表外国国家的部门或机关接收之日起两个月后方可提起。

六、当法院对外国国家作出缺席判决时，法院可以依判决对其有利的一方的请求，根据其认为应适用的规定及条件，允许该判决在本条第一款所述期限届满以前，对外国国家予以执行。

第二十九条 同意免责的权力

一、依据本条第二款，法院可以对外国国家作出任何命令（包括临时救济或终局救济的命令），除与本法中的豁免权不符外，属于合法。

二、法院不可以发布命令使外国国家雇用某人或恢复雇用某人。

第四部分 执 行

第三十条 执行的豁免

除本部分的规定外，外国国家的财产不受任何澳大利亚的法院发布的为抵偿或执行判决、命令、仲裁裁决、海事诉讼中的扣押、留置或变卖财产的司法程序或命令的限制。

第三十一条 执行豁免权的放弃

一、外国国家可以在任何时候以协议放弃第三十条对其财产的适用。

二、放弃可以有特殊的限制。

三、外国国家放弃第三十条中的豁免的协议，具有放弃该豁免的效力，且该放弃除根据协议中的条款外不被撤回。

四、放弃不适用于外交财产或军事财产，除非协议明确表示该财产属于放弃豁免的适用范围内。

五、除有权代表外国国家或外国国家的独立团体放弃适用第三十条中的人员外，其时在该国驻澳大利亚外交使团中履行团长职责的人员也具有该权限。

第三十二条　对商业财产的执行

一、基于第十条而有效的接受之实施，第三十条中的规定不适用于商业财产。

二、外国国家在涉及船舶或货物的诉讼中不享有豁免，在以下情况下，第三十条不禁止扣押、留置或出卖船舶或货物：

1. 该船舶或货物属于商业财产；并且

2. 在货物被属于同一外国国家或其他国家的船舶运走时，该船舶是商业财产。

三、就本条而言：

1. 商业财产是指，除外交财产或军事财产以外，外国国家主要为商业目的而使用的财产；并且

2. 在表面上是无人占有的或表面上不使用的财产，应被视为用于商业目的，除非法院认为该财产并非用于商业目的。

第三十三条　对不动产及其他的执行

当：

1. 财产：

（1）是由于继承或赠与而取得；或者

（2）是不动产；并且

2. 财产上的权利已经由第十四条提及的针对外国国家的诉讼作出的判决或命令确立；

那么，为执行该判决或命令，第三十条不适用于该财产。

第三十四条　对某些救济措施的限制

不能为执行由法院作出的针对外国国家的命令，向有失误的外国国家或代表外国国家的人员以罚金或履行义务形式作出的处罚。

第三十五条　适用于独立实体的申请

一、若本部分适用于外国国家，则也适用于外国政府的中央银行或金融主管当局这样的外国国家的独立实体。

二、根据本条第一款，本部分在以下相关程序中，对于外国国家的独立实体与外国国家同样适用：

1. 除第十条的规定外，独立实体享有管辖豁免；并且
2. 已经接受了管辖。

第五部分　其他规定

第三十六条　外国首脑

一、依据本条的以下款项，1967 年的《外交特权与豁免法》在作必要修改后，适用于某人在一段时间内作为：

1. 外国国家的元首；或
2. 外国国家元首的配偶；

该法适用于一个人作为外交使团的团长期间。

二、本条不影响任何澳大利亚有关征税的法律规定的适用。

三、本条不影响本法任何其他关于外国国家元首在其任期内的规定的适用。

四、本法第三部分适用于有关外国国家，也适用于以私人身份行事的该外国国家元首，基于此，第三部分提及的外国国家可解释为包括以私人身份行事的外国国家元首。

第三十七条　关于独立团体协议的效力

外国国家签署的适用于该国独立团体的协议，依本法规定，将独立团体视为协议一方而生效。

第三十八条　撤销程序及其他的权限

如外国国家或外国国家的独立团体提出申请，且法院认为其在有关外国国家或独立团体诉讼中作出或签发的判决、命令，或法庭程序与本法规定的豁免权不符，法院应撤销该判决、命令或法庭程序。

第三十九条　透露

一、以罚金或履行义务形式进行的处罚，不应由于外国国家或代表外国国家的人员在披露、提供文件或为诉讼提供资料上的失误或拒绝，而加诸该外国国家或代表外国国家的人员。

二、失误或拒绝本身不足以否定答辩或答辩的组成部分。

第四十条　给外国国家的证明书

一、为本法目的，外交部长可以以书面形式证明：

1. 特定国家，是或在特定时期曾是外国国家；
2. 指定地区是或不是，在特定时期曾是或不是外国国家的一部分；

3. 特定人员是，或在特定时期曾是外国国家或前外国国家的政府或政府部门的首脑；或者

4. 第二十四条或第二十八条中的特定文件的送达，于特定日期生效。

二、外交部长可以一般性地或根据授权文书规定，以书面文书形式，将他或她在本条第一款中享有的有关文书送达的权力授予他人。

三、被代理的权力，当由代表行使时，依本法目的，应被视为是由部长行使的。

四、本条第二款中的授权，不影响部长行使权力。

五、本节中的证明书，可作为其所述内容和事件的可接受的证据，并对这些事实和事件具有最终决定效力。

第四十一条　证明书的使用

为本法的目的，由澳大利亚境内的外国外交使团的团长在履行其公职时，作出的书面证明书以证明证明书中的特定财产，是：

1. 外国国家或外国国家的独立实体具有利益的财产；或

2. 由外国国家或外国国家的独立实体占有或控制的财产；

是或在特定时间曾是为证明书中的特定目的而使用，可作为其所述内容和事件的可接受的证据。

第四十二条　特权与豁免的限制和延伸

一、当外交部长认为本法授予外国国家的特权与豁免，与外国国家涉及澳大利亚的法律不符时，总督可以制定规章修改本法对该外国国家的特权与豁免的实施。

二、当外交部长认为本法授予外国国家的特权与豁免，不同于已经接受的条约、公约或其他该外国国家和澳大利亚作为缔约方的协议时，总督可以制定规章修改本法对该外国国家的特权与豁免的实施，以使其与条约、公约或协议相符合。

三、根据上述第一款或第二款可视为对豁免的限制和延伸的规定，可以被视为延伸至在该规定生效之前被提起的、没有最终判决的诉讼。

四、根据上述第一款或第二款可被视为对执行豁免或其他救济措施的限制和延伸的规定，可以被视为延伸至在该规定生效之前被提起的诉讼、使执行命令生效的程序未完成的诉讼，或其他救济措施的命令的诉讼。

五、对于规定中特定的诉讼，适用第三款或第四款的可以制定财产的保有或财产出售后收益的保有的条款，包括授权法院的官员管理、控制或保管该财产，或者，如果由于财产的状况，需要出卖或以其他方式处理该财产。

六、无论本节中的规定与某项该规定实施时有效的法律（除本法外）是否相符，该规定都有效。

七、因该规定产生的事宜，管辖权授予澳大利亚联邦法院，在宪法允许的范围内，也授予各领地法院和州法院，但各领地法院不应将授予其的任何管辖权行使于不在该领地的财产或联邦法院可行使管辖权的领地的财产，且州法院不应将授予其的任何管辖权行使于不在该州的财产。

第四十二（A）条　豁免的延长——危机事件预防和管理

一、如外交部长认为外国国家（或外国国家的独立实体）正在或将要提供协助或便利：

1. 给澳大利亚政府，或州或领地政府；且

2. 是为了准备、预防或管理澳大利亚的危机事件或灾害（不论是自然灾害还是其他灾害）

则适用本条规定。

二、总督可制定规定，对外国国家（或外国国家的独立实体）在提供协助或便利过程中的作为或不作为排除或修改适用第十三条（人身伤害和财产损失）。

（注：第二十二条适用第十三条对外国国家独立实体的规定。）

第四十三条　规定

在不与本法相抵触的情况下，总督可以制定规定，规定：

1. 本法要求或许可规定的事项；或者

2. 对执行或实施本法有必要或有利的事项。

1995年阿根廷法院对外国国家管辖豁免法

法律编号：24，488

批准日期：1995年5月31日

部分立法：1995年6月22日

阿根廷参议院、众议院与国会共同批准了本法的效力：

《阿根廷法院对外国国家管辖豁免法》

第一条

依据本法如下规定，外国国家免于阿根廷法院的管辖。

第二条

在下列情况下，外国国家不可享有法院管辖的豁免：

1. 依据国际条约、书面协议或任何情况下的宣言，已经明示服从法院管辖的；

2. 外国国家提起的反诉与该国首先提起的本诉直接相关；

3. 诉讼涉及外国国家进行的商业或工业活动，依据相关合同或国际法，阿根廷法院管辖权可以适用的情况下；

4. 外国国家与阿根廷国民或居民因雇佣合同而产生的诉讼，该合同的履行地为阿根廷或者虽在国外履行但对阿根廷产生影响；

5. 外国国家因在阿根廷的犯罪或违法行为而产生的损失或赔偿的诉讼；

6. 因在阿根廷境内的不动产而产生的诉讼；

7. 外国国家因作为在阿根廷境内的财产继承人或受益人而产生的诉讼；

8. 外国国家书面同意将有关商业交易的争议提交仲裁，则该外国国家不得在有关仲裁裁定的有效性或解释、仲裁程序、仲裁裁决的撤销等事项的诉讼中享有豁免，但仲裁协定另有规定者除外。

第三条①

如在阿根廷法院针对外国国家提起的诉讼是依据国际法的违反人权之

---

① 第3条依据849/95法令已失效。

诉，受理法院应告知原告，法院仅局限于依据可适用的本国管辖或普遍管辖提交至国际机构。同时，法院应向外交部、国际商务和文化部提交诉讼的副本，以便可以依据国际管辖权审查该诉讼并采取相应的措施。

第四条

外国国家在阿根廷法院出庭主张管辖豁免，不应被解释为该外国国家同意接受阿根廷法院的管辖。在争议解决之前依据管辖豁免发起的抗辩应中止转移或传讯的程序期限。

第五条

应外国国家的请求，法官可以审慎地就诉讼和例外请求延长期限。

第六条

本法规定不影响依据1961年《维也纳外交关系公约》和1963年《维也纳领事关系公约》给予的特权与豁免。

第七条

如发生对外国国家的诉讼，外交部、国际商务文化部作为法庭之友可以在法院审理案件之前对案件的事实或法律问题发表意见。

第八条

本法应告知行政机关。议员：艾伯托·R. 皮埃尔里、爱德华·梅纳姆、埃斯蒂斯·H. 佩雷拉·佩雷斯·帕多、埃德加多埃·皮乌西。

本法1995年5月31日在布宜诺斯艾利斯阿根廷国会大厅制定。

2005 年中华人民共和国外国中央银行财产司法强制措施豁免法

(2005 年 10 月 25 日第十届全国人民代表大会常务委员会第十八次会议通过)

第一条

中华人民共和国对外国中央银行财产给予财产保全和执行的司法强制措施的豁免；但是，外国中央银行或者其所属国政府书面放弃豁免的或者指定用于财产保全和执行的财产除外。

第二条

本法所称外国中央银行，是指外国的和区域经济一体化组织的中央银行或者履行中央银行职能的金融管理机构。

本法所称外国中央银行财产，是指外国中央银行的现金、票据、银行存款、有价证券、外汇储备、黄金储备以及该银行的不动产和其他财产。

第三条

外国不给予中华人民共和国中央银行或者中华人民共和国特别行政区金融管理机构的财产以豁免，或者所给予的豁免低于本法的规定的，中华人民共和国根据对等原则办理。

第四条

本法自公布之日起施行。

2008 年以色列外国国家豁免法

第一章 定 义

第一条 定义

为本法目的：

"中央银行"，指任何作为中央财政机关的外国国家机构；

"独立机构"，指具有独立于外国政府资格的法人实体；

"外国国家"，包括构成联邦国家的政治单位、政府机构、在其职务活动中对外代表国家的官方机构，及独立机构；

"商业资产"，指外国国家在以色列境内控制的，包括外交领事资产、军事资产和中央银行资产在内的任何资产，非用于特定目的的，均视为商业资产；

"军事资产"，指具有军事性质，或由军事机构控制的，用于军事目的或在军事活动中使用的资产；

"商业交易"，是指由民商事法律调整，且依行为性质不涉及行使国家权力的任何商业交易或活动；包括货物买卖或服务合同，金融借款或其他金融交易，担保或补偿。

第二章 管辖豁免

第一节 外国国家豁免

第二条 外国国家的管辖豁免

外国国家依本法规定，除刑事案件外，对以色列法院享有司法管辖豁免（以下简称"管辖豁免"）。

第二节 豁免的例外

第三条 商业交易

外国国家因其从事商业交易而引起的诉讼，不享有管辖豁免。

第四条　雇佣合同

一、下列情形全部满足时，外国国家在雇员或求职者提起的诉讼中不享有豁免：

（一）诉讼行为依法律规定属于地方劳动法庭专属管辖事项的；

（二）诉讼属于劳动争议，且部分或全部在以色列境内履行；

（三）诉讼发生时，该雇员或求职者是以色列公民，或常住以色列或其一地区的居民；本款中的"地区"由《紧急状态法第 5728—1967 号》规定。

二、如诉讼发生时，该雇员或求职者非以色列公民或常住居民，本条规定不适用。

三、如未满足本条所列条件，即使诉讼属于第三条规定的商业交易，外国国家在其雇员或求职者提起的诉讼中亦不享有豁免。

第五条　侵权行为

外国国家对在以色列领土内发生的人身侵权或有形财产侵权不享有管辖豁免。

第六条　财产权利

符合下列情形的，外国国家不享有管辖豁免：

（一）外国国家所有、占有、使用以色列境内的不动产权利引起的诉讼；

（二）外国国家通过继承、赠与、无主物取得对以色列境内资产享有的权利；或基于上述权利承担的义务所引起的诉讼；

（三）被监护人的动产或不动产，或企业清算、信托监管引起的诉讼。

第七条　知识产权

外国国家对《法院法》[《法院法》5744—1984 号（合并版本）] 第 40 部分第 4 款规定的下列知识产权不享受豁免：

（一）知识产权中的外国国家权利；

（二）对外国在以色列违反知识产权法律的指控。

第八条　船舶和货物

一、外国国家对在诉讼开始时所有或经营的船舶，或诉讼开始所有的在船货物，用于商业目的的，该外国国家不得对其主张管辖豁免。

二、本条中"所有"指外国国家占有、控制船舶或在船货物，或其他专属管控的法律事实。

第三节 豁免的放弃

第九条 协议放弃豁免

一、外国国家以书面形式明示放弃豁免，或以书面或口头形式通知法院放弃豁免的，不再享有豁免。

二、本条款项下的豁免放弃可具有普遍效力，亦可针对特定事项有效；可事前或事后作出；并可受例外的限制。

三、外国国家驻以色列外交使团团长，或其他行使该职权者得以该外国名义放弃本条所指的豁免；对外国国家缔结的合同引起的诉讼，以该国名义缔约者有权放弃本条所指的豁免；本款规定不得减损授予任何其他人以外国名义放弃豁免的权利。

第十条 管辖豁免的默示放弃

一、外国国家反诉或参与第三方诉讼，即外国国家通过起诉或参与诉讼程序而成为当事方的，不得主张管辖豁免。

二、外国国家因下列事由参与诉讼的，前款规定不适用：

（一）外国国家出庭主张豁免的；

（二）外国国家出庭的目的是主张其诉讼涉及或受裁判结果影响的财产权利的。

三、本条中，"反诉"指民事诉讼中就同一标的，或基于相同法律事实，或诉讼请求无异于且不超出本诉诉求的诉讼。

第十一条 仲裁

一、外国国家书面约定对已经发生的争议或可预期争议适用仲裁的，除仲裁协议另有规定外，不得对因仲裁程序引起的司法管辖主张管辖豁免。

二、仲裁协议缔约方均是国家时，适用国际公法相关规定，前款规定不适用；但缔约一方是非中央银行的独立实体除外。

第十二条 管辖豁免的主张期间

一、外国国家应在其提交实质主张之前尽快对法院主张管辖豁免。

二、第一款规定期间内外国国家未主张管辖豁免的，视为豁免的放弃。

三、该国家在第一款规定的时间内不知，且不能合理知道其可以主张豁免的事项，且在知道该事项后立即主张管辖豁免的，第二款规定不适用。

第四节 程序

第十三条 文件送达外国国家

一、起诉外国国家或对其进行缺席判决的相关文件应通过外交部送达该国外交部门。

二、前款未列举的审判文件应通过该国诉讼代理人送达该国；该方式不能送达的，依前款规定送达。

三、外国国家应自收到起诉或缺席判决文书之日起六十日内回复；法院可以延长此期限。

四、对独立实体送达上述文件的，不适用本条规定。

第十四条　缺席判决

外国国家为被告且未在规定期间内答辩的，当且仅当法院确定该国依本法不享有管辖豁免时，得对该国进行缺席判决。

第三章　执行豁免

第十五条　外国国家的执行豁免

1. 外国国家资产得享受以色列司法或其他执行程序豁免。

2. 外国国家或以该国名义行事的个人不履行以色列法院对该国作出的裁判或其他决定的，不得对其适用监禁或罚款。

3. 本条规定不适用于以色列法院作出的刑事判决。

第十六条　限制性条款

除第十五条第一款规定外，外国国家的下列财产不享受执行豁免：

（1）商业资产；

（2）其对以色列境内的资产，依继承、赠与、无主物取得主张权利的；

（3）以色列境内的不动产。

第十七条　执行豁免的放弃

1. 外国国家书面宣示放弃，或以书面或口头形式向法院表示放弃的，不得主张执行豁免。

2. 本条豁免放弃可具有普遍效力，或针对特定事项作出；可事前约定或事后作出；且可受例外限制；但对外交、领事、中央银行资产的执行豁免需单独明示作出。

3. 外国国家依第九条或第十条对管辖豁免的放弃，不得视为对执行豁免的放弃。

4. 本条规定不适用于军事财产的执行豁免。

5. 外国国家驻以色列的外交使团团长，或行使该职权者有权依据本条以该国名义放弃执行豁免；本款规定不排除其他依授权以外国国家名义放弃执行豁免者的行为。

第十八条 独立实体财产的执行

除第十五条第一款规定外，对依据以色列法院判决或其他决定实施的执行程序，非为中央银行的独立实体的财产不享有豁免；但判决或决定以该独立实体依第九条或第十条规定放弃其享有的管辖豁免为前提的除外。

第四章 其他规定

第十九条 通知司法部长

1. 依本法提出豁免申请的外国国家，应通知司法部长。
2. 外国国家依本法提出豁免申请，未按上述规定通知司法部长的，受理法院应通知司法部长。

第二十条 豁免规定对非国家实体的适用

外交部长会同司法部长，并经政府和国会宪法法律委员会批准，可通过行政指令，授予不具有国际法律人格的政治实体本法第二章或第三章规定的豁免权；该法令可具有普遍适用效力，也可适用于特定事项或特定类型事项，或在限定时间内有效。

第二十一条 外交和领事豁免

本法不得与在以色列有效的任何外交和领事豁免法律和习惯冲突。

第二十二条 外国军队的地位

除本法规定外，如外国军队依以色列与该军队所属国订立的协议享有法律地位和权利，对该军队的作为或不作为的法律程序应由该协议调整。

第二十三条 实施和规章

本法由司法部保障实施；司法部长可会同外交部长制定规章或其他保障实施的文件。

第二十四条 适用

本法对在生效之前已进入诉讼程序但还没开始审理的诉讼有效。

总理　埃胡德·奥尔默特
总统　西蒙·佩雷斯
司法部长　丹尼尔·弗里德曼
国会议长　戴利亚·伊奇克

2009 年日本对外国国家民事管辖法

(2009 年 4 月 24 日第 24 号法律)

第一章 总 则

第一条 宗旨

本法确立与外国国家相关的日本民事管辖权（指除有关刑事以外的管辖权，第四条亦同）的范围，以及与外国国家相关的民事诉讼审判程序的管辖权和特别规则。

第二条 定义

本法中所述"外国国家"是指以下所列主体（"国家"），不包括日本及其相关组织：

（一）国家及其政府机关；

（二）联邦制国家的州，以及一国内与州等同的有权行使国家主权权能的行政区域；

（三）除前两项规定以外的，被授权行使主权权能的实体团体（仅限于该实体团体行使主权的行为）；

（四）前三项规定所列实体中履行相应职责的代表。

第三条 基于条约等规定的特权或豁免关系

本法的规定不影响外国国家基于条约或已确立的国际法规则所享有的特权或豁免。

第二章 对外国国家管辖权的范围

第一节 豁免的原则

第四条

除本法另有规定，外国国家享有管辖豁免（日本的民事管辖豁免，下同）。

第二节 司法程序中不予豁免的情形

第五条 外国国家的同意

一、外国国家已通过以下任一方式，就某一特定事项接受管辖或就案件明确表示同意的，在关于该事项或案件的诉讼程序或其他法庭程序（以下在本节称"司法程序"，其中对外国财产的临时禁制令以及民事执行令除外）中，该外国国家不享有管辖豁免：

（一）条约或其他国际协议；

（二）书面合同；

（三）对上述诉讼程序向法院或其他当事方作出的声明或书面通知。

二、外国国家就特定事项同意适用日本法律，不应被视为对前款管辖权的同意。

第六条 推定同意

一、外国国家有下列行为的，视为对前条第一款（同意接受管辖权）的同意：

（一）向法院提起诉讼或启动其他诉讼审判程序；

（二）参加诉讼审判程序（但以主张管辖豁免为目的而参加诉讼的除外）；

（三）对诉讼实体问题作出辩论或陈述，又不对诉讼审判程序提出异议的。

二、如有令人信服的理由证明当事国在作出上述行为之前，不可能知晓有据以主张管辖豁免的事由存在，且当事国在知晓该豁免事由后立即予以证明的，不适用前款第二项和第三项的规定。

三、在法庭口头辩论期间及其他诉讼程序期间，外国国家缺席以及外国国家的代表仅作为证人出庭的，不得视为前条第一款规定的接受管辖。

第七条

一、在外国国家提起的诉讼或作为当事人参加的诉讼中，若提起反诉，应视为该外国国家对反诉存在第五条第一款（同意接受管辖权）的同意。

二、外国国家在以其自身为被告的诉讼中提起反诉的，应视为该外国国家存在第五条第一款中的同意。

第八条 商业交易

一、对外国国家与其他国家（对于非国家实体而言指其所属的国家，本款下文同此处理）的公民或与根据该其他国家或州的法律法规设立的法人或其他任何实体之间的商业交易（指与民商事货物买卖、服务获取、金钱借贷及其他事项有关的合同或交易，不包括雇佣合同。下款以及第十六条中的"商业交易"同此处理），该外国国家不享有与司法程序相关的管辖豁免。

二、前款规定在以下所列的情形中不予适用：

（一）该外国国家与其他国家之间的商业交易；

（二）该商业交易的各当事方明确同意以其他方式处理的情况。

第九条　劳动合同

一、对于外国国家与个人签订的劳动合同，若劳动之全部或部分系在或将在日本提供，则该外国国家对有关司法程序不享有管辖豁免。

二、对以下所列情形，前款规定不予适用：

（一）该个人系以下规定的人员：

1.《维也纳外交关系公约》第一条第五项规定的外交官员；

2.《维也纳领事关系公约》第一条第四项规定的领事官员；

3. 向国际组织派遣的常驻使团或特别使团的外交职员，或国际会议中为代表外国国家（如系非国家实体，则指其所属国家；本款下文依此处理）而雇佣的人员；

4. 除第 1 目至第 3 目规定之外享有外交豁免的人员。

（二）除前项所列情形外，还包括被雇用从事与该外国国家安全、外交秘密或其他重大利益有关的职责的个人。

（三）有关是否存在雇用或再雇用该个人的合同的诉讼或请求（但损害赔偿请求除外）。

（四）与解雇的效力或其他解除劳动合同有关的诉讼或请求（但损害赔偿请求除外），且该外国国家元首、政府首脑或外交部长认为与该诉讼请求相关的司法程序存在可能损害该外国国家安全利益的风险。

（五）提起诉讼或启动其他司法程序时该个人系该外国国家国民，但该个人在日本有惯常居所的情形不在此限。

（六）该劳动合同的各当事方另有书面约定的情形，但从保护劳动者的角度出发，如果日本法院对与该劳动合同有关的诉讼缺乏管辖权将违反公共秩序的则不在此限。

第十条　人员伤亡或有体物的灭失

对外国国家应负责任的行为导致人员伤亡或有体物灭失损毁的情形，

如该侵害行为的全部或部分系在日本实施且行为人实施该行为时在日本境内，则该外国国家对由此造成的金钱损害赔偿诉讼程序不享有管辖豁免。

第十一条　与不动产有关的权益

一、外国国家在涉及与日本国内不动产相关的下列事项的诉讼程序中，不享有管辖豁免：

（一）该外国国家的权益，或该外国国家占有或使用的权益；

（二）该外国国家的权益或其占有或使用的权益产生的该外国国家的义务。

二、对因动产或不动产的继承及其他概括继承、赠与或无主物取得而产生的该外国国家的权益，外国国家在有关司法程序中不享有管辖豁免。

第十二条　法院参与下财产管理或处分的有关权益

对于日本法院监督或以其他形式参与的信托财产、破产实体财产、公司清算财产或其他财产的管理或处分，外国国家对与此有关的处理该国权益的相关司法程序不享有管辖豁免。

第十三条　知识产权

外国国家对下列事项的相关司法程序不享有管辖豁免：

一、该外国国家主张拥有的知识产权（指与《2002年第122号知识产权基本法》第二条第一款规定的知识产权有关的日本法律法规确立的权利或日本法律保护的与法律利益有关的权利，下款规定亦同）存在与否、效力、归属或内容；

二、该外国国家被控在日本造成的知识产权侵权。

第十四条　有关实体成员资格

一、对外国国家系下列各项法人或其他任何实体的成员或组成部分的情形，该外国国家对与相关资格或基于该资格享有的权利或承担的义务有关的司法程序不享有管辖豁免：

（一）包含国家或国际组织以外成员或其他组成部分的实体；

（二）根据日本法律法规设立的或其主营业地或其他主要办事机构设立在日本的实体。

二、对司法程序当事方书面约定该外国国家享有管辖豁免，或该实体的章程、设立文件或任何其他类似规章等作出同样规定的情形，前款规定不予适用。

第十五条　船舶的运营等

一、对涉及外国国家所有或运营的船舶在运营中产生的争议，如果造成该争议的有关事实发生时该船舶系被用于政府非商业目的之外的用途，则该外国国家对于与该争议有关的司法程序不享有管辖豁免。

二、上述船舶系军舰或海军用辅助舰艇时，前款规定不予适用。

三、对外国国家所有或运营的船舶所载货物产生的争议，如果造成该争议的有关事实发生时该船舶系被用于政府非商业目的之外的用途，则该外国国家对于该争议相关的司法程序不享有管辖豁免。

四、对货物是由军舰或海军用辅助舰艇运送，或该货物由外国国家所有且专门用于或意图用于政府非商业目的的，前款规定不予适用。

第十六条　仲裁协议

对外国国家与其他国家（对于非国家而言，按其所属国家处理，本条下同）的公民或按照该其他国家或该其他国家所属的实体的法律法规设立的法人或其他任何实体之间订立的与商业交易有关的书面仲裁协议，该外国国家对与该仲裁协议成立与否、效力以及该仲裁协议规定的仲裁程序有关的司法程序不享有管辖豁免；但当事方之间的书面协议另有约定的情形除外。

第三节　对外国国家财产的临时禁制令及民事执行令不予豁免的情形

第十七条　外国国家的同意

一、对外国国家已通过以下任一方式明示同意接受对其所有的财产执行临时禁制令或民事执行令的情形，该外国国家对与该临时禁制令或民事执行令有关的程序不享有管辖豁免：

（一）条约或其他国际协议；

（二）关于仲裁的协议；

（三）书面合同；

（四）在执行该临时禁制令或者民事执行令过程中所作声明，或向法院或对方当事人所作书面通知（在向对方当事人作出通知的情形中，限于涉及权利关系的争议发生后所作的通知，且此种情形中该权利关系系请求执行临时禁制令或民事执行令的原因）。

二、对外国国家为实现临时禁制令或民事执行令的目的指定的特定财产，或提供的作为担保的特定财产，该外国国家对于就该财产执行临时禁制令或民事执行令有关的程序不享有管辖豁免。

三、本法第五条第一款项下的同意①不得视为本条第一款项下的同意。

第十八条　用于特殊用途的财产

一、对针对外国国家所有的专门用于或意图用于政府非商业目的用途之外的财产采取的民事执行程序，该外国国家不享有管辖豁免。

二、前款规定的财产不包括以下外国国家所有的财产：

（一）用于或意图用于履行外交使团、领事机构、特别使团、向国际组织派遣的使团、向国际组织机关或向国际会议派遣的代表团的职责的财产。

（二）具有军事性质的财产，或用于或意图用于执行军事任务的财产。

（三）以下所列的非售卖或非意图售卖的财产：

1. 与该外国国家有关的文化遗产；
2. 该外国国家管理的官方文件或其他文档；
3. 具有科学、文化或历史意义的展览品。

三、前款规定并不排除前条第一款及第二款规定的适用②。

第十九条　对外国中央银行的处理

一、日本以外的国家的中央银行或类似的金融主管部门（下款称"外国中央银行"）在对其所有的财产执行临时禁制令或民事执行令时应被视为"外国国家"，包括不符合本法第二条第一项至第三项要求的情形；同时第四条及第十七条第一款和第二款的规定应予适用。

二、对外国中央银行不适用前条第一款的规定③。

第三章　民事审判程序的特别规定

第二十条　诉状等的送达

一、对外国国家的诉状或其他类似文书及法院诉讼程序或其他程序起始日期的传票（本条及下条第一款称"诉状"）的送达，按以下方式送达：

（一）依照条约及其他国际协议规定的方式；

（二）前项没有规定的情形，按以下方式：

1. 通过外交途径的方式；

---

① 对司法程序的管辖豁免的同意。——编者注
② 明示同意执行或指定执行财产。——编者注
③ 商业目的的财产属于执行豁免例外的规定。——编者注

2. 该外国国家接受的送达方式及其他方式（限于《民事诉讼法》[1996年第109号法律]规定的方式）。

二、如按照前款第二项第一目规定的方式送达，则外国国家（国家以外的情形指其所属国）的外务省或相当于外务省的部门机关接受诉状的视为送达。

三、外国国家对案件不提出异议并参加口头辩论或进行陈述的，将丧失对诉状等的送达方式提出异议的权利。

四、除适用第一款和第二款规定外，对外国诉状等的送达其他相关必要事项依照日本最高法院规则确定。

第二十一条 《民事诉讼法》对外国国家缺席审判的特别规定

一、如外国国家在法庭辩论期间缺席且不提交答辩状或其他文书，法院得根据前条第二款的规定在诉状送达或视为送达之日起的四个月期限届满后作出对外国国家的不利判决。

二、对于《民事诉讼法》第二百五十四条第二款项下对外国国家的判决书或记录（在下款及第四款中称为"判决书"）的送达，比照适用前条第一款及第二款的规定。

三、除前款规定外，判决书送达的相关必要事项依照最高法院规则确定。

四、尽管存在《民事诉讼法》第二百八十五条主要条款［包括比照适用该法第三百一十三条（包括比照适用该法第三百一十八条第五款的规定）］或第三百五十七条主要条款（包括比照适用该法第三百六十七条第二款的规定）或第三百七十八条第一款主要条款，外国国家对本条第一款的判决提出上诉或异议的，必须在判决书送达或根据本条第二款比照适用于前条第二款的规定视为送达的四个月内做出，此期限不可延长。

第二十二条 传唤及罚款规定的适用例外

《民事诉讼法》或其他法律法规关于因未服从在庭审期间提交文书及其他文件、作证或其他命令而被传唤或罚款的规定，不适用于外国国家。

2015 年西班牙有关外国政府等享有的特权与豁免的组织法

2015 年 10 月 27 日颁布的本年度第 16 号组织法——《有关外国政府、总部设在西班牙或在西班牙设有办事处的国际组织以及在西班牙举办的国际会议所享有的特权与豁免权的组织法》

费利佩六世

西班牙国王

所有阅见本组织法并理解其内涵的人士，

请知晓：议会通过，且我批准颁布本组织法，其内容如下：

序　　言

一

　　国家主权豁免是国际法的基本原则，传统意义上该原则基于国家独立、主权平等原则（平等者之间无统治权）。其法律内涵基本上是诉讼法层面的，即一国法院不得审判另一国政权。主权豁免既意味着一国政府不应在另一国司法机构被起诉或被审判（管辖豁免），也意味着司法机构不得执行其裁决内容（执行豁免）。

　　由于当今的国际合作日益紧密，主权豁免的内涵得以拓展，豁免权也延伸至国际组织、国际会议、国家元首、政府首脑、外交部长、军舰、国有舰艇和航天器以及国外武装力量等主体，呈现出较为复杂的格局。其中，一些主体的豁免权有完善的规范，而另一些主体豁免权的规范则仍具有分散性和不确定性。

　　豁免权的国际法律规范来源于国际司法惯例，并由习惯法逐渐演变为成文法。然而，当前的成文法未能囊括实务中的问题，且规范内容也不尽如人意，其中尤其棘手的是豁免权的边界问题，因为主张绝对豁免的旧学说正逐渐给更为严格的新理论让步：新学说下，立法者应兼顾豁免权与法治国家的"有效司法救济"原则。

因此，在制定豁免权的国际规范时，应顾及三个层面：成文法层面、习惯法层面和判例层面。

成文法层面上，当今多项国际条约并存，其内容各异，且对国内法的制定也有不同的要求。这些条约有的是专门规范一国政权的有关机构在东道国享有的豁免权的；还有一些并非是规范主权豁免的，但其个别条款对豁免权的规范有重要意义。

首先，全面规范国家机构的外交与领事活动领域豁免权的相关国际条约主要有三个，这三个条约所规范的内容无须内化，它们分别是1961年4月18日通过的《维也纳外交关系公约》、1963年4月24日通过的《维也纳领事关系公约》以及1969年12月16日通过的《特别使团公约》。西班牙是这三个公约的缔约国，其规范已并入我国法律体系［分别通过1968年1月24日发布的该年度第21号《国家官方简报》（后被1968年4月2日发布的该年度第80号《国家官方简报》修正）、1970年3月6日发布的该年度第56号《国家官方简报》以及2001年7月4日发布的该年度第159号《国家官方简报》］。

其次，有关外国政府在国外享有的豁免权，2004年12月2日公布的《联合国国家及其财产管辖豁免公约》（以下简称《公约》）是该领域的主要规范。该《公约》于2005年1月17日开放签署，但至今尚未生效，且亦不能在短期内生效，因为依据第三十条第一款的规定，应至少有30国加入《公约》其才会正式生效，但目前只有17国同意缔约。然而，联合国大会认为《公约》中有关豁免权的规范符合"国际习惯法中广泛认可的原则"，因此遵守《公约》"将会巩固法律的至高地位以及法律安全，尤其在调整国家与自然人或法人的关系"；同时，联合国大会还强调了《公约》有关"国家及其财产的管辖豁免权的统一性和明确性"。西班牙于2011年9月11日签署了该《公约》，且西班牙对于保证豁免权的实施一贯持坚定立场。

再次，除了2004年《公约》外还存在其他的非专门规范豁免权的现行条约，这些条约内包含了主权豁免领域的重要条款。值得一提的是，这些条约依内容可分为三类，第一类诸如1982年12月10日颁布的《联合国海洋法公约》中第三十二条、第九十五条和第九十六条的有关国家战舰豁免权的规范。西班牙是《联合国海洋法公约》的缔约国，其相关规范已通过1997年2月14日发布的该年度第39号《国家官方简报》并入西班牙法律体系。

第二类是有关驻军地位的规范。实践中驻军豁免地位常常在特别协议中规定，这类协议的英文缩写（Status of Foreign Forces Agreement，SOFAs）广为人知。西班牙缔约的相关协议主要是 1951 年 6 月 19 日在伦敦通过的《北约驻军地位协议》，该协议已通过 1998 年 5 月 29 日发布的该年度第 128 号《国家官方简报》并入西班牙法律体系。此外，1988 年 12 月 1 日签署的《防御合作协议》中有部分条文规范了美国驻军在西班牙的地位，该协议后分别经 2002 年 4 月 10 日和 2012 年 10 月 10 日通过的修正案议定书修正。（《防御合作协议》及其两次修正案分别通过 1989 年 5 月 6 日发布的该年度第 108 号《国家官方简报》、2003 年 2 月 21 日发布的该年度第 45 号《国家官方简报》以及 2013 年 6 月 10 日发布的该年度第 138 号《国家官方简报》并入西班牙司法体系。）

第三类是三十几个总部设在西班牙或者在西班牙设有办事处的国际组织的豁免权的相关规范，这类国际条约又可分为两小类。一方面，一些国际组织拥有其所有成员国达成的协约，比如欧盟（附属于《欧盟运行条约》的 7 号议定书——《关于欧盟特权与豁免权的议定书》），联合国（1946 年 2 月 13 日通过的《联合国特权和豁免公约》，该公约已经由 1974 年 11 月 25 日发布的该年度第 282 号《国家官方简报》并入西班牙法律体系），或联合国机构（1947 年 11 月 21 日通过的《联合国专门机构特权和豁免公约》，该公约已经由 1974 年 11 月 25 日发布的该年度第 282 号《国家官方简报》并入西班牙法律体系）。另一方面，其余的国际组织拥有与西班牙王国签署的相关协议。

除了成文法外，国际习惯法对国际法的主体在西班牙所享有的豁免权也有直接规范意义，例如国有航天器的豁免权就不在 1944 年 12 月 7 日通过的《芝加哥协议》第三条第一款所规范的国际民航豁免权的范畴内。再如国家政府官员的刑事豁免规范（如国家元首、政府首脑和外交部长的豁免制度），当前正日益成为国际法委员会的关注重点。此外，主权豁免的一些领域中出现了某些国际惯例，例如放弃管辖豁免不意味着同时放弃执行豁免。然而对于很多豁免权的相关规范，各国仍就其是否属于国际习惯而争议不断，这些规范也包罗万象：一些是实体规范层面的，另一些则属于程序规则。

最后，国际法院的判例既是豁免权制度的重要组成部分，亦是西班牙司法机构进行审判活动的重要参考。其中比较重要的国际法院有联合国国际法院、国际海事法庭和欧洲人权法院，这些法院的判例对豁免法的发展起着日益显著的作用。

也许当前最引人注目的法律漏洞仍是国际会议参加方的相关豁免制度，因为该领域内既无国际成文法或国际习惯法、亦无丰富的司法判例。西班牙当前的做法是在会议召开前签署特别的相关临时协议，这些协议会因国际会议结束而终止效力。

二

国内法层面，豁免权的相关立法既要考虑到《宪法》与现行立法，又要顾及宪法法院建立的判例体系。

《宪法》第二十四条保障所有人"对于其合法权益取得法院'有效司法救济'的权利，且不得在任何情况下出现救济不力"。《宪法》第一百一十七条第三款规定"一切司法诉讼权力，包括审判权和执行权，都应由法律指定的法院依据正当程序行使"。然而《宪法》中并无外国政府豁免权的相关规定。

另一方面，《宪法》第九十三条至第九十六条明确要求西班牙履行国际法的相关义务，而这些义务中自然包括了在豁免权领域西班牙缔约的国际条约以及来源于国际习惯法和国际法院判例的国际法义务。

国内立法层面上，据1985年7月1日颁布的该年度第6号法典——《司法权力组织法》第二十一条第一款的规定，"西班牙的法院依据本组织法和西班牙缔约的国际协议和条约的有关规定受理西班牙人之间的、西班牙人与外国人间的以及外国人之间的诉讼"。然而，该条第二款规定"国际公法所规定的管辖和执行豁免构成前款之例外"。这项规定为西班牙履行国际义务铺平了道路，在当时具有重要的进步意义。同样地，依据2000年1月7日颁布的该年度第1号法典——《民事诉讼法》第三十六条的规定，有关民事管辖豁免权的规范，应参照"西班牙缔约的国际协议和条约"。总之，这些条文都与国际法的规范保持了一致的步调。

另外，宪法法院已判定"来源于外国政府豁免权的消极边界"完全合宪，因此"立法者必须兼顾国际法施加给国家政府的积极边界和消极边界"①，如此"（……）管辖豁免权将能基于更为客观与合理的理由"，因为"如果国家坚持在国际法未能规范的领域内实施司法管辖权，将会违背国际义务，并有违其对另一国的国际责任"（宪法法院1995年9月28日该年度

---

① "积极边界"与"消极边界"分别指什么，该文件中并未明确。其西班牙文原文分别是"límite positivo"与"límite negativo"，英文直译分别为"positive limit"与"negative limit"。——译者注

第 140 号判决书之第 9 号法律事实）。有关执行豁免权的法律规范，宪法法院认为其"存在于国际公法的多样的法律渊源中，包括国际公约和各国的实践"（宪法法院 1997 年 2 月 10 日该年度第 18 号判决书之第 6 号法律事实）。

然而对国际法的泛泛而指会对国内法律安全构成一定的威胁，甚至可能造成判例中的个案分化，进而导致错误与矛盾判决的出现，使西班牙担负国际性的责任。事实上，宪法法院已公开建议立法者在吸纳某些管辖与执行豁免相关学说的基础上制定外国政府在西班牙的豁免权规范，以保障国内司法领域的法律确定性（宪法法院 1992 年 7 月 1 日之该年度第 107 号判决书）。

因此在《司法权力组织法》颁布实施近三十年后的今天，西班牙似乎应当在充分尊重我国所承诺的国际义务的基础上，颁布一部系统规范豁免制度的组织法。因为正如前文所述，现行法所指向的国际法存在不足与缺陷，且其规范过于分散，不利于保障国内的法律安全。此外，考虑到国家间日益紧密的合作关系，西班牙亦当规范国家政府或其代表以外主体的豁免制度，这些主体主要有国际组织、驻军、国有舰艇与航空器以及在我国举行的国际会议。这部组织法应将豁免制度对"有效司法救济"权的影响降至最低，并在政府有能力调整的既定法律规范的领域内，保障议会控制权的实施。

这部组织法将成为其他规范国际法律关系法典的理想的规范补充，这些法典分别是 2014 年 3 月 25 日颁布的该年度第 2 号法典——《国家外交及外事服务法》（刊登于 2014 年 3 月 26 日发布的该年度第 74 号《国家官方简报》）以及 2014 年 11 月 27 日颁布的该年度第 25 号法典——《国际条约法》（刊登于 2014 年 11 月 28 日发布的该年度第 288 号《国家官方简报》）。

三

本组织法共分八篇。其中前篇规定了本组织法的目的、词语定义以及适用范围。第一篇是本组织法的核心篇，规范了外国政府在西班牙的司法豁免权，并将管辖豁免权与执行豁免权规定在不同的章节中。该篇的豁免权可明示或默示放弃，且东道国对此并不负担绝对性的义务，因为该篇明确了豁免权的边界。之后，本组织法依次规范了国家元首、政府首脑和外交部长的特权与豁免权（第二篇）、军舰及国有舰艇和航空器的豁免权（第三篇）、驻军地位（第四篇）、总部设在西班牙或在西班牙设有办事机构的国际组织的特权与豁免权（第五篇），以及国际会议的特权与豁免权（第六篇）。本组织法的最后一篇是程序性规范（第七篇），并以相应的附加条款、废止条款和最终条款结尾。

最后，值得一提的是，本组织法中并无外交与领事规范，因为西班牙的法律体系自几十年前就设立了相关的国际法律制度。另外，任何组织机构或个人都不得对本组织法的内容作不利于我国审判国际犯罪以及履行国际刑事法庭相关义务的解释。

前　篇

第一条　目的

本组织法用于规范西班牙司法机构的豁免事项，以及下列主体享有的特权：

（一）外国政府及外国政府的资产；

（二）任职期内以及非任职期内的国家元首、政府首脑和外交部长；

（三）军舰以及国有船舶和航天器；

（四）驻军；

（五）在西班牙设办事处的国际组织；以及

（六）在西班牙举办的国际会议。

第二条　定义

本组织法中出现的词语作下列解释：

（一）管辖豁免：国家、组织或个人享有的不得在另一国司法机关被起诉或审判的特权；

（二）执行豁免：国家、组织或个人以及其财产享有的不得在另一国司法机关被施行强制措施或执行法院裁决的特权；

（三）国家政府：

1. 政府及各政府部门；

2. 得为行使国家主权的联邦政府或政府分支的各部门；

3. 得为行使国家主权的政府各机构以及其他公共机构，且无关乎其法律性质；和

4. 得为行使国家主权的政府代表。

（四）国家元首：根据其国家宪法，行使元首职务的个人或者集体，且无关乎其职务名称；

（五）政府首脑：行使政府首脑职务之个人，且无关乎其职务名称；

（六）外交部长：外国政府中的外事负责人，且无关乎其职务名称；

（七）国有船舶：非商业用途的外国船舶，为国家所有或仅供公共使用；

（八）军舰：隶属于国外武装力量、有国家军舰标志的主舰或从舰，舰艇应听命于该国政府指定官员的指挥，且该官员应登记在政府官员名册或类似名册，舰艇船员接受该国武装力量的常规纪律管理；

（九）国有航空器：外国政府之航空器，由政府操作，且仅供公共使用、无商业用途，如军用、海关用或警用；

（十）驻军：受西班牙邀请或经西班牙同意，负有官方任务的位于西班牙境内的外国部队，但西班牙与外国政府可经协商同意上述个人或集体不属于本组织法定义下的驻军；

（十一）驻军的平民：陪同驻军、受该国军队雇用的平民，但不得为无国籍人士，或未经西班牙同意入境的第三国公民，抑或西班牙公民或者在西班牙有经常居所的人士；

（十二）国际组织：总部在西班牙或者在西班牙设有办事处的跨政府组织，具国际法人人格，且受国际法约束；

（十三）国际会议：由西班牙政府主办，或由国际组织主办、西班牙参与的，且经西班牙政府同意的在西班牙召开的政府间或非政府间会议；和

（十四）商业合同：一切货物或服务合同或交易；一切借贷合同或金融交易，包括依附该合同或交易的一切担保或赔偿；一切其他商业、工业和租赁实物或服务的合同，但不包括个人劳动合同。在界定合同是否属于"商业合同"之时，应主要参考合同或交易的性质，但若缔约方在合同中明确了合同目的，则该目的也作为参考；其中，若国家为缔约方，且据该国法律实务，合同中明确的合同目的可确定其非商业之性质，则该合同不是商业合同。

第三条 其他被国际法认可且不受本组织法影响的特权和豁免

本组织法之规定不妨害国际法承认的任何特权和豁免，尤其是下列主体的特权：

（一）一国的外交机构、领馆和特别机构；

（二）国际组织和国际组织的内部人员；和

（三）国有的或由国家操控的航空器、航天器和其他特殊物品。

第一篇　外国政府在西班牙的豁免权

第四条　外国政府的豁免权

一切外国政府及其财产都在本组织法规定的条件内于西班牙的司法机构中享有管辖豁免权和执行豁免权。

第一章　管辖豁免

第一节　外国政府接受西班牙司法机构之管辖权

第五条　明示许可

若外国政府通过下列方式明示许可西班牙司法机构之管辖，则不享有管辖豁免权：

（一）国际条约；

（二）书面合同；或

（三）在法院声明或在某诉讼中书面声明。

第六条　默示许可

若出现下列情况，则在诉讼中外国政府不享有管辖豁免权：

（一）起诉方为该国政府；

（二）该国政府介入诉讼或为任何实质性的诉讼行为；

（三）该国政府基于本诉的法律关系或法律事实提起反诉；或

（四）被告方提起反诉，且反诉基于之法律关系或法律事实与该国政府提起的诉讼相同。

第七条　不属于许可管辖的行为

下列行为不被看作外国政府对西班牙司法机构对其行使管辖权的许可：

（一）外国政府介入诉讼以主张其管辖豁免权；

（二）外国政府代表以证人身份出庭；

（三）外国政府不出庭；或

（四）外国政府明示或默示许可适用西班牙法律裁判诉讼标的。

第八条　许可之撤销

外国政府一旦作出本组织法第五条和第六条所规定之许可，则西班牙司法机构的诉讼开始后该国政府不得撤销该许可。

第二节 外国政府管辖豁免权之例外

第九条 商业合同类诉讼

一、若为商业合同类诉讼，且外国政府为缔约方，对方为非该国国籍的自然人或法人，则该国政府不得主张管辖豁免，除非：

（一）缔约方均为国家政府；或

（二）合同中约定了该国政府的管辖豁免。

二、若缔约方为国有企业或者由国家政府创办的企业，则该国政府不是缔约方，但该企业须具有法人资格和下述权能：

（一）起诉和被起诉；且

（二）能通过合约取得财产的所有权或占有财产，包括国家政府授权其开发、管理或拥有的财产。

第十条 劳动合同类诉讼

一、除非西班牙和外国政府另有协议，在该国政府与自然人的劳动纠纷中，若劳动已经开始且部分或全部劳动在西班牙境内进行，那么该国政府不得主张管辖豁免。

二、然而在下列情况下外国政府可主张管辖豁免：

（一）若劳动合同之内容为行使公共权力；

（二）若劳方为：

1. 《1961年维也纳外交关系公约》定义的外交代表；

2. 《1963年维也纳领事关系公约》定义的领事官员；或

3. 国际组织常设机构或国际会议中被指定代表外国政府的特别机构的外交人员。

（三）若诉讼是为了达成劳动合同、延续劳动合同或再次雇用劳方；

（四）若诉讼是为了辞退劳方、撤销合同或者外国政府的相关部门声明该诉讼有损其安全利益；

（五）若提起诉讼时劳方为该国公民，除非劳方在西班牙拥有经常居所；或

（六）若外国政府与劳方在劳动合同中约定了该国政府的管辖豁免，除非西班牙是唯一具有管辖权的国家。

第十一条 人身或财产损害赔偿类诉讼

除非西班牙和外国政府另有协议，在请求人身或财产侵权之金钱赔偿的案件中，若损害被指控由该国政府的故意或过失行为造成，那么该国政府不得主张管辖豁免，只要：

（一）该故意或过失行为部分或全部发生在西班牙；且

（二）该故意或过失行为发生时行为人在西班牙境内。

第十二条 有关确定财产类纠纷的权利义务的诉讼

除非西班牙和外国政府另有协议，在确定下列权利义务的诉讼中该国政府不得主张管辖豁免权：

（一）该国政府对位于西班牙的不动产的物权、占有权或使用权；

（二）该国政府享有的第（一）项中的权利所对应的义务；

（三）该国政府因继承、捐赠和时效而取得的动产或不动产；或

（四）该国政府在遗产信托关系中，或者在企业破产或清算中取得的财产管理权。

第十三条 知识产权确权类诉讼

除非西班牙和外国政府另有协议，该国政府不得在下列诉讼中主张管辖豁免：

（一）该国的知识产权确权类诉讼，且该权利受西班牙法律的保护；或

（二）该国政府因侵犯第三人知识产权而成为被告的诉讼，且该权利受西班牙法律的保护。

第十四条 有关国家政府参与法人或其他组织的诉讼

除非西班牙和外国政府另有协议，若该国政府参与到企业、社团、基金会或其他营利性的或非营利性的、具有法人资格或不具有法人资格的组织中，那么在处理该国政府与该组织的关系，抑或与该组织成员的关系的诉讼中，该国政府不得主张管辖权豁免，只要：

（一）该组织依据西班牙相关法律组建，或其中央行政部门或主要机构设立在西班牙；而且

（二）该组织非全部由国际法的主体构成。

第十五条 有关国有船舶之使用或舰艇之货物的诉讼

一、除非西班牙和拥有舰艇之所有权的外国政府另有协议，该国政府不得在下列诉讼中主张管辖豁免：

（一）与使用该舰艇相关的诉讼，尤其是与因碰撞、共同海损或其他与海难相关的事件而签署的协助、救援、维修、餐食供应合同以及与海域污染治理相关合同的相关诉讼，只要诉讼所基于的主要事实发生时该舰艇未被以非商业的公共目的使用；或者

（二）诉讼与舰艇所运货物相关，只要诉讼所基于的主要事实发生时该货物未被以非商业的公共目的的使用或该货物的最终用途不是非商业的公共用途。

二、前款之"使用"包括对舰艇的占有、控制、管理和租用，其中租用方式包括期租、程租和光租。

三、若在诉讼中对于本条第一款所述的"非商业的公共目的"或"非商业的公共用途"出现相关争议，则经西班牙政府承认的外国相关机构长官签字的证明书具有完全证明效力；或者在该国无经西班牙承认的相关机构的前提下，由该国相关部门签字的证明书同样具有完全证明效力。

四、本条第一款在任何条件下都不适用于外国军舰或外国的全面享有豁免权的舰艇。

第十六条　有关仲裁条约效力的诉讼

若一国政府已与另一国籍的自然人或法人达成商业交易的仲裁协议，除非双方在仲裁协议或仲裁条款中另有规定，该国政府在有关下列事项的诉讼中不得主张管辖豁免权：

（一）仲裁条款或仲裁条约的效力、解释或适用；

（二）仲裁程序，包括仲裁委员会的任命；

（三）仲裁裁决的确认、取消和复审；或

（四）国外仲裁裁决的效力认证。

第二章　执行豁免

第十七条　外国政府执行豁免

一、西班牙司法机构不得在作出裁决前或作出裁决后执行他国财产或对其采取其他强制性措施，除非有该国政府的明示或默示许可。

二、作出裁决后，若可确定执行标的的当前或将来用途不是非商业的官方用途，则西班牙司法机构可执行该标的，只要其位于西班牙境内且与被起诉的外国政府有牵连性，且无须其与诉讼所基于的事实依据有关联性。

第十八条　执行许可

一、本组织法第十七条第一款所指之"明示或默示许可"须经由下列途径传达：

（一）国际协约；

（二）书面合同；或

（三）法院庭上声明或在特定诉讼中的书面通知。

二、本组织法第十七条第一款所指之"默示许可"仅指外国政府指定其名下财产以偿付诉讼请求之情形。

三、外国政府作出本组织法第五条和第六条所指之管辖许可，在任何前提下都不意味着其同时作出执行许可。

第十九条　执行许可之撤销

外国政府一旦作出本组织法第十八条所规定之执行许可，则西班牙司法机构的诉讼开始后该国政府不得撤销该许可。

第二十条　外国政府之非商用的公用财产

一、下列外国政府所有的、占有的或者控制的财产，在任何情况下都被看作非商用的公用财产：

（一）包括银行账户在内的，用于维持政府外交机构、领事办公室和专门机构以及国际组织常驻代表机构、国际组织或国际会议的代表机构正常运行的资金；

（二）外国政府的军事财产或有军事用途的财产；

（三）外国政府的中央银行或其他官方金融机构的用于机构自身运行发展的财产；

（四）国外文化遗产、国家档案或展会展出的有科技、文化或历史价值的物品，但不包括可供公众购买的展览物；以及

（五）国有舰艇和航天器。

二、本条第一款第（一）项中的"银行账户"不包括无公共用途的账户。

三、本条所列之财产不得被作为执行标的，除非有外国政府的许可。

第二篇　现任国家元首、政府首脑及外交部长之特权与豁免

第一章　现任国家元首、政府首脑及外交部长的不可侵犯性与豁免权

第二十一条　不可侵犯性

一、任职期内的外国元首、政府首脑及外交部长，无论在官方场合还是在私人场所，在西班牙境内都不可侵犯。任职期内的外国元首、政府首脑及外交部长不得被拘捕，且应被给予应有的尊重，西班牙将采取一切合理措施保护其人身安全、自由和尊严。

二、本条第一款所指之"不可侵犯"，其主体还包括任职期内的外国元首、政府首脑及外交部长在西班牙的住所、来往信件、私人财物和其使用

的交通工具。

第二十二条 管辖与执行豁免

一、任职期内的外国元首、政府首脑及外交部长无论在西班牙境内还是在西班牙境外，在西班牙一切法律部门的司法机构中都享有管辖和执行豁免。若任职期内的外国元首、政府首脑及外交部长身处西班牙境内，则无论是官方访问还是私下来访，其都享有豁免权，且无论诉讼所基于的事实依据发生在任职期内的外国元首、政府首脑及外交部长的任职期之前还是任职期之内，也无论其被起诉的行为是官方行为还是私人行为，其都享有豁免权。

二、任职期内的外国元首、政府首脑及外交部长无须到西班牙的司法机构出庭作证。

第二章 前国家元首、政府首脑及外交部长的豁免权

第二十三条 任职期间职务行为之豁免权的连续性

一、任职期结束后，前国家元首、政府首脑及外交部长仅在国际法许可的范围内对于任职期内的职务行为继续享有刑事豁免权。但是在任何情况下前国家元首、政府首脑及外交部长对于其种族灭绝、强迫失踪、战争及反人类行为都不享有豁免权。

二、任职期结束后，前国家元首、政府首脑及外交部长仅对于任职期内的职务行为享有民事法、劳动法、行政法、商事法和财政法豁免权，本组织法第九条至第十五条所规定之例外对其适用。

第二十四条 对任职期内非职务行为之管辖权

任职期结束后，前国家元首、政府首脑及外交部长对于任职期内的非职务行为不得于西班牙的司法机构主张豁免。

第二十五条 对任职前行为之管辖权

任职期结束后，前国家元首、政府首脑及外交部长对于任职前的一切行为不得于西班牙的司法机构主张豁免权。

第三章 共同规定

第二十六条 国家元首、政府首脑及外交部长豁免权之对等原则

除非有国际法之明令禁止，现任或前任国家元首、政府首脑及外交部长的豁免权可因对等原则而被剥夺或削减。

第二十七条　国家元首、政府首脑及外交部长豁免权之放弃

一、外国政府可于西班牙司法机构声明放弃其现任或前任国家元首、政府首脑及外交部长的豁免权。

二、豁免权须明示放弃。

三、若现任或前任国家元首、政府首脑及外交部长提起司法诉讼，那么其对于直接基于本诉的反诉不得主张豁免权。

四、放弃管辖豁免不意味着放弃执行豁免，放弃后者须再为声明。

第二十八条　豁免放弃之撤销

本组织法第二十七条所规定之豁免放弃声明一旦作出，西班牙司法机构的诉讼开始后作出该声明的主体不得撤销其声明。

第二十九条　国际犯罪

本篇之规定不妨害西班牙履行对国际犯罪实施审判之义务，也不妨害西班牙向国际刑事法院履行其相关承诺。

第三篇　军舰和国有船舶、航空器之豁免权

第三十条　军舰和国有舰艇的豁免

除非相关国家间另有协议，外国军舰和国有舰艇于西班牙司法机构享有管辖和执行豁免权，且即使该军舰或舰艇位于西班牙领海或内海也适用豁免。

第三十一条　国有航空器之豁免

本组织法定义下的外国国有航天器于西班牙司法机构享有管辖和执行豁免，且即使该航天器位于西班牙领空或领土也适用豁免。

第三十二条　外国政府许可管辖或执行

有关外国政府许可西班牙司法机构对其依照本组织法享有豁免权的军舰和国有舰艇、航空器行使管辖权或许可西班牙司法机构执行上述财产的规定，参照本组织法第五条至第八条及第十八条和第十九条。

第四篇　驻军地位

第三十三条　驻军及其军事人员、平民和财产的地位

一、受西班牙邀请或经过西班牙同意得为身处西班牙境内的北约成员国或北约"和平伙伴关系计划"成员国的驻军及其军事人员、平民和财产，其地位适用 1951 年 6 月 19 日签署的《北约驻军地位协议》的有关规定。

二、受西班牙邀请或经过西班牙同意得为身处西班牙境内的其他国家的驻军及其军事人员、平民和财产，其地位部分或全部适用1951年6月19日签署的《北约驻军地位协议》（以下简称《协议》）的有关规定。上述《协议》的适用参照对等原则以及西班牙国防部与该国对等部门签署的相关协议。

三、本条规定适用于驻扎或过境西班牙主权地以及西班牙的舰艇和航天器的一切驻军及其军事人员、平民和财产。

第五篇　总部在西班牙或在西班牙设有办事处的国际组织之特权及豁免权

第三十四条　国际组织的不可侵犯性

一、无论身在何处，国际组织所在的建筑物（无论建筑物的所有人为何）、国际组织的文件、官方信件以及一切为其所有或受其控制以及一切供其以官方目的使用的文件都不可侵犯。

二、国际组织所在的建筑物以及其在西班牙的一切交通工具和财产都不得成为搜查、征用、没收、征收或任何其他执行性的、行政性的、司法性的或立法性的强制手段的施行对象。

第三十五条　国际组织的豁免权

一、若无可适用的国际双边或多边协议，则国际组织在西班牙的司法机构对于其所为的一切官方行为都享有管辖豁免和执行豁免，豁免的条件规定在本组织法中。

然而若提起的是私法或劳动法程序，且起诉人是国际组织的内部员工，那么国际组织不得主张豁免权，除非其能够证明在组织章程、内部规章或其他可适用的规范性文件中规范了解决此类纠纷的非司法途径。

二、除非另有协议，对于第三人因国际组织所有的或所操作的机动车造成损害而提起的民事诉讼，或对于第三人提起的交通事故类民事赔偿诉讼，且国际组织所有的或所操作的机动车与该事故有牵连性的，本条第一款规定的豁免权不再适用。

第三十六条　国际组织的内部人员

一、国际组织的最高代表人在西班牙享有国际法给予外交机构长官的同等级豁免权，且该豁免权延伸至最高代表人的无西班牙国籍且在西班牙无经常居所的家人。国际组织的最高代表人及其家人，以及他们的居所、信件和行李都同样不可侵犯。

二、国际组织的最高代表人的临时替代人在职位替代期间享有本条第一款所规定的豁免权。

三、国际组织的其余内部人员，无论其国籍为何，都不得因属于职务行为的口头言语、书面文字和行为而被逮捕，且享有管辖豁免权。

四、国际组织临时雇用的专家和其余人员不得因属于职务行为的口头言语、书面文字和行为而被逮捕，且享有管辖豁免权。

五、国际组织的最高代表人、其余内部人员以及临时雇用的专家和其余人员在离职后，对于其在职期间的职务行为依然享有管辖豁免权。

第三十七条 国际组织许可西班牙司法机构之管辖权

一、若国际组织已通过下列方式明确授意西班牙司法机构对某事件的管辖权，则该国际组织不得主张管辖豁免：

（一）国际条约；

（二）书面合同；或

（三）在法院声明或在特定诉讼中进行书面声明。

二、若出现下列情形，则国际组织在特定诉讼中不得主张管辖权豁免：

（一）起诉方为该国际组织；

（二）该国际组织作出实质性的诉讼行为；

（三）该国际组织基于本诉的法律关系或法律事实提起反诉；或

（四）被告方提起反诉，且反诉基于之法律关系或法律事实与该国际组织提起的诉讼的法律关系或法律事实相同。

三、若在国际组织为缔约方的合同之中，该国际组织于某条款内承认了西班牙任一普通司法机构的管辖权，则该条款应被视为该国际组织对管辖豁免权的放弃。

第三十八条 不构成许可管辖权的行为

下列行为不被看作国际组织对西班牙司法机构对其行使管辖权的许可：

（一）国际组织介入诉讼以主张其管辖豁免权；

（二）国际组织代表以证人身份出庭；

（三）国际组织不出庭；或

（四）国际组织明示或默示许可适用西班牙法律裁判诉讼标的。

第三十九条 许可之撤销

国际组织一旦作出本组织法第三十七条所规定之许可，则西班牙司法机构的诉讼开始后该组织不得撤销其许可。

第四十条 国际组织的成员国以及观察员国之代表

一、国际组织成员国的常任代表和观察员国派驻机构代表在西班牙享有外交机构长官的同等级豁免权，且该豁免权延伸至代表人的无西班牙国籍且在西班牙无经常居所的家人。代表人及其家人，以及他们的居所、信件和行李都同样不可侵犯。

二、国际组织成员国及观察员国代表团的外交事务工作人员在西班牙享有外交官的同等级豁免权，且该豁免权延伸至工作人员的无西班牙国籍且在西班牙无经常居所的家人。外交事务工作人员及其家人，以及他们的居所、信件和行李都同样不可侵犯。

三、国际组织成员国及观察员国代表团的其余内部人员，不得因属于职务行为的口头言语、书面文字和行为而被逮捕，且享有管辖豁免权。

第四十一条 外国政府许可管辖和执行

若无相关国际条约的规定，则有关国际组织的成员国或观察员国的国家政府许可西班牙司法机构对其代表机构或机构成员行使管辖权以及采取执行措施的规范，参照本组织法第五条至第八条以及第十八条和第十九条。

第六篇　国际会议的特权及豁免权

第四十二条 适用范围

一、若无西班牙缔约的可适用的相关条约，则有关西班牙举办的国际会议所享有的特权和豁免权的相关规范应参照本篇的规定，且无论该会议的具体名称为何。

二、若存在西班牙缔约的可适用的相关条约，则优先适用条约的相关规定，本组织法作补充规范。

第四十三条 特权及豁免权的期限

通常，国际会议的特权及豁免权始于会议召开前的第十天，止于会议结束后的第五天。

第四十四条 为举行国际会议而提供的便利、特权和豁免权

一、举办国际会议的场所，无论其所有人为何，都不可侵犯。在无会议组织方最高官员或代表人的明示授权下，任何西班牙的公务人员不得擅入会议举办地，除非有火情或其他类似紧急情况发生。

二、国际会议的举办场所以及其在西班牙的一切交通工具和财产都不得成为搜查、征用、没收、征收或任何其他执行性的、行政性的、司法性的或立法性的强制手段的施行对象。

三、在欧盟关税条例允许的条件内，国际会议组织方为举办会议而进口的行政、技术材料以及其他用于工作的官方文件和送给高官的常规礼品都免收关税，只要组织方承诺会议结束后，已消耗物品外的其余物料均会运出西班牙国境。

四、国际会议组织方的最高代表人或者会议主席在西班牙享有一国外交机构长官的同等级的特权和豁免权，且该特权及豁免权延伸至最高代表或会议主席的无西班牙国籍且在西班牙无经常居所的家人。

第四十五条　国际会议被邀请国代表

一、国际会议被邀请国代表团长官在西班牙享有一国外交机构长官的同等级的特权和豁免权。

二、国际会议被邀请国在国际会议召开前应将其代表团的内部成员名单经由外交途径递交给西班牙政府，名单内的代表团内部成员在西班牙享有一国外交官的同等级的特权及豁免权，该特权与豁免权之例外见本条第四款。

三、国际会议被邀请国代表团的其余工作人员享有管辖豁免权，且不得因属于职务行为的口头言语、书面文字和行为而被逮捕。

四、对于第三人因机动车造成损害而提起的民事诉讼，或对于第三人提起的交通事故类民事赔偿诉讼，且国际会议被邀请国代表团的内部成员所有的或所操作的机动车与该事故有牵连性的，本条第二款规定的豁免权不再适用。

五、国际会议被邀请国代表团所在的建筑物，无论其所有人为何，都不可侵犯。在无代表团长官或其代职人的明示授权下，任何西班牙的公务人员不得擅入该建筑物，除非有火情或其他类似紧急情况发生。

六、国际会议被邀请国代表团所在的建筑物以及其在西班牙的一切交通工具和财产都不得成为搜查、征用、没收、征收或任何其他执行性的、行政性的、司法性的或立法性的强制手段的施行对象。

七、西班牙允许国际会议被邀请国各代表团间的与会议相关的自由通信。各代表团可使用任何合适的通信方式，包括外交邮件、外交信函和设密码的或经特殊编码的信件。

八、在欧盟关税条例允许的条件内，国际会议被邀请国代表团为参加会议而进口的行政、技术材料以及其他用于工作的官方文件和送给高官的常规礼品都免收关税，只要被邀请国政府承诺会议结束后，已消耗物品外的其余物料均会运出西班牙国境。

第四十六条 国际会议组织方邀请的其他人员和组织方官员

国际会议组织方邀请的不属于被邀请国代表团成员的其他人员以及国际会议组织方来到西班牙的官员,只要无西班牙国籍且在西班牙无经常居所地,在西班牙都不得以任何形式被拘捕,且其随身物品不得被没收,除非其罪行显著;而且对于属于职务行为的口头言语、书面文字和行为,上述人士享有管辖豁免权。

第四十七条 联合国及联合国专门机构组织的国际会议

一、若联合国或联合国专门机构受西班牙政府邀请、与西班牙政府合作或征得西班牙政府同意,在西班牙举办国际会议,则根据具体情况适用《联合国特权和豁免公约》(1946年2月13日联合国大会通过)或《联合国专门机构特权和豁免公约》(1947年11月21日联合国大会通过),且具体的适用规则见以下款项。

二、联合国或联合国专门机构在举办国际会议前应将成员国代表的名单经由外交途径递交西班牙政府,名单中的代表根据具体情况享有1946年《联合国特权和豁免公约》第四条规定的特权和豁免权,或享有1947年《联合国专门机构特权和豁免公约》第五条规定的特权和豁免权。

三、受联合国或联合国专门机构邀请的,或受西班牙政府邀请的,或受两者同时邀请的不属于本条前款所指的成员国代表的国际会议参加人,若其名单在国际会议开始前已经由外交途径递交西班牙政府,则其享有1946年《联合国特权和豁免公约》第六条中规定的联合国机构专家所享有的同等级的特权和豁免权。

四、参加国际会议或履行国际会议相关职务的联合国或联合国专门机构的官员,若其名单在会议召开前已经由外交途径递交西班牙政府,则其分别享有1946年《联合国特权和豁免公约》第五条、第七条或1947年《联合国专门机构特权和豁免公约》第六条、第八条所规定的特权和豁免权。

五、本篇之规定作补充规范。

第四十八条 欧盟组织的国际会议

若欧盟或欧盟某机构受西班牙政府邀请、与西班牙政府合作或征得西班牙政府同意,在西班牙举办国际会议,则应适用《议定书七:关于欧盟特权与豁免权的议定书》中的有关特权和豁免权的规范。

第七篇　程序问题

第四十九条　司法机构依职权豁免

西班牙司法机构应依据本组织法之规定依职权适用豁免，不受理或驳回针对依据本组织法享有豁免权的单位、个人或财产提起的诉讼或执行请求。

第五十条　申请豁免

除非外国政府默示放弃管辖豁免权，在任何程序中，外国政府都可依照2000年1月7日通过的该年度第1号法典——《民事诉讼法》中第六十三条及以下条款的相关规定提起管辖权异议，且应在第六十四条第一款规定的时效内提出。

第五十一条　针对国家政府、国际组织和有豁免权的人士提起的诉讼

若在西班牙司法机构提起的某诉讼的被告方当事人是依据本组织法之规范享有豁免权的机构或个人，则认为该诉讼是针对上述有豁免权的主体提起的诉讼。①

第五十二条　向外国政府发出司法送达

传票、司法命令和其他一切向外国政府发出的司法送达文件，以及向西班牙外交与合作部发出的控告外国政府的、以便该部撰写和发出被告方管辖与执行豁免权报告的知悉通告，均应依据2015年7月30日通过的该年度第29号法典——《国际民事司法合作法》的相关规范施行。

第五十三条　外国政府及国际组织发出的通告

外国政府及国际组织应通过外交途径，经由西班牙外交与合作部向西班牙的司法机构发出有关其在本组织法规定下的明示许可西班牙司法机关的管辖权或放弃自身豁免权的通告。

第五十四条　西班牙外交与合作部与西班牙司法机构间的通告程序

一、西班牙司法机构向外国政府和国际组织发出的通告，应经由西班牙外交与合作部，向其外交机构或常驻西班牙代表处转递，以便其转交给该国外交部或该国际组织的相关机构。

---

① 本条文的翻译存在难度，其中心意思是要判断某诉讼是不是针对有豁免权的主体提起的，其标准在于该诉的被告方当事人是否是依据本组织法享有豁免权的机构或人士。——译者注

二、对于在西班牙提起的诉讼，西班牙外交与合作部应向西班牙的相关司法机构转递外国政府和国际组织依据 2015 年 7 月 30 日通过的该年度第 29 号法典——《国际民事司法合作法》第二十七条的相关规定撰写和发出的"无约束力报告"以及其他关于豁免权问题的经由外交途径向西班牙外交与合作部发出的通告。

三、西班牙的相关司法机构应尽快向西班牙外交与合作部发出依据 2015 年 7 月 30 日通过的该年度第 29 号法典——《国际民事司法合作法》第二十七条的相关规定撰写的报告，以便外交与合作部将其转递给外国政府。

第五十五条　缺席判决

西班牙的司法机构不得针对外国政府或国际组织作出缺席判决，除非同时满足下列三个条件：

（一）已完成通告要求；

（二）自外国政府或国际组织收到起诉通知或其他启动诉讼的文件起已经过四个月；且

（三）本组织法不禁止西班牙司法机构实施管辖权。

第五十六条　诉讼审理期间的外国政府与国际组织的特权及豁免权

一、若外国政府或国际组织未履行或拒绝履行西班牙司法机构向其发出的为某行为或停止某行为、递交某文件或提供某诉讼相关信息的命令，则其后果仅限于案件的实质裁判层面，西班牙司法机构不得因此处罚外国政府或国际组织或向其征收罚款。

二、若外国政府或国际组织为被告方当事人，则西班牙司法机构不得以保证诉讼费的收缴为由向其收取保证金或押金。

附加条款　通知其他国际法主体

西班牙外交与合作部将本组织法通知给所有与西班牙保持关系的国际法主体，包括西班牙身为成员国的国际组织。

废止条款　废止规范

本组织法废止一切与其规范有冲突的同阶的或低阶的法律规范。

最终条款第一条　立法权

本组织法的制定基于《宪法》第一百四十九条第一款第（三）项和第（六）项集中赋予国家的外交关系及程序规范领域的立法权。

最终条款第二条　组织法特定条款的普通法性质

本法之性质为组织法，但第四十九条至第五十五条以及最终条款第四条之性质为普通法。

最终条款第三条　1985 年 7 月 1 日颁布的该年度第 6 号组织法——《司法权力组织法》之修改

1985 年 7 月 1 日颁布的该年度第 6 号组织法——《司法权力组织法》第二十一条第二款之修改后的条文如下：

"二、然而，西班牙司法机构不受理针对依据西班牙立法和国际公法之规范享有管辖豁免和执行豁免的主体及财产提起的诉讼。"

最终条款第四条　2000 年 1 月 7 日颁布的该年度第 1 号法典——《民事诉讼法》之修改

2000 年 1 月 7 日颁布的该年度第 1 号法典——《民事诉讼法》第三十六条第二款第（一）项之修改后的条文如下：

"一、当提起诉讼或申请执行的对象是依据西班牙立法和国际公法之规范享有管辖豁免或执行豁免的主体或财产时。"

最终条款第五条　规范之发展

本组织法授权政府出台必要的法律法规以发展本组织法之规范。

最终条款第六条　国际条约的优先性

若本组织法之规定与西班牙缔约的国际条约之相关规定竞合，则优先适用国际条约的相关规范。

最终条款第七条　生效

本组织法于《国家官方简报》发布之日起的二十天后生效。

因此，

我命令所有的西班牙人，无论个人还是官方机构，保存且要求保存本组织法。

马德里，2015 年 10 月 27 日。

费利佩六世

政府首相

马里亚诺·拉霍伊·布莱依

2015 年俄罗斯关于外国国家和财产在俄罗斯联邦的管辖豁免法

俄罗斯联邦联邦法
2015 年 10 月 23 日通过国家杜马审议
2015 年 10 月 28 日经联邦委员会批准

第一条 本联邦法的管辖权

一、本联邦法适用于与俄罗斯联邦对某外国国家及其财产管辖豁免有关的关系。

二、外国国家依据本联邦法就其自身和财产享有管辖豁免。

三、俄罗斯联邦和外国国家之间无其他相关约定时适用于本联邦法的规定。

第二条 联邦法中使用的基本概念

为本联邦法之目的，使用以下概念：

一、外国国家

（一）除俄罗斯联邦以外的国家及其国家机关；

（二）该外国国家的组成部分（外国联邦国家的成员邦或外国国家政府分支机构）及其机构，有权依法行使主权权力并以该身份行事的；

（三）其他有权行使并且实际行使国家主权权力的实体或机构，无论它们的法人地位如何；

（四）以外国国家代表身份行事的代表；

二、外国国家财产是指：在俄罗斯联邦领土内属于外国国家的财产；

三、外国国家及其财产的管辖豁免是指：司法豁免，裁决前措施的国家豁免以及裁决后措施的国家豁免；

四、司法豁免是指：俄罗斯联邦法院避免使某外国国家陷入法院诉讼的法律义务；[①]

[①] 对应部分英文拼写有误：refrain form 应为 refrain from，下同。——译者注

五、判决前措施豁免是指：俄罗斯联邦法院不得对外国国家及其财产发布旨在推动司法程序和执行裁决的临时禁令和其他强制措施的法律义务；

六、判决后措施豁免是指：俄罗斯联邦法院或有权执行司法裁决、其他机构和当局命令的联邦行政机关，不得罚没外国国家财产，以及为执行裁决采取其他措施的法律义务；

七、俄罗斯联邦法院是指：依照《俄罗斯联邦宪法》、俄罗斯联邦宪法性法律和其他联邦法设立的俄罗斯联邦最高法院、享有普遍管辖权的联邦法院和仲裁法院；

八、主权权力是指：外国国家依照主权享有并为实现主权而行使的权力。

第三条　不受本联邦法影响的特权和豁免

一、本联邦法不妨碍给予外国国家根据国际法原则行使外交代表机构、领事机构、特别使团、驻国际组织代表团，或派往国际组织的机关或国际会议及与其相关人员的特权与豁免。

二、本联邦法不妨碍根据国际法原则给予外国国家元首、政府首脑和外交部长的特权和豁免。

三、本联邦法不妨碍外国国家根据国际法原则在拥有或运营航空器或空间物体、军舰，及其他以非商业目的运营的国家航空器方面享有的豁免。

第四条　管辖豁免适用的互惠原则

一、如俄罗斯联邦及其财产在外国国家所享有的管辖豁免受到限制，则在相互性原则基础上，外国国家及其财产根据本联邦法享有的管辖豁免范围同样可能受到限制。①

二、在俄罗斯联邦对外关系领域行使制定和执行国家政策、法律法规调节职能的联邦行政机关，依照现行俄罗斯联邦诉讼法规，有权针对俄罗斯联邦及其财产在外国国家享有管辖豁免问题作出认定。

第五条　外国国家同意行使管辖权

一、如果某外国国家通过以下方式，已明确同意俄罗斯联邦法院在诉讼中对某具体案件行使管辖权，则其不能援引管辖权豁免：②

（一）国际协定；

（二）不属于国际协定的书面协议；

（三）在针对具体纠纷的诉讼程序框架内，在俄罗斯联邦法院发表的声明或书面函件，或通过外交渠道转交给俄罗斯联邦的书面函件。

---

① 此处对应的英文中 ins 应为 its，下同。——译者注

② 此处对应英文 canon 应为 cannot，下同。——译者注

二、依照本条第一款之规定，外国国家对俄罗斯联邦法院管辖具体案件的同意不可撤销，并对法院诉讼的所有阶段有效。

三、在下列情形下，不得视为外国国家已同意俄罗斯联邦法院行使管辖权：

（一）只是为主张管辖豁免或主张诉讼中某项有争议财产的权利之目的，而介入法院诉讼或采取其他任何程序性的行动；

（二）外国国家同意在具体案件中适用俄罗斯联邦的法律；

（三）外国国家未能在俄罗斯联邦法院的一项诉讼程序中出庭；

（四）外国国家代表为提供证据或作为专家在俄罗斯联邦法院出庭。

四、外国国家同意俄罗斯联邦法院对具体案件行使管辖权不影响该外国国家享有的法院强制措施和判决执行的豁免。

第六条 放弃司法豁免权

一、如外国国家在俄罗斯联邦法院提起诉讼，介入俄罗斯联邦法院的诉讼程序，或对案件实质采取其他任何步骤，则视为该外国国家放弃司法豁免权。

二、如外国国家已签署一项仲裁协定或仲裁条款，以解决已经或可能出现的关于义务履行的争议，该外国国家被视为已放弃与仲裁协定或仲裁条款相关争议的司法豁免权。

三、如外国国家在俄罗斯联邦法院提起诉讼，则视为该国已放弃对任何反诉的司法豁免权。

四、如外国国家在俄罗斯联邦法院提起反诉，则视为该国已放弃对最初请求权的司法豁免权。

五、外国国家对具体诉讼司法豁免权的放弃不可撤销，并延伸至诉讼的所有阶段。

六、外国国家在具体诉讼中放弃司法豁免权不视为该国放弃法院强制措施和判决执行的豁免。

第七条 外国国家参与商业交易和（或）实施商业和其他经济活动的争议不适用司法豁免。

一、外国国家与其他国家的自然人或法人，或另一国家任何其他不具备法人地位的实体进行商业交易产生的争端，如根据可适用的法律俄罗斯联邦法院对该争议享有管辖权，且该交易与该外国国家行使主权权威性权力无关时，则该外国国家不享有司法豁免权。

二、如商业交易发生于国家之间，或商业交易中当事方另有约定时，则本条第一款之规定不适用。

三、如外国国家在俄罗斯联邦领土内实施商业和其他经济活动，或在其他国家实施上述活动的结果与俄罗斯联邦的领土有联系，该外国国家对与此相关的争议在俄罗斯联邦不得援引司法豁免权。

四、在认定由外国国家从事的商业交易是否与其行使主权权威性权力相关的问题时，俄罗斯联邦法院会考虑该交易的性质与目的。

第八条　雇佣争议不适用司法豁免

一、如外国国家与其雇员有关劳动合同产生纠纷，而该雇员所做工作已经或应该全部或部分在俄罗斯联邦领土上完成时，该外国国家在俄罗斯联邦不享有司法豁免权。

二、本条第一款规定不适用于以下情况：

（一）雇用该雇员是为了执行该外国国家主权权力的职能；

（二）该雇员是：

1. 国际条约所界定的外交代表；

2. 国际条约所界定的领事官员；

3. 常驻国际组织代表团外交人员、特别使团成员或受聘成为外国国家在国际组织的代表团成员，或代表该国出席国际会议的人员；

4. 享有外交豁免的任何其他人员；

（三）诉讼的事由涉及个人的招聘、雇佣期的延长或复职；

（四）诉讼的事由涉及解雇个人或终止雇用，且外国的国家元首、政府首脑或外交部长以书面方式认定该诉讼将有碍该外国国家安全利益；

（五）该雇员在俄罗斯联邦法院提起诉讼时是外国国家的公民，除非此人在俄罗斯联邦有永久居住权。

第九条　涉及法人或其他不具备法人地位实体的纠纷不适用司法豁免

一、如外国国家的法人或其他不具备法人地位的实体，与依照俄罗斯联邦现行法律设立并（或）在俄罗斯联邦领土内开展活动的法人，或在俄罗斯联邦领土内开展活动的其他不具备法人地位的实体产生的争议，以及外国国家和其他国家和（或）国家间组织和（或）政府间组织的法人和不具备法人地位的实体产生的争议，该外国国家不能在俄罗斯联邦援引司法豁免权。

二、本条第一款规定不适用于以下情况：

（一）是相关国家间协定中已有规定的；

（二）是由法律实体或机构的宪法性文件所规定的；

（三）是经争议各方书面达成协定的。

第十条　财产权争议不适用司法豁免权

外国国家在下列争议中不享有俄罗斯联邦的司法豁免权：

（一）该外国国家对处于俄罗斯联邦领土内的不动产的权利和义务；

（二）该外国国家通过继承、赠与或无主物取得动产或不动产而产生的权利和义务；

（三）该外国国家对财产进行管理产生的权利和义务。

第十一条 与人身伤害赔偿和财产损害赔偿有关的争议不适用司法豁免

在对外国国家主张由可归因于该国的作为或不作为引起的对个人的生命、人身、财产、荣誉和尊严、商业信誉的损害赔偿，或对法人的财产和商业信誉损害的赔偿诉讼中，如果该作为或不作为或其他情形全部或部分发生在俄罗斯联邦领土内，且加害方在作为或不作为发生时在俄罗斯联邦领土内，该外国国家不能在俄罗斯联邦援引司法豁免。

第十二条 知识产权争议不适用司法豁免

外国国家对下列争议不能在俄罗斯联邦援引司法豁免权：

（一）涉及外国国家对知识产权、商业名称或企业名称、商标、著作权的权利的确定与实施；

（二）涉及外国国家指控第三方侵犯其知识产权、商业名称或企业名称、商标、著作权的权利。

第十三条 船舶营运争议不适用司法豁免

一、在与外国国家拥有或运营的船舶，或所载货物有关的诉讼中，如在引发诉讼的事实发生时，该船舶是用于非商业性用途以外的目的和（或者）所载货物不属于该外国国家并被该外国国家专门用于或将用于行使政府权力的目的，则该外国国家不能在俄罗斯联邦援引司法豁免权。

二、为执行这一条款，下列定义可理解为：

（一）船舶：用作或将用作水上交通工具的所有种类的船只；

（二）用于非商业性通途的船舶：外国国家为实施政府权威而使用的船舶，包括军舰和用作非商业用途的国家船舶；

（三）涉及船舶运营的争议包括：

1. 船舶碰撞事故，破坏港口和水利工程建筑或其他海运事故；
2. 援助、营救和普通事故；
3. 维修和其他工作的供给，与船舶有关的服务条款；
4. 海洋污染的影响；
5. 打捞沉没财产。

第十四条 判决前措施的国家豁免

外国国家享有判决前措施管辖豁免，除非外国国家：

一、已明确通过本联邦法第五条第一款规定的方法之一同意采取此类措施；

二、外国国家已经拨出或专门指定该财产用于清偿该诉讼标的的请求。

第十五条 判决后措施的国家豁免

外国国家对判决后措施方面享有管辖豁免，除非：

一、外国国家已明确通过本联邦法第五条第一款规定的方法之一同意采取此类措施；

二、外国国家已经拨出或专门指定该财产用于清偿该诉讼标的的请求；

三、经确认外国国家非为实施主权权威之目的专门使用和（或）将使用该财产。

第十六条 外国国家财产享有判决前和判决后措施豁免

一、下列外国国家所有的财产，意图用于或用于以其名义实施的与实现主权权力有关的活动，享有判决前和判决后措施的豁免：

（一）用于或意图用于外国国家外交代表机构、领事机构、特别使团、驻国际组织代表团、派往国际组织的机关或国际会议的代表团履行职能的财产（包括银行账户款项）；

（二）被俄罗斯联邦认可，用于或意图用于军事目的，或用于维和行动的具有军事性质的财产；

（三）构成国家文化遗产或其档案的一部分，且非供出售或意图出售的财产；

（四）构成具有科学、文化或历史价值的展品，且非供出售或意图出售的财产；

（五）外国国家中央银行或其他具有银行监督职能机构的财产。

二、本条第一款之规定的适用将适当考虑本联邦法第十四条和第十五条第一款、第二款的相关规定。

第十七条 涉及外国国家参与的案件审理程序

涉及外国国家参与的案件由俄罗斯联邦法院依照俄罗斯联邦现行诉讼法的相关程序进行审理。

第十八条 本联邦法的生效

本联邦法于 2016 年 1 月 1 日起生效。

俄罗斯联邦总统

弗·普京

（俄罗斯联邦总统办公厅印）

莫斯科，克里姆林宫

2015 年 11 月 3 日

第 297 号联邦法

第二部分 国际公约

1972年《国家豁免欧洲公约》及其附加议定书

序　言

签署本公约的欧洲委员会成员国,

考虑到欧洲委员会的目的在于实现其成员国相互间的更大的团结;

注意到在国际法内有一种对一国在外国法院被诉案件中得主张的豁免权加以限制的趋势;

为了制定关于在它们相互关系中,一国得免于受另一国法院管辖的范围及有利于保证对另一国作出的判决能被遵从的共同规则;

考虑到采行此项规则将有助于欧洲委员会成员国在法律范围内承担的协调工作的进展,

兹议定如下:

第一章　司法管辖的豁免

第一条

一、缔约国在另一缔约国法院提起或参加诉讼时,即系就各该诉讼自愿接受该法院的管辖。

二、该缔约国不得向另一缔约国法院就下列任何反诉主张豁免:

(一) 反诉所根据的法律关系或事实与本诉相同者;

(二) 反诉如以独立的诉讼程序单独提出,依本公约的规定,该国亦不得主张豁免者;

三、缔约国在另一缔约国法院提起反诉时,即不仅单就反诉部分而且并就本诉部分,也自愿接受了该国法院的管辖。

第二条

缔约国不得在另一缔约国法院主张豁免,如果由于下列缘由,该国已承担了接受该法院管辖的义务:

(一) 由于国际协定;

(二) 由于在书面合同中包含了一项明示的条款;或

（三）由于在双方当事人间发生争端以后，曾作出一项明示的同意。

第三条

一、缔约国如在主张豁免前，已经参加有关实质性问题的诉讼程序，即不得再主张免于另一缔约国法院的管辖。但如该国能使法院确信，倘非先参加此项程序，即无法获悉可据以提出豁免的事实时，得根据这些事实主张豁免，但以尽可能及时提出此项主张为限。

二、如果缔约国为了主张豁免而在另一缔约国出庭，该缔约国不得视为已放弃豁免。

第四条

一、除第五条另有规定外，缔约国不得主张免于另一缔约国法院的管辖，如果该诉讼涉及该国的一项债务，而依照合同，此项债务应在法庭地国家的领土内履行者。

二、第一款不适用于：

（一）合同是由国家相互间缔结的情况；

（二）合同双方当事人另有书面约定时；

（三）以某国为一方的合同是在该国缔结的，而其所承担的债务又是受其行政法支配的。

第五条

一、缔约国不得主张免于另一缔约国法院的管辖，如果该诉讼涉及该国与个人的雇佣合同而其工作又必须在法庭地国家领土内履行者。

二、第一款不适用于下列情况：

（一）在提起诉讼时，该个人系雇佣国的国民；

（二）在订立合同时，该个人既非法庭地国家的国民，又非其惯常居住户；或

（三）合同双方当事人另有相反的书面约定，但合同的主要内容依法庭地国的法律系专属该国法院管辖者除外。

三、对于受雇于第七条所述的办事处、代理机构或其他组织的工作人员，本条第二款第（一）项和第（二）项仅适用于在订立合同时，该个人在雇用他的缔约国有惯常居所的为限。

第六条

一、缔约国不得主张免于另一国法院的管辖，如它参加了与私人，一人或若干人共同组织的、设在法庭地国领土内或在其领土内有实际和法定所在地、登记事务所或主营业所的公司、社团或其他法律实体，而该诉讼

涉及以该国为一方，以该实体或其他参加者为另一方之间，在由于参加了此项实体而发生的事件中的相互关系。

二、如有相反的书面约定，第一款不适用。

第七条

一、如缔约国在法庭地国的领土上设有办事处、代理机构或其任何形式的组织，通过它，和私人一样，从事于商业、工业或金融业的活动，而诉讼与该办事处、代理机构或其他任何形式的组织的此项活动有关时，不得主张免于另一缔约国的司法管辖。

二、如各方当事人均为国家或如另有相反的书面约定时，第一款不适用。

第八条

缔约国不得主张免于另一缔约国法院的管辖，如诉讼涉及：

（一）专利、工业设计、商标、服务标志或其他类似权利，此项权利在法庭地国已申请、登记或注册或得到其他保护，而该国即是此项权利的申请者或所有者；

（二）被指控在法庭地国领土内，侵害属于第三者的并受法庭地国保护的此项权利；

（三）被指控在法庭地国领土内，侵害属于第三者的并受法庭地国保护的著作权；

（四）在法庭地国使用商号的权利。

第九条

缔约国不得主张免于另一缔约国法院的管辖，如诉讼涉及：

（一）其对不动产的权利或利益，或其使用或占有；或

（二）由于对不动产的权利或利益，或其使用或占有而发生的债务或责任，而且该财产系位于裁判地国领土之内的。

第十条

缔约国不得主张免于另一缔约国法院的管辖，如诉讼涉及由于继承、赠与或无主物取得而产生的关于动产或不动产的权利。

第十一条

缔约国不得主张免于另一缔约国法院的管辖，如诉讼涉及因人身伤害或毁损有形财物而请求损害赔偿，而造成伤害或毁损的事实又发生于法庭地国的领域内，其伤害和毁损的肇事者在发生此项事实时，亦在该领域内。

第十二条

一、缔约国已书面同意将已发生或可能发生的民事或商事争议交付仲

裁时，该国不得主张免于另一缔约国法院的管辖，如仲裁系或将在该国领土内，或依照该国的法律进行，而诉讼又涉及下列有关事项：

（一）仲裁协议的效力及其解释；

（二）仲裁程序；

（三）仲裁裁决的废弃；

但仲裁协议另有相反规定时，不在此限。

二、第一款不适用于国家间的仲裁协议。

第十三条

非当事人的缔约国就涉讼于另一缔约国法院中作为诉讼标的的财产主张享有权利或利益，而依其情况，如向该缔约国提起诉讼，该缔约国应有权享受豁免时，则不适用第一条第一款的规定。

第十四条

不得援用本公约的任何条款以另一缔约国对该项财产享有权利或利益这个唯一事实为理由，阻止各缔约国法院对财产的管理，诸如为信托财产、破产财团进行管理、监督或调解。

第十五条

缔约国应有享受免受另一缔约国法院管辖之权，如诉讼不属于第一条至第十四条的范围；法院应拒绝受理此类诉讼，即使相关国家并未到庭。

第二章　程序规则

第十六条

一、在另一缔约国法院对缔约国进行诉讼，应适用下列规则。

二、法庭地国主管部门应将下列文件

（一）起诉文件的原本或副本；

（二）对被告国所为任何缺席判决的副本，

通过外交途径送交被告国的外交部；如认为恰当，并请转送其他主管部门这些文件，必要时，应附具被告国官方语言或官方语言之一种的译本。

三、在该外交部收到时，第二款所述的文件应认为已完成送达。

四、一国应出庭或就缺席判决提出上诉的期限为两个月，自该国外交部收到起诉文件或判决书副本之日后起算。

五、如出庭或就缺席判决提出上诉的期限系由法院规定时，则法院应给予该国不少于两个月的期限，自该国外交部收到起诉文件或判决书副本之日后起算。

六、缔约国到庭应诉应视为已放弃对送达方法的异议。

七、缔约国如不到庭，只有在证实起诉文件已依照第二款送达以及第四款和第五款规定的到庭应诉期限已经遵守的情况下，才能对之作出缺席判决。

第十七条

法庭地国如对其国民或在其国内有住所或居所之人并不要求为缴纳裁判费用或开支提供担保，则缔约国亦不得被要求提供担保，不论是何种保证书或担保品。缔约国如在另一缔约国法院为原告时，应支付可能应由其负担的一切裁判费用和开支。

第十八条

缔约国在另一缔约国法院的诉讼中为当事人时，不得由于其未能提示或拒绝提示任何文件或其他证据而对之采用任何强制措施或加以处罚。但法院得根据其未能提示或拒绝提示作出它认为适当的任何结论。

第十九条

一、法院对以缔约国为当事人而提起的诉讼，应在一方当事人的请求下，或如其本国法律许可，得依职权拒绝该案件的进行或中止诉讼程序，如该同一当事人之间，根据同一事实，并为了同一目的已另有诉讼，

（一）正由该缔约国法院受理并系首先提起的；或

（二）正由任何另一缔约国法院受理，并系首先提起，而可能导致一项判决，依照第二十条或第二十五条的规定，该诉讼中的国家一方必须赋予效力的。

二、任何缔约国，如其法律对于在同一当事人之间，根据同一事实，并为了同一目的，正涉讼于另一缔约国法院的案件，规定由法院斟酌情况拒绝该案的进行或中止诉讼程序者，得向欧洲委员会秘书长发出通知，宣布该法院不受第一款规定的约束。

第三章　判决的效力

第二十条

一、缔约国应给另一缔约国法院作出的判决以效力，如：

（一）依照第一条至第十三条的规定，该国不得主张司法豁免者；以及

（二）为缺席判决而不得或不得再予以废弃，或该判决为不得，或不得再进行上诉，或依其他通常程序请求复审或予以撤销者。

二、但有下列任何情况之一时，缔约国对该项判决并无给予效力的义务：

（一）给予效力明显将违反该国的公共政策，或依其情况，有一方当事人未曾有适当的机会以充分地陈述其案情时；

（二）在同一当事人之间，根据同一事实，并为了同一目的，已另有诉讼：

1. 正在该国法院涉讼，而且系首先提出者；以及

2. 正在另一缔约国法院涉讼，而且系首先提出，并可能导致一项判决，而对该项判决根据本公约条款，该诉讼中的国家一方必须给予效力者；

（三）该判决的结果与对同一当事人所作另一判决的结果互相矛盾或不一致：

1. 该另一判决系由该缔约国的法院作出，而诉讼系在该法院首先提出者，或该另一判决系在该判决前已作出并符合第一款第（二）项规定的条件者；或

2. 该另一判决系由另一缔约国法院作出而且系首先符合本公约规定的要求者；

（四）第十六条规定未被遵守，而该国亦未到庭或对缺席判决提起上诉者。

三、此外，第十条规定的案件，缔约国对其判决无给予效力的义务：

（一）判决地国法院若准用了被诉国奉行的司法管辖权的规定（本公约附件以外者），即不得享有管辖权者；

（二）如该法院未依照被诉国国际私法规则适用应适用的法律而适用了其他法律，从而导致结果不同的判决。

但缔约国不得援用上述第（一）项和第（二）项列举的拒绝理由，如该国受其与法庭地国所订的关于承认和执行判决的协定的约束，而该判决又符合协定中有关管辖的要求；或协定中尚有有关适用法律的要求，而该判决亦符合此项要求。

第二十一条

一、如向缔约国作出判决而该缔约国不给以效力，引用该判决的一方当事人有权要求该国主管法院作出应否依第二十条赋予效力的决定。此项诉讼亦可由被判决的国家向该法院提出，如果其法律是这样允许的。

二、除为适用第二十条而有此必要，该主管法院不得就该判决的实质性问题进行审查。

三、依第一款向一国法院提起诉讼时：

（一）在诉讼进行中应给予各方当事人以到庭陈述的机会；

（二）要引用该判决的一方当事人提供的文件无须再经过合法认可或其他类似手续；

（三）不得由于国籍、住所或居所的原因向要引用该判决的一方当事人要求提供任何种类的担保、保证书或保证金；

（四）引用该判决的一方当事人应有享受司法救助的权利，其待遇应不低于定居或住在该国的国民的条件。

四、各缔约国在交存其批准书、接受书或加入书等文件时，应指定第一款所述的法院一所或若干所，并将此通知欧洲委员会秘书长。

第二十二条

一、缔约国对该国作为当事人一方在另一缔约国法院进行的诉讼中所作的和解应给予效力；第二十条规定不适用于此项和解。

二、如该国不使此项和解生效，得适用第二十一条规定的程序。

第二十三条

不得对缔约国在另一缔约国领土内的财产采取任何执行措施或保全措施，但个别案件，经缔约国以书面明示同意时，在其同意的范围内，不在此限。

第四章　任意选择条款

第二十四条

一、虽有第十五条的规定，但任何国家均得在签署本公约时或交存其批准书、接受书或加入书时，或其后任何日期，以向欧洲委员会秘书长发出通知书的方式，声明凡不属于第一条至第十三条的案件，该国法院应有权受理对另一缔约国的诉讼，其范围与受理对非缔约国的诉讼相同。此项声明应无损于外国就其行使国家主权的行为，享有司法豁免权。

二、但曾为第一款声明的国家的法院仍无权受理对另一缔约国的诉讼，如其管辖权系完全根据本公约附件所述的一项或多项理由，除非另一缔约国已经参加涉及实质性问题的诉讼程序而未首先对法院的管辖权提出异议。

三、依本条对缔约国提起的诉讼，适用第二章的规定。

四、依第一款作出的声明得以向欧洲委员会秘书长发出通知书的方式予以撤销。撤销应在通知书收到之日后经过三个月发生效力，但并不影响在撤销生效日期以前已提出的诉讼。

第二十五条

一、曾为第二十四条声明的任何缔约国，应给予为同样声明的其他缔约国的法院对不属第一条至第十三条的案件所为的判决以效力：

（一）如第二十条第一款第（二）项规定的条件已完成，并且

（二）如该法院依下列各款应认为具有管辖权。

二、但缔约国对此项判决亦得不给予效力，如：

（一）具有第二十条第二款规定的拒绝给予效力的理由；或

（二）第二十四条第二款的规定未被遵守。

三、除应受第四款规定的约束外，缔约国法院应被认为依第一款第（二）项规定具有管辖权，如：

（一）经法庭地国和另一缔约国参加的协议条款承认其管辖权时；

（二）两国间对民事判决的承认和执行无协议，如法庭地国法院准用被判决的国家国内施行的管辖权规则（在本公约附件规定以外者）；应视为有权受理。本条款不适用于由于合同所发生的问题。

四、缔约国在为第二十四条规定的声明后，通过对本公约的补充协议，得确定其法院依本条第一款第（二）项规定应认为具有管辖权的情事。

五、如缔约国对该判决不给以效力，得适用第二十一条规定的程序。

第二十六条

尽管有第二十三条的规定，缔约国和私人一样从事于工业或商业活动从而在诉讼中被判决败诉时，法庭地国对其专用于此项活动的国家的财产，得根据判决予以执行，如：

（一）法庭地国及被判决的国家均曾为第二十四条的声明；

（二）导致判决的诉讼属于第一条至第十三条规定或是依照第二十四条第一款和第二款提出的；

（三）该判决是符合第二十条第一款第（二）项规定的要求的。

第五章　一般规定

第二十七条

一、本公约所称"缔约国"不包括与其有区别的、可以起诉或被诉的缔约国的任何法律实体，亦不因该实体已被授予公共职能而有所不同。

二、对第一款所述的实体得和对私人一样在另一缔约国法院提起诉讼，但针对有关实体行使国家主权的行为提起的诉讼，法院不得受理。

三、如果在相应情况下针对缔约国提起诉讼时法院具有管辖权，则无论如何可在法院对此类实体提起诉讼。

第二十八条

一、在不影响第二十七条规定的情况下，组成联邦国家的各邦不享有豁免权。

二、但作为本公约一方的联邦国家得向欧洲委员会秘书长发出通知，声明其所属各邦得援引适用于缔约国的规定并承担相同的义务。

三、在联邦国家依据第二款作出声明后，对联邦各邦送达文件应依照第十六条向联邦国家的外交部为之。

四、只有联邦国家有权作出本公约规定的各种声明、通知或照会，也只有联邦国家得为依第三十四条所为诉讼的当事人。

第二十九条

本公约不适用于涉及下列事项的诉讼：

（一）社会保障；

（二）同核有关的损失及损害；

（三）进出口税收、国内税收或罚金。

第三十条

本公约不适用于涉及关于缔约国所有或经营的航行远洋船舶的活动，或关于此项船舶的货运及客运，或关于缔约国所有的货物通过商船运输所发生的请求权的诉讼。

第三十一条

本公约任何条款均不得影响缔约国武装部队在另一缔约国领土内，就其一切作为或不作为或其他有关事项，享有的豁免权或特权。

第三十二条

本公约任何条款均不影响与外交使团、领事馆及其有关人员的执行职务有关的特权和豁免权。

第三十三条

本公约任何条款均不影响现有的或将来的涉及本公约所述各事项而在特殊方面缔结的国际条约。

第三十四条

一、在两个以上的缔约国之间，就本公约的解释或适用发生的任何争议，应依争议一方的申请或依特别协议，提交国际法院，但有关各方同意他种和平解决争议的方法时，不在此限。

二、但是，不得向国际法院提出涉及下列事项的诉讼：

（一）在缔约国于另一缔约国法院被控告的诉讼中所发生的争议，在该院尚未作出符合第二十条第一款第（二）项的判决以前者；

（二）在依照第二十一条第一款向缔约国法院提出的诉讼中发生的争议，在该院尚未就此项诉讼作出终局决定以前者。

第三十五条

一、本公约只适用于在其生效后提出的诉讼。

二、在本公约生效后才成为本公约成员的国家，本公约只适用于其对该国生效以后提出的诉讼。

三、本公约任何条款均不适用于由于在其开放签字日期以前的作为、不作为或事实而发生的诉讼，或以其为根据的判决。

第六章　最后条款

第三十六条

一、本公约对欧洲委员会的成员国开放签字，并须经批准或接受。批准书或接受书应交存欧洲委员会秘书长处。

二、自交存第三份批准书或接受书之日后满三个月，本公约应即生效。

三、关于其后批准或接受的签字国，本公约应自其交存批准书或接受书之日后满三个月开始生效。

第三十七条

一、本公约生效以后，欧洲委员会的部长会议得经投票国一致的同意票，邀请任何非成员国参加本公约。

二、参加以向欧洲委员会秘书长交存参加书为之，并自交存参加书之日后满三个月生效。

三、但是，如在该参加尚未生效前，已参加本公约的国家已通知欧洲委员会秘书长其反对该非会员国的参加，则本公约不得适用于该两国之间的关系。

第三十八条

一、任何国家均得在签署或交存其批准书、接受书或参加书时，限制本公约仅适用于其特定领土的一处或若干处。

二、任何国家在交存其批准书、接受书或参加书时，或在其后任何日期，均得向欧洲委员会秘书长提出声明，将本公约扩及适用于其声明中具体规定的,由该国对其国际关系负有责任并有权代其承担义务的其他一处或若干处领土。

三、依照前款所作的任何声明,就关于此项声明中所述的任何领土,得根据本公约第四十条规定的程序予以撤销。

第三十九条

对于本公约不允许作任何保留。

第四十条

一、任何缔约国,就其本国一切有关事项,得向欧洲委员会秘书长发出通知,废止本公约。

二、此项废止应在秘书长收到通知之日后满六个月开始生效。但本公约仍应适用于在通知生效前已经提出的诉讼及此项诉讼中作出的判决。

第四十一条

一、欧洲委员会秘书长应通知欧洲委员会成员国及已参加本公约的任何国家:

(一)任何签署;

(二)任何批准书、接受书或参加书的交存;

(三)依照本公约第三十六条及第三十七条,本公约开始生效的日期;

(四)依照第十九条第二款的规定收到的任何通知;

(五)依照第二十一条第四款的规定收到的任何照会;

(六)依照第二十四条第一款的规定收到的任何通知;

(七)依照第二十四条第四款的规定作出的撤销通知;

(八)依照第二十八条第二款的规定收到的任何通知;

(九)依照第三十七条第三款的规定收到的任何通知;

(十)依照第三十八条的规定收到的任何声明;

(十一)依照第四十条的规定收到的任何通知及废止生效的日期。

二、下列签署人,经本国政府正式授权,签署本公约,以资证明。

1972年5月16日订于巴塞尔,用英文和法文写成,两种文本具有同等效力,合成正本一份,交存欧洲委员会档案库。欧洲委员会秘书长应将经核证无误的副本分送各签字国和加入国。

附件

一、确定第二十条第三款第(一)项、第二十四条第二款及第二十五条第三款第(二)项所提及的管辖权的根据如下:

(一)在法庭地国领土内属被告所有的财产,或原告经依法占有或扣押的位于法庭地国领土内的财产，但下列情况除外：

1. 诉讼的目的在于主张确认该财产之所有权或占有权，或诉讼的发生与有关该财产的另一争议有关，或

2. 诉讼的主题为债务而该财产系属此项债务的担保品；

（二）原告之国籍；

（三）原告的住所、惯常居所或一般居所在法庭地国领土内，但对于某种类的合同得例外地根据其特殊内容及性质准许如此确定管辖权者除外。

（四）被告曾在法庭地国经营商业，但以诉讼系由于此项商业业务而发生者为限。

（五）原告单方面指明了法庭，特别是记载于发票者。

二、法人的实际和法定所在地，经登记的事务所所在地或主营业地应视为其住所地或惯常居所地。

《国家豁免欧洲公约》的附加议定书

1972年5月16日订于巴塞尔

欧洲委员会成员国，本议定书的签字国，

注意到《国家豁免欧洲公约》（以下简称《公约》），尤其是其中的第二十一条和第三十四条；

为了通过增补一些条款以规定欧洲的解决争议的程序，从而促进在公约涉及事项的范围内的协调工作，

兹同意下列条款：

第一章

第一条

一、对缔约国作出判决，而该国并未使之生效，谋求适用该判决的一方当事人应有权要求对依照公约第二十条或第二十五条应否使之生效的问题作出决定，并得为此向下列机构之一提起诉讼：

（一）适用公约第二十一条向该国主管法院；或

（二）向依本议定书第三章规定组成的欧洲法院，但该国应为本议定书的成员国且未作出第四章所述的保留。

两者任选其一，一经选定，不得变更。

二、意欲依照公约第二十一条第一款的规定向其本国法院提出诉讼的国家，应将其意图通知判决中胜诉的一方。如该方在收到通知后三个月内未向欧洲法院提出诉讼，该国才可提出此项诉讼。此项限期一经届满，胜诉一方即不得再向欧洲法院提出诉讼。

三、除非为了适用公约第二十条和第二十五条而有此必要，欧洲法院不得审查判决的实质性部分。

第二章

第二条

一、发生在本议定书的两个或两个以上的缔约国之间的有关公约的解释或适用的任何争议，应依争议一方的申请或依特别协议，提交依本议定书第三章规定组成的欧洲法院。本议定书缔约国承担不把此类争议提交另一种不同方式解决的义务。

二、如争议涉及在公约一缔约国法院对公约另一缔约国提出的诉讼中的问题，或依公约第二十一条向公约一缔约国法院提出的诉讼中的问题，在各该法院对此项诉讼作出终局判决前，此项争议不得交付欧洲法院。

三、有关判决的争议如依本议定书第一章，欧洲法院曾就此作过决定或正在被要求作出决定时，不得向欧洲法院起诉。

第三条

本议定书的任何条款不得解释为意在阻止欧洲法院就两国或两国以上的公约缔约国之间可能发生的有关公约的解释或适用的争议作出决定，而此项争议，其有关国家或其中任何有关国家即使非为本议定书的缔约国时，亦得通过特别协议提交欧洲法院。

第三章

第四条

一、关于国家豁免权方面应设立一欧洲法院以决定依本议定书第一章及第二章向其提出的案件。

二、欧洲法院应包括欧洲人权法院的成员，已经加入本议定书的各非欧洲委员会成员国政府得就其具有该法院成员应有资格的人员中各指定一人，并经欧洲委员会部长委员会同意，其任期为九年。

三、欧洲法院院长应为欧洲人权法院院长。

第五条

一、依照本议定书第一章规定向欧洲法院提起诉讼时，欧洲法院审判庭应由七名成员组成。原判决中被告国国民的欧洲法院成员及法庭地国国民的欧洲法院成员均为该庭的当然成员。缺少符合上述条件的任何一个成员时，则由有关政府任命一人，以该庭成员身份参加审判。其余五名成员应由欧洲法院院长在书记官长前以抽签方式选择之。

二、依本议定书第二章规定向欧洲法院提起诉讼时，其审判庭应按前款的方式组成，但争议的当事国国民的欧洲法院成员应为该庭的当然成员。如无符合上述条件的成员时，则由有关政府任命一人以该庭成员身份参加审判。

三、审判庭在案件的审判中发生重大的有关公约或本议定书的解释问题时，该庭得随时放弃管辖权而让欧洲法院全体会议受理。如该问题的解决可能导致与欧洲法院的审判庭或欧洲法院全体会议以前所作出的判决不一致的结果时，放弃管辖权应是必需的。管辖权的放弃应是终局的。放弃管辖权无须说明理由。

第六条

一、欧洲法院应就对该法院是否有管辖权的一切争议作出决定。

二、欧洲法院审讯应公开进行，但法院就例外情况另有决定时，不在此限。

三、欧洲法院的判决，由出席成员的过半数决定，并在公开庭宣布。欧洲法院的判决应附有理由。如判决的全部或一部分不代表欧洲法院的一致意见，则任何成员均有权发表其个别意见。

四、欧洲法院的判决应为终局的，并对当事各方有约束力。

第七条

一、欧洲法院应起草其自己的规则，并确定其自己的程序。

二、欧洲法院的书记处人员应由欧洲人权法院的书记官长调配。

第八条

一、欧洲法院的经营费应由欧洲委员会负担。加入本议定书的非欧洲委员会的成员国亦应提供经费，其方式由部长委员会与这些国家商定。

二、欧洲法院的成员应按每一值勤日收取报酬，由部长委员会核定。

第四章

第九条

一、任何国家,得在签署本议定书时,或在交存其批准书、接受书或加入书时,向欧洲委员会秘书长发出通知,声明其仅受第二章至第五章的约束。

二、此项通知得随时予以撤销。

第五章

第十条

一、本议定书应对已经签署公约的欧洲委员会成员国开放签字。本议定书应经批准或接受,批准书或接受书应向欧洲委员会秘书长交存。

二、本议定书应自交存第五份批准书或接受书之日后满三个月开始生效。

三、对于嗣后批准或接受的签字国,本议定书应在交存其批准书或接受书之日后满三个月开始生效。

四、欧洲委员会的成员国在未经批准或接受公约前,不得批准或接受本议定书。

第十一条

一、在本议定书生效后,凡已经加入公约的国家,均得加入本议定书。

二、此项加入应以向欧洲委员会秘书长交存加入书为之,在交存加入书之日后满三个月开始生效。

第十二条

对于本议定书不允许作任何保留。

第十三条

一、任何缔约国,就与其有关的范围而言,得以向欧洲委员会秘书长发致通知的方式,废止本议定书。

二、废止应自秘书长接到此项通知之日后满六个月开始生效。但在废止生效前,依本议定书规定提出的诉讼,仍得继续适用本议定书。

三、凡废止公约均应被认为亦当然废止本议定书。

第十四条

欧洲委员会秘书长应通知委员会成员国及任何已加入公约的国家:

（一）本议定书的任何签署；

（二）批准书、接受书或加入书的交存；

（三）依照本议定书第十条和第十一条，本议定书开始生效的日期；

（四）依照第四章的规定收到的任何通知及此项通知的撤销；

（五）依照第十三条的规定收到的通知及其废止生效的日期。

下列签署人，经正式授权，签署本议定书，以资证明。

1972年5月16日订于巴塞尔，用英文和法文写成，两种文本具有同等效力，合成正本一份，交存欧洲委员会档案库。欧洲委员会秘书长应将经核证无误的副本分送每一签字国和加入国。

2004 年联合国国家及其财产管辖豁免公约

本公约缔约国,

考虑到国家及其财产的管辖豁免为一项普遍接受的习惯国际法原则,

铭记《联合国宪章》所体现的国际法原则,

相信一项关于国家及其财产的管辖豁免国际公约将加强法治和法律的确定性,特别是在国家与自然人或法人的交易方面,并将有助于国际法的编纂与发展及此领域实践的协调,

考虑到国家及其财产的管辖豁免方面国家实践的发展,

申明习惯国际法的规则仍然适用于本公约没有规定的事项,

议定如下:

第一部分 导 言

第一条 本公约的范围

本公约适用于国家及其财产在另一国法院的管辖豁免。

第二条 用语

一、为本公约的目的:

(一)"法院"是指一国有权行使司法职能的不论名称为何的任何机关;

(二)"国家"是指:

1. 国家及其政府的各种机关;

2. 有权行使主权权力并以该身份行事的联邦国家的组成单位或国家政治区分单位;

3. 国家机构、部门或其他实体,但须它们有权行使并且实际在行使国家的主权权力;

4. 以国家代表身份行事的国家代表。

(三)"商业交易"是指:

1. 为销售货物或为提供服务而订立的任何商业合同或交易；

2. 任何贷款或其他金融性质之交易的合同，包括涉及任何此类贷款或交易的任何担保义务或补偿义务；

3. 商业、工业、贸易或专业性质的任何其他合同或交易，但不包括雇佣人员的合同。

二、在确定一项合同或交易是否为第一款第（三）项所述的"商业交易"时，应主要参考该合同或交易的性质，但如果合同或交易的当事方已达成一致，或者根据法院地国的实践，合同或交易的目的与确定其非商业性质有关，则其目的也应予以考虑。

三、关于本公约用语的第一款和第二款的规定不妨碍其他国际文书或任何国家的国内法对这些用语的使用或给予的含义。

第三条 不受本公约影响的特权和豁免

一、本公约不妨碍国家根据国际法所享有的有关行使下列职能的特权和豁免：

（一）其外交代表机构、领事机构、特别使团、驻国际组织代表团，或派往国际组织的机关或国际会议的代表团的职能；和

（二）与上述机构有关联的人员的职能。

二、本公约不妨碍根据国际法给予国家元首个人的特权和豁免。

三、本公约不妨碍国家根据国际法对国家拥有或运营的航空器或空间物体所享有的豁免。

第四条 本公约不溯及既往

在不妨碍本公约所述关于国家及其财产依国际法而非依本公约享有管辖豁免的任何规则的适用的前提下，本公约不应适用于在本公约对有关国家生效前，在一国法院对另一国提起的诉讼所引起的任何国家及其财产的管辖豁免问题。

第二部分 一般原则

第五条 国家豁免

一国本身及其财产遵照本公约的规定在另一国法院享有管辖豁免。

第六条 实行国家豁免的方式

一、一国应避免对在其法院对另一国提起的诉讼行使管辖，以实行第五条所规定的国家豁免；并应为此保证其法院主动地确定该另一国根据第五条享有的豁免得到尊重。

二、在一国法院中的诉讼应视为对另一国提起的诉讼，如果该另一国：

（一）被指名为该诉讼的当事一方；或

（二）未被指名为该诉讼的当事一方，但该诉讼实际上企图影响该另一国的财产、权利、利益或活动。

第七条　明示同意行使管辖

一、一国如以下列方式明示同意另一国对某一事项或案件行使管辖，则不得在该法院就该事项或案件提起的诉讼中援引管辖豁免：

（一）国际协定；

（二）书面合同；或

（三）在法院发表的声明或在特定诉讼中提出的书面函件。

二、一国同意适用另一国的法律，不应被解释为同意该另一国的法院行使管辖权。

第八条　参加法院诉讼的效果

一、在下列情况下，一国不得在另一国法院的诉讼中援引管辖豁免：

（一）该国本身提起该诉讼；或

（二）介入该诉讼或采取与案件实体有关的任何其他步骤。但如该国使法院确信它在采取这一步骤之前不可能知道可据以主张豁免的事实，则它可以根据那些事实主张豁免，条件是它必须尽早这样做。

二、一国不应被视为同意另一国的法院行使管辖权，如果该国仅为下列目的介入诉讼或采取任何其他步骤：

（一）援引豁免；或

（二）对诉讼中有待裁决的财产主张一项权利或利益。

三、一国代表在另一国法院出庭作证不应被解释为前一国同意法院行使管辖权。

四、一国未在另一国法院的诉讼中出庭不应被解释为前一国同意法院行使管辖权。

第九条　反诉

一、一国在另一国法院提起一项诉讼，不得就与本诉相同的法律关系或事实所引起的任何反诉向法院援引管辖豁免。

二、一国介入另一国法院的诉讼中提出诉讼请求，则不得就与该国提出的诉讼请求相同的法律关系或事实所引起的任何反诉援引管辖豁免。

三、一国在另一国法院对该国提起的诉讼中提出反诉，则不得就本诉向法院援引管辖豁免。

第三部分　不得援引国家豁免的诉讼

第十条　商业交易

一、一国如与外国一自然人或法人进行一项商业交易，而根据国际私法适用的规则，有关该商业交易的争议应由另一国法院管辖，则该国不得在该商业交易引起的诉讼中援引管辖豁免。

二、第一款不适用于下列情况：

（一）国家之间进行的商业交易；或

（二）该商业交易的当事方另有明确协议。

三、当国家企业或国家所设其他实体具有独立的法人资格，并有能力

（一）起诉或被诉；和

（二）获得、拥有或占有和处置财产，包括国家授权其经营或管理的财产，其卷入与其从事的商业交易有关的诉讼时，该国享有的管辖豁免不应受影响。

第十一条　雇佣合同

一、除有关国家间另有协议外，一国在该国和个人间关于已全部或部分在另一国领土进行，或将进行的工作之雇佣合同的诉讼中，不得向该另一国原应管辖的法院援引管辖豁免。

二、第一款不适用于下列情况：

（一）招聘该雇员是为了履行行使政府权力方面的特定职能；

（二）该雇员是：

1. 1961 年《维也纳外交关系公约》所述的外交代表；

2. 1963 年《维也纳领事关系公约》所述的领事官员；

3. 常驻国际组织代表团外交工作人员、特别使团成员或获招聘代表一国出席国际会议的人员；或

4. 享有外交豁免的任何其他人员；

（三）诉讼的事由是个人的招聘、雇佣期的延长或复职；

（四）诉讼的事由是解雇个人或终止雇用，且雇佣国的国家元首、政府首脑或外交部长认定该诉讼有碍该国安全利益；

（五）该雇员在诉讼提起时是雇佣国的国民，除非此人长期居住在法院地国；或

（六）该雇员和雇佣国另有书面协议，但由于公共政策的任何考虑，因该诉讼的事由内容而赋予法院地国法院专属管辖权者不在此限。

第十二条　人身伤害和财产损害

除有关国家间另有协议外，一国在对主张由可归因于该国的作为或不作为引起的死亡或人身伤害，或有形财产的损害或灭失要求金钱赔偿的诉讼中，如果该作为或不作为全部或部分发生在法院地国领土内，而且作为或不作为的行为人在作为或不作为发生时处于法院地国领土内，则不得向另一国原应管辖的法院援引管辖豁免。

第十三条　财产的所有、占有和使用

除有关国家间另有协议外，一国在涉及确定下列问题的诉讼中，不得对另一国原应管辖的法院援引管辖豁免：

（一）该国对位于法院地国的不动产的任何权利或利益，或该国对该不动产的占有或使用，或该国由于对该不动产的利益或占有或使用而产生的任何义务；

（二）该国对动产或不动产由于继承、赠予或无主物取得而产生的任何权利或利益；或

（三）该国对托管财产、破产者财产或公司解散前清理之财产的管理的任何权利或利益。

第十四条　知识产权和工业产权

除有关国家间另有协议外，一国在有关下列事项的诉讼中不得向另一国原应管辖的法院援引管辖豁免：

（一）确定该国对在法院地国享受某种程度，即使是暂时的法律保护的专利、工业设计、商业名称或企业名称、商标、版权或任何其他形式的知识产权或工业产权的任何权利；或

（二）据称该国在法院地国领土内侵犯在法院地国受到保护的、属于第三者的第（一）项所述性质的权利。

第十五条　参加公司或其他集体机构

一、一国在有关该国参加具有或不具有法人资格的公司或其他集体机构的诉讼中，即在关于该国与该机构或该机构其他参加者之间关系的诉讼中，不得向另一国原应管辖的法院援引管辖豁免，但有以下条件：

（一）该机构的参加者不限于国家或国际组织；而且

（二）该机构是按照法院地国法律注册或组成，或其所在地或主要营业地位于法院地国。

二、但是，如果有关国家同意，或如果争端当事方之间的书面协议作此规定，或如果据以建立或管理有关机构的文书中载有此一规定，则一国

可以在此诉讼中援引管辖豁免。

第十六条　国家拥有或经营的船舶

一、除有关国家间另有协议外，拥有或经营一艘船舶的一国，在另一国原应管辖的法院有关该船舶经营的一项诉讼中，只要在诉讼事由产生时该船舶是用于政府非商业性用途以外的目的，即不得援引管辖豁免。

二、第一款不适用于军舰或辅助舰艇，也不适用于一国拥有或经营的、专门用于政府非商业性活动的其他船舶。

三、除有关国家间另有协议外，一国在有关该国拥有或经营的船舶所载货物之运输的一项诉讼中，只要在诉讼事由产生时该船舶是用于政府非商业性用途以外的目的，即不得向另一国原应管辖的法院援引管辖豁免。

四、第三款不适用于第二款所指船舶所载运的任何货物，也不适用于国家拥有的、专门用于或意图专门用于政府非商业性用途的任何货物。

五、国家可提出私有船舶、货物及其所有人所能利用的一切抗辩措施、时效和责任限制。

六、如果在一项诉讼中产生有关一国拥有或经营的一艘船舶，或一国拥有的货物的政府非商业性质问题，由该国的一个外交代表或其他主管当局签署并送交法院的证明，应作为该船舶或货物性质的证据。

第十七条　仲裁协定的效果

一国如与外国一自然人或法人订立书面协议，将有关商业交易的争议提交仲裁，则该国不得在另一国原应管辖的法院有关下列事项的诉讼中援引管辖豁免：

（一）仲裁协议的有效性、解释或适用；

（二）仲裁程序；或

（三）裁决的确认或撤销，但仲裁协议另有规定者除外。

第四部分　在法院诉讼中免于强制措施的国家豁免

第十八条　免于判决前的强制措施的国家豁免

不得在另一国法院的诉讼中针对一国财产采取判决前的强制措施，例如查封和扣押措施，除非：

（一）该国以下列方式明示同意采取此类措施：

1. 国际协定；

2. 仲裁协议或书面合同；或

3. 在法院发表的声明或在当事方发生争端后提出的书面函件；或

（二）该国已经拨出或专门指定该财产用于清偿该诉讼标的的请求。

第十九条　免于判决后的强制措施的国家豁免

不得在另一国法院的诉讼中针对一国财产采取判决后的强制措施，例如查封、扣押和执行措施，除非：

（一）该国以下列方式明示同意采取此类措施：

1. 国际协定；

2. 仲裁协议或书面合同；或

3. 在法院发表的声明或在当事方发生争端后提出的书面函件；或

（二）该国已经拨出或专门指定该财产用于清偿该诉讼标的的请求；或

（三）已经证明该财产被该国具体用于或意图用于政府非商业性用途以外的目的，并且处于法院地国领土内，但条件是只可对与被诉实体有联系的财产采取判决后强制措施。

第二十条　同意管辖对强制措施的效力

虽然必须按照第十八条和第十九条表示同意采取强制措施，但按照第七条的规定同意行使管辖并不构成默示同意采取强制措施。

第二十一条　特定种类的财产

一、一国的以下各类财产尤其不应被视为第十九条第（三）项所指被一国具体用于或意图用于政府非商业性用途以外目的的财产：

（一）该国外交代表机构、领事机构、特别使团、驻国际组织代表团、派往国际组织的机关或国际会议的代表团履行公务所用或意图所用的财产，包括任何银行账户款项；

（二）属于军事性质，或用于或意图用于军事目的的财产；

（三）该国中央银行或其他货币当局的财产；

（四）构成该国文化遗产的一部分或该国档案的一部分，且非供出售或意图出售的财产；

（五）构成具有科学、文化或历史价值的物品展览的一部分，且非供出售或意图出售的财产。

二、第一款不妨碍第十八条和第十九条第（一）项和第（二）项。

第五部分　其他规定

第二十二条　诉讼文书的送达

一、送达传票或对一国提起诉讼的其他文书应按以下方式进行：

（一）按照对法院地国和有关国家有约束力的任何可适用的国际公约；或

（二）如果法院地国法律未作禁止，则按照求偿方和有关国家关于送达诉讼文书的特殊安排；或

（三）如无此公约或特殊安排，则：

1. 通过外交渠道送交有关国家的外交部；或

2. 采取有关国家接受的不受法院地国法律禁止的任何其他方式。

二、以第一款第（三）项第一目所指的方式送达诉讼文书时，外交部收到该项文书即视为该项文书已送达。

三、在必要时，送达的文书应附有译成有关国家正式语文或正式语文之一的译本。

四、任何国家在对其提起的诉讼中就实质问题出庭，其后即不得声称诉讼文书的送达不符合第一款和第三款的规定。

第二十三条　缺席判决

一、不得对一国作出缺席判决，除非法院已查明：

（一）第二十三条第一款和第三款规定的要求已获遵守；

（二）从按照第二十二条第一款和第二款送达传票或其他起诉文书之日算起，或视为已送达之日算起至少四个月；并且

（三）本公约不禁止法院行使管辖权。

二、对一国作出任何缺席判决，应通过第二十二条第一款所指的一种方式并按该款规定将判决书的副本送交该有关国家，必要时附上译成有关国家正式语文或正式语文之一的译本。

三、申请撤销一项缺席判决的时限不应少于四个月，时限应从有关国家收到判决书副本或视为有关国家收到判决书副本之日算起。

第二十四条　法院诉讼期间的特权和豁免

一、如一国未能或拒绝遵守另一国法院为一项诉讼的目的所下达的关于要求它实行或不实行一项特定行为，或提供任何文件，或透露任何其他资料的命令，则这种行为除了对该案的实质可能产生的后果外，不应产生任何其他后果。特别是，不应因此对该国处以任何罚款或罚金。

二、一国对它在另一国法院作为被告方的任何诉讼，均无须出具无论何种名称的担保、保证书或保证金保证支付司法费用或开支。

第六部分　最后条款

第二十五条　附件

本公约附件为公约的组成部分。

第二十六条　其他国际协定

本公约不影响与本公约所涉事项有关的现有国际协定对缔约国所规定的，适用于这些协定缔约方之间的权利和义务。

第二十七条　争端的解决

一、缔约国应致力通过谈判解决关于本公约的解释或适用方面的争端。

二、两个或两个以上的缔约国之间关于本公约的解释或适用方面的任何争端，不能在六个月内谈判解决的，经前述任一缔约国要求，应交付仲裁。如果自要求仲裁之日起六个月内，前述缔约国不能就仲裁的组成达成协定，其中任一缔约国可以依照《国际法院规约》提出请求，将争端提交国际法院审理。

三、每一个缔约国在签署、批准、接受或核准本公约或加入本公约时，可以声明本国不受第二款的约束。相对于作出这项保留的任何缔约国，其他缔约国也不受第二款的约束。

四、依照第三款的规定作出保留的任何缔约国，可以随时通知联合国秘书长撤回该项保留。

第二十八条　签署

本公约应在 2007 年 1 月 17 日之前开放给所有国家在纽约联合国总部签署。

第二十九条　批准、接受、核准或加入

一、本公约须经批准、接受、核准或加入。

二、本公约持续开放给任何国家加入。

三、批准书、接受书、核准书或加入书应交存联合国秘书长。

第三十条　生效

一、本公约应自第三十份批准书、接受书、核准书或加入书交存联合国秘书长之日后第三十天生效。

二、对于在第三十份批准书、接受书、核准书或加入书交存以后批准、接受、核准或加入本公约的每一国家，本公约应在该国将批准书、接受书、核准书或加入书交存之后第三十天生效。

第三十一条　退出

一、任何缔约国可书面通知联合国秘书长退出本公约。

二、退出应自联合国秘书长接到通知之日起一年后生效。但本公约应继续适用于在退出对任何有关国家生效前，在一国法院对另一国提起的诉讼所引起的任何国家及其财产的管辖豁免问题。

三、退出决不影响任何缔约国按照国际法而非依本公约即应担负的履行本公约所载任何义务的责任。

第三十二条　保存机关和通知

一、联合国秘书长应为本公约的保存机关。

二、联合国秘书长作为本公约的保存机关，应将以下事项通知所有国家：

（一）本公约的签署及按照第二十九条和第三十一条交存批准书、接受书、核准书或加入书或退出通知的情况；

（二）本公约按照第三十条生效之日期；

（三）与本公约有关的任何文书、通知或来文。

第三十三条　作准文本

本公约的阿拉伯文、中文、英文、法文、俄文和西班牙文文本同等作准。

本公约于 2005 年 1 月 17 日在纽约联合国总部开放供签字。下列签署人经各自政府正式授权在本公约上签字，以昭信守。

公约附件

对公约若干规定的理解

本附件旨在列出对有关规定的理解。

关于第十条

第十条中的"豁免"一词应根据本公约全文来理解。

第十条第三款并不预断"掀开公司面纱"的问题，涉及国家实体故意虚报其财务状况或继而减少其资产，以避免清偿索赔要求的问题，或其他有关问题。

关于第十一条

第十一条第二款第（四）项所提到的雇佣国"安全利益"主要是针对国家安全事项以及外交使团和领事馆的安全而言。

1961 年《维也纳外交关系公约》第四十一条和 1963 年《维也纳领事关系公约》第五十五条规定，条款提及的所有个人都有义务遵守东道国的法律规章，包括遵守东道国的劳工法。同时，1961 年《维也纳外交关系公约》

第三十八条和 1963 年《维也纳领事关系公约》第七十一条规定，接受国有义务在行使管辖时，不对使团或领馆开展工作造成不当妨碍。

关于第十三条和第十四条

"确定"一词不仅指查明或核查是否有受保护的权利，而且也指评价或评估此类权利的实质，包括其内容、范围和程度。

关于第十七条

"商业交易"一词包括投资事项。

关于第十九条

第（三）项"实体"一词系指作为独立法人的国家，以及具有独立法人地位的联邦制国家的组成部分、国家政治区分单位、国家的机构或部门或其他实体。

第（三）项"与被诉实体有联系的财产"一语应理解为具有比"所有"或"占有"更广泛的含义。

第十九条并不预断"掀开公司面纱"的问题，涉及国家实体故意虚报其财务状况或随后减少其资产，以避免清偿索赔要求，或其他有关问题。

第三部分 其他国际文件

1991年联合国国际法委员会国家及其财产的管辖豁免条款草案

第一部分 导 言

第一条 本条款的范围

本条款适用于国家及其财产对另一国法院的管辖豁免。

第二条 用语

一、为本条款的目的：

（一）"法院"是指一国有权行使司法职能的不论名称为何的任何机关；

（二）"国家"是指：

1. 国家及其政府的各种机关；

2. 联邦国家的组成单位；

3. 授权为行使国家主权权力而行为的国家政治区分单位；

4. 国家机构或部门和其他实体，只要它们授权为行使国家主权权力而行为；

5. 以国家代表身份行为的国家代表；

（三）"商业交易"是指：

1. 为出售货物或为提供服务而订立的任何商业合同或交易；

2. 任何贷款或其他金融性质之交易的合同，包括与任何此类贷款或交易有关的任何担保义务或保赔义务；

3. 商业、工业、贸易或专业性质的任何其他合同或交易，但不包括雇佣人员的合同。

二、确定本条第一款第（三）项下的合同或交易是否属于"商业交易"时，首先应考虑合同或交易的性质。但是，如果在作为其缔约一方的国家的实践中该合同或交易的目的与确定其非商业性质有关，则也应予以考虑。

三、关于本条款用语的第一款和第二款的规定不妨碍其他国际文书或任何国家的国内法对这些用语的使用或给予的含义。

第三条　不受本条款影响的特权和豁免

一、本条款不妨碍一国根据国际法所享有的有关行使下列职能的特权和豁免：

（一）其使馆、领馆、特别使团、驻国际组织代表团或派往国际组织的机关或国际会议的代表团的职能；和

（二）与上述机构有关联的人员的职能。

二、本条款同样不妨碍根据国际法给予国家元首个人的特权和豁免。

第四条　本条款不溯及既往

在不妨碍本条款所列、不以本条款为转移而根据国际法制约国家及其财产的管辖豁免的任何规则之适用的条件下，本条款不应适用于在本条款对有关国家生效前，在另一国法院对该国提起的诉讼所引起的任何国家及其财产的管辖豁免问题。

第二部分　一般原则

第五条　国家豁免

国家本身及其财产遵照本条款的规定对另一国法院享有管辖豁免。

第六条　实行国家豁免的方式

一、一国应避免对在其法院对另一国提起的诉讼行使管辖，以实行第五条所规定的国家豁免；并应为此保证其法院主动地确定第五条所规定的对该另一国的豁免得到遵守。

二、在一国法院中的诉讼应视为对另一国提起的诉讼，如果该另一国：

（一）被指名为该诉讼的当事一方；

（二）未被指名为该诉讼的当事一方，但该诉讼实际上企图影响该另一国的财产、权利、利益或活动。

第七条　明示同意行使管辖

一、一国如以下列方式明示同意另一国对一个事项或案件行使管辖，则不得在该法院就该事项或案件提起的诉讼中援引管辖豁免：

（一）国际协定；

（二）书面合同；或

（三）法院对特定诉讼发表的声明或对特定诉讼的书面函件。

二、一国同意适用另一国的法律，不应被解释为同意该另一国的法院行使管辖权。

第八条　参加法院诉讼的效果

一、一国如有下列情况，则在另一国法院的诉讼中不得援引管辖豁免：

（一）该国本身提起该诉讼；或

（二）介入该诉讼或采取与案情实质有关的任何其他步骤。但如该国使法院确信它在采取这一步骤之前不可能知道可据以主张豁免的事实，则它可以根据那些事实主张豁免，条件是它必须尽早这样做。

二、一国不应被视为同意另一国的法院行使管辖权，如果该国仅为下列目的介入诉讼或采取任何其他步骤：

（一）援引豁免；或

（二）对诉讼中有待裁决的财产主张一项权利或利益。

三、一国代表在另一国法院出庭作证不应被解释为前一国同意法院行使管辖权。

四、一国未在另一国法院的诉讼中出庭不应被解释为前一国同意法院行使管辖权。

第九条　反诉

一、一国在另一国法院提起一项诉讼，不得就与本诉相同的法律关系或事实所引起的任何反诉援引法院的管辖豁免。

二、一国介入另一国法院的诉讼中提出诉讼要求，则不得就与该国提出的诉讼要求相同的法律关系或事实所引起的任何反诉援引管辖豁免。

三、一国在另一国法院对该国提起的诉讼中提出反诉，则不得就本诉援引法院的管辖豁免。

第三部分　不得援引国家豁免的诉讼

第十条　商业交易

一、一国如与一外国自然人或法人进行一项商业交易，而根据国际私法适用的规则，有关该商业交易的争议应由另一国法院管辖，则该国不得在该商业交易引起的诉讼中援引管辖豁免。

二、第一款不适用于下列情况：

（一）国家之间进行的商业交易；或

（二）该商业交易的当事方另有明确协议。

三、国家享有的管辖豁免在一个国家企业或国家设立的其他实体所从事商业交易的有关诉讼中不应受影响，该国家企业或其他实体具有法人资格，并有能力：

（一）起诉或被诉；和

（二）获得、拥有或占有和处置财产，包括国家授权其经营或管理的财产。

第十一条　雇佣合同

一、除有关国家间另有协议外，一国在该国和个人间关于已全部或部分在另一国领土进行或将进行的工作之雇佣合同的诉讼中，不得对该另一国原应管辖的法院援引管辖豁免。

二、第一款不适用于下列情况：

（一）征聘该雇员是为了履行与行使政府权力密切有关的职务；

（二）该诉讼的主题是个人的征聘、雇佣期的延长或复职；

（三）该雇员在签订合同时既非法院地国的国民，也非其长期居民；

（四）该雇员在提起诉讼时是雇佣国的国民；或

（五）该雇员和雇佣国另有书面协议，但由于公共政策的任何考虑，因该诉讼的事项内容而赋予法院地国法院专属管辖权者不在此限。

第十二条　人身伤害和财产损害

除有关国家间另有协议外，一国在对据称由归因于该国的作为或不作为引起的人身死亡或伤害或有形财产的损害或灭失要求金钱补偿的诉讼中，如果该作为或不作为全部或部分发生在法院地国领土内，而且作为或不作为的行为人在作为或不作为发生时处于法院地国领土内，则不得对另一国原应管辖的法院援引管辖豁免。

第十三条　财产的所有权、占有和使用

除有关国家间另有协议外，一国在涉及下列问题之确定的诉讼中，不得对另一国原应管辖的法院援引管辖豁免：

（一）该国对位于法院地国的不动产的任何权利或利益，或该国对该不动产的占有或使用，或该国由于对该不动产的利益或占有或使用而产生的任何义务；

（二）该国对动产或不动产由于继承、赠与或无主物取得而产生的任何权利或利益；或

（三）该国对托管财产、破产者财产或公司解散前清理财产的管理的任何权利或利益。

第十四条　知识产权和工业产权

除有关国家另有协议外，一国在有关下列事项的诉讼中不得对另一国

原应管辖的法院援引管辖豁免：

（一）确定该国对在法院地国享受某种程度，即使是暂时的法律保护的专利、工业设计、商业名称或企业名称、商标、版权或任何其他形式的知识产权或工业产权的任何权利；或

（二）据称该国在法院地国领土内侵犯在法院地国受到保护的、属于第三者的第（一）项所述性质的权利。

第十五条　参加公司或其他集体机构

一、一国在有关该国参加具有或不具有法人资格的公司或其他集体机构的诉讼中，即在关于该国与该机构或该机构其他参加者之间关系的诉讼中，不得对另一国原应管辖的法院援引管辖豁免，但有以下条件：

（一）该机构的参加者不限于国家或国际组织；而且

（二）该机构是按照法院地国的法律注册或组成，或其所在地或主要营业所位于法院地国。

二、但是，如果有关国家同意，或如果争端当事方之间的书面协议作此规定，或如果据以建立或管理有关机构的文书中载有此一规定，则一国可以在此诉讼中援引管辖豁免。

第十六条　国家拥有或经营的船舶

一、除有关国家间另有协议外，拥有或经营一艘船舶的一国，在另一国原应管辖的法院有关该船舶经营的一项诉讼中，只要在诉讼事由产生时该船舶是用于政府非商业性用途以外的目的，即不得援引管辖豁免。

二、第一款不适用于军舰、辅助舰艇，也不适用于一国拥有或经营的、专门用于政府非商业性活动的其他船舶。

三、为本条的目的，"有关该船舶经营的诉讼"一语，除其他外，是指同确定下列要求有关的任何诉讼：

（一）碰撞或其他航行事故；

（二）协助、救助和共同海损；

（三）修理、供应或有关船舶的其他合同；

（四）海洋环境污染引起的后果。

四、除有关国家间另有协议外，一国在有关该国拥有或经营的船舶所载货物之运输的一项诉讼中，只要在诉讼事由产生时该船舶是用于政府非商业性用途以外的目的，即不得对另一国原应管辖的法院援引管辖豁免。

五、第四款不适用于第二款所指船舶所载运的任何货物，也不适用于国家拥有的、专门用于或意图专门用于政府非商业性用途的任何货物。

六、国家可提出私有船舶、货物及其所有人所能利用的一切抗辩措施、时效和责任限制。

七、如果在一项诉讼中产生有关一国拥有或经营的一艘船舶，或一国拥有的货物的政府非商业性质问题，由该国的一个外交代表或其他主管当局签署并送达法院的证件，应作为该船舶或货物性质的证据。

第十七条　仲裁协定的效力

一国如与一外国自然人或法人订立书面协定，将有关商业交易的争讼提交仲裁，则该国不得在另一国原应管辖的法院就有关下列事项的诉讼中援引管辖豁免：

（一）仲裁协定的有效性或解释；

（二）仲裁程序；或

（三）裁决的撤销；

但仲裁协定另有规定者除外。

第四部分　在法院诉讼中免于强制措施的国家豁免

第十八条　免于强制措施的国家豁免

一、不得在另一国法院的诉讼中采取针对一国财产的强制措施，例如查封、扣押和执行措施，除非：

（一）该国以下列方式明示同意就该有关财产采取此类措施：

1. 国际协定；

2. 仲裁协定或书面合同；或

3. 在法院发表的声明或在当事方发生争端后提出的书面函件；

（二）该国已经拨出或专门指定该财产用于清偿该诉讼标的的要求；或

（三）该财产在法院地国领土上，并且被该国具体用于或意图用于政府非商业性用途以外的目的，而且与诉讼标的的要求有关，或者与被诉的机构或部门有关。

二、按照第七条的规定同意行使管辖并非默示同意按第一款采取强制措施，关于强制措施必须另行表示同意。

第十九条　特定种类的财产

一、一国的以下各类财产尤其不应被视为第十八条第一款第（三）项所指被一国具体用于或意图用于政府非商业性用途以外目的的财产：

（一）用于或意图用于该国使馆、领馆、特别使团、驻国际组织代表团、派往国际组织的机关或国际会议的代表团用途的财产，包括任何银行账户款项；

（二）属于军事性质，或用于或意图用于军事目的的财产；

（三）该国中央银行或其他货币当局的财产；

（四）构成该国文化遗产的一部分或该国档案的一部分，且非供出售或意图出售的财产；

（五）构成具有科学、文化或历史价值的物品展览的一部分，且非供出售或意图出售的财产。

二、第一款不妨碍第十八条第一款第（一）项和第（二）项。

第五部分　其他规定

第二十条　诉讼文书的送达

一、送达传票或对一国提起诉讼的其他文件应按以下方式进行：

（一）按照对法院地国和有关国家有约束力的任何可适用的国际公约；或

（二）如无此公约，则：

1. 通过外交渠道送交有关国家的外交部；或
2. 采取有关国家接受的不受法院地国法律禁止的任何其他方式。

二、以第一款第（二）项第一目所指的方式送达诉讼文书时，外交部收到该项文书即视为该项文书已送达。

三、在必要时，送达的文书应附有译成有关国家正式语文或正式语文之一的译本。

四、任何国家在对其提起的诉讼中就实质问题出庭，其后即不得声称诉讼文书的送达不符合第一款和第三款的规定。

第二十一条　缺席判决

一、不得对一国作出缺席判决，除非法院已查明：

（一）第二十条第一款和第三款规定的要求已获遵守；

（二）从按照第二十条第一款和第二款送达传票或其他起诉文件之日算起，或视为已送达之日算起至少四个月；并且

（三）本条款不禁止法院行使管辖权。

二、对一国作出任何缺席判决，应通过第二十条第一款所指的一种方式并按该款规定将判决书的副本送交该有关国家，必要时附上译成有关国家正式语文或正式语文之一的译本。

三、提请撤销一项缺席判决的时限不应少于四个月，时限应从有关国家收到判决书副本或认为有关国家收到判决书副本之日算起。

第二十二条 法院诉讼期间的特权和豁免

一、如一国未能或拒绝遵守另一国法院为一项诉讼的目的所下达的关于要求它实行或不实行一项特定行为，或提供任何文件，或透露任何其他资料的命令，则除了这种行为对该案的实质可能产生的后果外，不应产生任何其他后果。特别是，不应因此对该国处以任何罚款或罚金。

二、一国对它在另一国法院作为当事一方的任何诉讼，均无须出具无论何种名称的担保、保证书或保证金保证支付司法费用或开支。

1991年国际法研究院关于国家豁免在管辖和执行方面的一些现实问题的决议

(第十四委员会，特别报告员：伊恩·布朗利先生，英文文本为作准文体，法文文本为翻译文本)

国际法研究院，

鉴于自1954年本研究院在普罗旺斯艾克斯的会议通过的关于外国国家豁免的决议以来，在国家实践、学理和司法判例上出现了重大趋势；

鉴于在不同国家法律制度范围内提出与国家管辖豁免适用有关的规则，意在限制豁免的同时保持对必要国家利益的保护是有帮助的；

通过以下决议：

第一条　决议的范围

本决议仅涉及法院地国有关机关管辖某个国家的作为或不作为的权限问题，该国在法院地国法院或其他准司法性质机关的有关诉讼中作为当事方。

第二条　法院地国的法院或其他相关机关在管辖豁免方面的权限的认定标准

一、在确定法院地国有关机关的权限问题时，每个案件应根据有关事实以及关于权限和超越权限的标准分别确定；不应对任何一类标准预设优先顺序。

二、如果没有相反的协议，尽管作为当事方的外国国家主张管辖豁免，但以下标准对认定法院地国有关机关有权管辖诉求的实质内容具有参考意义：

（一）法院地国的机关有权管辖与商业交易有关的诉讼，且某外国国家（或其代理人）是商业交易的一方。

（二）法院地国的机关有权管辖由私法性质的关系引发的法律争端，而某外国国家（或其代理人）作为争端一方；所涉及的争端包括（但不限于）以下法律类别：商业合同，服务合约，贷款和融资安排，有关金融义务的担保或补偿，财产的所有权、占有和使用，保护工业和知识产权，附属于法人团体、非法人团体和社团、合伙的法律事件，对船舶和货物的对物诉讼，汇票。

（三）法院地国的机关有权管辖与雇佣合同和专业服务合同有关的诉讼，且某外国国家（或其代理人）是合同的一方。

（四）法院地国的机关有权管辖基于本地法律中的善意和信赖因素的法律关系产生的法律争端的诉讼，尽管有关法律关系不被法院认为具有"私法性质"。

（五）法院地国的机关有权管辖涉及死亡、人身伤害或有形财产的灭失或损坏的诉讼，且在法院地国的管辖范围内上述行为可归因于外国国家及其代理人。

（六）法院地国的机关有权管辖与外国国家涉及动产或不动产的利益有关的诉讼，不论该权利或利益来自于继承、赠予或无主物取得；或管理死者、心智不健全的人或破产人的部分财产而产生的权利或利益；或在解散或清算时管理公司财产而产生的权利或利益；或管理信托财产或其他设立信托的财产而产生的权利或利益。

（七）法院地国的机关有权管辖外国国家与自然人或法人之间的仲裁协议，如该机关具有监督管辖权。

（八）法院地国的机关有权管辖依合理推断当事方并不会通过外交方式解决争端的事务。

（九）法院地国的机关有权管辖有关财政负债、所得税、关税、印花税、登记费和类似税负的诉讼，只要这些负债是正常发生的或是在当地法律体系下属于商业或其他法律关系的。

三、如果没有相反的协议，在涉及外国国家管辖豁免的情况下，以下标准对认定法院地国有关机关无权管辖诉求的实质内容具有参考意义：

（一）争议的主题与被告国交易在国际公法方面的效力之间的关系。

（二）争议的主题与被告国国内行政和立法行为在国际公法方面的效力之间的关系。

（三）法院地国的机关不应被视为有权管辖已经安排有另外救济措施的事项。

（四）法院地国的机关不应被视为有权询问被告国的国防和安全政策的内容或执行情况。

（五）法院地国的机关不应被视为有权管辖根据国际公法规则设立机构、组织或基金的政府间协定或决定的有效性、含义和执行。

第三条 国家机构和国家的政治分支

一、上列适格与不适格的一般标准适用于外国国家机构及其政治分支的活动，不论它们在相关国家的正式名称或宪法地位为何。

二、外国国家机构或政治分支根据外国国家法律由于公司化或其他而具有独立的法律人格的事实本身并不排除对其活动享有豁免。

三、某个实体根据外国国家法律具有联邦国家组成单位地位或类似特别自治区的地位这个事实本身并不排除对其活动享有豁免。

第四条 强制措施

一、除本条及第五条规定外，外国国家财产不因为执行法院判决或命令或作为执行准备的中间措施（以下简称强制措施），接受法院地国法院或其他机关的程序或命令。

二、下列种类的国家财产尤其豁免于强制措施：

（一）一国的外交或领事机构、特别使团或驻国际组织的代表团正在使用或供其使用的财产；

（二）一国的武装力量为军事目的正在使用或供其使用的财产；

（三）一国的中央银行或金融监管机构为行使其职能正在使用或供其使用的财产；

（四）作为一国文化遗产或档案的一部分且不用于或意图用于销售的财产。

三、根据上述第二款，下列国家财产不能豁免于强制措施：

（一）一国分配或指定用来抵偿有关请求的财产；

（二）在第（一）项所述财产已用尽或显示明显不足以抵偿请求时，其他在所在国领土内的正用于或意图用于商业目的的国家财产。

四、本条适用于国家机构和国家政治分支持有的财产，不论它们的正式名称和宪法地位为何；但这不影响对下列事项的恰当认定：

（一）对请求负有责任的法律实体，以及

（二）属于上述实体且根据第三款为抵偿债务而可能在诉前被扣押和诉后被没收的财产。

五、法院地国法院和其他机关应在救济和执行措施的后果之间适当注意比例原则。

第五条　同意或放弃

一、如外国国家法院以下列方式明确同意接受法院地国有关法院或其他机关的有关种类的管辖，该外国国家不能主张管辖豁免或强制执行豁免：

（一）通过国际协议；

（二）载于书面合同；

（三）通过对特定案件发表的声明；

（四）以在法院地国相关机关主动提起有关程序的方式，或为解决有关程序所涉的实体问题而参与程序，或通过其他相应步骤参与程序的方式自愿接受管辖。

二、同意接受管辖不意味着同意接受强制执行措施，后者要求有单独和清楚的同意。

第六条　善意原则

在适用当前决议的时候，善意原则应被给予适当尊重。

第七条　保留条款

一、当前决议并不意图直接或间接表明影响国内法庭管辖权学说的有效性及其他方面，这些学说形成国内法的一套或多套制度，国家行为主义就是其中的一个例子。

二、当前决议并不意图规制对外国政府行为有效性的承认问题，这是国际私法领域内的事项。

三、外国国家向法院地国相关机关主张有关某一请求的管辖豁免，并不因此排除其基于管辖豁免以外的原因主张该机关无权管辖诉求的实质内容。

四、当前决议不妨碍国际法给予一国供其下列机构行使职能的特权与豁免：

（一）其外交使团、领事机构、特别使团、驻国际组织的代表团、向国际组织机构或为参加国际会议派出的代表团；以及

（二）与上述机构有关的人员。

五、当前决议不妨碍国际法给予国家元首个人的特权与豁免。

2009年国际法研究院关于国家和代表国家行事的个人犯下国际罪行时的管辖豁免的决议

(特别报告员：福克斯女士)

决 议

国际法研究院，

注意到该研究院已经在1891年《汉堡决议》中处理了国家的管辖豁免，该决议涉及法院对外国国家、君主和国家元首的诉讼的管辖权，1954年在普罗旺斯艾克斯通过的《关于外国国家管辖和执行豁免的决议》和1991年在巴塞尔通过的《关于国家豁免在管辖和执行方面的一些现实问题的决议》以及2001年在温哥华通过的《关于国家元首和政府首脑在国际法上的管辖和执行豁免的决议》；

意识到根据协约和习惯国际法，一国有义务尊重和确保其管辖范围内的所有人的人权；

考虑到国家及其代理人的管辖豁免和国际罪行引起的声索之间的潜在冲突；

希望在解决此种冲突方面取得进展；

认识到在国家法院诉讼程序中剥夺豁免是实现对国际罪行的有效赔偿的一种方式；

通过以下决议：

第一条 定义

一、为本决议的目的，"国际罪行"是指国际法规定的严重罪行，如种族灭绝、危害人类罪、酷刑和战争罪，这反映在有关条约及国际法院和法庭的规约和判例中。

二、为了本决议的目的，"管辖权"是指一个国家的国家法院的刑事、民事和行政管辖权，此种管辖与另一国或其代理人依条约或习惯国际法享有的豁免有关。

第二条 原则

一、豁免的给予是为了确保在有关国家的诉讼中依照国际法有秩序地分配和行使管辖权，尊重国家主权平等，并使代表国家行事的人员能有效履行职能。

二、根据条约和习惯国际法，各国有义务预防和制止国际罪行。豁免不应构成本决议所涉罪行的受害者有权获得适当赔偿的障碍。

三、当国家的代理人被指控犯有国际罪行时，国家应考虑放弃豁免权。

第三条 代表国家行事的人的豁免

一、除符合国际法的个人豁免权外，管辖豁免不适用于国际罪行。

二、任何享有个人豁免权的人的职位或使命若已到期或结束，个人豁免权就会终止。

三、上述规定不妨碍：

（一）前款规定的人的国际法责任；

（二）将构成国际罪行的任何人的行为归于一国。

第四条 国家豁免

上述规定不处理某一国家在另一国国家法院有关该国代理人所犯国际罪行的民事诉讼中是否及何时享有管辖豁免。

2013年欧洲委员会国有文化财产管辖豁免声明

我们签署，

希望加强在文化领域的国际合作；

认识到文化财产的交流将极大地促进国家的相互理解；

决心通过临时跨境展览提升国有文化财产的流动性；

意识到有必要根据2004年《联合国关于国家及其财产的管辖豁免公约》（以下简称《公约》）所编纂的有关国家豁免的习惯国际法规则，重申适用于国有文化财产在另一国公开展览的国际法律框架；

联合声明如下：

按照《公约》编纂的习惯国际法，

构成一国文化遗产或其档案的国家财产或构成具有科学、文化或历史价值的展览品，且不是用于或计划用于出售的财产，在另一国免于查封、扣押或执行等任何限制措施；和

因此，这种限制措施只能在拥有该财产的国家主管当局明确放弃该特定财产的豁免的情况下，或者该财产作为有关诉讼针对的对象已被该国分配或指定用于满足有关诉求。

在此背景下，对任何这种财产的跨境公开展览可能引发的争端，我们重申对上述关于国有文化财产的习惯国际法规则的承诺。

在昭信守，经正式授权，签署了宣言。

Declaration on Jurisdictional Immunities of State Owned Cultural Property, 2013 (Council of Europe)

We, the undersigned,

Desirous to strengthen international cooperation in the field of culture;

Recognizing that the exchange of cultural property significantly contributes to the mutual understanding of nations;

Resolved to promote the mobility of State-owned cultural property through temporary cross border loans for public display;

Aware of the need to reaffirm the international legal framework applicable to State-owned cultural property on public display in another State on the basis of the customary international law on State immunity, as codified in the United Nations Convention on Jurisdictional Immunities of States and Their Property of 2004 (hereinafter the "Convention");

Jointly declare the following:

In accordance with customary international law as codified in the Convention

· property of a State forming part of its cultural heritage or its archives or forming part of an exhibition of objects of scientific, cultural or historical interest, and not placed or intended to be placed on sale cannot be subject to any measure of constraint, such as attachment, arrest or execution, in another State; and

· therefore, such measures of constraint can only be taken if immunity is expressly waived for a clearly specified property by the competent national authorities of the State owning the property or if the property has been allocated or earmarked by that State for the satisfaction of the claim which is the object of the proceeding concerned.

In this context, we reaffirm our commitment to the rules of customary international law on State owned cultural property as outlined above, in relation to any dispute that may arise in connection with cross-border loans of such property intended for public display.

In witness whereof the undersigned, being duly authorised thereto, have signed the Declaration.

2. For the purposes of this Resolution "jurisdiction" means the criminal, civil and administrative jurisdiction of national courts of one State as it relates to the immunity of another State or its agents conferred by treaties or customary international law.

Article II Principles

1. Immunities are conferred to ensure an orderly allocation and exercise of jurisdiction in accordance with international law in proceedings concerning States, to respect the sovereign equality of States and to permit the effective performance of the functions of persons who act on behalf of States.

2. Pursuant to treaties and customary international law, States have an obligation to prevent and suppress international crimes. Immunities should not constitute an obstacle to the appropriate reparation to which victims of crimes addressed by this Resolution are entitled.

3. States should consider waiving immunity where international crimes are allegedly committed by their agents.

Article III Immunity of persons who act on behalf of a State

1. No immunity from jurisdiction other than personal immunity in accordance with international law applies with regard to international crimes.

2. When the position or mission of any person enjoying personal immunity has come to an end, such personal immunity ceases.

3. The above provisions are without prejudice to:

(a) the responsibility under international law of a person referred to in the preceding paragraphs;

(b) the attribution to a State of the act of any such person constituting an international crime.

Article IV Immunity of States

The above provisions are without prejudice to the issue whether and when a State enjoys immunity from jurisdiction before the national courts of another State in civil proceedings relating to an international crime committed by an agent of the former State.

Resolution on the Immunity from Jurisdiction of the State and of Persons Who Act on Behalf of the State in Case of International Crimes, 2009 (IDI)

Rapporteur : Lady Fox

RESOLUTION

The Institute of International Law,

Mindful that the Institute has addressed jurisdictional immunities of States in the 1891 Hamburg Resolution on the jurisdiction of courts in proceedings against foreign States, sovereigns and heads of State, the 1954 Aix-en-Provence Resolution on immunity of foreign States from jurisdiction and measures of execution, the 1991 Basle Resolution on the contemporary problems concerning immunity of States in relation to questions of jurisdiction and enforcement and in the 2001 Vancouver Resolution on immunities from jurisdiction and execution of heads of State and of Government in international law;

Conscious that under conventional and customary international law a State has an obligation to respect and to ensure the human rights of all persons within its jurisdiction;

Considering the underlying conflict between immunity from jurisdiction of States and their agents and claims arising from international crimes;

Desirous of making progress towards a resolution of that conflict;

Recognizing that the removal of immunity from proceedings in national courts is one way by which effective reparation for the commission of international crimes may be achieved;

Adopts the following Resolution:

Article I Definitions

1. For the purposes of this Resolution "international crimes" means serious crimes under international law such as genocide, crimes against humanity, torture and war crimes, as reflected in relevant treaties and the statutes and jurisprudence of international courts and tribunals.

Article 5 Consent or Waiver

1. A foreign State may not invoke immunity from jurisdiction or from measures of constraint if it has expressly consented to the exercise of the relevant type of jurisdiction by the relevant court or other organs of the forum State:

a) by international agreement;

b) in a written contract;

c) by a declaration relating to the specific case;

d) by a voluntary submission to jurisdiction in the form of the institution of proceedings in the relevant organs of the forum State, or of intervention in proceedings for the purpose of pursuing issues related to the merits of those proceedings, or of a comparable step in the proceedings.

2. Consent to the exercise of jurisdiction does not imply consent to measures of constraint, for which separate and explicit consent is required.

Article 6 The Principle of Good Faith

The principle of good faith is to be given appropriate weight in applying the present Resolution.

Article 7 Saving Clauses

1. The present Resolution is not intended to indicate either directly or indirectly the validity or otherwise of doctrines affecting the competence of municipal courts which form part of one or more systems of municipal law and of which the act of State doctrine is an example.

2. The present Resolution is not intended to regulate the general question of the recognition, as a matter of private international law, of the validity of foreign governmental acts.

3. A foreign State which asserts its jurisdictional immunity in respect of a claim before a relevant organ of the forum State is not thereby precluded from arguing that the organ lacks competence to determine the subject-matter of the claim for reasons other than jurisdictional immunity.

4. The present Resolution is without prejudice to the privileges and immunities accorded to a State under international law in relation to the exercise of the functions of:

a) its diplomatic missions, consular posts, special missions, missions to international organizations or delegations to organs of international organizations or to international conferences; and

b) persons connected with them.

5. The present Resolution is without prejudice to the personal privileges and immunities accorded to Heads of States under international law.

d) The organs of the forum State should not assume competence to inquire into the content or implementation of the foreign defence and security policies of the defendant State.

e) The organs of the forum State should not assume competence in respect of the validity, meaning and implementation of an intergovernmental agreement or decision creating agencies, institutions or funds subject to the rules of public international law.

Article 3 State Agencies and Political Subdivisions

1. The general criteria of competence and incompetence set forth above are applicable to the activities of the agencies and political subdivisions of foreign States whatever their formal designation or constitutional status in the State concerned.

2. The fact that an agency or political subdivision of a foreign State possesses a separate legal personality as a consequence of incorporation or otherwise under the law of the foreign State does not in itself preclude immunity in respect of its activities.

3. The fact that an entity has the status of a constituent unit of a federal State, or a comparable status of special autonomy, under the law of the foreign State does not preclude immunity in respect of its activities.

Article 4 Measures of Constraint

1. The property of a foreign State is not subject to any process or order of the courts or other organs of the forum State for the satisfaction or enforcement of a judgment or order, or for the purpose of prejudgment measures in preparation for execution (hereafter referred to as measures of constraint), except as provided for by this Article and by Article 5.

2. The following categories of property of a State in particular are immune from measures of constraint:

a) property used or set aside for use by the State's diplomatic or consular missions, its special missions or its missions to international organizations;

b) property in use or set aside for use by the armed forces of the State for military purposes;

c) property of the central bank or monetary authority of the State in use or set aside for use for the purposes of the central bank or monetary authority;

d) property identified as part of the cultural heritage of the State, or of its archives, and not placed or intended to be placed on sale.

3. Subject to paragraph (2) above, the following property of a State is not immune from measures of constraint:

a) property allocated or earmarked by the State for the satisfaction of the claim in question;

b) where the property referred to in sub-paragraph (a) has been exhausted or is shown to be clearly inadequate to satisfy the claim, other property of the State within the territory of the forum State which is in use or intended for use for commercial purposes.

4. This Article applies to property of or in the possession of State agencies and political subdivisions of a State, whatever their formal designation or constitutional status ; but this is without prejudice to the due identification of:

a) the legal entity liable in respect of the claim, and

b) the property which belongs to that entity and which may accordingly be liable in accordance with paragraph (3) to measures of prejudgment attachment and seizure in execution to satisfy its liabilities.

5. The courts and other organs of the forum State shall give appropriate effect to the principle of proportionality as between the remedy sought and the consequences of enforcement measures.

b) The organs of the forum State are competent in respect of proceedings concerning legal disputes arising from relationships of a private law character to which a foreign State (or its agent) is a party; the class of relationships referred to includes (but is not confined to) the following legal categories: commercial contracts; contracts for the supply of services; loans and financing arrangements; guarantees or indemnities in respect of financial obligations; ownership, possession and use of property; the protection of industrial and intellectual property; the legal incidents attaching to incorporated bodies, unincorporated bodies and associations, and partnerships; actions *in rem* against ships and cargoes; and bills of exchange.

c) The organs of the forum State are competent in respect of proceedings concerning contracts of employment and contracts for professional services to which a foreign State (or its agent) is a party.

d) The organs of the forum State are competent in respect of proceedings concerning legal disputes arising from relationships which are not classified in the forum as having a "private law character" but which nevertheless are based upon elements of good faith and reliance (legal security) within the context of the local law.

e) The organs of the forum State are competent in respect of proceedings concerning the death of, or personal injury to, a person, or loss of or damage to tangible property, which are attributable to activities of a foreign State and its agents within the national jurisdiction of the forum State.

f) The organs of the forum State are competent in respect of proceedings relating to any interests of a foreign State in movable or immovable property, being a right or interest arising by way of succession, gift or *bona vacantia*; or a right or interest in the administration of property forming part of the estate of a deceased person or a person of unsound mind or a bankrupt; or a right or interest in the administration of property of a company in the event of its dissolution or winding up; or a right or interest in the administration of trust property or property otherwise held on a fiduciary basis.

g) The organs of the forum State are competent in so far as it has a supervisory jurisdiction in respect of an agreement to arbitrate between a foreign State and a natural or juridical person.

h) The organs of the forum State are competent in respect of transactions in relation to which the reasonable inference is that the parties did not intend that the settlement of disputes would be on the basis of a diplomatic claim.

i) The organs of the forum State are competent in respect of proceedings relating to fiscal liabilities, income tax, customs duties, stamp duty, registration fees, and similar impositions provided that such liabilities are the normal concomitant or commercial and other legal relationships in the context of the local legal system.

3. In the absence of agreement to the contrary, the following criteria are indicative of the incompetence of the organs of the forum State to determine the substance of the claim, in a case where the jurisdictional immunity of a foreign State party is in issue:

a) The relation between the subject-matter of the dispute and the validity of the transactions of the defendant State in terms of public international law.

b) The relation between the subject-matter of the dispute and the validity of the internal administrative and legislative acts of the defendant State in terms of public international law.

c) The organs of the forum State should not assume competence in respect of issues the Resolution of which has been allocated to another remedial context.

Contemporary Problems Concerning the Immunity of States in Relation to Questions of Jurisdiction and Enforcement, 1991 (IDI)

(Fourteenth Commission, Rapporteur : Mr. Ian Brownlie)
(The English text is authoritative. The French text is a translation.)

The Institute of International Law,

Whereas significant trends have appeared both in the practice of States and in doctrine and jurisprudence since the Resolution on the immunities of foreign States adopted at the Aix-en-Provence Session of the Institute in 1954;

Whereas it is helpful to propose formulations pertinent to the application within the various national legal systems of the rules relating to the jurisdictional immunity of States with a view to limiting the immunity, while maintaining the protection of essential States interests;

Adopts the following Resolution:

Article 1 Scope of the Resolution

The present Resolution is concerned exclusively with the competence of the relevant organs of the State of the forum in respect of the acts or omissions of a State which is a party to proceedings in the courts of the forum State or in other organs of that State with powers of a quasi-judicial character.

Article 2 Criteria Indicating the Competence of Courts or Other Relevant Organs of the Forum State in Relation to Jurisdictional Immunity

1. In determining the question of the competence of the relevant organs of the forum State, each case is to be separately characterised in the light of the relevant facts and the relevant criteria, both of competence and incompetence; no presumption is to be applied concerning the priority of either group of criteria.

2. In the absence of agreement to the contrary, the following criteria are indicative of the competence of the relevant organs of the forum State to determine the substance of the claim, notwithstanding a claim to jurisdictional immunity by a foreign State which is a party:

a) The organs of the forum State are competent in respect of proceedings relating to a commercial transaction to which a foreign State (or its agent) is a party.

2. A copy of any default judgement rendered against a State, accompanied if necessary by a translation into the official language or one of the official languages of the State concerned, shall be transmitted to it through one of the means specified in paragraph 1 of article 20 and in accordance with the provisions of that paragraph.

3. The time-limit for applying to have a default judgement set aside shall not be less than four months and shall begin to run from the date on which the copy of the judgement is received or is deemed to have been received by the State concerned.

Article 22 Privileges and immunities during court proceedings

1. Any failure or refusal by a State to comply with an order of a court of another State enjoining it to perform or refrain from performing a specific act or to produce any document or disclose any other information for the purposes of a proceeding shall entail no consequences other than those which may result from such conduct in relation to the merits of the case. In particular, no fine or penalty shall be imposed on the State by reason of such failure or refusal.

2. A State shall not be required to provide any security, bond or deposit, however described, to guarantee the payment of judicial costs or expenses in any proceeding to which it is a party before a court of another State.

(a) property, including any bank account, which is used or intended for use for the purposes of the diplomatic mission of the State or its consular posts, special missions, missions to international organizations, or delegations to organs of international organizations or to international conferences;

(b) property of a military character or used or intended for use for military purposes;

(c) property of the central bank or other monetary authority of the State;

(d) property forming part of the cultural heritage of the State or part of its archives and not placed or intended to be placed on sale;

(e) property forming part of an exhibition of objects of scientific, cultural or historical interest and not placed or intended to be placed on sale.

2. Paragraph 1 is without prejudice to paragraph 1 (a) and (b) of article 18.

Part V Miscellaneous provisions

Article 20 Service of process

1. Service of process by writ or other document instituting a proceeding against a State shall be effected:

(a) in accordance with any applicable international convention binding on the State of the forum and the State concerned; or

(b) in the absence of such a convention:

(i) by transmission through diplomatic channels to the Ministry of Foreign Affairs of the State concerned; or

(ii) by any other means accepted by the State concerned, if not precluded by the law of the State of the forum.

2. Service of process referred to in paragraph 1 (b) (i) is deemed to have been effected by receipt of the documents by the Ministry of Foreign Affairs.

3. These documents shall be accompanied, if necessary, by a translation into the official language, or one of the official languages, of the State concerned.

4. Any State that enters an appearance on the merits in a proceeding instituted against it may not thereafter assert that service of process did not comply with the provisions of paragraphs 1 and 3.

Article 21 Default judgement

1. A default judgement shall not be rendered against a State unless the court has found that:

(a) the requirements laid down in paragraphs 1 and 3 of article 20 have been complied with;

(b) a period of not less than four months has expired from the date on which the service of the writ or other document instituting a proceeding has been effected or deemed to have been effected in accordance with paragraphs 1 and 2 of article 20; and

(c) the present articles do not preclude it from exercising jurisdiction.

6. States may plead all measures of defence, prescription and limitation of liability which are available to private ships and cargoes and their owners.

7. If in a proceeding there arises a question relating to the government and non-commercial character of a ship owned or operated by a State or cargo owned by a State, a certificate signed by a diplomatic representative or other competent authority of that State and communicated to the court shall serve as evidence of the character of that ship or cargo.

Article 17 Effect of an arbitration agreement

If a State enters into an agreement in writing with a foreign natural or juridical person to submit to arbitration differences relating to a commercial transaction, that State cannot invoke immunity from jurisdiction before a court of another State which is otherwise competent in a proceeding which relates to:

(a) the validity or interpretation of the arbitration agreement;

(b) the arbitration procedure; or

(c) the setting aside of the award;

unless the arbitration agreement otherwise provides.

Part IV State immunity from measures of constraint in connection with proceedings before a court

Article 18 State immunity from measures of constraint

1. No measures of constraint, such as attachment, arrest and execution, against property of a Stare may be taken in connection with a proceeding before a court of another State unless and except to the extent that:

(a) the State has expressly consented to the taking of such measures as indicated:

(i) by international agreement;

(ii) by an arbitration agreement or in a written contract; or

(iii) by a declaration before the court or by a written communication after a dispute between the parties has arisen;

(b) the State has allocated or earmarked property for the satisfaction of the claim which is the object of that proceeding; or

(c) the property is specifically in use or intended for use by the State for other than government non-commercial purposes and is in the territory of the State of the forum and has a connection with the claim which is the object of the proceeding or with the agency or instrumentality against which the proceeding was directed.

2. Consent to the exercise of jurisdiction under article 7 shall not imply consent to the taking of measures of constraint under paragraph 1, for which separate consent shall be necessary.

Article 19 Specific categories of property

1. The following categories, in particular, of property of a State shall not be considered as property specifically in use or intended for use by the State for other than government non-commercial purposes under paragraph 1 (c) of article 18:

munity from jurisdiction before a court of another State which is otherwise competent in a proceeding which relates to:

(a) the determination of any right of the State in a patent, industrial design, trade name or business name, trade mark, copyright or any other form of intellectual or industrial property, which enjoys a measure of legal protection, even if provisional, in the State of the forum; or

(b) an alleged infringement by the State, in the territory of the State of the forum, of a right of the nature mentioned in subparagraph (a) which belongs to a third person and is protected in the State of the forum.

Article 15 Participation in companies or other collective bodies

1. A State cannot invoke immunity from jurisdiction before a court of another State which is otherwise competent in a proceeding which relates to its participation in a company or other collective body, whether incorporated or unincorporated, being a proceeding concerning the relationship between the State and the body or the other participants therein, provided that the body:

(a) has participants other than States or international organizations; and

(b) is incorporated or constituted under the law of the State of the forum or has its seat or principal place of business in that State.

2. A State can, however, invoke immunity from jurisdiction in such a proceeding if the States concerned have so agreed or if the parties to the dispute have so provided by an agreement in writing or if the instrument establishing or regulating the body in question contains provisions to that effect.

Article 16 Ships owned or operated by a State

1. Unless otherwise agreed between the States concerned, a State which owns or operates a ship cannot invoke immunity from jurisdiction before a court of another State which is otherwise competent in a proceeding which relates to the operation of that ship, if at the time the cause of action arose, the ship was used for other than government noncommercial purposes.

2. Paragraph 1 does not apply to warships and naval auxiliaries nor does it apply to other ships owned or operated by a State and used exclusively on government non-commercial service.

3. For the purposes of this article, "proceeding which relates to the operation of that Ship" means, inter alia, any proceeding involving the determination of a claim in respect of:

(a) collision or other accidents of navigation;

(b) assistance, salvage and general average;

(c) repairs, supplies or other contracts relating to the ship;

(d) consequences of pollution of the marine environment.

4. Unless otherwise agreed between the States concerned, a State cannot invoke immunity from jurisdiction before a court of another State which is otherwise competent in a proceeding which relates to the carnage of cargo on board a ship owned or operated by that State if, at the time the cause of action arose, the ship was used for other than government non-commercial purposes.

5. Paragraph 4 does not apply to any cargo carried on board the ships referred to in paragraph 2 nor does it apply to any cargo owned by a State and used or intended for use exclusively for government non-commercial purposes.

terprise or other entity established by the State which has an independent legal personality and is capable of:

(a) suing or being sued; and

(b) acquiring, owning or possessing and disposing of property, including property which the State has authorized it to operate or manage.

Article 11 Contracts of employment

1. Unless otherwise agreed between the States concerned, a State cannot invoke immunity from jurisdiction before a court of another State which is otherwise competent in a proceeding which relates to a contract of employment between the State and an individual for work performed or to be performed, in whole or in part, in the territory of that other State.

2. Paragraph 1 does not apply if:

(a) the employee has been recruited to perform functions closely related to the exercise of governmental authority;

(b) the subject of the proceeding is the recruitment, renewal of employment or reinstatement of an individual;

(c) the employee was neither a national nor a habitual resident of the State of the forum at the time when the contract of employment was concluded;

(d) the employee is a national of the employer State at the time when the proceeding is instituted; or

(e) the employer State and the employee have otherwise agreed in writing, subject to any considerations of public policy conferring on the courts of the State of the forum exclusive jurisdiction by reason of the subject-matter of the proceeding.

Article 12 Personal injuries and damage to properly

Unless otherwise agreed between the States concerned, a State cannot invoke immunity from jurisdiction before a court of another State which is otherwise competent in a proceeding which relates to pecuniary compensation for death or injury to the person, or damage to or loss of tangible property, caused by an act or omission which is alleged to be attributable to the State, if the act or omission occurred in whole or in part in the territory of that other State and if the author of the act or omission was present in that territory at the time of the act or omission.

Article 13 Ownership, possession and use of property

Unless otherwise agreed between the States concerned, a State cannot invoke immunity from jurisdiction before a court of another State which is otherwise competent in a proceeding which relates to the determination of:

(a) any right or interest of the State in, or its possession or use of, or any obligation of the State arising out of its interest in, or its possession or use of, immovable property situated in the State of the forum;

(b) any right or interest of the State in movable or immovable property arising by way of succession, gift or *bona vacantia*; or

(c) any right or interest of the State in the administration of property, such as trust property, the estate of a bankrupt or the property of a company in the event of its winding-up.

Article 14 Intellectual and industrial property

Unless otherwise agreed between the States concerned, a State cannot invoke im-

Article 8 Effect of participation in a proceeding before a court

1. State cannot invoke immunity from jurisdiction in a proceeding before a court of another State if it has:

(a) itself instituted the proceeding; or

(b) intervened in the proceeding or taken any other step relating to the merits. However, if the State satisfies the court that it could not have acquired knowledge of facts on which a claim to immunity can be based until after it took such a step, it can claim immunity based on those facts, provided it does so at the earliest possible moment.

2. A State shall not be considered to have consented to the exercise of jurisdiction by a court of another State if it intervenes in a proceeding or takes any other step for the sole purpose of:

(a) invoking immunity; or

(b) asserting a right or interest in property at issue in the proceeding.

3. The appearance of a representative of a State before a court of another State as a witness shall not be interpreted as consent by the former State to the exercise of jurisdiction by the court.

4. Failure on the part of a State to enter an appearance in a proceeding before a court of another State shall not be interpreted as consent by the former State to the exercise of jurisdiction by the court.

Article 9 Counter-claims

1. A State instituting a proceeding before a court of another State cannot invoke immunity from the jurisdiction of the court in respect of any counter-claim arising out of the same legal relationship or facts as the principal claim.

2. A State intervening to present a claim in a proceeding before a court of another State cannot invoke immunity from the jurisdiction of the court in respect of any counter-claim arising out of the same legal relationship or facts as the claim presented by the State.

3. A State making a counter-claim in a proceeding instituted against it before a court of another State cannot invoke immunity from the jurisdiction of the court in respect of the principal claim.

Part III Proceedings in which State immunity cannot be invoked

Article 10 Commercial transactions

1. If a State engages in a commercial transaction with a foreign natural or juridical person and, by virtue of the applicable rules of private international law, differences relating to the commercial transaction fall within the jurisdiction of a court of another State, the State cannot invoke immunity from that jurisdiction in a proceeding arising out of that commercial transaction.

2. Paragraph 1 does not apply:

(a) in the case of a commercial transaction between States; or

(b) if the parties to the commercial transaction have expressly agreed otherwise.

3. The immunity from jurisdiction enjoyed by a State shall not be affected with regard to a proceeding which relates to a commercial transaction engaged in by a State en-

Article 3 Privileges and immunities not affected by the present articles

1. The present articles are without prejudice to the privileges and immunities enjoyed by a State under international law in relation to the exercise of the functions of:

(a) its diplomatic missions, consular posts, special missions, missions to international organizations, or delegations to organs of international organizations or to international conferences; and

(b) persons connected with them.

2. The present articles are likewise without prejudice to privileges and immunities accorded under international law to Heads of State ratione personae.

Article 4 Non-retroactivity of the present articles

Without prejudice to the application of any rules set forth in the present articles to which jurisdictional immunities of States and their property are subject under international law independently of the present articles, the articles shall not apply to any question of jurisdictional immunities of States or their property arising in a proceeding instituted against a State before a court of another State prior to the entry into force of the present articles for the States concerned.

Part II General principles

Article 5 State immunity

A State enjoys immunity, in respect of itself and its property, from the jurisdiction of the courts of another State subject to the provisions of the present articles.

Article 6 Modalities for giving effect to State immunity

1. A State shall give effect to State immunity under article 5 by refraining from exercising jurisdiction in a proceeding before its courts against another State and to that end shall ensure that its courts determine on their own initiative that the immunity of that other State under article 5 is respected.

2. A proceeding before a court of a State shall be considered to have been instituted against another State if that other State:

(a) is named as a party to that proceeding; or

(b) is not named as a party to the proceeding but the proceeding in effect seeks to affect the property, rights, interests or activities of that other State.

Article 7 Express consent to exercise of jurisdiction

1. A State cannot invoke immunity from jurisdiction in a proceeding before a court of another State with regard to a matter or case if it has expressly consented to the exercise of jurisdiction by the court with regard to the matter or case:

(a) by international agreement;

(b) in a written contract; or

(c) by a declaration before the court or by a written communication in a specific proceeding.

2. Agreement by a State for the application of the law of another State shall not be interpreted as consent to the exercise of jurisdiction by the courts of that other State.

Draft Articles on Jurisdictional Immunities of States and Their Property, 1991 (ILC)

Part I Introduction

Article 1 Scope of the present articles

The present articles apply to the immunity of a State and its property from the jurisdiction of the courts of another State.

Article 2 Use of terms

1. For the purposes of the present articles:

(a) "court" means any organ of a State, however named, entitled to exercise judicial functions;

(b) "State" means:

(i) the State and its various organs of government;

(ii) constituent units of a federal State;

(iii) political subdivisions of the State which are entitled to perform acts in the exercise of the sovereign authority of the State;

(iv) agencies or instrumentalities of the State and other entities, to the extent that they are entitled to perform acts in the exercise of the sovereign authority of the State;

(v) representatives of the State acting in that capacity;

(c) "commercial transaction" means:

(i) any commercial contract or transaction for the sale of goods or supply of services;

(ii) any contract for a loan or other transaction of a financial nature, including any obligation of guarantee or of indemnity in respect of any such loan or transaction;

(iii) any other contract or transaction of a commercial, industrial, trading or professional nature, but not including a contract of employment of persons.

2. In determining whether a contract or transaction is a "commercial transaction" under paragraph 1 (c), reference should be made primarily to the nature of the contract or transaction, but its purpose should also be taken into account if, in the practice of the State which is a party to it, that purpose is relevant to determining the non-commercial character of the contract or transaction.

3. The provisions of paragraphs 1 and 2 regarding the use of terms in the present articles are without prejudice to the use of those terms or to the meanings which may be given to them in other international instruments or in the internal law of any State.

Part III
Other International Instruments

those articles have the duty to respect the laws and regulations, including labour laws, of the host country. At the same time, under article 38 of the 1961 Vienna Convention on Diplomatic Relations and article 71 of the 1963 Vienna Convention on Consular Relations, the receiving State has a duty to exercise its jurisdiction in such a manner as not to interfere unduly with the performance of the functions of the mission or the consular post.

With respect to articles 13 and 14

The expression "determination" is used to refer not only to the ascertainment or verification of the existence of the rights protected, but also to the evaluation or assessment of the substance, including content, scope and extent, of such rights.

With respect to article 17

The expression "commercial transaction" includes investment matters.

With respect to article 19

The expression "entity" in subparagraph (c) means the State as an independent legal personality, a constituent unit of a federal State, a subdivision of a State, an agency or instrumentality of a State or other entity, which enjoys independent legal personality.

The words "property that has a connection with the entity" in subparagraph (c) are to be understood as broader than ownership or possession.

Article 19 does not prejudge the question of "piercing the corporate veil", questions relating to a situation where a State entity has deliberately misrepresented its financial position or subsequently reduced its assets to avoid satisfying a claim, or other related issues.

Article 31 Denunciation

1. Any State Party may denounce the present Convention by written notification to the Secretary-General of the United Nations.

2. Denunciation shall take effect one year following the date on which notification is received by the Secretary-General of the United Nations. The present Convention shall, however, continue to apply to any question of jurisdictional immunities of States or their property arising in a proceeding instituted against a State before a court of another State prior to the date on which the denunciation takes effect for any of the States concerned.

3. The denunciation shall not in any way affect the duty of any State Party to fulfil any obligation embodied in the present Convention to which it would be subject under international law independently of the present Convention.

Article 32 Depositary and notifications

1. The Secretary-General of the United Nations is designated the depositary of the present Convention.

2. As depositary of the present Convention, the Secretary-General of the United Nations shall inform all States of the following:

(a) signatures of the present Convention and the deposit of instruments of ratification, acceptance, approval or accession or notifications of denunciation, in accordance with articles 29 and 31;

(b) the date on which the present Convention will enter into force, in accordance with article 30;

(c) any acts, notifications or communications relating to the present Convention.

Article 33 Authentic texts

The Arabic, Chinese, English, French, Russian and Spanish texts of the present Convention are equally authentic.

IN WITNESS WHEREOF, the undersigned, being duly authorized thereto by their respective Governments, have signed this Convention opened for signature at United Nations Headquarters in New York on 17 January 2005.

Annex to the Convention

Understandings with respect to certain provisions of the Convention

The present annex is for the purpose of setting out understandings relating to the provisions concerned.

With respect to article 10

The term "immunity" in article 10 is to be understood in the context of the present Convention as a whole.

Article 10, paragraph 3, does not prejudge the question of "piercing the corporate veil", questions relating to a situation where a State entity has deliberately misrepresented its financial position or subsequently reduced its assets to avoid satisfying a claim, or other related issues.

With respect to article 11

The reference in article 11, paragraph 2 (d), to the "security interests" of the employer State is intended primarily to address matters of national security and the security of diplomatic missions and consular posts.

Under article 41 of the 1961 Vienna Convention on Diplomatic Relations and article 55 of the 1963 Vienna Convention on Consular Relations, all persons referred to in

Part VI Final clauses

Article 25 Annex
The annex to the present Convention forms an integral part of the Convention.

Article 26 Other international agreements
Nothing in the present Convention shall affect the rights and obligations of States Parties under existing international agreements which relate to matters dealt with in the present Convention as between the parties to those agreements.

Article 27 Settlement of disputes
1. States Parties shall endeavour to settle disputes concerning the interpretation or application of the present Convention through negotiation.

2. Any dispute between two or more States Parties concerning the interpretation or application of the present Convention which cannot be settled through negotiation within six months shall, at the request of any of those States Parties, be submitted to arbitration. If, six months after the date of the request for arbitration, those States Parties are unable to agree on the organization of the arbitration, any of those States Parties may refer the dispute to the International Court of Justice by request in accordance with the Statute of the Court.

3. Each State Party may, at the time of signature, ratification, acceptance or approval of, or accession to, the present Convention, declare that it does not consider itself bound by paragraph 2. The other States Parties shall not be bound by paragraph 2 with respect to any State Party which has made such a declaration.

4. Any State Party that has made a declaration in accordance with paragraph 3 may at any time withdraw that declaration by notification to the Secretary-General of the United Nations.

Article 28 Signature
The present Convention shall be open for signature by all States until 17 January 2007, at United Nations Headquarters, New York.

Article 29 Ratification, acceptance, approval or accession
1. The present Convention shall be subject to ratification, acceptance or approval.

2. The present Convention shall remain open for accession by any State.

3. The instruments of ratification, acceptance, approval or accession shall be deposited with the Secretary-General of the United Nations.

Article 30 Entry into force
1. The present Convention shall enter into force on the thirtieth day following the date of deposit of the thirtieth instrument of ratification, acceptance, approval or accession with the Secretary-General of the United Nations.

2. For each State ratifying, accepting, approving or acceding to the present Convention after the deposit of the thirtieth instrument of ratification, acceptance, approval or accession, the Convention shall enter into force on the thirtieth day after the deposit by such State of its instrument of ratification, acceptance, approval or accession.

1. Service of process by writ or other document instituting a proceeding against a State shall be effected:

(a) in accordance with any applicable international convention binding on the State of the forum and the State concerned; or

(b) in accordance with any special arrangement for service between the claimant and the State concerned, if not precluded by the law of the State of the forum; or

(c) in the absence of such a convention or special arrangement:

(i) by transmission through diplomatic channels to the Ministry of Foreign Affairs of the State concerned; or

(ii) by any other means accepted by the State concerned, if not precluded by the law of the State of the forum.

2. Service of process referred to in paragraph 1 (c) (i) is deemed to have been effected by receipt of the documents by the Ministry of Foreign Affairs.

3. These documents shall be accompanied, if necessary, by a translation into the official language, or one of the official languages, of the State concerned.

4. Any State that enters an appearance on the merits in a proceeding instituted against it may not thereafter assert that service of process did not comply with the provisions of paragraphs 1 and 3.

Article 23 Default judgment

1. A default judgment shall not be rendered against a State unless the court has found that:

(a) the requirements laid down in article 22, paragraphs 1 and 3, have been complied with;

(b) a period of not less than four months has expired from the date on which the service of the writ or other document instituting a proceeding has been effected or deemed to have been effected in accordance with article 22, paragraphs 1 and 2; and

(c) the present Convention does not preclude it from exercising jurisdiction.

2. A copy of any default judgment rendered against a State, accompanied if necessary by a translation into the official language or one of the official languages of the State concerned, shall be transmitted to it through one of the means specified in article 22, paragraph 1, and in accordance with the provisions of that paragraph.

3. The time-limit for applying to have a default judgment set aside shall not be less than four months and shall begin to run from the date on which the copy of the judgment is received or is deemed to have been received by the State concerned.

Article 24 Privileges and immunities during court proceedings

1. Any failure or refusal by a State to comply with an order of a court of another State enjoining it to perform or refrain from performing a specific act or to produce any document or disclose any other information for the purposes of a proceeding shall entail no consequences other than those which may result from such conduct in relation to the merits of the case. In particular, no fine or penalty shall be imposed on the State by reason of such failure or refusal.

2. A State shall not be required to provide any security, bond or deposit, however described, to guarantee the payment of judicial costs or expenses in any proceeding to which it is a respondent party before a court of another State.

(iii) by a declaration before the court or by a written communication after a dispute between the parties has arisen; or

(b) the State has allocated or earmarked property for the satisfaction of the claim which is the object of that proceeding.

Article 19 State immunity from post-judgment measures of constraint

No post-judgment measures of constraint, such as attachment, arrest or execution, against property of a State may be taken in connection with a proceeding before a court of another State unless and except to the extent that:

(a) the State has expressly consented to the taking of such measures as indicated:

(i) by international agreement;

(ii) by an arbitration agreement or in a written contract; or

(iii) by a declaration before the court or by a written communication after a dispute between the parties has arisen; or

(b) the State has allocated or earmarked property for the satisfaction of the claim which is the object of that proceeding; or

(c) it has been established that the property is specifically in use or intended for use by the State for other than government non-commercial purposes and is in the territory of the State of the forum, provided that post-judgment measures of constraint may only be taken against property that has a connection with the entity against which the proceeding was directed.

Article 20 Effect of consent to jurisdiction to measures of constraint

Where consent to the measures of constraint is required under articles 18 and 19, consent to the exercise of jurisdiction under article 7 shall not imply consent to the taking of measures of constraint.

Article 21 Specific categories of property

1. The following categories, in particular, of property of a State shall not be considered as property specifically in use or intended for use by the State for other than government non-commercial purposes under article 19, subparagraph (c):

(a) property, including any bank account, which is used or intended for use in the performance of the functions of the diplomatic mission of the State or its consular posts, special missions, missions to international organizations or delegations to organs of international organizations or to international conferences;

(b) property of a military character or used or intended for use in the performance of military functions;

(c) property of the central bank or other monetary authority of the State;

(d) property forming part of the cultural heritage of the State or part of its archives and not placed or intended to be placed on sale;

(e) property forming part of an exhibition of objects of scientific, cultural or historical interest and not placed or intended to be placed on sale.

2. Paragraph 1 is without prejudice to article 18 and article 19, subparagraphs (a) and (b).

Part V Miscellaneous provisions

Article 22 Service of process

by an agreement in writing or if the instrument establishing or regulating the body in question contains provisions to that effect.

Article 16 Ships owned or operated by a State

1. Unless otherwise agreed between the States concerned, a State which owns or operates a ship cannot invoke immunity from jurisdiction before a court of another State which is otherwise competent in a proceeding which relates to the operation of that ship if, at the time the cause of action arose, the ship was used for other than government non-commercial purposes.

2. Paragraph 1 does not apply to warships, or naval auxiliaries, nor does it apply to other vessels owned or operated by a State and used, for the time being, only on government non-commercial service.

3. Unless otherwise agreed between the States concerned, a State cannot invoke immunity from jurisdiction before a court of another State which is otherwise competent in a proceeding which relates to the carriage of cargo on board a ship owned or operated by that State if, at the time the cause of action arose, the ship was used for other than government non-commercial purposes.

4. Paragraph 3 does not apply to any cargo carried on board the ships referred to in paragraph 2, nor does it apply to any cargo owned by a State and used or intended for use exclusively for government non-commercial purposes.

5. States may plead all measures of defence, prescription and limitation of liability which are available to private ships and cargoes and their owners.

6. If in a proceeding there arises a question relating to the government and non-commercial character of a ship owned or operated by a State or cargo owned by a State, a certificate signed by a diplomatic representative or other competent authority of that State and communicated to the court shall serve as evidence of the character of that ship or cargo.

Article 17 Effect of an arbitration agreement

If a State enters into an agreement in writing with a foreign natural or juridical person to submit to arbitration differences relating to a commercial transaction, that State cannot invoke immunity from jurisdiction before a court of another State which is otherwise competent in a proceeding which relates to:

(a) the validity, interpretation or application of the arbitration agreement;

(b) the arbitration procedure; or

(c) the confirmation or the setting aside of the award, unless the arbitration agreement otherwise provides.

Part IV State immunity from measures of constraint in connection with proceedings before a court

Article 18 State immunity from pre-judgment measures of constraint

No pre-judgment measures of constraint, such as attachment or arrest, against property of a State may be taken in connection with a proceeding before a court of another State unless and except to the extent that:

(a) the State has expressly consented to the taking of such measures as indicated:

(i) by international agreement;

(ii) by an arbitration agreement or in a written contract; or

Article 12 Personal injuries and damage to property

Unless otherwise agreed between the States concerned, a State cannot invoke immunity from jurisdiction before a court of another State which is otherwise competent in a proceeding which relates to pecuniary compensation for death or injury to the person, or damage to or loss of tangible property, caused by an act or omission which is alleged to be attributable to the State, if the act or omission occurred in whole or in part in the territory of that other State and if the author of the act or omission was present in that territory at the time of the act or omission.

Article 13 Ownership, possession and use of property

Unless otherwise agreed between the States concerned, a State cannot invoke immunity from jurisdiction before a court of another State which is otherwise competent in a proceeding which relates to the determination of:

(a) any right or interest of the State in, or its possession or use of, or any obligation of the State arising out of its interest in, or its possession or use of, immovable property situated in the State of the forum;

(b) any right or interest of the State in movable or immovable property arising by way of succession, gift or *bona vacantia*; or

(c) any right or interest of the State in the administration of property, such as trust property, the estate of a bankrupt or the property of a company in the event of its winding up.

Article 14 Intellectual and industrial property

Unless otherwise agreed between the States concerned, a State cannot invoke immunity from jurisdiction before a court of another State which is otherwise competent in a proceeding which relates to:

(a) the determination of any right of the State in a patent, industrial design, trade name or business name, trademark, copyright or any other form of intellectual or industrial property which enjoys a measure of legal protection, even if provisional, in the State of the forum; or

(b) an alleged infringement by the State, in the territory of the State of the forum, of a right of the nature mentioned in subparagraph (a) which belongs to a third person and is protected in the State of the forum.

Article 15 Participation in companies or other collective bodies

1. A State cannot invoke immunity from jurisdiction before a court of another State which is otherwise competent in a proceeding which relates to its participation in a company or other collective body, whether incorporated or unincorporated, being a proceeding concerning the relationship between the State and the body or the other participants therein, provided that the body:

(a) has participants other than States or international organizations; and

(b) is incorporated or constituted under the law of the State of the forum or has its seat or principal place of business in that State.

2. A State can, however, invoke immunity from jurisdiction in such a proceeding if the States concerned have so agreed or if the parties to the dispute have so provided

Part III   Proceedings in which State immunity cannot be invoked

Article 10   Commercial transactions

1. If a State engages in a commercial transaction with a foreign natural or juridical person and, by virtue of the applicable rules of private international law, differences relating to the commercial transaction fall within the jurisdiction of a court of another State, the State cannot invoke immunity from that jurisdiction in a proceeding arising out of that commercial transaction.

2. Paragraph 1 does not apply:

(a) in the case of a commercial transaction between States; or

(b) if the parties to the commercial transaction have expressly agreed otherwise.

3. Where a State enterprise or other entity established by a State which has an independent legal personality and is capable of:

(a) suing or being sued; and

(b) acquiring, owning or possessing and disposing of property, including property which that State has authorized it to operate or manage, is involved in a proceeding which relates to a commercial transaction in which that entity is engaged, the immunity from jurisdiction enjoyed by that State shall not be affected.

Article 11   Contracts of employment

1. Unless otherwise agreed between the States concerned, a State cannot invoke immunity from jurisdiction before a court of another State which is otherwise competent in a proceeding which relates to a contract of employment between the State and an individual for work performed or to be performed, in whole or in part, in the territory of that other State.

2. Paragraph 1 does not apply if:

(a) the employee has been recruited to perform particular functions in the exercise of governmental authority;

(b) the employee is:

(i) a diplomatic agent, as defined in the Vienna Convention on Diplomatic Relations of 1961;

(ii) a consular officer, as defined in the Vienna Convention on Consular Relations of 1963;

(iii) a member of the diplomatic staff of a permanent mission to an international organization or of a special mission, or is recruited to represent a State at an international conference; or

(iv) any other person enjoying diplomatic immunity;

(c) the subject-matter of the proceeding is the recruitment, renewal of employment or reinstatement of an individual;

(d) the subject-matter of the proceeding is the dismissal or termination of employment of an individual and, as determined by the head of State, the head of Government or the Minister for Foreign Affairs of the employer State, such a proceeding would interfere with the security interests of that State;

(e) the employee is a national of the employer State at the time when the proceeding is instituted, unless this person has the permanent residence in the State of the forum; or

(f) the employer State and the employee have otherwise agreed in writing, subject to any considerations of public policy conferring on the courts of the State of the forum exclusive jurisdiction by reason of the subject-matter of the proceeding.

2. A proceeding before a court of a State shall be considered to have been instituted against another State if that other State:

(a) is named as a party to that proceeding; or

(b) is not named as a party to the proceeding but the proceeding in effect seeks to affect the property, rights, interests or activities of that other State.

Article 7 Express consent to exercise of jurisdiction

1. A State cannot invoke immunity from jurisdiction in a proceeding before a court of another State with regard to a matter or case if it has expressly consented to the exercise of jurisdiction by the court with regard to the matter or case:

(a) by international agreement;

(b) in a written contract; or

(c) by a declaration before the court or by a written communication in a specific proceeding.

2. Agreement by a State for the application of the law of another State shall not be interpreted as consent to the exercise of jurisdiction by the courts of that other State.

Article 8 Effect of participation in a proceeding before a court

1. A State cannot invoke immunity from jurisdiction in a proceeding before a court of another State if it has:

(a) itself instituted the proceeding; or

(b) intervened in the proceeding or taken any other step relating to the merits. However, if the State satisfies the court that it could not have acquired knowledge of facts on which a claim to immunity can be based until after it took such a step, it can claim immunity based on those facts, provided it does so at the earliest possible moment.

2. A State shall not be considered to have consented to the exercise of jurisdiction by a court of another State if it intervenes in a proceeding or takes any other step for the sole purpose of:

(a) invoking immunity; or

(b) asserting a right or interest in property at issue in the proceeding.

3. The appearance of a representative of a State before a court of another State as a witness shall not be interpreted as consent by the former State to the exercise of jurisdiction by the court.

4. Failure on the part of a State to enter an appearance in a proceeding before a court of another State shall not be interpreted as consent by the former State to the exercise of jurisdiction by the court.

Article 9 Counterclaims

1. A State instituting a proceeding before a court of another State cannot invoke immunity from the jurisdiction of the court in respect of any counterclaim arising out of the same legal relationship or facts as the principal claim.

2. A State intervening to present a claim in a proceeding before a court of another State cannot invoke immunity from the jurisdiction of the court in respect of any counterclaim arising out of the same legal relationship or facts as the claim presented by the State.

3. A State making a counterclaim in a proceeding instituted against it before a court of another State cannot invoke immunity from the jurisdiction of the court in respect of the principal claim.

(i) any commercial contract or transaction for the sale of goods or supply of services;

(ii) any contract for a loan or other transaction of a financial nature, including any obligation of guarantee or of indemnity in respect of any such loan or transaction;

(iii) any other contract or transaction of a commercial, industrial, trading or professional nature, but not including a contract of employment of persons.

2. In determining whether a contract or transaction is a "commercial transaction" under paragraph 1 (c), reference should be made primarily to the nature of the contract or transaction, but its purpose should also be taken into account if the parties to the contract or transaction have so agreed, or if, in the practice of the State of the forum, that purpose is relevant to determining the non-commercial character of the contract or transaction.

3. The provisions of paragraphs 1 and 2 regarding the use of terms in the present Convention are without prejudice to the use of those terms or to the meanings which may be given to them in other international instruments or in the internal law of any State.

Article 3 Privileges and immunities not affected by the present Convention

1. The present Convention is without prejudice to the privileges and immunities enjoyed by a State under international law in relation to the exercise of the functions of:

(a) its diplomatic missions, consular posts, special missions, missions to international organizations or delegations to organs of international organizations or to international conferences; and

(b) persons connected with them.

2. The present Convention is without prejudice to privileges and immunities accorded under international law to heads of State ratione personae.

3. The present Convention is without prejudice to the immunities enjoyed by a State under international law with respect to aircraft or space objects owned or operated by a State.

Article 4 Non-retroactivity of the present Convention

Without prejudice to the application of any rules set forth in the present Convention to which jurisdictional immunities of States and their property are subject under international law independently of the present Convention, the present Convention shall not apply to any question of jurisdictional immunities of States or their property arising in a proceeding instituted against a State before a court of another State prior to the entry into force of the present Convention for the States concerned.

Part II General principles

Article 5 State immunity

A State enjoys immunity, in respect of itself and its property, from the jurisdiction of the courts of another State subject to the provisions of the present Convention.

Article 6 Modalities for giving effect to State immunity

1. A State shall give effect to State immunity under article 5 by refraining from exercising jurisdiction in a proceeding before its courts against another State and to that end shall ensure that its courts determine on their own initiative that the immunity of that other State under article 5 is respected.

United Nations Convention on Jurisdictional Immunities of States and Their Property, 2004

The States Parties to the present Convention,

Considering that the jurisdictional immunities of States and their property are generally accepted as a principle of customary international law,

Having in mind the principles of international law embodied in the Charter of the United Nations,

Believing that an international convention on the jurisdictional immunities of States and their property would enhance the rule of law and legal certainty, particularly in dealings of States with natural or juridical persons, and would contribute to the codification and development of international law and the harmonization of practice in this area,

Taking into account developments in State practice with regard to the jurisdictional immunities of States and their property,

Affirming that the rules of customary international law continue to govern matters not regulated by the provisions of the present Convention,

Have agreed as follows:

Part I Introduction

Article 1 Scope of the present Convention

The present Convention applies to the immunity of a State and its property from the jurisdiction of the courts of another State.

Article 2 Use of terms

1. For the purposes of the present Convention:

(a) "court" means any organ of a State, however named, entitled to exercise judicial functions;

(b) "State" means:

(i) the State and its various organs of government;

(ii) constituent units of a federal State or political subdivisions of the State, which are entitled to perform acts in the exercise of sovereign authority, and are acting in that capacity;

(iii) agencies or instrumentalities of the State or other entities, to the extent that they are entitled to perform and are actually performing acts in the exercise of sovereign authority of the State;

(iv) representatives of the State acting in that capacity;

(c) "commercial transaction" means:

a) any signature of the present Protocol;

b) any deposit of an instrument of ratification, acceptance or accession;

c) any date of entry into force of the present Protocol in accordance with Articles 10 and 11 thereof;

d) any notification received in pursuance of the provisions of Part IV and any withdrawal of any such notification;

e) any notification received in pursuance of the provisions of Article 13 and the date on which such denunciation takes effect.

In witness whereof the undersigned, being duly authorised thereto, have signed the present Protocol.

Done at Basle, this 16th day of May 1972, in English and French, both texts being equally authoritative, in a single copy which shall remain deposited in the archives of the Council of Europe. The Secretary General of the Council of Europe shall transmit certified copies to each of the signatory and acceding States.

Part IV

Article 9

1. Any State may, by notification addressed to the Secretary General of the Council of Europe at the moment of its signature of the present Protocol, or of the deposit of its instrument of ratification, acceptance or accession thereto, declare that it will only be bound by Parts II to V of the present Protocol.

2. Such a notification may be withdrawn at any time.

Part V

Article 10

1. The present Protocol shall be open to signature by the member States of the Council of Europe which have signed the Convention. It shall be subject to ratification or acceptance. Instruments of ratification or acceptance shall be deposited with the Secretary General of the Council of Europe.

2. The present Protocol shall enter into force three months after the date of the deposit of the fifth instrument of ratification or acceptance.

3. In respect of a signatory State ratifying or accepting subsequently, the Protocol shall enter into force three months after the date of the deposit of its instrument of ratification or acceptance.

4. A member State of the Council of Europe may not ratify or accept the present Protocol without having ratified or accepted the Convention.

Article 11

1. A State which has acceded to the Convention may accede to the present Protocol after the Protocol has entered into force.

2. Such accession shall be effected by depositing with the Secretary General of the Council of Europe an instrument of accession which shall take effect three months after the date of its deposit.

Article 12

No reservation is permitted to the present Protocol.

Article 13

1. Any Contracting State may, in so far as it is concerned, denounce the present Protocol by means of a notification addressed to the Secretary General of the Council of Europe.

2. Such denunciation shall take effect six months after the date of receipt by the Secretary General of such notification. The Protocol shall, however, continue to apply to proceedings introduced in conformity with the provisions of the protocol before the date on which such denunciation takes effect.

3. Denunciation of the Convention shall automatically entail denunciation of the present Protocol.

Article 14

1. The Secretary General of the Council of Europe shall notify the member States of the Council and any State which has acceded to the Convention of:

3. The President of the European Tribunal shall be the President of the European Court of Human Rights.

Article 5

1. Where proceedings are instituted before the European Tribunal in accordance with the provisions of Part I of the present Protocol, the European Tribunal shall consist of a Chamber composed of seven members. There shall sit as ex officio members of the Chamber the member of the European Tribunal who is a national of the State against which the judgment has been given and the member of the European Tribunal who is a national of the State of the forum, or, should there be no such member in one or the other case, a person designated by the government of the State concerned to sit in the capacity of a member of the Chamber. The names of the other five members shall be chosen by lot by the President of the European Tribunal in the presence of the Registrar.

2. Where proceedings are instituted before the European Tribunal in accordance with the provisions of Part II of the present Protocol, the Chamber shall be constituted in the manner provided for in the preceding paragraph. However, there shall sit as ex officio members of the Chamber the members of the European Tribunal who are nationals of the States parties to the dispute or, should there be no such member, a person designated by the government of the State concerned to sit in the capacity of a member of the Chamber.

3. Where a case pending before a Chamber raises a serious question affecting the interpretation of the Convention or of the present Protocol, the Chamber may, at any time, relinquish jurisdiction in favour of the European Tribunal meeting in plenary session. The relinquishment of jurisdiction shall be obligatory where the resolution of such question might have a result inconsistent with a judgment previously delivered by a Chamber or by the European Tribunal meeting in plenary session. The relinquishment of jurisdiction shall be final. Reasons need not be given for the decision to relinquish jurisdiction.

Article 6

1. The European Tribunal shall decide any disputes as to whether the Tribunal has jurisdiction.

2. The hearings of the European Tribunal shall be public unless the Tribunal in exceptional circumstances decides otherwise.

3. The judgments of the European Tribunal, taken by a majority of the members present, are to be delivered in public session. Reasons shall be given for the judgment of the European Tribunal. If the judgment does not represent in whole or in part the unanimous opinion of the European Tribunal, any member shall be entitled to deliver a separate opinion.

4. The judgments of the European Tribunal shall be final and binding upon the parties.

Article 7

1. The European Tribunal shall draw up its own rules and fix its own procedure.

2. The Registry of the European Tribunal shall be provided by the Registrar of the European Court of Human Rights.

Article 8

1. The operating costs of the European Tribunal shall be borne by the Council of Europe. States non-members of the Council of Europe having acceded to the present Protocol shall contribute thereto in a manner to be decided by the Committee of Ministers after agreement with these States.

2. The members of the European Tribunal shall receive for each day of duty a compensation to be determined by the Committee of Ministers.

2. If the State intends to institute proceedings before its court in accordance with the provisions of paragraph 1 or Article 21 of the Convention, it must give notice of its intention to do so to the party in whose favour the judgment has been given; the State may thereafter institute such proceedings only if the party has not, within three months of receiving notice, instituted proceedings before the European Tribunal. Once this period has elapsed, the party in whose favour the judgment has been given may no longer institute proceedings before the European Tribunal.

3. Save in so far as may be necessary for the application of Articles 20 and 25 of the Convention, the European Tribunal may not review the merits of the judgment.

Part II

Article 2

1. Any dispute which might arise between two or more States parties to the present Protocol concerning the interpretation or application of the Convention shall be submitted, on the application of one of the parties to the dispute or by special agreement, to the European Tribunal constituted in conformity with the provisions of Part III of the present Protocol. The States parties to the present Protocol undertake not to submit such a dispute to a different mode of settlement.

2. If the dispute concerns a question arising in proceedings instituted before a court of one State Party to the Convention against another State Party to the Convention, or a question arising in proceedings instituted before a court of a State Party to the Convention in accordance with Article 21 of the Convention, it may not be referred to the European Tribunal until the court has given a final decision in such proceedings.

3. Proceedings may not be instituted before the European Tribunal which relate to a dispute concerning a judgment which it has already determined or is required to determine by virtue of Part I of this Protocol.

Article 3

Nothing in the present Protocol shall be interpreted as preventing the European Tribunal from determining any dispute which might arise between two or more States parties to the Convention concerning the interpretation or application thereof and which might be submitted to it by special agreement, even if these States, or any of them, are not parties to the present Protocol.

Part III

Article 4

1. There shall be established a European Tribunal in matters of State Immunity to determine cases brought before it in conformity with the provisions of Parts I and II of the present Protocol.

2. The European Tribunal shall consist of the members of the European Court of Human Rights and, in respect of each non-member State of the Council of Europe which has acceded to the present Protocol, a person possessing the qualifications required of members of that Court designated, with the agreement of the Committee of Ministers of the Council of Europe, by the government of that State for a period of nine years.

the defendant, or the seizure by the plaintiff of property situated there, unless:

i) the action is brought to assert proprietary or possessory rights in that property, or arises from another issue relating to such property;

ii) or the property constitutes the security for a debt which is the subject-matter of the action;

b) the nationality of the plaintiff;

c) the domicile, habitual residence or ordinary residence of the plaintiff within the territory of the State of the forum unless the assumption of jurisdiction on such a ground is permitted by way of an exception made on account of the particular subject-matter of a class of contracts;

d) the fact that the defendant carried on business within the territory of the State of the forum, unless the action arises from that business;

e) a unilateral specification of the forum by the plaintiff, particularly in an invoice.

2. A legal person shall be considered to have its domicile or habitual residence where it has its seat, registered office or principal place of business.

ADDITIONAL PROTOCOL TO THE EUROPEAN CONVENTION ON STATE IMMUNITY

Basle, 16. V. 1972

The member States of the Council of Europe, signatory to the present Protocol,

Having taken note of the European Convention on State Immunity—hereinafter referred to as "the Convention" —and in particular Articles 21 and 34 thereof;

Desiring to develop the work of harmonisation in the field covered by the Convention by the addition of provisions concerning a European procedure for the settlement of disputes,

Have agreed as follows:

Part I

Article 1

1. Where a judgment has been given against a State Party to the Convention and that State does not give effect thereto, the party which seeks to invoke the judgment shall be entitled to have determined the question whether effect should be given to the judgment in conformity with Article 20 or Article 25 of the Convention, by instituting proceedings before either:

a) the competent court of that State in application of Article 21 of the Convention; or

b) the European Tribunal constituted in conformity with the provisions of Part III of the present Protocol, provided that that State is a Party to the present Protocol and has not made the declaration referred to in Part IV thereof.

The choice between these two possibilites shall be final.

Council of Europe, extend this Convention to any other territory or territories specified in the declaration and for whose international relations it is responsible or on whose behalf it is authorised to give undertakings.

3. Any declaration made in pursuance of the preceding paragraph may, in respect of any territory mentioned in such declaration, be withdrawn according to the procedure laid down in Article 40 of this Convention.

Article 39

No reservation is permitted to the present Convention.

Article 40

1. Any Contracting State may, in so far as it is concerned, denounce this Convention by means of notification addressed to the Secretary General of the Council of Europe.

2. Such denunciation shall take effect six months after the date of receipt by the Secretary General of such notification. This Convention shall, however, continue to apply to proceedings introduced before the date on which the denunciation takes effect, and to judgments given in such proceedings.

Article 41

1. The Secretary General of the Council of Europe shall notify the member States of the Council of Europe and any State which has acceded to this Convention of:

a) any signature;

b) any deposit of an instrument of ratification, acceptance or accession;

c) any date of entry into force of this Convention in accordance with Articles 36 and 37 thereof;

d) any notification received in pursuance of the provisions of paragraph 2 of Article 19;

e) any communication received in pursuance of the provisions of paragraph 4 of Article 21;

f) any notification received in pursuance of the provisions of paragraph 1 of Article 24;

g) the withdrawal of any notification made in pursuance of the provisions of paragraph 4 of Article 24;

h) any notification received in pursuance of the provisions of paragraph 2 of Article 28;

i) any notification received in pursuance of the provisions of paragraph 3 or Article 37;

j) any declaration received in pursuance of the provisions of Article 38;

k) any notification received in pursuance of the provisions of Article 40 and the date on which denunciation takes effect.

2. In witness whereof the undersigned, being duly authorised thereto, have signed this Convention.

Done at Basle, this 16th day of May 1972, in English and French, both texts being equally authoritative, in a single copy which shall remain deposited in the archives of the Council of Europe. The Secretary General of the Council of Europe shall transmit certified copies to each of the signatory and acceding States.

ANNEX

1. The grounds of jurisdiction referred to in paragraph 3, sub-paragraph a, of Article 20, paragraph 2 of Article 24 and paragraph 3, sub-paragraph b, of Article 25 are the following:

a) the presence in the territory of the State of the forum of property belonging to

2. However, proceedings may not be instituted before the International Court of Justice which relate to:

a) a dispute concerning a question arising in proceedings instituted against a Contracting State before a court of another Contracting State, before the court has given a judgment which fulfils the condition provided for in paragraph 1. b of Article 20;

b) a dispute concerning a question arising in proceedings instituted before a court of a Contracting State in accordance with paragraph 1 of Article 21, before the court has rendered a final decision in such proceedings.

Article 35

1. The present Convention shall apply only to proceedings introduced after its entry into force.

2. When a State has become Party to this Convention after it has entered into force, the Convention shall apply only to proceedings introduced after it has entered into force with respect to that State.

3. Nothing in this Convention shall apply to proceedings arising out of, or judgments based on, acts, omissions or facts prior to the date on which the present Convention is opened for signature.

Chapter VI Final provisions

Article 36

1. The present Convention shall be open to signature by the member States of the Council of Europe. It shall be subject to ratification or acceptance. Instruments of ratification or acceptance shall be deposited with the Secretary General of the Council of Europe.

2. The Convention shall enter into force three months after the date of the deposit of the third instrument of ratification or acceptance.

3. In respect of a signatory State ratifying or accepting subsequently, the Convention shall enter into force three months after the date of the deposit of its instrument of ratification or acceptance.

Article 37

1. After the entry into force of the present Convention, the Committee of Ministers of the Council of Europe may, by a decision taken by a unanimous vote of the members casting a vote, invite any non-member State to accede thereto.

2. Such accession shall be effected by depositing with the Secretary General of the Council of Europe an instrument of accession which shall take effect three months after the date of its deposit.

3. However, if a State having already acceded to the Convention notifies the Secretary General of the Council of Europe of its objection to the accession of another non-member State, before the entry into force of this accession, the Convention shall not apply to the relations between these two States.

Article 38

1. Any State may, at the time of signature or when depositing its instrument of ratification, acceptance or accession, specify the territory or territories to which the present Convention shall apply.

2. Any State may, when depositing its instrument of ratification, acceptance or accession or at any later date, by declaration addressed to the Secretary General of the

3. Proceedings may in any event be instituted against any such entity before those courts if, in corresponding circumstances, the courts would have had jurisdiction if the proceedings had been instituted against a Contracting State.

Article 28

1. Without prejudice to the provisions of Article 27, the constituent States of a Federal State do not enjoy immunity.

2. However, a Federal State Party to the present Convention, may, by notification addressed to the Secretary General of the Council of Europe, declare that its constituent States may invoke the provisions of the Convention applicable to Contracting States, and have the same obligations.

3. Where a Federal State has made a declaration in accordance with paragraph 2, service of documents on a constituent State of a Federation shall be made on the Ministry of Foreign Affairs of the Federal State, in conformity with Article 16.

4. The Federal State alone is competent to make the declarations, notifications and communications provided for in the present Convention, and the Federal State alone may be party to proceedings pursuant to Article 34.

Article 29

The present Convention shall not apply to proceedings concerning:

a) social security;

b) damage or injury in nuclear matters;

c) customs duties, taxes or penalties.

Article 30

The present Convention shall not apply to proceedings in respect of claims relating to the operation of seagoing vessels owned or operated by a Contracting State or to the carriage of cargoes and of passengers by such vessels or to the carriage of cargoes owned by a Contracting State and carried on board merchant vessels.

Article 31

Nothing in this Convention shall affect any immunities or privileges enjoyed by a Contracting State in respect of anything done or omitted to be done by, or in relation to, its armed forces when on the territory of another Contracting State.

Article 32

Nothing in the present Convention shall affect privileges and immunities relating to the exercise of the functions of diplomatic missions and consular posts and of persons connected with them.

Article 33

Nothing in the present Convention shall affect existing or future international agreements in special fields which relate to matters dealt with in the present Convention.

Article 34

1. Any dispute which might arise between two or more Contracting States concerning the interpretation or application of the present Convention shall be submitted to the International Court of Justice on the application of one of the parties to the dispute or by special agreement unless the parties agree on a different method of peaceful settlement of the dispute.

Article 25

1. Any Contracting State which has made a declaration under Article 24 shall, in cases not falling within Articles 1 to 13, give effect to a judgment given by a court of another Contracting State which has made a like declaration:

a) if the conditions prescribed in paragraph 1. b of Article 20 have been fulfilled; and

b) if the court is considered to have jurisdiction in accordance with the following paragraphs.

2. However, the Contracting State is not obliged to give effect to such a judgment:

a) if there is a ground for refusal as provided for in paragraph 2 of Article 20; or

b) if the provisions of paragraph 2 of Article 24 have not been observed.

3. Subject to the provisions of paragraph 4, a court of a Contracting State shall be considered to have jurisdiction for the purpose of paragraph 1. b:

a) if its jurisdiction is recognised in accordance with the provisions of an agreement to which the State of the forum and the other Contracting State are Parties;

b) where there is no agreement between the two States concerning the recognition and enforcement of judgments in civil matters, if the courts of the State of the forum would have been entitled to assume jurisdiction had they applied, *mutatis mutandis*, the rules of jurisdiction (other than those mentioned in the annex to the present Convention) which operate in the State against which the judgment was given. This provision does not apply to questions arising out of contracts.

4. The Contracting States having made the declaration provided for in Article 24 may, by means of a supplementary agreement to this Convention, determine the circumstances in which their courts shall be considered to have jurisdiction for the purposes of paragraph 1. b of this article.

5. If the Contracting State does not give effect to the judgment, the procedure provided for in Article 21 may be used.

Article 26

Notwithstanding the provisions of Article 23, a judgment rendered against a Contracting State in proceedings relating to an industrial or commercial activity, in which the State is engaged in the same manner as a private person, may be enforced in the State of the forum against property of the State against which judgment has been given, used exclusively in connection with such an activity, if:

a) both the State of the forum and the State against which the judgment has been given have made declarations under Article 24;

b) the proceedings which resulted in the judgment fell within Articles 1 to 13 or were instituted in accordance with paragraphs 1 and 2 of Article 24; and

c) the judgment satisfies the requirements laid down in paragraph 1. b of Article 20.

Chapter V General provisions

Article 27

1. For the purposes of the present Convention, the expression "Contracting State" shall not include any legal entity of a Contracting State which is distinct therefrom and is capable of suing or being sued, even if that entity has been entrusted with public functions.

2. Proceedings may be instituted against any entity referred to in paragraph 1 before the courts of another Contracting State in the same manner as against a private person; however, the courts may not entertain proceedings in respect of acts performed by the entity in the exercise of sovereign authority (*acta jure imperii*).

3. Where proceedings are instituted before a court of a State in accordance with paragraph 1:

a) the parties shall be given an opportunity to be heard in the proceedings;

b) documents produced by the party seeking to invoke the judgment shall not be subject to legislation or any other like formality;

c) no security, bond or deposit, however described, shall be required of the party invoking the judgment by reason of his nationality, domicile or residence;

d) the party invoking the judgment shall be entitled to legal aid under conditions no less favourable than those applicable to nationals of the State who are domiciled and resident therein.

4. Each Contracting State shall, when depositing its instrument of ratification, acceptance or accession, designate the court or courts referred to in paragraph 1, and inform the Secretary General of the Council of Europe thereof.

Article 22

1. A Contracting State shall give effect to a settlement to which it is a party and which has been made before a court of another Contracting State in the course of the proceedings; the provisions of Article 20 do not apply to such a settlement.

2. If the State does not give effect to the settlement, the procedure provided for in Article 21 may be used.

Article 23

No measures of execution or preventive measures against the property of a Contracting-State may be taken in the territory of another Contracting State except where and to the extent that the State has expressly consented thereto in writing in any particular case.

Chapter IV   Optional provisions

Article 24

1. Notwithstanding the provisions of Article 15, any State may, when signing this Convention or depositing its instrument of ratification, acceptance or accession, or at any later date, by notification addressed to the Secretary General of the Council of Europe, declare that, in cases not falling within Articles 1 to 13, its courts shall be entitled to entertain proceedings against another Contracting State to the extent that its courts are entitled to entertain proceedings against States not party to the present Convention. Such a declaration shall be without prejudice to the immunity from jurisdiction which foreign States enjoy in respect of acts performed in the exercise of sovereign authority (*acta jure imperii*).

2. The courts of a State which has made the declaration provided for in paragraph 1 shall not however be entitled to entertain such proceedings against another Contracting State if their jurisdiction could have been based solely on one or more of the grounds mentioned in the annex to the present Convention, unless that other Contracting State has taken a step in the proceedings relating to the merits without first challenging the jurisdiction of the court.

3. The provisions of Chapter II apply to proceedings instituted against a Contracting State in accordance with the present article.

4. The declaration made under paragraph 1 may be withdrawn by notification addressed to the Secretary General of the Council of Europe. The withdrawal shall take effect three months after the date of its receipt, but this shall not affect proceedings instituted before the date on which the withdrawal becomes effective.

2. Nevertheless, a Contracting State is not obliged to give effect to such a judgment in any case:

a) where it would be manifestly contrary to public policy in that State to do so, or where, in the circumstances, either party had no adequate opportunity fairly to present his case;

b) where proceedings between the same parties, based on the same facts and having the same purpose:

i) are pending before a court of that State and were the first to be instituted;

ii) are pending before a court of another Contracting State, were the first to be instituted and may result in a judgment to which the State party to the proceedings must give effect under the terms of this Convention;

c) where the result of the judgment is inconsistent with the result of another judgment given between the same parties:

i) by a court of the Contracting State, if the proceedings before that court were the first to be instituted or if the other judgment has been given before the judgment satisfied the conditions specified in paragraph 1. b; or

ii) by a court of another Contracting State where the other judgment is the first to satisfy the requirements laid down in the present Convention;

d) where the provisions of Article 16 have not been observed and the State has not entered an appearance or has not appealed against a judgment by default.

3. In addition, in the cases provided for in Article 10, a Contracting State is not obliged to give effect to the judgment:

a) if the courts of the State of the forum would not have been entitled to assume jurisdiction had they applied, *mutatis mutandis*, the rules of jurisdiction (other than those mentioned in the annex to the present Convention) which operate in the State against which judgment is given; or

b) if the court, by applying a law other than that which would have been applied in accordance with the rules of private international law of that State, has reached a result different from that which would have been reached by applying the law determined by those rules.

However, a Contracting State may not rely upon the grounds of refusal specified in sub-paragraphs a and b above if it is bound by an agreement with the State of the forum on the recognition and enforcement of judgments and the judgment fulfils the requirement of that agreement as regards jurisdiction and, where appropriate, the law applied.

Article 21

1. Where a judgment has been given against a Contracting State and that State does not give effect thereto, the party which seeks to invoke the judgment shall be entitled to have determined by the competent court of that State the question whether effect should be given to the judgment in accordance with Article 20. Proceedings may also be brought before this court by the State against which judgment has been given, if its law so permits.

2. Save in so far as may be necessary for the application of Article 20, the competent court of the State in question may not review the merits of the judgment.

6. A Contracting State which appears in the proceedings is deemed to have waived any objection to the method of service.

7. If the Contracting State has not appeared, judgment by default may be given against it only if it is established that the document by which the proceedings were instituted has been transmitted in conformity with paragraph 2, and that the time-limits for entering an appearance provided for in paragraphs 4 and 5 have been observed.

Article 17

No security, bond or deposit, however described, which could not have been required in the State of the forum of a national of that State or a person domiciled or resident there, shall be required of a Contracting State to guarantee the payment of judicial costs or expenses. A State which is a claimant in the courts of another Contracting State shall pay any judicial costs or expenses for which it may become liable.

Article 18

A Contracting State party to proceedings before a court of another Contracting State may not be subjected to any measure of coercion, or any penalty, by reason of its failure or refusal to disclose any documents or other evidence. However the court may draw any conclusion it thinks fit from such failure or refusal.

Article 19

1. A court before which proceedings to which a Contracting State is a party are instituted shall, at the request of one of the parties or, if its national law so permits, of its own motion, decline to proceed with the case or shall stay the proceedings if other proceedings between the same parties, based on the same facts and having the same purpose:

a) are pending before a court of that Contracting State, and were the first to be instituted; or

b) are pending before a court of any other Contracting State, were the first to be instituted and may result in a judgment to which the State party to the proceedings must give effect by virtue of Article 20 or Article 25.

2. Any Contracting State whose law gives the courts a discretion to decline to proceed with a case or to stay the the proceedings in cases where proceedings between the same parties, based on the same facts and having the same purpose, are pending before a court of another Contracting State, may, by notification addressed to the Secretary General of the Council of Europe, declare that its courts shall not be bound by the provisions of paragraph 1.

Chapter III   Effect of Judgment

Article 20

1. A Contracting State shall give effect to a judgment given against it by a court of another Contracting State:

a) if, in accordance with the provisions of Articles 1 to 13, the State could not claim immunity from jurisdiction; and

b) if the judgment cannot or can no longer be set aside if obtained by default, or if it is not or is no longer subject to appeal or any other form of ordinary review or to annulment.

claim immunity from the jurisdiction of a court of another Contracting State on the territory or according to the law of which the arbitration has taken or will take place in respect of any proceedings relating to:
   a) the validity or interpretation of the arbitration agreement;
   b) the arbitration procedure;
   c) the setting aside of the award, unless the arbitration agreement otherwise provides.
   2. Paragraph 1 shall not apply to an arbitration agreement between States.

Article 13

Paragraph 1 of Article 1 shall not apply where a Contracting State asserts, in proceedings pending before a court of another Contracting State to which it is not a party, that it has a right or interest in property which is the subject-matter of the proceedings, and the circumstances are such that it would have been entitled to immunity if the proceedings had been brought against it.

Article 14

Nothing in this Convention shall be interpreted as preventing a court of a Contracting State from administering or supervising or arranging for the administration of property, such as trust property or the estate of a bankrupt, solely on account of the fact that another Contracting State has a right or interest in the property.

Article 15

A Contracting State shall be entitled to immunity from the jurisdiction of the courts of another Contracting State if the proceedings do not fall within Articles 1 to 14; the court shall decline to entertain such proceedings even if the State does not appear.

Chapter II   Procedural rules

Article 16

1. In proceedings against a Contracting State in a court of another Contracting State, the following rules shall apply.

2. The competent authorities of the State of the forum shall transmit
   —the original or a copy of the document by which the proceedings are instituted;
   —a copy of any judgment given by default against a State which was defendant in the proceedings,
through the diplomatic channel to the Ministry of Foreign Affairs of the defendant-State, for onward transmission, where appropriate, to the competent authority. These documents shall be accompanied, if necessary, by a translation into the official language, or one of the official languages, of the defendant State.

3. Service of the documents referred to in paragraph 2 is deemed to have been effected by their receipt by the Ministry of Foreign Affairs.

4. The time-limits within which the State must enter an appearance or appeal against any judgment given by default shall begin to run two months after the date on which the document by which the proceedings were instituted or the copy of the judgement is received by the Ministry of Foreign Affairs.

5. If it rests with the court to prescribe the time-limits for entering an appearance or for appealing against a judgment given by default, the court shall allow the State not less than two months after the date on which the document by which the proceedings are instituted or the copy of the judgment is received by the Ministry of Foreign Affairs.

business on the territory of the State of the forum, and the proceedings concern the relationship, in matters arising out of that participation, between the State on the one hand and the entity or any other participant on the other hand.

2. Paragraph 1 shall not apply if it is otherwise agreed in writing.

Article 7

1. A Contracting State cannot claim immunity from the jurisdiction of a court of another Contracting State if it has on the territory of the State of the forum an office, agency or other establishment through which it engages, in the same manner as a private person, in an industrial, commercial or financial activity, and the proceedings relate to that activity of the office, agency or establishment.

2. Paragraph 1 shall not apply if all the parties to the dispute are States, or if the parties have otherwise agreed in writing.

Article 8

A Contracting State cannot claim immunity from the jurisdiction of a court of another Contracting State if the proceedings relate:

a) to a patent, industrial design, trade-mark, service mark or other similar right which, in the State of the forum, has been applied for, registered or deposited or is otherwise protected, and in respect of which the State is the applicant or owner;

b) to an alleged infringement by it, in the territory of the State of the forum, of such a right belonging to a third person and protected in that State;

c) to an alleged infringement by it, in the territory of the State of the forum, of copyright belonging to a third person and protected in that State;

d) to the right to use a trade name in the State of the forum.

Article 9

A Contracting State cannot claim immunity from the jurisdiction of a court of another Contracting State if the proceedings relate to:

a) its rights or interests in, or its use or possession of, immovable property; or

b) its obligations arising out of its rights or interests in, or use or possession of, immovable property and the property is situated in the territory of the State of the forum.

Article 10

A Contracting State cannot claim immunity from the jurisdiction of a court of another Contracting State if the proceedings relate to a right in movable or immovable property arising by way of succession, gift or *bona vacantia*.

Article 11

A Contracting State cannot claim immunity from the jurisdiction of a court of another Contracting State in proceedings which relate to redress for injury to the person or damage to tangible property, if the facts which occasioned the injury or damage occurred in the territory of the State of the forum, and if the author of the injury or damage was present in that territory at the time when those facts occurred.

Article 12

1. Where a Contracting State has agreed in writing to submit to arbitration a dispute which has arisen or may arise out of a civil or commercial matter, that State may not

c) by an express consent given after a dispute between the parties has arisen.

Article 3

1. A Contracting State cannot claim immunity from the jurisdiction of a court of another Contracting State if, before claiming immunity, it takes any step in the proceedings relating to the merits. However, if the State satisfies the Court that it could not have acquired knowledge of facts on which a claim to immunity can be based until after it has taken such a step, it can claim immunity based on these facts if it does so at the earliest possible moment.

2. A Contracting State is not deemed to have waived immunity if it appears before a court of another Contracting State in order to assert immunity.

Article 4

1. Subject to the provisions of Article 5, a Contracting State cannot claim immunity from the jurisdiction of the courts of another Contracting State if the proceedings relate to an obligation of the State, which, by virtue of a contract, falls to be discharged in the territory of the State of the forum.

2. Paragraph 1 shall not apply:

a) in the case of a contract concluded between States;

b) if the parties to the contract have otherwise agreed in writing;

c) if the State is party to a contract concluded on its territory and the obligation of the State is governed by its administrative law.

Article 5

1. A Contracting State cannot claim immunity from the jurisdiction of a court of another Contracting State if the proceedings relate to a contract of employment between the State and an individual where the work has to be performed on the territory of the State of the forum.

2. Paragraph 1 shall not apply where:

a) the individual is a national of the employing State at the time when the proceedings are brought;

b) at the time when the contract was entered into the individual was neither a national of the State of the forum nor habitually resident in that State; or

c) the parties to the contract have otherwise agreed in writing, unless, in accordance with the law of the State of the forum, the courts of that State have exclusive jurisdiction by reason of the subject-matter.

3. Where the work is done for an office, agency or other establishment referred to in Article 7, paragraphs 2. a and b of the present article apply only if, at the time the contract was entered into, the individual had his habitual residence in the Contracting State which employs him.

Article 6

1. A Contracting State cannot claim immunity from the jurisdiction of a court of another Contracting State if it participates with one or more private persons in a company, association or other legal entity having its seat, registered office or principal place of

European Convention on State Immunity and Additional Protocol, 1972

Preamble

The member States of the Council of Europe, signatory hereto,
Considering that the aim of the Council of Europe is to achieve a greater unity between its members;
Taking into account the fact that there is in international law a tendency to restrict the cases in which a State may claim immunity before foreign courts;
Desiring to establish in their mutual relations common rules relating to the scope of the immunity of one State from the jurisdiction of the courts of another State, and designed to ensure compliance with judgments given against another State;
Considering that the adoption of such rules will tend to advance the work of harmonisation undertaken by the member States of the Council of Europe in the legal field,
Have agreed as follows:

Chapter I Immunity from jurisdiction

Article 1

1. A Contracting State which institutes or intervenes in proceedings before a court of another Contracting State submits, for the purpose of those proceedings, to the jurisdiction of the courts of that State.

2. Such a Contracting State cannot claim immunity from the jurisdiction of the courts of the other Contracting State in respect of any counterclaim:

a) arising out of the legal relationship or the facts on which the principal claim is based;

b) if, according to the provisions of this Convention, it would not have been entitled to invoke immunity in respect of that counterclaim had separate proceedings been brought against it in those courts.

3. A Contracting State which makes a counterclaim in proceedings before a court of another Contracting State submits to the jurisdiction of the courts of that State with respect not only to the counterclaim but also to the principal claim.

Article 2

A Contracting State cannot claim immunity from the jurisdiction of a court of another Contracting State if it has undertaken to submit to the jurisdiction of that court either:

a) by international agreement;

b) by an express term contained in a contract in writing; or

Part II
International Conventions

1. Has expressly consented to the taking of such measures by one of the means as provided in part 1 article 5 of the present Federal Law;

2. Has allocated or earmarked property for the satisfaction of the claim which is the object of that proceeding.

Article 15 State immunity from post-judgment measures

A foreign State enjoys judicial immunity in regard to post-judgment measures unless:

1. The foreign State has expressly consented to the taking of such measures by one of the means as provided in part 1 article 5 of the present Federal Law;

2. The foreign State has allocated or earmarked property for the satisfaction of the claim which is the object of that proceeding;

3. it has been established that the property is specifically in use and (or) intended for use by the foreign State for the purposes other than sovereign authoritative power realization.

Article 16 Property of a foreign State that enjoys immunity form pre-judgment and post-judgment measures

1. The following property owned by a foreign State, intended to used or used under its own name in activity related to sovereign authoritative power realization enjoys immunity from pre-judgment and post-judgment measures:

   a. Property (including any bank accounts), which is used or intended for use in the performance of the functions of the diplomatic mission of the foreign State or its consular posts, special missions, missions to international organization or to international conferences;

   b. Property of military character of used or intended for use in the performance of military functions or peacemaking operation, recognized by the Russian Federation;

   c. Property forming part of the cultural heritage of the State or part of its archives and not placed or intended to be placed on sale;

   d. Property forming part of an exhibition of objects of scientific, cultural or historical interest and not placed or intended to be placed for sale;

   e. Property of the central bank or any other supervisory organ of a foreign State which is entitled to banking supervisory.

2. Paragraph 1 of the present article is applied with due regard to provisions of articles 14 and article 15 subparagraphs 1 and 2 of the present Federal Law.

Article 17 Judicial proceedings on claims with the involvement of a foreign State

Legal actions with the involvement of a foreign State are heard by a Court of the Russian Federation in accordance with procedural legislation of the Russian Federation.

Article 18 Entering into force of the present Federal Law

The present Federal law enters into force from 1 January 2016.

PRESINDENT OF
THE RUSSIAN FEDRATION
V. PUTIN
MOSCOW, THE KREMLIN
3 NOVEMBER 2015
No. 297-FZ

1. Rights and obligations of the foreign State in regard to immovable property situated in the Russian Federation;

2. Rights and obligations of the foreign State in regard to movable or immovable property arising by the way of succession, gift or *bona vacantia*;

3. Rights and obligations of the foreign State in regard to administration of the property.

Article 11 Non-application of judicial immunity in regard to the disputes which relate to compensating personal injuries and damage to property

A foreign State cannon invoke judicial immunity in the Russian Federation in regard to the disputes which relate to compensation by the foreign State for injury caused to life, health, property, honor and dignity, business reputation of a natural person or property and business reputation of a legal entity, if the claim arose from causing injury to life, health, property, honor and dignity, business reputation by an act or omission or due to other circumstances which occurred in whole or in part in the territory of the Russian Federation and the author of the injury was present in the territory of the Russian Federation at the time of the act or omission.

Article 12 Non-application of judicial immunity in regard to the disputes which relate to intellectual property

A foreign State cannon invoke judicial immunity in the Russian Federation in regard to the disputes which relate to:

1. Determination and realization of a foreign State rights to intellectual property and trade or business name, trademark, copyright;

2. Alleged infringement by a foreign State of a right of third person to intellectual property and trade or business name, trademark, copyright.

Article 13 Non-application of judicial immunity in regard to the disputes which relate to operation of a ship

1. A foreign State cannon invoke judicial immunity in the Russian Federation in regard to the disputes which relate to a foreign State operation of a ship which is in its ownership or operated by a foreign State, or carriage of a cargo by this ship if at the time the cause of action arose, the ship was used for other that non-commercial purposes and (or) the cargo was not the cargo owned by the foreign State and used or intended to be used by the for foreign state exclusively for government authority purposes.

2. For the purposes of application of the article, the terms are follows:

a. A ship—all types of water crafts which are used or intended to be used as a means of transport on the water;

b. A ship used for non-commercial purposes—ships which are used by a foreign State to realize its governmental authority, including warships and operated for non-commercial purposes governmental ships;

c. Disputes relating to operation of a ship, disputes in context of:
i. Collisions, damage to port and hydraulic structures and other shipping accidents
ii. Assistance, rescue and general accidents;
iii. Supply of repair and other works, provision of services related to the ship;
iv. Effect of marine pollution;
v. Lifting the sunken property.

Article 14 State immunity form post-judgment measures

A foreign State enjoys judicial immunity in regard to pre-judgment measures unless the foreign State:

to the disputes related to realizing business activities or any other financial activities on the territory of the Russian Federation, as well as on the territory of another State if the consequences of that activity are connected with the territory of Russian Federation.

4. A court in deciding the question of whether the transaction a foreign State engaged in is connected with realization of its sovereign authoritative power a Court of the Russian Federation takes into consideration the nature and the purpose of the transaction.

Article 8 Non-application of judicial immunity in regard to employment disputes

1. A foreign State cannon invoke judicial immunity in the Russian Federation in regard to the disputes which relate to a contract of employment between the foreign State and an employee for work performed or to be performed in whole or in part in the territory of the Russian Federation.

2. The provisions of paragraph 1 do not apply if

a. The employee has been recruited to perform functions in the exercise of governmental authority of a foreign State;

b. The employee is

i. A diplomatic agent, as defined by international treaties;

ii. A consular officer, as defined by international treaties;

iii. A member of the diplomatic staff of a permanent mission to an international organization or of a special mission, or is recruited to represent a State at an international conference;

iv. Any other person enjoying diplomatic immunity;

c. The subject-matter of the proceedings is the recruitment, renewal of employment or reinstatement of an individual;

d. The subject-matter of the proceedings is the dismissal or termination of employment of an individual, and as determined in writing by the head of the foreign State, the head of Government of the foreign State or the Minister for Foreign Affairs of the foreign State that such a proceeding would interfere with the security interests of the foreign State;

e. The employee is a national of the foreign employer State at the time when the proceeding is instituted in the Russian Federation, unless this person has the permanent residence in the Russian Federation.

Article 9 Non-application of judicial immunity in regard to participation in companies or other collective bodies without the status of legal entity

1. A foreign State cannon invoke judicial immunity in the Russian Federation in regard to the disputes which relate to participation of a foreign State in companies or other collective bodies without the status of a legal entity, and have arose between a foreign State and a legal entity, incorporated in the established by legislation of the Russian Federation procedure and (or) realizing its activities in the territory of the Russian Federation or other institution without the status of legal entity realizing its activities in the territory of the Russian Federation, or between a foreign State and other participants of such legal entity or an institution, if such an institution has participants other than the States or international organizations.

2. The provision of paragraph 1 do not apply in cases if other:

a. Is provided by an agreement between the concerned States;

b. Is provided by the constitutional documents of the legal entity or an institution;

c. Is provided by an agreement in writing by the parties to the dispute.

Article 10 Non-application of judicial immunity in regard to the disputes in the context of rights of property

A foreign State cannon invoke judicial immunity in the Russian Federation in regard to the disputes which relate to:

2. Consent of a foreign State to the jurisdiction of the Russian Federation in regard to a specific case according to the clause 1 of the present article cannot be withdrawn and is valid to all the stages of court proceedings.

3. A foreign State shall not considered to have consented to the exercise of jurisdiction of the court of the Russian Federation in the following cases;

    a. Intervention in the court proceedings or taking any other procedural action for the sole purpose to claim jurisdictional immunities or to assert a property right at issue in the proceeding;

    b. Consent of a foreign State to the application of the legislation of the Russian Federation with regard to a specific case;

    c. Failure on the part of a State to enter an appearance in a proceeding in the court of the Russian Federation;

    d. The Appearance of a representative of a foreign State before a court of the Russian Federation as a witness or an expert.

4. Consent of a foreign State to the jurisdiction of the Russian Federation in regard to a specific case cannot interfere the immunity of a foreign State in respect to the interim remedies immunity and (or) the immunity for the execution.

Article 6 Waiver of judicial immunity

1. A foreign State is considered to have waived its right to judicial immunity if the foreign State itself instituted the proceeding in a Court of Russian Federation, intervened in the proceeding in a Court of Russian Federation or taken any other step relating to the merits.

2. A foreign State is considered to have waived its right to judicial immunity in regard to the disputes in relation to arbitration agreement or arbitration clause if the State concluded an arbitration agreement or an arbitration clause for dispute settlement with its intervention which have arose or may arise in the future in regard to obligations fulfillment.

3. A foreign State is considered to have waived its right to judicial immunity in regard to any counterclaim if the foreign State institutes a proceeding in a Court of Russian Federation.

4. A foreign State is considered to have waived its right to judicial immunity from the initial claim if the foreign State makes a counterclaim in a Court of Russian Federation.

5. The waiver of judicial immunity of a foreign State in regard of a specific proceeding cannot be withdrawn and extend to all the stages of the proceedings.

6. The waiver of judicial immunity of a foreign State in regard to a specific proceeding is not considered as a waiver of immunity from interim measures and immunity from execution of the judgment.

Article 7 Non-application of judicial immunity in regard to disputes in the context of a foreign State participation in commercial transactions and (or) realizing business activities or any other financial activities

1. A foreign State cannon invoke judicial immunity in the Russian Federation in regard to the disputes in the context of a foreign State engagement in commercial transactions with a foreign natural person or legal entities or any other institutions without the status of a legal entity of another State, if such disputes in accordance with the applicable law fall under jurisdiction of a Court of the Russian Federation and if the transactions are not be related to a foreign State realization of its sovereign authoritative power.

2. The provisions of paragraph 1 do not apply in the case of commercial transactions between States or if the parties to the commercial transaction have expressly agreed otherwise.

3. A foreign State cannon invoke judicial immunity in the Russian Federation in regard

5. State immunity from pre-judgment measures—the legal duty of a Court of the Russian Federation to refrain from granting interim injunction and other interim remedies intending to further judicial proceedings and execution of a judgment in respect of a foreign State and its property;

6. State immunity from post—judgment measures the legal duty of a Court of the Russian Federation or of a federal executive body which is entitled to enforce judicial decisions, acts of other bodies and authorities to refrain from imposing claims to property of a foreign State and taking other actions in respect of the enforcement of a judgment;

7. Court of the Russian Federation—the Supreme Court of the Russian Federation, a federal Court of General Jurisdiction, an Arbitration Court established in accordance with the Constitution of the Russian Federation, Federal Constitutional Laws and Federal Laws;

8. Sovereign authority—the competence that a foreign State possesses in accordance with its sovereignty and which it exercises for the purpose of realization of the sovereign power.

Article 3 Privileges and immunities not affected by the present Federal Law

1. Present Federal Law is without prejudice to the privileges and immunities enjoyed by a foreign State under international law, in relation to the exercise of the functions of its diplomatic missions and consular posts, special missions, headquarters and missions to international organizations or delegations to the organs of international organizations or to international conferences and persons connected with then.

2. The present Federal Law is without prejudice to privileges and immunities accorded under international law to heads of the States, heads of Governments and ministers of foreign affairs.

3. The present Federal Law is without prejudice to the privileges and immunities enjoyed by the State under international law, with respect to aircrafts and space objects owned and operated by a foreign State as well as war-ships and other vehicles, operated by a State for non-commercial purposes.

Article 4 The principle of reciprocity in application of jurisdictional immunities

1. Jurisdictional immunities of a foreign State and its property in the scope enjoyed by a foreign State according to the present Federal Law can be limited in respect to the principle of reciprocity, there will be found existence of restrictions to the scope of immunities enjoyed by the Russian Federation and ins property in that foreign State.

2. Federal executive body entitled to developing and implementation of the state policy and regulation in the sphere of international affairs, according to procedural rule of the Russian Federation gives legal opinions on the issues of granting jurisdictional immunities to the Russian Federation and its property in a foreign State.

Article 5 Consent of a Foreign State to exercise of jurisdiction

1. A foreign State cannot invoke immunity from the jurisdiction if it has expressly consented to the exercise of jurisdiction in a proceeding before a court of the Russian Federation with regard to a specific case:

a. By an international agreement;

b. In a written contract, which is no an international agreement;

c. By a declaration before the court of the Russian Federation, by a written communication before the court if the Russian Federation delivered to the Russian Federation through the diplomatic channels in relation to the specific proceeding.

Law on Jurisdictional Immunities of Foreign State and Property of Foreign State in the Russian Federation, 2015 (Russia)

Adopted by the State Duma On 23 October 2015
Approved by the Federation Council On 28 October 2015

Article 1 Competence of the present Federal law

1. The present Federal law applies to the relations connected with application of jurisdictional immunities of a foreign State and its property by the Russian Federation.

2. A foreign State enjoys jurisdictional immunities in respect of itself and its property in accordance with the provisions of the present Federal Law.

3. The provisions of the present Federal Law should be applied if the Russian Federation and a Foreign State have not agreed otherwise.

Article 2 Basic terms used in the present Federal Law

For the purpose of the present Federal Law the following basic terms are used:

1. foreign State:

a. A State, different from the Russian Federation and state bodies of the Russian Federation;

b. Constituent units of the foreign State (subjects of a foreign federal State or political subdivisions of a foreign State) and their bodies to the extent to which they are entitled to perform acts in the exercise of the sovereign authority and are acting in such capacity;

c. Agencies and other entities irrespective of their legal persons status to the extent they are entitled to perform and actually performing acts in exercise of sovereign authority of the State;

d. Representatives of a foreign State, acting in that capacity;

2. Property of a foreign State—is a property that belongs to a foreign State and that is situated on the territory of the Russian Federation.

3. Jurisdictional immunities of a foreign State and its property—are judicial immunity, State immunity from pre-judgment measures and State immunity from post-judgment measures;

4. Judicial immunity—the legal duty of a Court of the Russian Federation to refrain form involving a foreign State to the court proceedings;

Disposición final tercera. Modificación de la Ley Orgánica 6/1985, de 1 de julio, del Poder Judicial.

El artículo 21.2 de la Ley Orgánica 6/1985, de 1 de julio, del Poder Judicial pasa a tener la siguiente redacción:

2. No obstante, no conocerán de las pretensiones formuladas respecto de sujetos o bienes que gocen de inmunidad de jurisdicción y de ejecución de conformidad con la legislación española y las normas de Derecho Internacional Público.

Disposición final cuarta. Modificación de la Ley 1/2000, de 7 de enero, de Enjuiciamiento Civil.

La circunstancia 1.a del apartado 2 del artículo 36 de la Ley 1/2000, de 7 de enero, de Enjuiciamiento Civil queda redactada como sigue:

1.a Cuando se haya formulado demanda o solicitado ejecución respecto de sujetos o bienes que gocen de inmunidad de jurisdicción o de ejecución de conformidad con la legislación española y las normas de Derecho Internacional Público.

Disposición final quinta. Desarrollo normativo.

Se autoriza al Gobierno a dictar las disposiciones que resulten necesarias para el adecuado desarrollo de lo establecido en la presente Ley Orgánica.

Disposición final sexta. Preferencia de los tratados internacionales.

En caso de concurrencia normativa de la presente Ley Orgánica con las previsiones recogidas en un tratado internacional del que el Reino de España sea Estado Parte se aplicará con carácter preferente el tratado internacional.

Disposición final séptima. Entrada en vigor.

La presente Ley Orgánica entrará en vigor a los veinte días de su publicación en el ñBoletín Oficial del Estado.

Por tanto,

Mando a todos los españoles, particulares y autoridades, que guarden y hagan guardar esta ley orgánica.

Madrid, 27 de octubre de 2015.
FELIPE R.
El Presidente del Gobierno,
MARIANO RAJOY BREY

2. El Ministerio de Asuntos Exteriores y de Cooperación dará traslado al órgano jurisdiccional competente del informe no vinculante previsto en el artículo 27 de la Ley 29/2015, de 30 de julio, de Cooperación Jurídica Internacional en Materia Civil y de cualquier comunicación que, en materia de inmunidad, le remita por vía diplomática un Estado extranjero o una organización internacional en relación con un proceso incoado en España.

3. El órgano jurisdiccional competente, a la mayor brevedad posible, dará traslado al Ministerio de Asuntos Exteriores y de Cooperación de las peticiones del informe previsto en el artículo 27 de la Ley 29/2015, de 30 de julio, de Cooperación Jurídica Internacional en Materia Civil y de las comunicaciones que dirija al Estado extranjero.

Artículo 55. Sentencias dictadas en rebeldía.

Los órganos jurisdiccionales españoles no dictarán sentencia en rebeldía contra el Estado extranjero o la organización internacional, salvo que concurran las siguientes condiciones:

a) Que se hayan cumplido los requisitos de notificación;

b) Que haya transcurrido un plazo de cuatro meses a contar desde la fecha de recepción de la notificación de la demanda u otro documento por el que se incoe el proceso; y

c) Que la presente Ley Orgánica no impida el ejercicio de la jurisdicción.

Artículo 56. Privilegios e inmunidades de los Estados extranjeros y de las organizaciones internacionales durante la sustanciación del proceso.

1. El hecho de que el Estado extranjero o la organización internacional incumpla o rehúse cumplir el requerimiento de un órgano jurisdiccional español por el que se le inste a realizar o abstenerse de realizar determinado acto, a presentar cualquier documento o a revelar cualquier otra información a los efectos del proceso no tendrá más consecuencias que las que resulten de tal comportamiento en relación con el fondo del asunto. En particular, no se impondrá ninguna sanción o pena al Estado u organización internacional que haya incumplido o rehusado cumplir tal requerimiento.

2. Ningún Estado extranjero u organización internacional estará obligado a prestar caución, fianza o depósito, para garantizar el pago de las costas o gastos judiciales de cualquier proceso en el que sea parte demandada ante un órgano jurisdiccional español.

Disposición adicional única. Comunicación a otros sujetos de Derecho Internacional.

El Ministerio de Asuntos Exteriores y de Cooperación comunicará la presente Ley Orgánica a todos los sujetos de Derecho Internacional con los que España mantiene relaciones, incluidas las organizaciones internacionales de las que es miembro.

Disposición derogatoria única. Derogación normativa.

Quedan derogadas cuantas disposiciones de igual o inferior rango se opongan a la presente Ley Orgánica.

Disposición final primera. Título competencial.

La presente Ley Orgánica se dicta en ejercicio de las competencias exclusivas atribuidas al Estado en materia de relaciones internacionales y de legislación procesal por el artículo 149. 1. 3. a y 6. a de la Constitución.

Disposición final segunda. Carácter ordinario de determinados artículos de la Ley.

Sin perjuicio del carácter orgánico de la presente Ley, los artículos 49 a 55 y la disposición final cuarta, tienen carácter ordinario.

TÍTULO VII Cuestiones procedimentales

Artículo 49. Apreciación de oficio de la inmunidad por los órganos jurisdiccionales.

Los órganos jurisdiccionales españoles apreciarán de oficio las cuestiones relativas a la inmunidad a las que se refiere la presente Ley Orgánica y se abstendrán de conocer de los asuntos que se les sometan cuando se haya formulado demanda, querella o se haya iniciado el proceso de cualquier otra forma o cuando se solicite una medida ejecutiva respecto de cualquiera de los entes, personas o bienes que gocen de inmunidad conforme a la presente Ley Orgánica.

Artículo 50. Invocación de la inmunidad.

Salvo que hubiese renunciado tácitamente a la inmunidad de jurisdicción, y sea cual sea el tipo de procedimiento, el Estado extranjero podrá hacerla valer por el cauce de la declinatoria, de conformidad con lo dispuesto en los artículos 63 y siguientes de la Ley 1/2000, de 7 de enero, de Enjuiciamiento Civil, con excepción de los plazos previstos en el apartado 1 del artículo 64.

Artículo 51. Proceso incoado contra Estados u organizaciones internacionales o contra personas con inmunidad.

A los efectos de la presente Ley Orgánica, se entenderá que se ha incoado un proceso ante los órganos jurisdiccionales españoles contra cualquiera de los entes o personas que, de conformidad con la presente Ley Orgánica, gozan de inmunidad, si alguno de ellos es mencionado como parte contra la que se dirige el mismo.

Artículo 52. Comunicaciones judiciales dirigidas a Estados extranjeros.

Los emplazamientos, citaciones, requerimientos y cualesquiera otros actos de comunicación judicial dirigidos a Estados extranjeros, así como la comunicación al Ministerio de Asuntos Exteriores y de Cooperación de la existencia de cualquier procedimiento contra un Estado extranjero, a los solos efectos de que aquel emita informe en relación con las cuestiones relativas a la inmunidad de jurisdicción y ejecución, se realizarán en la forma prevista en la Ley 29/2015, de 30 de julio, de Cooperación Jurídica Internacional en Materia Civil.

Artículo 53. Comunicaciones de los Estados extranjeros y de las organizaciones internacionales.

Las comunicaciones de los Estados extranjeros por las que se haga constar expresamente su consentimiento al ejercicio de la jurisdicción por órganos jurisdiccionales españoles o la renuncia a la inmunidad en todos los casos previstos en la presente Ley Orgánica, así como las de las organizaciones internacionales que tengan la misma finalidad, se cursarán por vía diplomática, a través del Ministerio de Asuntos Exteriores y de Cooperación.

Artículo 54. Procedimiento de comunicación entre el Ministerio de Asuntos Exteriores y de Cooperación y los órganos jurisdiccionales españoles.

1. El Ministerio de Asuntos Exteriores y de Cooperación remitirá el emplazamiento o la notificación del órgano jurisdiccional a la misión diplomática o a la representación permanente española correspondiente, a los efectos de su traslado al Ministerio de Asuntos Exteriores del Estado extranjero o al órgano competente de la organización internacional.

Artículo 46. Otros invitados y funcionarios de la organización.
Los invitados a la conferencia o reunión internacional que no formen parte de delegaciones de Estados y los miembros del personal de la organización desplazados a España para participar en el evento o en su organización, siempre que no tengan nacionalidad española ni residencia habitual en España, no podrán ser objeto de ninguna forma de detención ni de confiscación de equipaje personal, salvo en caso de flagrante delito. Gozarán, igualmente, de inmunidad de jurisdicción por cualesquiera palabras, escritos y actos realizados en relación con la conferencia o reunión internacional.

Artículo 47. Conferencias o reuniones internacionales organizadas por las Naciones Unidas o sus organismos especializados.
1. En el caso de que las Naciones Unidas o alguno de sus organismos especializados celebre en España, a invitación del Gobierno español, en colaboración con este o con su consentimiento, una conferencia o reunión internacional, se aplicará el régimen de privilegios e inmunidades previsto en la Convención sobre privilegios e inmunidades de las Naciones Unidas, aprobada por la Asamblea General el 13 de febrero de 1946 o en la Convención sobre privilegios e inmunidades de los organismos especializados, aprobada por la Asamblea General el 21 de noviembre de 1947, según corresponda, de la forma expresada en los siguientes apartados.

2. Los representantes de los Estados miembros de la organización o del organismo, cuyo nombre haya sido comunicado por la organización o el organismo al Gobierno español por vía diplomática con antelación al inicio de la conferencia o reunión internacional, gozarán de las prerrogativas e inmunidades previstas en el artículo IV de la Convención sobre privilegios e inmunidades de las Naciones Unidas de 1946 o en el artículo V de la Convención sobre privilegios e inmunidades de los organismos especializados de 1947, según corresponda.

3. Los participantes en la conferencia o reunión internacional que no sean representantes de los Estados miembros a los que se refiere el artículo anterior, invitados bien por Naciones Unidas o el organismo especializado organizador, bien por el Gobierno de España o por ambos, cuyo nombre haya sido comunicado al Gobierno de España por vía diplomática con antelación al inicio del evento, gozarán de las prerrogativas e inmunidades reconocidas a los expertos que forman parte de las misiones de Naciones Unidas previstas en el artículo VI de la Convención sobre privilegios e inmunidades de las Naciones Unidas de 1946.

4. Los funcionarios de Naciones Unidas o de sus organismos especializados que participen en la conferencia o reunión internacional o desarrollen funciones relacionadas con esta y cuyo nombre haya sido comunicado al Gobierno de España con antelación al inicio del evento gozarán de las prerrogativas e inmunidades reconocidas en los artículos V y VII de la Convención de 1946 y los artículos VI y VIII de la Convención de 1947, respectivamente.

5. Supletoriamente, se aplicará lo dispuesto en el presente Título.

Artículo 48. Conferencias o reuniones internacionales organizadas por la Unión Europea.
En el caso de que la Unión Europea o alguna de sus instituciones, órganos u organismos celebre en España, a invitación del Gobierno español, en colaboración con este o con su consentimiento, una conferencia o reunión internacional, se aplicará el régimen de privilegios e inmunidades previsto en el Protocolo número 7 sobre los privilegios y las inmunidades de la Unión Europea y, supletoriamente, lo dispuesto en el presente Título.

registro, requisa, confiscación, expropiación o de cualquier otra medida coercitiva de carácter ejecutivo, administrativo, judicial o legislativo.

3. Estarán exentos de derechos de aduana y tasas de importación, en los casos y condiciones en que lo permita la normativa aduanera de la Unión Europea, el material administrativo, técnico y científico suministrado por la organización para la celebración de la conferencia o reunión internacional, las publicaciones y demás documentos oficiales de la organización destinados a sus trabajos y los regalos habituales ofrecidos o recibidos por los altos funcionarios de la misma, siempre que la organización se comprometa a su reexportación al término del evento, con excepción de los consumidos in situ.

4. El máximo representante de la organización en la conferencia o reunión internacional y quien ostente la presidencia de dicho evento, si no fueran la misma persona, gozarán de las prerrogativas y privilegios concedidos a los Jefes de misión diplomática en España, que se extenderán a los familiares que le acompañen, siempre que no tengan nacionalidad española ni residencia habitual en España.

Artículo 45. Delegaciones de Estados invitados a la conferencia o reunión internacional.

1. El Jefe de la delegación gozará de las prerrogativas y privilegios reconocidos en España a los Jefes de misión diplomática.

2. Los miembros del personal de las delegaciones de los Estados invitados, cuyos nombres deberán ser comunicados al Gobierno español por vía diplomática con antelación al inicio de la conferencia o reunión internacional, gozarán de las prerrogativas y privilegios reconocidos a los agentes diplomáticos en España, con la excepción prevista en el apartado 4.

3. Los restantes miembros de la delegación gozarán de inmunidad de jurisdicción y no podrán ser objeto de ninguna forma de detención por cualesquiera palabras, escritos y actos realizados en relación con la conferencia o reunión internacional.

4. No obstante lo dispuesto en el apartado 2, los miembros del personal de las delegaciones no gozarán de inmunidad en relación con acciones de naturaleza civil iniciadas por terceros por daños resultantes de accidente causado por vehículos de motor o relacionadas con una infracción de tráfico en la que se encuentren involucrados tales vehículos.

5. Los locales asignados a las delegaciones, cualquiera que sea su propietario, serán inviolables. Ningún agente de las autoridades españolas podrá entrar en ellos sin consentimiento expreso del Jefe de la delegación o quien le sustituya, si bien el consentimiento se presumirá en caso de incendio o emergencia equiparable.

6. Los locales, medios de transporte, archivos y documentos no podrán ser objeto de registro, requisa, confiscación, expropiación o de cualquier otra medida coercitiva de carácter ejecutivo, administrativo, judicial o legislativo.

7. Se permitirá la libre comunicación de las delegaciones para todos los fines relacionados con la conferencia o reunión internacional. A este fin, podrán utilizar todos los medios de comunicación adecuados, incluidos correos diplomáticos, valija diplomática y mensajes en clave o en cifra.

8. Estarán exentos de derechos de aduana y tasas de importación, en los casos y condiciones en que lo permita la normativa aduanera de la Unión Europea, el material administrativo y técnico destinado a la celebración de la conferencia o reunión internacional, las publicaciones y demás documentos oficiales de la delegación destinados a sus trabajos y los regalos habituales ofrecidos o recibidos, siempre que el Estado extranjero que envía la delegación se comprometa a su reexportación al término del evento, con excepción de los consumidos in situ.

Artículo 39. Revocación del consentimiento.

El consentimiento de la organización internacional al que se refiere el artículo 37 no podrá ser revocado una vez iniciado el proceso ante un órgano jurisdiccional español.

Artículo 40. Representantes de los Estados miembros y Estados observadores ante la organización internacional.

1. Los Representantes Permanentes ante la organización internacional y los Jefes de las misiones de observación gozarán de la inmunidad acordada a los Jefes de misión diplomática acreditados en España, que se extenderá a los familiares a su cargo que no tengan nacionalidad española ni residencia habitual en España. Igualmente gozarán de inviolabilidad personal, así como de residencia, correspondencia y equipaje.

2. Los miembros del personal diplomático de las delegaciones de los Estados miembros y Estados observadores ante la organización internacional gozarán de la inmunidad acordada a los agentes diplomáticos en España, que se extenderá a los familiares a su cargo que no tengan nacionalidad española ni residencia habitual en España. Igualmente gozarán de inviolabilidad personal, así como de residencia, correspondencia y equipaje.

3. Los restantes miembros de las delegaciones de los Estados miembros y Estados observadores ante la organización internacional gozarán de inmunidad de jurisdicción y de detención en relación con cualesquiera palabras, escritos y actos realizados en el ejercicio de sus funciones.

Artículo 41. Consentimiento del Estado extranjero al ejercicio de la jurisdicción y a la adopción de medidas de ejecución.

El consentimiento del Estado extranjero al ejercicio de la jurisdicción y a la adopción de medidas de ejecución por órganos jurisdiccionales españoles en relación con sus representaciones permanentes o de observación y los miembros de estas se regirá, en ausencia de acuerdo internacional que lo regule, por lo dispuesto en los artículos 5 a 8, 18 y 19.

TÍTULO VI Privilegios e inmunidades aplicables a las conferencias y reuniones internacionales

Artículo 42. Ámbito de aplicación.

1. En ausencia de acuerdo específico celebrado por España, el régimen establecido en el presente Título regulará los privilegios e inmunidades aplicables a la celebración en España de una conferencia o reunión internacional, cualquiera que sea su denominación particular.

2. En los casos en que España haya celebrado un acuerdo específico en la materia, el régimen aplicable será el estipulado en dicho acuerdo y, supletoriamente, el establecido en la presente Ley Orgánica.

Artículo 43. Duración de los privilegios e inmunidades.

Con carácter general, la duración de los privilegios e inmunidades reconocidos se extenderá durante toda la duración de la conferencia o reunión internacional y sendos periodos de diez días anteriores y cinco días posteriores a esta.

Artículo 44. Facilidades, privilegios e inmunidades para la celebración de la conferencia o reunión internacional.

1. Los locales asignados a la conferencia o reunión internacional, cualquiera que sea su propietario, serán inviolables. Ningún agente de las autoridades españolas podrá entrar en ellos sin consentimiento expreso de la máxima autoridad de la organización o representante autorizado, si bien el consentimiento se presumirá en caso de incendio o emergencia equiparable.

2. Los locales, medios de transporte, archivos y documentos y cualesquiera bienes y haberes asignados a la conferencia o reunión internacional no podrán ser objeto de

2. La persona que sustituya temporalmente al máximo representante de la organización gozará de la inmunidad a la que se refiere el apartado anterior durante el periodo de duración de la sustitución.

3. El resto del personal de las organizaciones internacionales cualquiera que sea su nacionalidad, gozará de inmunidad de jurisdicción y no podrá ser objeto de ninguna forma de detención en relación con cualesquiera palabras, escritos y actos ejecutados en el ejercicio de sus funciones.

4. Los expertos y otras personas contratadas por las organizaciones internacionales para el desempeño de misiones específicas durante un tiempo limitado gozarán de inmunidad de jurisdicción y no podrán ser objeto de ninguna forma de detención en relación con cualesquiera palabras, escritos y actos realizados en el ejercicio de sus funciones.

5. La inmunidad de jurisdicción a la que se refiere este artículo subsistirá después de haber cesado en la condición de representante, miembro del personal, experto o contratado de la organización por los actos realizados en el ejercicio de sus funciones durante su permanencia en el cargo de que se trate.

Artículo 37. Consentimiento de las organizaciones internacionales al ejercicio de la jurisdicción por parte de los órganos jurisdiccionales españoles.

1. Las organizaciones internacionales no podrán hacer valer la inmunidad de jurisdicción ante un órgano jurisdiccional español respecto de una cuestión en relación con la cual hayan consentido de forma expresa el ejercicio de dicha jurisdicción:

a) Por acuerdo internacional;

b) En un contrato escrito; o

c) Por una declaración ante el tribunal o por una comunicación escrita en un proceso determinado.

2. Las organizaciones internacionales no podrán hacer valer la inmunidad de jurisdicción ante un órgano jurisdiccional español en relación con un determinado proceso:

a) Cuando este haya sido iniciado mediante la interposición de demanda o querella por la propia organización;

b) Cuando la organización internacional haya realizado cualquier acto relativo al fondo del proceso;

c) Cuando la organización internacional haya formulado reconvención basada en la misma relación jurídica o los mismos hechos que la demanda principal; o

d) Cuando se haya formulado reconvención basada en la misma relación jurídica o los mismos hechos que la demanda presentada por la organización internacional.

3. La inclusión en un contrato en el que sean parte las organizaciones internacionales de una cláusula en la que se reconozca la jurisdicción de un órgano jurisdiccional ordinario español constituirá una renuncia a la inmunidad de jurisdicción.

Artículo 38. Comportamientos que no constituyen consentimiento a la jurisdicción.

No se interpretará como consentimiento de la organización internacional al ejercicio de la jurisdicción por órganos jurisdiccionales españoles respecto de determinado proceso:

a) La intervención de la organización internacional en el proceso para hacer valer la inmunidad;

b) La comparecencia de un representante de la organización internacional en el proceso en calidad de testigo;

c) La incomparecencia de la organización internacional en el proceso; o

d) El consentimiento expreso o tácito, otorgado por la organización internacional a la aplicación de la ley española a la cuestión objeto del proceso.

2. A las Fuerzas Armadas visitantes de cualquier otro Estado extranjero, a su personal militar y civil y a sus bienes, cuando se encuentren en territorio español a invitación o con consentimiento de España, se les aplicarán, de forma total o parcial, las disposiciones del Convenio entre los Estados Partes del Tratado del Atlántico Norte relativo al estatuto de sus fuerzas, de 19 de junio de 1951. Dicha aplicación se hará, atendiendo al principio de reciprocidad y en virtud del acuerdo que sea suscrito a tal efecto por el Ministerio de Defensa de España con el homólogo del Estado extranjero.

3. Las disposiciones de este artículo se aplicarán a cualquier parte del territorio bajo soberanía española donde estén situadas las Fuerzas Armadas visitantes, su personal militar y civil y sus bienes, ya se encuentren estacionadas o en tránsito, así como a los buques y aeronaves de España.

TÍTULO V Privilegios e inmunidades de las organizaciones internacionales con sede u oficina en España

Artículo 34. Inviolabilidad de las organizaciones internacionales.

1. Los locales de las organizaciones internacionales, cualquiera que sea su propietario, sus archivos, su correspondencia oficial y, en general, todos los documentos que les pertenezcan u obren en su poder y estén destinados a su uso oficial serán inviolables dondequiera que se encuentren.

2. Los locales de las organizaciones internacionales, así como todos sus medios de transporte, bienes y haberes en España no podrán ser objeto de registro, requisa, confiscación, expropiación o de cualquier otra medida coercitiva de carácter ejecutivo, administrativo, judicial o legislativo.

Artículo 35. Inmunidad de las organizaciones internacionales.

1. En ausencia de acuerdo internacional bilateral o multilateral aplicable, las organizaciones internacionales gozarán, respecto de toda actuación vinculada al cumplimiento de sus funciones, de inmunidad de jurisdicción y de ejecución ante los órganos jurisdiccionales españoles de todos los órdenes, en los términos y condiciones establecidos en la presente Ley Orgánica.

No obstante lo dispuesto en el párrafo anterior, cuando se trate de procedimientos de Derecho privado o de procesos del ámbito laboral relativos a miembros del personal de las organizaciones internacionales, estas no podrán hacer valer la inmunidad, salvo que acrediten disponer de un mecanismo alternativo de resolución de la controversia, ya esté previsto en el tratado constitutivo, los estatutos, el reglamento interno o en cualquier otro instrumento aplicable de las organizaciones internacionales.

2. Salvo acuerdo en otro sentido, las organizaciones internacionales no gozarán de la inmunidad prevista en el apartado 1 en relación con acciones de naturaleza civil iniciadas por terceros por daños resultantes de accidente causado por vehículos de motor pertenecientes u operados por la organización en su beneficio o relacionadas con una infracción de tráfico en la que se encuentren involucrados tales vehículos.

Artículo 36. Personal propio de las organizaciones internacionales.

1. El máximo representante de las organizaciones internacionales en España gozará de la inmunidad acordada por el Derecho Internacional a los Jefes de misión diplomática, que se extenderá a los familiares a su cargo que no tengan nacionalidad española ni residencia habitual en España. Igualmente gozarán de inviolabilidad personal, así como de residencia, correspondencia y equipaje.

Artículo 27. Renuncia a la inmunidad del Jefe de Estado, Jefe de Gobierno y Ministro de Asuntos Exteriores.

1. El Estado extranjero podrá renunciar a la inmunidad de jurisdicción ante los órganos jurisdiccionales españoles de su Jefe del Estado, Jefe de Gobierno o Ministro de Asuntos Exteriores o de las personas que hubieran ocupado estos cargos en el pasado.

2. La renuncia habrá de ser siempre expresa.

3. Si cualquiera de las personas que gocen de inmunidad, de conformidad con lo dispuesto en el presente Título, entablase una acción judicial, no podrá hacer valer la inmunidad de jurisdicción respecto de cualquier reconvención directamente ligada a la demanda principal.

4. La renuncia a la inmunidad de jurisdicción no implicará renuncia a la inmunidad de ejecución, que requerirá una nueva renuncia expresa.

Artículo 28. Revocación de la renuncia.

La renuncia del Estado extranjero a la que se refiere el artículo anterior no podrá ser revocada una vez iniciado el proceso ante un órgano jurisdiccional español.

Artículo 29. Crímenes internacionales.

Lo dispuesto en el presente Título no afectará a las obligaciones internacionales asumidas por España respecto del enjuiciamiento de crímenes internacionales, ni a sus compromisos con la Corte Penal Internacional.

TÍTULO III Inmunidades de los buques de guerra y de los buques y aeronaves de Estado

Artículo 30. Inmunidad de buques de guerra y buques de Estado.

Salvo que por acuerdo entre los Estados interesados se haya dispuesto otra cosa, los buques de guerra y los buques de Estado extranjeros gozarán de inmunidad de jurisdicción y ejecución ante los órganos jurisdiccionales españoles, incluso cuando se encuentren en aguas interiores o en mar territorial españoles.

Artículo 31. Inmunidad de aeronaves de Estado.

Las aeronaves de Estado extranjeras, tal como se definen en la presente Ley Orgánica, gozarán de inmunidad de jurisdicción y ejecución ante los órganos jurisdiccionales españoles, incluso cuando se encuentren en el espacio aéreo o terrestre español.

Artículo 32. Consentimiento del Estado extranjero al ejercicio de la jurisdicción o a la adopción de medidas de ejecución.

El consentimiento del Estado extranjero al ejercicio de la jurisdicción o a la adopción de medidas de ejecución por los órganos jurisdiccionales españoles en relación con sus buques de guerra y sus buques y aeronaves de Estado, en supuestos en los que gocen de inmunidad conforme a lo establecido en la presente Ley Orgánica, se regirá por lo dispuesto en los artículos 5 a 8, 18 y 19.

TÍTULO IV Estatuto de las Fuerzas Armadas visitantes

Artículo 33. Estatuto de las Fuerzas Armadas visitantes, de su personal militar y civil y de sus bienes.

1. A las Fuerzas Armadas visitantes de un Estado miembro de la OTAN o de la Asociación para la Paz, a su personal militar y civil y a sus bienes, cuando se encuentren en territorio español a invitación o con consentimiento de Españ se les aplicarán las disposiciones del Convenio entre los Estados Partes del Tratado del Atlántico Norte relativo al estatuto de sus fuerzas, de 19 de junio de 1951.

medios de transporte que utilicen.

Artículo 22. Inmunidad de jurisdicción y ejecución.

1. Las personas a las que se refiere el presente Capítulo disfrutarán de inmunidad de jurisdicción y ejecución ante los órganos jurisdiccionales españoles de todos los órdenes durante toda la duración de su mandato, ya se encuentren en España o en el extranjero. Si estuvieran en España, la inmunidad se extiende tanto a los viajes oficiales como a las visitas privadas, ya se trate de acciones judiciales en relación con actos oficiales o privados, ya sean relativas a actos realizados con anterioridad a su mandato o durante el ejercicio de este.

2. No estarán obligados a comparecer como testigos en procesos de los que conozcan los órganos jurisdiccionales españoles.

CAPÍTULO II Inmunidades de antiguos Jefes de Estado y de Gobierno y antiguos Ministros de Asuntos Exteriores

Artículo 23. Continuidad de la inmunidad respecto de los actos oficiales realizados durante el mandato.

1. Una vez finalizado su mandato, los antiguos Jefes de Estado y de Gobierno y los antiguos Ministros de Asuntos Exteriores continuarán disfrutando de inmunidad penal únicamente en relación con los actos realizados durante su mandato en el ejercicio de sus funciones oficiales, con el alcance que determina el Derecho Internacional. En todo caso, quedarán excluidos de la inmunidad los crímenes de genocidio, desaparición forzada, guerra y lesa humanidad.

2. También continuarán disfrutando de inmunidad civil, laboral, administrativa, mercantil y fiscal únicamente en relación con los actos realizados durante su mandato en el ejercicio de sus funciones oficiales, con las excepciones previstas en los artículos 9 a 16.

Artículo 24. Jurisdicción sobre los actos realizados a título privado durante el mandato.

Una vez finalizado su mandato, las personas a las que se refiere el presente Capítulo no podrán hacer valer la inmunidad ante los órganos jurisdiccionales españoles cuando se trate de acciones relacionadas con actos no realizados en el ejercicio de sus funciones oficiales durante su mandato.

Artículo 25. Jurisdicción sobre los actos realizados con anterioridad al comienzo del mandato.

Una vez finalizado su mandato, las personas a las que se refiere el presente Capítulo no podrán hacer valer la inmunidad de jurisdicción y ejecución ante los órganos jurisdiccionales españoles por actos realizados con anterioridad al comienzo de aquel.

CAPÍTULO III Disposiciones comunes

Artículo 26. Reciprocidad en la aplicación de la inmunidad del Jefe de Estado, Jefe de Gobierno y Ministro de Asuntos Exteriores.

Salvo que lo impida el Derecho Internacional, la inmunidad de los Jefes de Estado, Jefes de Gobierno o Ministros de Asuntos Exteriores o de las personas que hubieran ocupado estos cargos en el pasado podrá verse denegada o limitada en su aplicación atendiendo al principio de reciprocidad.

únicamente cuando el Estado extranjero ha asignado bienes de su propiedad a la satisfacción de la demanda objeto del proceso.

3. El consentimiento del Estado extranjero para el ejercicio de la jurisdicción, al que se refieren los artículos 5 y 6 no implicará, en ningún caso, consentimiento para la adopción de medidas de ejecución.

Artículo 19. Revocación del consentimiento a la adopción de medidas de ejecución.

El consentimiento del Estado extranjero al que se refiere el artículo anterior no podrá ser revocado una vez iniciado el proceso ante un órgano jurisdiccional español.

Artículo 20. Bienes del Estado dedicados a fines públicos no comerciales.

1. De los bienes propiedad del Estado extranjero o de los que este ostente su posesión o control, se consideran en todo caso específicamente utilizados o destinados a ser utilizados para fines públicos no comerciales los siguientes:

a) Los bienes, incluidas las cuentas bancarias, utilizados o destinados a ser utilizados en el desempeño de las funciones de la misión diplomática del Estado o de sus oficinas consulares, misiones especiales, representaciones permanentes ante organizaciones internacionales o delegaciones en órganos de organizaciones internacionales o en conferencias internacionales;

b) Los bienes del Estado de naturaleza militar o utilizados o destinados a ser utilizados en el desempeño de funciones militares;

c) Los bienes del banco central u otra autoridad monetaria del Estado que se destinen a los fines propios de dichas instituciones;

d) Los bienes que formen parte del patrimonio cultural o de los archivos del Estado o de una exposición de objetos de interés científico, cultural o histórico, siempre que no se hayan puesto ni estén destinados a ser puestos a la venta; y

e) Los buques y aeronaves de Estado.

2. Lo dispuesto en el punto a) del apartado anterior no será de aplicación a cuentas bancarias destinadas exclusivamente a fines distintos de los públicos no comerciales.

3. Los bienes enumerados en este artículo no podrán ser objeto de medidas de ejecución, salvo que el Estado extranjero haya prestado su consentimiento.

TÍTULO II Privilegios e inmunidades del Jefe del Estado, el Jefe de Gobierno y el Ministro de Asuntos Exteriores del Estado extranjero

CAPÍTULO I Inviolabilidad e inmunidades de los Jefes de Estado, Jefes de Gobierno y Ministros de Asuntos Exteriores en ejercicio

Artículo 21. Inviolabilidad.

1. Las personas del Jefe de Estado, el Jefe de Gobierno y el Ministro de Asuntos Exteriores del Estado extranjero serán inviolables cuando se hallen en territorio español, durante todo el periodo de duración de su mandato, con independencia de que se encuentren en misión oficial o en visita privada. No podrán ser objeto de ninguna forma de detención, se les tratará con el debido respeto y se adoptarán todas las medidas adecuadas para impedir cualquier atentado contra su persona, su libertad o su dignidad.

2. La inviolabilidad a la que se refiere el apartado anterior se extiende a su lugar de residencia en España, a su correspondencia y a sus propiedades y, en su caso, a los

momento de producirse el hecho que da lugar a la acción, el buque estuviera siendo utilizado para un fin distinto del servicio público no comercial; o

b) El transporte de su cargamento, siempre que, en el momento de producirse el hecho que da lugar a la acción, el cargamento estuviese siendo utilizado exclusivamente o estuviera destinado a ser utilizado exclusivamente para un fin distinto del servicio público no comercial.

2. A los efectos de lo dispuesto en el apartado anterior, el término explotación abarca la posesión del buque, su control, su gestión o su fletamento, ya sea por tiempo, por viaje, a casco desnudo u otro.

3. Cuando en el curso del proceso se planteen dudas sobre el carácter público no comercial del buque o de su cargamento, al que se refiere el apartado 1, la certificación acreditativa de tal carácter, firmada por el jefe de misión del Estado extranjero acreditado ante España o por la autoridad competente del Estado extranjero en el caso de que este no disponga de misión acreditada ante el Estado español, hará prueba plena.

4. Lo dispuesto en el apartado 1 no se aplica, en ningún caso, a los buques de guerra y buques de Estado extranjeros, que gozarán de inmunidad a todos los efectos.

Artículo 16. Procesos relativos a los efectos de un convenio arbitral.

Cuando un Estado extranjero haya convenido con una persona natural o jurídica nacional de otro Estado la sumisión a arbitraje de toda controversia relativa a una transacción mercantil, salvo acuerdo de las partes en otro sentido en el convenio arbitral o en la cláusula compromisoria, el Estado no podrá hacer valer la inmunidad ante un órgano jurisdiccional español en un proceso relativo a:

a) La validez, interpretación o aplicación de la cláusula compromisoria o del convenio arbitral;

b) El procedimiento de arbitraje, incluido el nombramiento judicial de los árbitros;

c) La confirmación, la anulación o la revisión del laudo arbitral; o

d) El reconocimiento de los efectos de los laudos extranjeros.

CAPÍTULO II Inmunidad de ejecución

Artículo 17. Inmunidad del Estado extranjero respecto de medidas de ejecución.

1. Los órganos jurisdiccionales españoles se abstendrán de adoptar medidas de ejecución u otras medidas coercitivas contra bienes del Estado extranjero, tanto antes como después de la resolución judicial, salvo que dicho Estado lo haya consentido, de manera expresa o tácita.

2. Después de la resolución judicial, los órganos jurisdiccionales españoles podrán también adoptar medidas de ejecución si se ha determinado que los bienes objeto de aquellas se utilizan o están destinados a ser utilizados por el Estado con fines distintos de los oficiales no comerciales, siempre que se encuentren en territorio español y tengan un nexo con el Estado contra el que se ha incoado el proceso, aunque se destinen a una actividad distinta de la que dio lugar al litigio.

Artículo 18. Consentimiento a la adopción de medidas de ejecución.

1. El consentimiento expreso del Estado extranjero al que se refiere el artículo anterior habrá de contenerse en:

a) acuerdo internacional;

b) un contrato escrito; o

c) una declaración ante el tribunal o una comunicación escrita en un proceso determinado.

2. Se considera que existe consentimiento tácito a los efectos del artículo anterior

un proceso relativo a una acción de indemnización pecuniaria por muerte o lesiones sufridas por una persona o por daño o pérdida de bienes, causados por un acto u omisión presuntamente atribuible a dicho Estado, siempre que:

a) El acto u omisión se hubiera producido total o parcialmente en territorio español; y

b) El autor material del acto u omisión se encontrara en territorio español en el momento en que dicho acto u omisión se produjo.

Artículo 12. Procesos relativos a la determinación de derechos u obligaciones respecto de bienes.

Salvo acuerdo en otro sentido entre España y un Estado extranjero, este no podrá hacer valer la inmunidad de jurisdicción ante los órganos jurisdiccionales españoles en un proceso relativo a la determinación de:

a) Derechos reales, la posesión o el uso del Estado extranjero respecto de bienes inmuebles situados en España;

b) Obligaciones del Estado extranjero derivadas de alguno de los derechos a los que se refiere el párrafo anterior;

c) Derechos del Estado extranjero sobre bienes muebles o inmuebles adquiridos por herencia, legado o cualquier otro título sucesorio, donación o prescripción; o

d) Derechos del Estado extranjero relativos a la administración de dichos bienes cuando estén afectos a un fideicomiso o pertenezcan a la masa activa en un procedimiento concursal o al patrimonio de sociedades en liquidación.

Artículo 13. Procesos relativos a la determinación de derechos de propiedad intelectual e industrial.

Salvo acuerdo en otro sentido entre España y un Estado extranjero, este no podrá hacer valer la inmunidad de jurisdicción ante los órganos jurisdiccionales españoles en un proceso relativo a:

a) La determinación de derechos de propiedad intelectual o industrial de dicho Estado extranjero, cuando estos derechos estén protegidos por la legislación española; o

b) La supuesta infracción por el Estado extranjero de los derechos de propiedad intelectual o industrial de un tercero, cuando estos derechos estén protegidos por la legislación española.

Artículo 14. Procesos relativos a la participación en personas jurídicas y otras entidades de carácter colectivo.

Salvo acuerdo en otro sentido entre España y un Estado extranjero, este no podrá hacer valer la inmunidad de jurisdicción ante los órganos jurisdiccionales españoles en procesos relativos a su participación en sociedades, asociaciones, fundaciones y otras entidades, con o sin ánimo de lucro, dotadas o no de personalidad jurídica, que conciernan a las relaciones de dicho Estado con la entidad o los demás participantes en ella, siempre que esta:

a) Se haya constituido con arreglo a la legislación española o bien su administración central o su establecimiento principal se encuentre en España; y

b) No esté formada exclusivamente por sujetos de Derecho Internacional.

Artículo 15. Procesos relativos a la explotación o cargamento de buques pertenecientes a un Estado o explotados por este.

1. Salvo acuerdo en otro sentido entre España y un Estado extranjero que sea propietario de un buque o lo explote, este no podrá hacer valer la inmunidad ante los órganos jurisdiccionales españoles en un proceso relativo a:

a) La explotación de dicho buque, incluyendo, en particular, las acciones relativas a abordajes y otros accidentes de la navegación, asistencia, salvamento, avería gruesa, reparaciones, avituallamiento y otros contratos concernientes al buque y las relativas a las consecuencias de la contaminación del medio marino, siempre que, en el

Sección 2. a Excepciones a la inmunidad de jurisdicción del estado extranjero
Artículo 9. Procesos relativos a transacciones mercantiles.

1. El Estado extranjero no podrá hacer valer la inmunidad ante los órganos jurisdiccionales españoles en relación con procesos relativos a transacciones mercantiles celebradas por dicho Estado con personas físicas o jurídicas que no tengan su nacionalidad, salvo en los siguientes supuestos:

   a) Cuando se trate de una transacción mercantil entre Estados; o
   b) Cuando las partes hayan pactado expresamente otra cosa.

2. No se considerará que un Estado extranjero es parte en una transacción mercantil cuando quien realiza la transacción sea una empresa estatal o una entidad creada por dicho Estado, siempre que dicha empresa o entidad esté dotada de personalidad jurídica propia y de capacidad para:

   a) Demandar o ser demandada; y
   b) Adquirir por cualquier título la propiedad o posesión de bienes, incluidos los que este Estado le haya autorizado a explotar o administrar y disponer de ellos.

Artículo 10. Procesos relativos a contratos de trabajo.

1. Salvo acuerdo en otro sentido entre España y un Estado extranjero, este no podrá hacer valer la inmunidad de jurisdicción ante los órganos jurisdiccionales españoles en un proceso relativo a un contrato de trabajo entre ese Estado y una persona física, cuando el trabajo haya sido ejecutado o haya de ejecutarse total o parcialmente en España.

2. No obstante lo dispuesto en el apartado anterior, el Estado extranjero podrá hacer valer la inmunidad de jurisdicción en los procesos a los que dicho apartado se refiere, en los siguientes supuestos:

   a) Cuando el trabajador hubiera sido contratado para desempeñar funciones que supongan el ejercicio del poder público;
   b) Cuando el empleado sea:
     i) Un agente diplomático, según se define en la Convención de Viena sobre Relaciones Diplomáticas de 1961;
     ii) Un funcionario consular, según se define en la Convención de Viena sobre Relaciones Consulares de 1963; o
     iii) Un miembro del personal diplomático de una misión permanente ante una organización internacional o de una misión especial o que haya sido designado para representar al Estado extranjero en una conferencia internacional.
   c) Cuando el proceso tenga por objeto la contratación, la renovación del contrato o la readmisión del trabajador;
   d) Cuando el proceso tenga por objeto el despido del trabajador o la rescisión del contrato y una autoridad competente del Estado extranjero comunique que dicho proceso menoscaba sus intereses de seguridad;
   e) Cuando el trabajador fuera nacional del Estado extranjero en el momento de interposición de la demanda, salvo que dicha persona tuviese su residencia habitual en España; o
   f) Cuando el Estado extranjero y el trabajador hayan convenido otra cosa por escrito, salvo que la competencia de los órganos jurisdiccionales españoles fuese irrenunciable para el trabajador.

Artículo 11. Procesos relativos a indemnización por lesiones a las personas y daños a los bienes.

Salvo acuerdo en otro sentido entre España y un Estado extranjero, este no podrá hacer valer la inmunidad de jurisdicción ante los órganos jurisdiccionales españoles en

a) Las misiones diplomáticas, oficinas consulares y misiones especiales de un Estado;
b) Las organizaciones internacionales y las personas adscritas a ellas; y
c) Los ingenios aeroespaciales y objetos espaciales propiedad de un Estado u operados por este.

TÍTULO I   Inmunidades del Estado extranjero en España

Artículo 4. Inmunidades del Estado extranjero.

Todo Estado extranjero y sus bienes disfrutarán de inmunidad de jurisdicción y ejecución ante los órganos jurisdiccionales españoles, en los términos y condiciones previstos en la presente Ley Orgánica.

CAPÍTULO I   Inmunidad de jurisdicción
Sección 1. a Consentimiento del estado extranjero al ejercicio de la jurisdicción por parte de órganos jurisdiccionales españoles

Artículo 5. Consentimiento expreso.

El Estado extranjero no podrá hacer valer la inmunidad de jurisdicción en un proceso ante un órgano jurisdiccional español respecto de una cuestión en relación con la cual haya consentido de forma expresa el ejercicio de dicha jurisdicción:

a) por acuerdo internacional;
b) en un contrato escrito; o
c) por una declaración ante el tribunal o por una comunicación escrita en un proceso determinado.

Artículo 6. Consentimiento tácito.

El Estado extranjero no podrá hacer valer la inmunidad de jurisdicción ante un órgano jurisdiccional español en relación con un determinado proceso:

a) Cuando este haya sido iniciado mediante la interposición de demanda o querella por el propio Estado extranjero;

b) Cuando el Estado extranjero haya intervenido en el proceso o haya realizado cualquier acto en relación con el fondo;

c) Cuando el Estado extranjero haya formulado reconvención basada en la misma relación jurídica o los mismos hechos que la demanda principal; o

d) Cuando se haya formulado reconvención basada en la misma relación jurídica o los mismos hechos que la demanda presentada por el Estado extranjero.

Artículo 7. Comportamientos que no constituyen consentimiento a la jurisdicción.

No se interpretará como consentimiento del Estado extranjero al ejercicio de la jurisdicción por órganos jurisdiccionales españoles respecto de un determinado proceso:

a) La intervención del Estado extranjero en el proceso para hacer valer la inmunidad;

b) La comparecencia de un representante del Estado extranjero en el proceso en calidad de testigo;

c) La incomparecencia del Estado extranjero en el proceso; o

d) El consentimiento expreso o tácito, otorgado por el Estado extranjero, a la aplicación de la ley española a la cuestión objeto del proceso.

Artículo 8. Revocación del consentimiento.

El consentimiento del Estado extranjero al que se refieren los artículos 5 y 6 no podrá ser revocado una vez iniciado el proceso ante un órgano jurisdiccional español.

de un órgano colegiado cuando, de conformidad con la Constitución respectiva, dicho órgano cumpla las funciones de tal;

e) Jefe de Gobierno: la persona que ejerce la jefatura del Gobierno de un Estado extranjero, cualquiera que sea la denominación de su cargo;

f) Ministro de Asuntos Exteriores: el miembro del Gobierno de un Estado extranjero responsable de las relaciones exteriores, cualquiera que sea la denominación de su cargo;

g) Buque de Estado: un buque de titularidad o uso público de un Estado extranjero siempre que preste, con carácter exclusivo, servicios públicos de carácter no comercial;

h) Buque de guerra: un buque y, en su caso, los buques auxiliares, adscritos a las Fuerzas Armadas de un Estado extranjero, que lleven los signos exteriores distintivos de los buques de guerra de su nacionalidad, se encuentren bajo el mando de un oficial debidamente designado por el Gobierno de ese Estado, cuyo nombre esté inscrito en el escalafón de oficiales o en un documento equivalente y cuyas dotaciones estén sometidas a la disciplina de las Fuerzas Armadas regulares;

i) Aeronave de Estado: una aeronave perteneciente a un Estado extranjero, operada o explotada por él y utilizada exclusivamente para un servicio público no comercial, tales como servicios militares, de aduana o de policía;

j) Fuerzas Armadas visitantes: el personal militar de un Estado extranjero que, a invitación o con consentimiento de España, se encuentre en territorio español en relación con sus deberes oficiales, en el bien entendido de que España y el Estado extranjero podrán convenir que determinados individuos, unidades o formaciones no se considere que forman parte o están incluidos en una Fuerza a los fines de la presente Ley Orgánica;

k) Personal civil de las Fuerzas Armadas visitantes: el personal civil que acompañe a una Fuerza Armada de un Estado extranjero y que esté empleado por uno de los ejércitos de dicho Estado, siempre que no sean personas apátridas, ni nacionales de un tercer Estado respecto del cual España no haya consentido su entrada en territorio español, ni tengan nacionalidad española o residencia habitual en España;

l) Organización internacional: una organización de carácter intergubernamental, dotada de personalidad jurídica internacional y regida por el Derecho Internacional que tenga sede u oficina en España;

m) Conferencia internacional: una reunión, ya sea de carácter intergubernamental o no, celebrada o que vaya a celebrarse en España a iniciativa del Gobierno de España o de una organización internacional de la que España sea parte con consentimiento del Gobierno español; y

n) Transacción mercantil: todo contrato o transacción mercantil de compraventa de bienes o prestación de servicios; todo contrato de préstamo u otra transacción de carácter financiero, incluida cualquier obligación de garantía o de indemnización concerniente a ese préstamo o a esa transacción; cualquier otro contrato o transacción de naturaleza mercantil, industrial o de arrendamiento de obra o de servicios, con exclusión de los contratos individuales de trabajo. Para determinar si un contrato o transacción es una ñtransacción mercantilñ, se atenderá principalmente a la naturaleza del contrato o de la transacción, pero se tendrá en cuenta también su finalidad si así lo acuerdan las partes en el contrato o la transacción o si, en la práctica del Estado que es parte en uno u otra, tal finalidad es pertinente para la determinación del carácter no mercantil del contrato o de la transacción.

Artículo 3. Otros privilegios e inmunidades reconocidos por el Derecho Internacional y no afectados por la presente Ley Orgánica.

Lo dispuesto en la presente Ley Orgánica se entenderá sin perjuicio de cualesquiera otros privilegios e inmunidades contemplados por el Derecho Internacional y, en particular, de los reconocidos a:

Orgánica se regulan las inmunidades jurisdiccionales del Estado extranjero en España (Título I), diferenciando en sendos capítulos entre inmunidad de jurisdicción e inmunidad de ejecución. Las inmunidades previstas en este título se conciben como un derecho renunciable, de manera expresa o tácita. Es, igualmente, una obligación de carácter no absoluto para el Estado del foro, ya que conoce ciertos límites. A partir de ahí, la presente Ley Orgánica trata los privilegios e inmunidades del Jefe del Estado, el Jefe del Gobierno y el Ministro de Asuntos Exteriores del Estado extranjero (Título II), la inmunidad del Estado respecto de los buques de guerra y los buques y aeronaves de Estado (Título III), el estatuto de las fuerzas armadas visitantes (Título IV), los privilegios e inmunidades de las organizaciones internacionales con sede u oficina en España (Título V) y los privilegios e inmunidades aplicables a las conferencias y reuniones internacionales (Título VI). La Ley Orgánica se cierra con unas disposiciones de carácter procedimental (Título VII) y las correspondientes disposiciones adicional, derogatoria y finales.

Cabe subrayar, por último, que la Ley Orgánica deja fuera el régimen diplomático y consular, por contar con una regulación internacional propia bien asentada que, desde hace décadas, forma ya parte del ordenamiento jurídico español. Por otro lado, su contenido ha de entenderse, en todo caso, sin perjuicio de las obligaciones internacionales de nuestro país respecto del enjuiciamiento de crímenes internacionales, así como de sus compromisos con la Corte Penal Internacional.

TÍTULO PRELIMINAR

Artículo 1. Objeto.

La presente Ley Orgánica tiene por objeto regular las inmunidades ante los órganos jurisdiccionales españoles y, en su caso, los privilegios aplicables a:

a) Los Estados extranjeros y sus bienes;

b) Los Jefes de Estado y de Gobierno y Ministros de Asuntos Exteriores extranjeros, durante el ejercicio de su cargo y una vez finalizado el mismo;

c) Los buques de guerra y buques y aeronaves de Estado;

d) Las Fuerzas Armadas visitantes;

e) Las organizaciones internacionales con sede u oficina en España y sus bienes; y

f) Las conferencias y reuniones internacionales celebradas en España.

Artículo 2. Definiciones.

A los efectos de la presente Ley Orgánica, se entiende por:

a) Inmunidad de jurisdicción: prerrogativa de un Estado, organización o persona de no ser demandado ni enjuiciado por los órganos jurisdiccionales de otro Estado;

b) Inmunidad de ejecución: prerrogativa por la que un Estado, organización o persona y sus bienes no pueden ser objeto de medidas coercitivas o de ejecución de decisiones dictadas por los órganos jurisdiccionales de otro Estado;

c) Estado:

i) El Estado y sus diversos órganos de gobierno;

ii) Los elementos constitutivos de un Estado federal o las subdivisiones políticas del Estado, que estén facultados para realizar actos en el ejercicio de la autoridad soberana y actúen en tal capacidad;

iii) Los organismos e instituciones del Estado y otras entidades públicas, aunque tengan personalidad jurídica diferenciada, siempre que estén facultados para realizar actos en el ejercicio de la autoridad soberana del Estado y que actúen en tal capacidad; y

iv) Los representantes del Estado cuando actúen en esa condición.

d) Jefe de Estado: la persona que ejerce la jefatura de un Estado extranjero, cualquiera que sea la denominación de su cargo, incluyendo cada uno de los miembros

Estados extranjeros». De este modo, «el legislador necesariamente ha de tener presentes los límites, positivos y negativos, que el Derecho Internacional impone a los Estados» y ello «viene a corroborar la justificación objetiva y razonable de la inmunidad de la jurisdicción (…)», porque «caso de que se extendiera más allá del ámbito delimitado por el Derecho Internacional y tratara de hacer efectiva en todo caso la tutela jurisdiccional en el orden interno, el Estado podría incurrir, al hacerlo así, en un hecho ilícito por la violación de una obligación internacional, lo que entrañaría su responsabilidad internacional frente a otro Estado» (STC 140/1995, de 28 de septiembre, Fundamento Jurídico 9). Por lo que se refiere a la inmunidad de ejecución, el Tribunal Constitucional también ha considerado que el régimen de esta inmunidad «se contiene en normas de Derecho Internacional público que se obtienen por inducción de datos de origen muy diverso, entre los que se encuentran las convenciones internacionales y la práctica de los Estados» (STC 18/1997, de 10 de febrero, Fundamento Jurídico 6).

Sin embargo, esta remisión genérica al Derecho Internacional provoca, en el plano judicial interno, cierta inseguridad jurídica e incluso un casuismo jurisprudencial que, en ocasiones, puede conducir a errores o contradicciones, susceptibles, en el plano externo, de comprometer la responsabilidad internacional de España. De hecho, el legislador ha recibido una abierta recomendación del propio Tribunal Constitucional para que regule el régimen de las inmunidades de los Estados extranjeros en España en aras a garantizar una mayor certeza en el ámbito jurisdiccional interno sobre la base de una doctrina restringida de la inmunidad de jurisdicción y de ejecución (STC 107/1992, de 1 de julio).

Por tanto, casi tres décadas después de la introducción del ya aludido precepto en la Ley Orgánica del Poder Judicial, parece conveniente desarrollar legislativamente la cuestión a través de una Ley Orgánica que, con pleno respeto de las obligaciones internacionales asumidas por nuestro país, regule de forma sistemática esta materia. Ello resulta tanto más necesario, en aras de lograr la necesaria seguridad jurídica, en cuanto el propio Derecho Internacional al que remite nuestra legislación presenta, como ya se ha mencionado, una regulación también insuficiente y fragmentada. Y conviene hacerlo, una vez emprendida la labor, de manera que se incluyan también aquellas otras inmunidades diferentes a las inmunidades del Estado extranjero y sus representantes, pero que ya son frecuentes como consecuencia de la intensidad de la cooperación internacional. Es el caso, básicamente, de las inmunidades de las organizaciones internacionales, las fuerzas armadas visitantes, los buques y aeronaves de Estado, así como el régimen de privilegios e inmunidades de las conferencias internacionales o reuniones que se celebren en nuestro país. Todo ello, velando por la reducción al mínimo imprescindible del efecto que dichas inmunidades tiene respecto al derecho al acceso efectivo a la justicia y garantizando, en aquellos ámbitos donde existe capacidad del Gobierno para modular el régimen establecido por la Ley, el ejercicio de la función de control del Parlamento.

Esta Ley Orgánica se erige, además, en complemento idóneo de las otras leyes en materia de Derecho Internacional aprobadas durante esta legislatura, a saber, la Ley 2/2014, de 25 de marzo, de la Acción y del Servicio Exterior del Estado (BOE núm. 74, de 26 de marzo de 2014) y la Ley 25/2014, de 27 de noviembre, de Tratados y otros Acuerdos Internacionales (BOE núm. 288, de 28 de noviembre de 2014).

III

El contenido de la presente Ley Orgánica se articula en torno a ocho títulos. El punto de partida lo configuran las disposiciones generales del título preliminar sobre objeto, definiciones y ámbito material. A continuación, como núcleo central de la Ley

jurisprudencia de creciente interés en la materia.

No obstante, al final, perviven lagunas importantes en el régimen internacional de las inmunidades. Ello, en último término, hace que, indirectamente, también la jurisprudencia sobre la materia de otros tribunales nacionales pueda servir en ocasiones como valioso elemento de referencia.

En estos momentos, quizá la laguna más llamativa sea la relativa a los privilegios e inmunidades aplicables a los participantes en conferencias y reuniones internacionales que se celebran en el territorio de un determinado Estado. No se regula la cuestión en ningún tratado internacional, tampoco existe Derecho consuetudinario al respecto y se carece de una respuesta jurisdiccional adecuada. Ante esta realidad, en el caso español, se celebran tratados internacionales ad hoc, que agotan sus efectos una vez celebrado el evento cuya inmediatez requiere, además, en muchas ocasiones, el recurso a la aplicación provisional.

II

Por lo que respecta al ámbito jurídico interno, el tratamiento de las inmunidades exige considerar tanto la perspectiva constitucional y legislativa, como el marco jurisprudencial establecido básicamente por la doctrina del Tribunal Constitucional sobre la materia.

Desde la perspectiva constitucional, el artículo 24 de la Carta Magna garantiza el derecho de todas las personas «a obtener la tutela judicial efectiva de los jueces y tribunales en el ejercicio de sus derechos e intereses legítimos, sin que, en ningún caso, pueda producirse indefensión». Por su parte, el artículo 117. 3 establece que «el ejercicio de la potestad jurisdiccional en todo tipo de procesos, juzgando y haciendo ejecutar lo juzgado corresponde exclusivamente a los Juzgados y Tribunales determinados por las leyes, según las normas de competencia y procedimiento que las mismas establezcan». No existe, empero, previsión alguna en relación a las inmunidades del Estado extranjero.

Por otro lado, la Constitución recoge igualmente una clara exigencia de cumplimiento de las obligaciones jurídicas derivadas del Derecho Internacional (arts. 93 a 96). Entre ellas, lógicamente, se incluyen las obligaciones contenidas en tratados internacionales celebrados por España en materia de inmunidades, así como otro tipo de obligaciones que puedan derivar del Derecho Internacional consuetudinario o de sentencias obligatorias de tribunales internacionales.

En el plano legislativo, la Ley Orgánica 6/1985, de 1 de julio, del Poder Judicial prevé en el apartado primero del artículo 21 que «los Juzgados y Tribunales españoles conocerán de los juicios que se susciten en territorio español entre españoles, entre extranjeros y españoles y extranjeros con arreglo a lo establecido en la presente ley y en los tratados y convenios internacionales en los que España sea Parte». Si bien, por lo que directamente afecta a la inmunidad, el apartado segundo fija que ñse exceptúan los supuestos de inmunidad de jurisdicción y de ejecución establecidos por las normas del Derecho Internacional Público. Esta disposición supuso, en su momento, una importante novedad, que permitía a España cumplir con sus obligaciones internacionales. En parecido sentido, la Ley 1/2000, de 7 de enero, de Enjuiciamiento Civil también recoge en su articulado la adecuada remisión a «los tratados y convenios internacionales de los que España sea parte», al referirse a aspectos de la jurisdicción civil concernidos por las inmunidades (art. 36). Estas previsiones normativas resultan, en suma, acordes con el Derecho Internacional.

Por su parte, el Tribunal Constitucional ha considerado plenamente conforme con la Constitución el «límite negativo que se deriva de la inmunidad jurisdiccional atribuida a los

Es también, en segundo término, el supuesto del régimen de las Fuerzas Armadas de un Estado presentes en el territorio de otro. Su estatuto de inmunidades se suele regular a través de convenios ad hoc que, en la práctica, son conocidos por su acrónimo inglés (SOFAs, Status of Foreign Forces Agreements). En el caso español se cuenta básicamente con los relativos a la OTAN (Convenio de Londres entre los Estados Partes del Tratado de Atlántico Norte relativo al estatuto de sus fuerzas, de 19 de junio de 1951; BOE núm. 128, de 29 de mayo de 1998). Por lo que concierne a los miembros de las fuerzas armadas de Estados Unidos presentes en España, ha de tenerse también en cuenta las previsiones recogidas en el relevante Convenio sobre cooperación para la defensa, de 1 de diciembre de 1988, revisado por los Protocolos de Enmienda, de 10 de abril de 2002 y de 10 de octubre de 2012 (BOE núm. 108, de 6 de mayo de 1989; BOE núm. 45, de 21 de febrero de 2003; y BOE núm. 138, de 10 de junio de 2013).

Finalmente, en relación con la treintena de organizaciones internacionales con sede u oficina en España, existen dos tipos de acuerdos internacionales para regular sus inmunidades. Por un lado, algunas organizaciones internacionales cuentan con convenios internacionales celebrados entre todos sus Estados miembros. Tal es el caso de la Unión Europea (Protocolo número 7, anejo al Tratado de Funcionamiento de la Unión Europea, sobre los privilegios y las inmunidades de la Unión Europea) o de las organizaciones del ámbito de Naciones Unidas, para las que existe un convenio general (Convención General sobre prerrogativas e inmunidades de Naciones Unidas, de 13 de febrero de 1946; BOE núm. 282, de 25 de noviembre de 1974) y otro para sus organismos especializados (Convención sobre privilegios e inmunidades de los organismos especializados, de 25 de noviembre de 1947; BOE núm. 282, de 25 de noviembre de 1974). En cambio, por otro lado, para el resto de organizaciones internacionales se han celebrado acuerdos de sede entre la organización concernida y el Reino de España.

Además de los convenios internacionales, concurren igualmente obligaciones derivadas del Derecho Internacional consuetudinario, que inciden directamente en el régimen de las inmunidades en España de los sujetos de Derecho Internacional. Es, entre otros, el caso de las aeronaves de Estado, cuyo régimen jurídico queda fuera del Convenio de Chicago, de 7 de diciembre de 1944, sobre aviación civil internacional, en virtud de su artículo 3 a). También encajan en esta categoría aspectos concretos de la inmunidad penal de los funcionarios del Estado (por ejemplo, el régimen aplicable a los Jefes de Estado, Presidentes de Gobierno y Ministros de Asuntos Exteriores), que en estos momentos está siendo objeto de atención incipiente por parte de la Comisión de Derecho Internacional. O incluso han cristalizado costumbres internacionales en torno a ámbitos específicos de las inmunidades del Estado, como aquella según la cual la renuncia a la inmunidad de jurisdicción no conlleva por sí misma una correlativa renuncia a la inmunidad de ejecución. Con todo, perviven amplias dudas a propósito del carácter consuetudinario o no de buen número de aspectos de las inmunidades, en cuestiones de índole tanto sustantiva como procesal.

Por último, los tribunales internacionales han contribuido a clarificar el régimen de las inmunidades con relevantes sentencias, que en aspectos fundamentales marcan la pauta de actuación de los órganos jurisdiccionales nacionales. Destaca, por encima de todos, la Corte Internacional de Justicia, pero también el Tribunal Internacional de Derecho del Mar o el Tribunal Europeo de Derechos Humanos, que han desplegado una

Particularmente delicada es la cuestión de los límites de las inmunidades, dado que la vieja doctrina absoluta de las inmunidades ha ido dando paso a una doctrina más restrictiva que haga compatible la existencia de tales inmunidades con las exigencias elementales de tutela judicial efectiva derivadas del principio de Estado de Derecho.

De ahí que, a la hora de fijar el estatuto internacional de las inmunidades, haya de tenerse en consideración tres planos diferentes, a saber, el convencional, el consuetudinario y el jurisprudencial.

Por lo que concierne al plano convencional, se constata la existencia de diversos tratados internacionales de dispar contenido y exigencia de desarrollo normativo nacional. Cabe diferenciar, en este sentido, entre tratados que regulan los privilegios e inmunidades de los órganos del Estado que participan en la acción exterior, los que tratan específicamente las inmunidades del Estado extranjero en el Estado del foro y otros tratados sobre ámbitos absolutamente ajenos a las inmunidades pero con disposiciones específicas de relevancia en la materia.

En primer lugar, en relación con los privilegios e inmunidades de los órganos del Estado que participan en la acción diplomática y consular existen, a su vez, tres tratados internacionales de carácter universal. Estos instrumentos configuran un ámbito plenamente asentado y no necesitado de desarrollo normativo interno. Se trata, en concreto, de los convenios relativos a las relaciones diplomáticas (Convención de Viena, de 18 de abril de 1961), las relaciones consulares (Convención de Viena, de 24 de abril de 1963) y, en menor medida, las misiones especiales (Convenio de Nueva York, de 16 de diciembre de 1969). España es Parte en estos tratados, que están incorporados a nuestro ordenamiento jurídico interno (respectivamente BOE núm. 21, de 24 de enero de 1968, con corrección de errores en BOE núm. 80, de 2 de abril de 1968; BOE núm. 56, de 6 de marzo de 1970; y BOE núm. 159, de 4 de julio de 2001).

En segundo lugar, por lo que concierne al régimen jurídico básico de las inmunidades de que gozan los Estados extranjeros en el Estado del foro, existe la Convención de las Naciones Unidas, de 2 de diciembre de 2004, sobre las inmunidades jurisdiccionales de los Estados y de sus bienes, que representa el principal intento codificador en la materia. Pero esta Convención, abierta a la firma en Nueva York el 17 de enero de 2005, no ha entrado aún en vigor ni es probable que lo haga en un futuro inmediato, ya que se precisa para ello el depósito de treinta instrumentos de ratificación o adhesión (art. 30.1) y por el momento solo diecisiete Estados lo han llevado a cabo. No obstante, la propia Asamblea General de Naciones Unidas considera que las inmunidades recogidas en este instrumento constituyen «un principio generalmente aceptado en el Derecho Internacional consuetudinario», de manera que su cumplimiento «fortalecería la preeminencia del derecho y la seguridad jurídica, particularmente en las relaciones de los Estados con las personas naturales o jurídicas»; igualmente, destaca «la importancia de la uniformidad y la claridad en el derecho de las inmunidades jurisdiccionales de los Estados y de sus bienes». En todo caso, España depositó su instrumento de adhesión a la Convención el 11 de septiembre de 2011 y ha mostrado siempre un firme compromiso internacional en defensa de los principios y garantías del régimen de inmunidades.

En tercer lugar, junto a esta Convención de 2004 se encuentran otros tratados en vigor en ámbitos diferentes a las inmunidades, pero que en su articulado contienen disposiciones relevantes sobre la materia. Cabe subrayar tres modalidades diferentes. Sería, en primer término, el caso de los artículos 32, 95 y 96 de la Convención de las Naciones Unidas sobre Derecho del mar, de 10 de diciembre de 1982, de la que España es Parte, en lo que se refiere a los buques de guerra que pertenezcan a un Estado (BOE núm. 39, de 14 de febrero de 1997).

Organic Law on Privileges and Immunities of Foreign States etc., 2015 (Spain)

Ley Orgánica 16/2015, de 27 de octubre, sobre privilegios e inmunidades de los Estados extranjeros, las Organizaciones Internacionales con sede u oficina en España y las Conferencias y Reuniones internacionales celebradas en España.

TEXTO

FELIPE VI

REY DE ESPAÑA

A todos los que la presente vieren y entendieren.

Sabed: Que las Cortes Generales han aprobado y Yo vengo en sancionar la siguiente ley orgánica:

PREÁMBULO

I

Las inmunidades soberanas del Estado encarnan, tradicionalmente, un principio básico del Derecho Internacional que deriva, a su vez, de los principios de independencia, soberanía e igualdad de los Estados (par in parem imperium non habet). Su contenido jurídico es básicamente de naturaleza procesal y supone que los jueces y tribunales de un Estado no pueden juzgar a otro Estado. Abarca tanto el derecho del Estado a no ser demandado ni sometido a juicio ante los órganos jurisdiccionales de otro Estado (inmunidad de jurisdicción), como el derecho a que no se ejecute lo juzgado (inmunidad de ejecución).

En la actualidad, como consecuencia de los fenómenos de cooperación internacional, las inmunidades internacionales abarcan también otros ámbitos, entre los que destacan el de las organizaciones internacionales y el de las conferencias y reuniones internacionales, sin olvidar las relativas a los Jefes de Estado, Jefes de Gobierno y Ministros de Asuntos Exteriores, los buques de guerra y buques y aeronaves de Estado y las fuerzas armadas extranjeras. Todo ello configura un panorama complejo en el que algunos sectores han alcanzado ya una regulación consolidada, mientras que en otros existe todavía cierta fragmentación e indeterminación.

El régimen jurídico internacional de estas inmunidades hunde sus raíces en la práctica judicial internacional y se ha ido configurando a través de normas consuetudinarias que posteriormente se han recogido en diversos tratados. Sin embargo, la regulación derivada de estos tratados no abarca la totalidad de las cuestiones que se plantean en la práctica y no ofrece todavía una respuesta suficientemente satisfactoria.

(b) Any methods that said Foreign State, etc. will accept as a method of service (limited to those methods provided for in the Code of Civil Procedure (Act No. 109 of 1996)).

(2) In cases where service has been carried out according to a method listed in item (ii) (a) of the preceding paragraph, service shall be deemed to have been effected when the body of said Foreign State, etc. (for those other than a State, the State to which they belong) corresponding to the Ministry of Foreign Affairs has received the Complaint, etc.

(3) A Foreign State, etc. shall lose the right to state an objection concerning the method of service of the Complaint, etc. when it has made an oral argument or a statement on the merits without making any objection.

(4) In addition to what is provided under paragraph (1) and paragraph (2), necessary matters concerning the service of a Complaint, etc. upon a Foreign State, etc. shall be specified by the Rules of the Supreme Court.

Article 21 Special Provisions of the Code of Civil Procedure in Cases of Nonappearance of a Foreign State, etc.

(1) In cases where a Foreign State, etc. has failed to appear on the date for oral argument and has not submitted a written answer or any other brief, a judgment upholding a claim against said Foreign State, etc. cannot be rendered until four months have elapsed since the day the Complaint, etc. was served or the day on which the Complaint, etc. was deemed to have been served pursuant to the provisions of paragraph (2) of the preceding Article.

(2) The provisions of paragraph (1) and paragraph (2) of the preceding Article shall apply *mutatis mutandis* to the service upon said Foreign State, etc., of the judgment document or the record under Article 254, paragraph (2) of the Code of Civil Procedure (referred to as "Judgment Document, etc." in the following paragraph and paragraph (4)) concerning the judgment provided for in the preceding paragraph.

(3) In addition to what is provided for in the preceding paragraph, the necessary matters concerning the service of Judgment Document, etc. shall be specified by the Rules of Supreme Court.

(4) Notwithstanding the provisions of the main clause of Article 285 of the Code of Civil Procedure (including cases where applied *mutatis mutandis* pursuant to Article 313 of the same Act (including cases where applied *mutatis mutandis* pursuant to Article 318 paragraph (5) of the same Act)) or of the main clause of Article 357 (including cases where applied *mutatis mutandis* pursuant to Article 367 paragraph (2) of the same Act) or the main clause of Article 378, paragraph (1), the filing of appeals or objections by a Foreign State, etc. to the judgment provided for in paragraph (1), must be done within an unextendable period of four months from the day the Judgment Document, etc. was served or the day service was deemed to have been effected pursuant to the provisions of paragraph (2) of the preceding Article as applied *mutatis mutandis* pursuant to paragraph (2).

Article 22 Exclusion from Application of Provisions Concerning Subpoenas and Non-penal Fines

The provisions of the Code of Civil Procedure or any other laws and regulations concerning subpoenas and non-penal fines due to failure to comply with an order to submit documents or any other article issued during Civil Court Proceedings, a summons of a witness, or any other order during said Civil Court Proceedings shall not apply to a Foreign State, etc.

(3) A consent under Article 5, paragraph (1) shall not be construed as being a consent under paragraph (1) of this Article.

Article 18 Property Used for a Specific Purpose

(1) A Foreign State, etc. shall not be immune from jurisdiction with respect to proceedings of a civil execution procedures against the property held by said Foreign State, etc. that is in use or intended for use by said Foreign State, etc. exclusively for other than government non-commercial purposes.

(2) The property a Foreign State, etc. holds listed below shall not be included in the property of the preceding paragraph:

(i) Property which is used or intended for use in the performance of the functions of the diplomatic mission, consular posts, special missions, missions to international organizations or delegations to organs of international organizations or to international conferences;

(ii) Property of a military character or used or intended for use in the performance of military functions;

(iii) Property listed below that is not being sold and is not intended to be sold:

(a) Cultural heritage pertaining to said Foreign State, etc. ;

(b) Official documents or any other records administered by said Foreign State, etc. ;

(c) Exhibits that have scientific, cultural, or historical significance.

(3) The provision of the preceding paragraph shall not preclude the application of the provisions of paragraph (1) and paragraph (2) of the preceding Article.

Article 19 Handling of Foreign Central Banks

(1) The central bank of a State other than Japan or the financial authorities equivalent thereto (referred to as a "Foreign Central Bank, etc." in the following paragraph) shall be deemed to be a Foreign State, etc. for purposes of an execution of a temporary restraining order or a civil execution procedures against property held by the Foreign Central Bank, etc., even in cases where it does not fall within the requirements of Article 2, item (i) through item (iii), and the provisions of Article 4 and Article 17, paragraph (1) and paragraph (2) shall apply.

(2) With respect to a Foreign Central Bank, etc., the provisions of paragraph (1) of the preceding Article shall not apply.

Chapter III   Special Provisions for Civil Court Proceedings

Article 20 Service of Complaints, etc.

(1) The service of a complaint or any other similar document and a writ of summons for the first date of litigation proceedings or any other proceedings in court (hereinafter referred to as a "Complaint, etc." in this Article and paragraph (1) of the following Article) upon a Foreign State, etc. shall be carried out according to the methods listed below:

(i) Methods prescribed by treaties or any other international agreements;

(ii) In cases where the methods listed in the preceding item do not exist, the methods listed in (a) or (b) below:

(a) Methods carried out through diplomatic channels;

Article 15 Operation of Ships, etc.

(1) A Foreign State, etc. which owns or operates a ship shall not be immune from jurisdiction with respect to Judicial Proceedings which relates to a dispute regarding the operation of that ship if, at the time the fact that causes said dispute arose, the ship was used for other than government noncommercial purposes.

(2) The provision of the preceding paragraph shall not apply in cases where said ship is a warship or a naval auxiliary.

(3) A Foreign State, etc. which owns or operates a ship shall not be immune from jurisdiction with respect to Judicial Proceedings which relates to a dispute regarding the carriage of cargo on board that ship if, at the time the fact that causes said dispute arose, the ship was used for other than government noncommercial purposes.

(4) The provision of the preceding paragraph shall not apply in cases where said freight was being carried on board a warship or a naval auxiliary or in cases where a State etc. owns said cargo and said cargo is used or intended for use exclusively for government non-commercial purposes.

Article 16 Arbitration Agreements

A Foreign State, etc. , with respect to the written arbitration agreements relating to commercial transactions between said Foreign State, etc. and a citizen of a State other than said Foreign State, etc. (for those other than a State, the State to which they belong; hereinafter the same shall apply in this Article) or a judicial person or any other entity established based on the laws and regulations of the State or the State, etc. which belongs to the State, shall not be immune from jurisdiction with respect to Judicial Proceedings concerning the existence or nonexistence or effect of said arbitration agreements or arbitration proceedings based on said arbitration agreements; provided however, this shall not apply in cases where the parties have agreed otherwise in writing.

Section 3   Cases of Non-Immunity from Proceedings of Execution of Temporary Restraining Orders and Civil Execution Procedures against Property of a Foreign State, etc.

Article 17 Consent of a Foreign State, etc.

(1) In cases where consent to an execution of a temporary restraining order or a civil execution against the property held by a Foreign State, etc. , has been given expressly by any of the following methods, the Foreign State, etc. shall not be immune from jurisdiction with regard to the proceedings of said execution of temporary restraining order or said civil execution procedure:

(i) Treaties or any other international agreements;

(ii) Agreements concerning arbitration;

(iii) Written contracts;

(iv) Statements made during the course of said proceedings of the execution of the temporary restraining order or the civil execution, or written notices to the court or the other party (in the case of notices to the other party, limited to notices made subsequent to the occurrence of the dispute pertaining to the relationship of rights that was the cause of the petition for said execution of temporary restraining order or said civil execution) .

(2) In cases where specific property is designated to enable achievement of the purpose of an execution of a temporary restraining order or a civil execution, or provided as security, a Foreign State, etc. shall not be immune from jurisdiction with respect to proceedings of said execution of temporary restraining order or said civil execution against said property.

ble object resulted from an act for which it is claimed a Foreign State, etc., should take responsibility, if all or part of said act took place in Japan and the person who performed said act was in Japan at the time it was committed, said Foreign State, etc. shall not be immune from jurisdiction with respect to Judicial Proceedings in which monetary compensation for the damage or loss resulting from said act is being sought.

Article 11 Rights and Interests, etc. Pertaining to Real Property

(1) A Foreign State, etc. shall not be immune from jurisdiction with respect to Judicial Proceedings regarding the matters listed below pertaining to real property in Japan:

(i) The rights or interests of said Foreign State, etc. or possession of or use by said Foreign State, etc.;

(ii) The obligations of said Foreign State, etc. arising from rights or interests of said Foreign State, etc. or the possession of or use by said Foreign State, etc.

(2) A Foreign State, etc. shall not be immune from jurisdiction with respect to Judicial Proceedings regarding rights or interests of said Foreign State, etc. arising due to inheritance or any other general succession, gifts, or acquisition of ownerless properties, concerning movables or real property.

Article 12 Rights and Interests Pertaining to the Administration or Disposition of Property in which the Court Participates

A Foreign State, etc. shall not be immune from jurisdiction with respect to Judicial Proceedings regarding the rights or interests of said Foreign State, etc. pertaining to the administration or disposition of trust property, property belonging to a bankruptcy estate, property of a company in liquidation, or any other property for which a Japanese court conducts supervision or any other participation.

Article 13 Intellectual Property Rights

A Foreign State, etc. shall not be immune from jurisdiction with respect to Judicial Proceedings regarding the matters listed below:

(1) The existence or nonexistence, effect, ownership, or contents of intellectual property rights (meaning rights established by the laws and regulations of Japan regarding intellectual property as provided for in the Intellectual Property Basic Act (Act No. 122 of 2002), Article 2, paragraph (1) or rights pertaining to interests legally protected under Japanese law; the same shall apply in the following item) that said Foreign State, etc., claims to hold;

(2) Infringement of intellectual property rights allegedly caused by said Foreign State, etc. in Japan.

Article 14 Qualification as a Constituent Member of an Entity

(1) In cases where a Foreign State, etc. is a member or any other constituent member of a juridical person or any other entity that falls under any of the following items, it shall not be immune from jurisdiction with respect to Judicial Proceedings concerning qualification, or the rights or obligations based on such qualification:

(i) An entity that has members or other constituent members other than a State, etc., or an international organization;

(ii) An entity established based on the laws and regulations of Japan or that has its principal business office or other principal office in Japan.

(2) The provision of the preceding paragraph shall not apply in cases where there is a written agreement between the parties to said Judicial Proceedings to the effect that said Foreign State, etc. shall have immunity from jurisdiction or in cases where the articles of incorporation, constitution, or any other similar regulations of said entity provide to that effect.

tions relating to the civil or commercial buying and selling of commodities, procurement of services, lending of money, or other matters (excluding labor contracts); the same shall apply in the following paragraph and Article 16) between said Foreign State, etc. and a citizen of a State other than said Foreign State, etc. (for those other than a State, the State to which they belong, hereinafter the same shall apply in this paragraph) or a judicial person or any other entity established based on the laws and regulations of the State or the State, etc. which belongs to the State.

(2) The provision of the preceding paragraph shall not apply in the cases listed below:

(i) Cases of commercial transactions between said Foreign State, etc. and a State, etc. other than said Foreign State, etc. ;

(ii) Cases in which parties to said commercial transactions have expressly agreed otherwise.

Article 9 Labor Contracts

(1) A Foreign State, etc. shall not be immune from jurisdiction with respect to Judicial Proceedings regarding labor contracts between said Foreign State, etc. and an individual wherein all or part of the labor is, or is to be, provided in Japan.

(2) The provision of the preceding paragraph shall not apply in the cases listed below:

(i) Where said individual is one of the following persons:

(a) A diplomat as provided in Article 1 (e) of the Vienna Convention on Diplomatic Relations;

(b) A consular officer as provided in Article 1 (d) of the Vienna Convention on Consular Relations;

(c) A diplomatic staff of a permanent missions or a special mission to an international organizations or a persons employed to represent said Foreign State, etc. , (for those other than a State, the State to which they belong; hereinafter the same shall apply in this paragraph) at international conferences;

(d) In addition to those persons listed in (a) through (c), persons enjoying diplomatic immunity.

(ii) In addition to the cases listed in the preceding item, cases where said individual has been employed in order to perform duties pertaining to the security, diplomatic secrets, or other important interests of said Foreign State, etc. ;

(iii) An action or petition regarding the existence or nonexistence of the contract for the employment or re-employment of the individual (excluding those seeking compensation for damages) ;

(iv) An action or petition regarding the effect of a dismissal or other termination of the labor contracts (excluding those seeking compensation for damages) where the head of said Foreign State, etc., the head of its government, or its Minister of Foreign Affairs finds that there is a risk that Judicial Proceedings pertaining to said action or petition would harm the security interests of said Foreign State, etc. ;

(v) Cases where the individual is a citizen of said Foreign State, etc. at the time of the filing of the action or any other petition for commencement of Judicial Proceedings; provided however, that this shall not apply where said individual has the permanent residence in Japan;

(vi) Cases where the parties to said labor contract have otherwise agreed in writing; provided however, that this shall not apply where the lack of jurisdiction over the action or petition regarding said labor contract by Japanese courts is contrary to public order from the viewpoint of protecting workers.

Article 10 Death or Injury of Persons or Loss, etc. of Tangible Objects

In cases where the death of or injury to a person or the loss of or damage to a tangi-

Section 2 Cases of Non-Immunity from Judicial Proceedings
Article 5 Consent of a Foreign State, etc.

(1) In cases where consent to submission to jurisdiction concerning a specific matter or case has been given expressly by any of the following methods, a Foreign State, etc. shall not be immune from jurisdiction concerning the proceedings related to said specific matter or case among the litigation proceedings or any other proceedings in court (excluding temporary restraining orders and civil execution procedures with respect to property held by a Foreign State, etc., hereinafter referred to as "Judicial Proceedings" in this Section):

(i) Treaties or any other international agreements;

(ii) Written contracts;

(iii) Statements made in said Judicial Proceedings or written notices to the court or the other party.

(2) The consent of a Foreign State, etc. to apply the laws of Japan to specific matter or case shall not be construed as the consent described in the preceding Paragraph.

Article 6 Constructive Consent

(1) In cases where a Foreign State, etc. carries out any of the acts listed below, it shall be deemed that the consent set forth in paragraph (1) of the preceding Article has been given:

(i) The filing of an action or any other petition for commencement of some other Judicial Proceeding;

(ii) Intervention in a Judicial Proceedings (excluding one whose object is to claim immunity from jurisdiction);

(iii) An oral argument or a statement on the merits of a Judicial Proceeding without making any objection.

(2) The provisions set forth in items (ii) and (iii) of the preceding paragraph shall not apply in cases where there are any compelling reasons that it could not be known that facts constituting grounds for immunity from jurisdiction existed before said Foreign State etc. carried out any of the listed acts, and where said reasons are promptly proven after said facts become known.

(3) The nonappearance of a Foreign State, etc. and the appearance of a representative of the Foreign State, etc. as a witness on the date for oral arguments or the date of other Judicial Proceedings shall not be interpreted as the consent set forth in paragraph (1) of the preceding Article.

Article 7

(1) In cases where a Foreign State, etc. has filed an action or has intervened in an action as a party, when a counterclaim has been filed, this shall be deemed to constitute consent as set forth in Article 5 paragraph (1) with respect to said counterclaim.

(2) The filing of a counterclaim by a Foreign State, etc. in an action in which said Foreign State, etc. is the defendant shall be deemed to constitute consent as set forth in Article 5, paragraph (1) with respect to said action.

Article 8 Commercial Transactions

(1) A Foreign State, etc. shall not be immune from jurisdiction with respect to Judicial Proceedings regarding commercial transactions (meaning contracts or transac-

Act on the Civil Jurisdiction of Japan with Respect to a Foreign State, 2009 (Japan)

(Act No. 24 of April 24, 2009)

Chapter I General Provisions

Article 1 Purpose

This Act establishes the scope of the civil jurisdiction (meaning the jurisdiction other than the one pertaining to criminal matters; the same shall apply in Article 4) of Japan with respect to a Foreign State, etc. jurisdiction and the special provisions of civil court proceedings pertaining to a Foreign State, etc.

Article 2 Definitions

In this Act, a "Foreign State, etc." shall mean the entities listed in the following items (hereinafter referred to as a "State, etc."), excluding Japan and any entity which pertains to Japan:

(ⅰ) A State and the governmental institutions thereof;

(ⅱ) A State within a Federal States and any other administrative divisions of a State equivalent thereto having the authority to exercise sovereign power;

(ⅲ) In addition to what is listed in the preceding two items, entities that are granted the authority to exercise sovereign power (limited to cases in which said power is exercised.);

(ⅳ) A representative of an entity listed in the previous three items acting based on its qualifications.

Article 3 Relationships with the privileges or immunities based on treaties, etc.

The provisions of this Act shall not affect the privileges or immunities enjoyed by a Foreign State, etc. based on treaties or the established international law.

Chapter II Scope of Jurisdiction with respect to a Foreign State, etc.

Section 1 Principle of Immunity

Article 4

A Foreign State, etc., except as otherwise provided by this Act, shall be immune from jurisdiction (meaning the civil jurisdiction of Japan; the same shall apply hereinafter).

the authority conferred on any other person to waive the immunity in the name of the foreign State.

18. Execution against assets of a separate entity

Notwithstanding the provisions of section 15 (a), the assets of a separate entity, excluding a central bank, shall not have immunity from execution of a judgment or other decision rendered by a court in Israel, except where the jurisdiction of the court originates in waiver of the jurisdiction, given under sections 9 or 10.

Chapter Four   Miscellaneous Provisions

19. Notice to the Attorney General

(a) Where a foreign State has raise a plea of immunity under this Statute, it shall give notice thereof to the Attorney General.

(b) Where a question of immunity of a foreign State under this statute has arises in court, and no notice thereof has been given under subsection (a), the court shall give notice thereof to the Attorney General.

20. Application of immunity to a political entity which is not a foreign State

The Minister of Foreign Affairs, in consultation with the Attorney General and with the approval of the Government and of the Constitution and Law Committee of the Knesset, may prescribe by order that a political entity shall have immunity under Chapters Two or Three of this statute, even

though its international legal status does not amount to that of a State; an order under this section may be general, for certain types of matters or for a specific matter, and may be restricted to a certain period.

21. Diplomatic and consular immunity

This statute shall not derogate from diplomatic or consular immunity or any other immunity applicable in Israel, under any law or usage.

22. Status of foreign military forces

Notwithstanding the provisions of this statute, legal actions based on any act or omission committed by foreign military forces whose rights and status in Israel were determined by agreement between the State of Israel and the State to which the foreign military forces belong shall be governed by that agreement.

23. Implementation and regulations

The Minister of Justice shall be in charge of implementing this statute, and he may, in consultation with Minister of Foreign Affairs, make regulations on any matter concerning its implementation.

24. Application

This statute shall also apply to proceedings brought before it came into force, provided that the hearing on those proceedings has not yet commenced.

Ehud Olmert	Daniel Friedmann
Prime Minister	Minister of Justice
Shimon Peres	Dalia Itzik
President of State	Speaker of the Knesset

ceedings against it or a judgment given against it in default of defence shall be served, through the Ministry of Foreign Affairs, on the Foreign Office of the foreign State.

(b) Court documents in a proceeding to which the foreign State is a party, not enumerated in sub-section (a), shall be served on that state through its attorney for that proceeding, but if this is not possible, they shall be served in the manner specified in sub-section (a).

(c) The response of the foreign State to the action brought against it or to a judgment in default of defence given against it shall be filed within 60 days from the day they were served on it; the court may however extend that period.

(d) This section shall not apply to service of documents on a separate entity.

14. Judgment in default of defense

Where an action has been brought against a foreign State, and that State has not submitted a defence in good time, the court shall only give judgment against it in default of defence if it is convinced that the foreign state does not have immunity from its jurisdiction under the provisions of this statute.

Chapter Three Immunity from Execution Proceedings

15. Immunity of a foreign State from execution proceedings

(a) The assets of a foreign State shall have immunity from proceedings for execution of a judgment or other decision of a court in Israel.

(b) No fine or prison sentence shall be imposed on a foreign State or on a person acting in its name for non-compliance with a judgment or other decision of a court in Israel given against that State.

(c) The provisions of this section shall not apply to a judgment or other decision of a court in Israel in criminal matters.

16. Proviso to immunity

Notwithstanding the provisions of section 15 (a), the assets of a foreign State detailed below shall not benefit from immunity under this section:

(1) commercial property;

(2) assets situated in Israel to which the foreign State is entitled by way of succession, gift or as *bona vacantia*;

(3) immovables situated in Israel.

17. Waiver of immunity

(a) Assets of a foreign state shall not benefit from immunity under section 15 if the foreign State has expressly waived such immunity in writing, or by written or oral notice to the court.

(b) A waiver under this section may be made generally or in respect of a specific matter, in advance or *ex post factum*, and may be limited by exceptions, provided that waiver in respect of a diplomatic or consular asset or an asset of a central bank shall be made expressly.

(c) A waiver by a foreign State of its immunity from the jurisdiction given under sections 9 or 10 shall not be considered a waiver under this section.

(d) Waiver under this section shall not apply to a military asset.

(e) The head of a diplomatic mission of a foreign State in Israel or any person acting in such capacity, shall be authorized to waive the immunity under this section, in the name of the foreign State; the provisions of this sub-section shall not derogate from

Part Three: Waiver of Immunity
9. Waiver of immunity by agreement

(a) A foreign State shall not have immunity from jurisdiction where it has expressly waived such immunity in writing, or where it has waived it by written or oral notice to the court.

(b) A waiver under this section may be made generally or in respect of a particular matter, in advance or *ex post factum*, and may be limited by exceptions.

(c) The head of a diplomatic mission of a foreign State in Israel or any person acting in such capacity, is authorized to waive the immunity under this section, in the name of the foreign State, and in respect of immunity in a proceeding originating in a contract to which the foreign State is a party, any person who has contracted in the name of the foreign State shall also be so authorized; the provisions of this sub-section shall not derogate from an authority conferred on any other person to waive the immunity in the name of the foreign State.

10. Waiver of immunity by way of conduct

(a) A foreign State shall not have immunity from jurisdiction in a counterclaim or in third-party proceedings, where it was the foreign State that initiated the court proceeding or joined them, thereby becoming a party to the proceedings.

(b) The provisions of sub-section (a) shall not apply to a foreign State which joined the proceeding in one of the following circumstances:

(1) the foreign State pleads immunity from the jurisdiction;

(2) the object of the foreign State in adhering to the proceeding is to put before the court submissions regarding a right or other interest it has in assets involved in the proceeding or regarding any other right which may be affected by the proceeding.

(c) In this section, "—counterclaim" means a counterclaim in a civil action having the same subject-matter, or where they both arise from the same circumstances or where the relief sought in the counterclaim is not different from and does not exceed the relief sought in the original action.

11. Arbitration

(a) Where a foreign State has agreed in writing to submit to arbitration a dispute which has arisen or is likely to arise in the future, the foreign State shall not have immunity from jurisdiction, in respect of court proceedings connected with the arbitration, unless it has been otherwise determined in the arbitration agreement.

(b) The provisions of this section shall not apply to an arbitration agreement between states to which the provisions of public international law apply, except such an agreement one of the parties to which is a separate entity, not being a central bank.

12. Time for raising plea of immunity

(a) A foreign State shall raise a plea of immunity from jurisdiction at the earliest opportunity, and no later than when it first submits its case regarding the substance of the action.

(b) Where the foreign State has not raised a plea of immunity from jurisdiction by the time limit specified in sub-section (a), it shall be regarded as having waived its immunity.

(c) Despite the provisions of sub-section (b), a foreign State shall not be regarded as having waived its immunity if it raised a plea of immunity immediately after the facts in respect of which it is entitled to immunity became known to it, and it did not know nor was it required to know those facts at the time specified in sub-section (a).

Part Four: Procedure
13. Service of documents on a foreign State

(a) An action brought against a foreign State with the object of commencing legal pro-

4. Contract of employment

(a) A foreign State shall not have immunity from jurisdiction in an action by an employee or by an applicant for employment, where all the following conditions are fulfilled:

(1) The cause of action is the exclusive jurisdiction of a Regional Labor Court, under any legal provision;

(2) the subject matter of action is labour, all or a part of which has been performed, or is to be performed, in Israel;

(3) When the cause of action arose, the employee or applicant for employment was an Israeli citizen or was habitually resident in Israel or in a region; in this context, the term "region" shall be as defined in the Emergency Regulations (Judea and Samaria-Adjudication of Offenses and Legal Assistance) Law, 5728-1967.

(b) The provisions of this section shall not apply if the employee or candidate for employment was, at the time of the commencement of the proceeding, a citizen of the foreign country and was not resident in Israel.

(c) In an action by an employee or applicant for employment where the conditions specified in this section are not fulfilled, the foreign State shall not have immunity from jurisdiction, even where the cause of action is a commercial transaction as provided in section 3.

5. Actions in Torts

A foreign State shall not have immunity from jurisdiction in an action in tort where personal injury or damage to tangible property has occurred, provided the tort was committed in Israel.

6. Property rights

A foreign State shall not have immunity from jurisdiction in an action or in the proceedings as detailed below:

(1) an action concerning a right or other interest that the foreign State has in immovable property situated in Israel, an action concerning possession or use by a foreign State of immovable property situated in Israel or an action concerning the obligation of the foreign State deriving from such right, other interest or use;

(2) an action or proceedings concerning a right or other interest of the foreign State in assets situated in Israel to which it is entitled by way of succession, gift, or as *bona vacantia*, or an action or proceedings concerning an obligation deriving from such right or other interest;

(3) proceedings concerning estates, property of persons under guardianship, proceedings for insolvency or administration of trusts.

7. Intellectual property

A foreign State shall not have immunity from jurisdiction in an action in matters of intellectual property as defined in section 40 (4) of the Courts Law [Consolidated Version] 5744 – 1984, which concerns—

(1) the right of the foreign State in intellectual property;

(2) allegation of a breach, in Israel, by the foreign State of a right in intellectual property.

8. Action against a ship or cargo

(a) A foreign State shall not have immunity from jurisdiction in an action against a ship which at the commencement of the proceeding was owned or operated by that foreign State, and in an action against a cargo of a ship, which cargo was owned by the foreign State at the commencement of the proceeding, provided that at the time the cause of action arose, the ship or the cargo, whichever is applicable, was being used for a commercial purposes.

(b) In this section "ownership" of a ship or cargo, includes possession, control or other proprietary connection of the foreign State to the ship or cargo.

Foreign States Immunity Law, 2008 (Israel)

Chapter One Definitions

1. Definitions

In this Law—

"central bank" including any agency that constituting the central monetary authority of foreign State;

"separate body" means a governmental authority of a foreign State having separate legal personality from that of the government of that State;

"foreign State" includes a political unit within a federal State, governmental agencies of a foreign State, official functionaries representing such a State in performing their functions, and a separate entity;

"commercial asset" means any asset, excluding a diplomatic or consular asset, a military asset or an asset of a central bank, which is held in Israel by a foreign State for a commercial purpose; in this matter, an asset held in Israel by a foreign State and not intended for a particular purpose shall be regarded as being held by that State for a commercial purpose, unless it is proved otherwise;

"military asset" means an asset used or intended for use in connection with military activity and which is of a military nature or is controlled by the military authorities;

"commercial transaction" means any transaction or activity within the sphere of private law which is of a commercial nature, including an agreement for the sale of goods or services, a loan or other transaction, for financing, guarantee or indemnity, and which by its nature does not involve the exercise of governmental authority.

Chapter Two Immunity from Jurisdiction

Part One: Immunity of the foreign State

2. Immunity of a foreign State from the jurisdiction

A foreign State shall have immunity from the jurisdiction of the courts in Israel, excluding jurisdiction in criminal matters (hereafter referred to as immunity from jurisdiction), subject to the provisions of this statute.

Part Two: Exceptions to Immunity

3. Commercial transactions

A foreign State shall not have immunity from jurisdiction where the cause of action is a commercial transaction.

Law on Judicial Immunity from Compulsory Measures Concerning the Property of Foreign Central Banks, 2005 (China)

(Adopted at the 18th Meeting of the Standing Committee of the Tenth National People's Congress on October 25, 2005)

Article 1

The People's Republic of China grants to foreign central banks' property the judicial immunity from the compulsory measures of property preservation and execution, except where a foreign central bank, or a government to which a central bank is subordinate, gives up such immunity in writing, and where the property which is designated to be used for property preservation and execution.

Article 2

For the purposes of this Law, a foreign central bank means the central bank of a foreign country and of a regional economic integration organization, or the financial administration institution exercising the functions of a central bank.

For the purposes of this Law, the property of foreign central banks includes the cash, notes, bank deposits, securities, foreign exchange reserve and gold reserve of the foreign central banks and the banks' immovable property and other property.

Article 3

Where a foreign country grants no immunity to the property of the central bank of the People's Republic of China or to the property of the financial administration institutions of the special administrative regions of the People's Republic of China, or the immunity granted covers less items than what are provided for in this Law, the People's Republic of China shall apply the principle of reciprocity.

Article 4

This Law shall go into effect as of the date of promulgation.

rights under international law, the intervening court shall restrict itself to indicating to the claimant the international body before which it may bring its claim, if applicable, under local or universal jurisdiction. Likewise, it shall forward a copy of the claim to the Ministry of Foreign Affairs, International Commerce and Culture, so that it may examine the claim and adopt the corresponding measures under international jurisdiction.

Article 4

The appearance of foreign States before Argentinean Courts in order to invoke jurisdictional immunity shall not be interpreted as an acceptance of the competence of the Argentinean Courts. The filing of a defence based on jurisdictional immunity shall suspend the procedural deadlines for the transfer or summons until the issue is resolved.

Article 5

The judges, at the foreign State's request, may prudently extend the deadlines in which to reply to the claim and present exceptions.

Article 6

The provisions of this Law shall not affect any immunity ro privilege conferred by virtue of the Vienna Convention of 1961 on diplomatic relations or the 1963 Convention on cousular relations.

Artice 7

If a claim is brought against a foreign State, the Ministry of Foreign Affairs, International Commerce and Culture may express its opinion on any factual or legal issue before the intervening court, in its role as "friend to the court".

Article 8

To be notified to the Executive—Alberto R Pierri—Eduardo Menem—Esther H Pereyra Arandía de Pérez Pardo—Edgardo Piuzzi.

Given in the Hall of Sessions of the Argentinean Congress, in Buenos Aires, on 31 May 1995.

Inmunidad Jurisdiccional De Los Estados Extranjeros Ante Los Tribunales Argentinos, 1995 (Argentina)

Immunity of Forejgn States from the Jurisdiction of Argentinean Courts
Law No. 24, 488
Approved: 31 May 1995
Partially Enacted: 22 June 1995

The Senate and the House of Representatives of Argentina, gathered in Congress, etc, approve with the force of Law:

Immunity of foreign States from the jurisdiction of Argentinean Courts

Article 1

Foreign States are immune from the jurisdiction of Argentinean Courts in accordance with the following provisions of this law.

Article 2

Foreign States may not invoke jurisdictional immunity in the following cases:

(a) where they have consented expressly to the jurisdiction of Argentinean Courts by virtue of an international treaty, written agreement or declaration in any particular case;

(b) where the foreign State is subject to a counterclaim directly linkend to a main claim which it initiated;

(c) where the claim affects a commercial or industrial activity carried out by the foreign State and the jurisdiction of Argentinean Courts is applicable under the corresponding contract or under international law;

(d) where the foreign State is subject to a claim by Argentineans or residents of Argentina, relating to a contract of employment executed in Argentina or abroad with effects in Argentina;

(e) where the foreign State is subject to a claim for losses or damages derived from crimes or offences committed in Argentina;

(f) in the event of actions over real estate located in Argentina;

(g) in the event of actions based on the foreign State's position as an heir or beneficiary of assets located in Argentina;

(h) where the foreign State, after agreeing in writing to submit a dispute arising from a commercial transaction to arbitration, wishes to invoke jurisdictional immunity from Argentinean Courts in proceedings involving the validity or interpretation of the arbitration agreement or the arbitration proceedings or the cancellation of the arbitration award, unless the arbitration agreement provides otherwise.

Article 3 [1]

If claims were brought before the Argentinean Courts against a foreign State based on a violation of human

---

[1] Art. 3 is not in force (see Decree 849/95 at 5.010 above and 5.020 below).

(6) Regulations under this section have effect notwithstanding that they are inconsistent with an Act (other than this Act) as in force at the time when the regulations came into operation.

(7) Jurisdiction is conferred on the Federal Court of Australia and, to the extent that the Constitution permits, on the courts of the Territories, and the courts of the States are invested with federal jurisdiction, in respect of matters arising under the regulations but a court of a Territory shall not exercise any jurisdiction so conferred in respect of property that is not within that Territory or a Territory in which the court may exercise jurisdiction and a court of a State shall not exercise any jurisdiction so invested in respect of property that is not within that State.

42. A Extension of immunities—emergency prevention and management

(1) This section applies if the Minister is satisfied that a foreign State (or a separate entity of a foreign State) is providing, or is to provide, assistance or facilities:

(a) to the Australian Government, or the government of a State or Territory; and

(b) for the purposes of preparing for, preventing or managing emergencies or disasters (whether natural or otherwise) in Australia.

(2) The Governor General may make regulations excluding or modifying the application of section 13 (personal injury and damage to property) with respect to the foreign State (or the separate entity of the foreign State) in relation to acts or omissions done or omitted to be done by the foreign State (or the entity) in the course of the provision of the assistance or facilities.

[Note: Section 22 applies section 13 to a separate entity of a foreign State.]

43. Regulations

The Governor General may make regulations, not inconsistent with this Act, prescribing matters:

(a) required or permitted by this Act to be prescribed; or

(b) necessary or convenient to be prescribed for carrying out or giving effect to this Act.

(c) a specified person is, or was at a specified time, the head of, or the government or part of the government of, a foreign State or a former foreign State; or

(d) service of a specified document as mentioned in section 24 or 28 was effected on a specified day.

(2) The Minister for Foreign Affairs may, either generally or as otherwise provided by the instrument of delegation, delegate by instrument in writing to a person his or her powers under subsection (1) in relation to the service of documents.

(3) A power so delegated, when exercised by the delegate, shall, for the purposes of this Act, be deemed to have been exercised by the Minister.

(4) A delegation under subsection (2) does not prevent the exercise of the power by the Minister.

(5) A certificate under this section is admissible as evidence of the facts and matters Stated in it and is conclusive as to those facts and matters.

41. Certificate as to use

For the purposes of this Act, a certificate in writing given by the person for the time being performing the functions of the head of a foreign State's diplomatic mission in Australia to the effect that property specified in the certificate, being property:

(a) in which the foreign State or a separate entity of the foreign State has an interest; or

(b) that is in the possession or under the control of the foreign State or of a separate entity of the foreign State;

is or was at a specified time in use for purposes specified in the certificate is admissible as prima facie evidence of the facts stated in the certificate.

42. Restrictions and extensions of immunities and privileges—general

(1) Where the Minister is satisfied that an immunity or privilege conferred by this Act in relation to a foreign State is not accorded by the law of the foreign State in relation to Australia, the Governor General may make regulations modifying the operation of this Act with respect to those immunities and privileges in relation to the foreign State.

(2) Where the Minister is satisfied that the immunities and privileges conferred by this Act in relation to a foreign State differ from those required by a treaty, convention or other agreement to which the foreign State and Australia are parties, the Governor General may make regulations modifying the operation of this Act with respect to those immunities and privileges in relation to the foreign State so that this Act as so modified conforms with the treaty, convention or agreement.

(3) Regulations made under subsection (1) or (2) that are expressed to extend or restrict an immunity from the jurisdiction may be expressed to extend to a proceeding that was instituted before the commencement of the regulations and has not been finally disposed of.

(4) Regulations made under subsection (1) or (2) that are expressed to extend or restrict an immunity from execution or other relief may be expressed to extend to a proceeding that was instituted before the commencement of the regulations and in which procedures to give effect to orders for execution or other relief have not been completed.

(5) Regulations in relation to which subsection (3) or (4) applies may make provision with respect to the keeping of property, or for the keeping of the proceeds of the sale of property, with which a proceeding specified in the regulations is concerned, including provision authorising an officer of a court to manage, control or preserve the property or, if, by reason of the condition of the property, it is necessary to do so, to sell or otherwise dispose of the property.

(a) the separate entity would, apart from the operation of section 10, have been immune from the jurisdiction; and

(b) it has submitted to the jurisdiction.

Part V Miscellaneous

36. Heads of foreign States

(1) Subject to the succeeding provisions of this section, the Diplomatic Privileges and Immunities Act 1967 extends, with such modifications as are necessary, in relation to the person who is for the time being:

(a) the head of a foreign State; or

(b) a spouse of the head of a foreign State;

as that Act applies in relation to a person at a time when he or she is the head of a diplomatic mission.

(2) This section does not affect the application of any law of Australia with respect to taxation.

(3) This section does not affect the application of any other provision of this Act in relation to a head of a foreign State in his or her public capacity.

(4) Part III extends in relation to the head of a foreign State in his or her private capacity as it applies in relation to the foreign State and, for the purpose of the application of Part III as it so extends, a reference in that Part to a foreign State shall be read as a reference to the head of the foreign State in his or her private capacity.

37. Effect of agreements on separate entities

An agreement made by a foreign State and applicable to a separate entity of that State has effect, for the purposes of this Act, as though the separate entity were a party to the agreement.

38. Power to set aside process etc.

Where, on the application of a foreign State or a separate entity of a foreign State, a court is satisfied that a judgment, order or process of the court made or issued in a proceeding with respect to the foreign State or entity is inconsistent with an immunity conferred by or under this Act, the court shall set aside the judgment, order or process so far as it is so inconsistent.

39. Discovery

(1) A penalty by way of fine or committal shall not be imposed in relation to a failure or refusal by a foreign State or by a person on behalf of a foreign State to disclose or produce a document or to furnish information for the purposes of a proceeding.

(2) Such a failure or refusal is not of itself sufficient ground to strike out a pleading or part of a pleading.

40. Certificate as to foreign State etc.

(1) The Minister for Foreign Affairs may certify in writing that, for the purposes of this Act:

(a) a specified country is, or was on a specified day, a foreign State;

(b) a specified territory is or is not, or was or was not on a specified day, part of a foreign State;

(4) A waiver does not apply in relation to property that is diplomatic property or military property unless a provision in the agreement expressly designates the property as property to which the waiver applies.

(5) In addition to any other person who has authority to waive the application of section 30 on behalf of a foreign State or a separate entity of the foreign State, the person for the time being performing the functions of the head of the State's diplomatic mission in Australia has that authority.

32. Execution against commercial property

(1) Subject to the operation of any submission that is effective by reason of section 10, section 30 does not apply in relation to commercial property.

(2) Where a foreign State is not immune in a proceeding against or in connection with a ship or cargo, section 30 does not prevent the arrest, detention or sale of the ship or cargo if, at the time of the arrest or detention:

(a) the ship or cargo was commercial property; and

(b) in the case of a cargo that was then being carried by a ship belonging to the same or to some other foreign State—the ship was commercial property.

(3) For the purposes of this section:

(a) commercial property is property, other than diplomatic property or military property, that is in use by the foreign State concerned substantially for commercial purposes; and

(b) property that is apparently vacant or apparently not in use shall be taken to be being used for commercial purposes unless the court is satisfied that it has been set aside otherwise than for commercial purposes.

33. Execution against immovable property etc.

Where:

(a) property:

(i) has been acquired by succession or gift; or

(ii) is immovable property; and

(b) a right in respect of the property has been established as against a foreign State by a judgment or order in a proceeding as mentioned in section 14;

then, for the purpose of enforcing that judgment or order, section 30 does not apply to the property.

34. Restrictions on certain other relief

A penalty by way of fine or committal shall not be imposed in relation to a failure by a foreign State or by a person on behalf of a foreign State to comply with an order made against the foreign State by a court.

35. Application of Part to separate entities

(1) This Part applies in relation to a separate entity of a foreign State that is the central bank or monetary authority of the foreign State as it applies in relation to the foreign State.

(2) Subject to subsection (1), this Part applies in relation to a separate entity of the foreign State as it applies in relation to the foreign State if, in the proceeding concerned:

(b) if English is not an official language of the foreign State:
(i) a translation of the judgment into an official language of the foreign State; and
(ii) a certificate in that language, signed by the translator, setting out particulars of his or her qualifications as a translator and stating that the translation is an accurate translation of the judgment;
has been effected in accordance with this section on the department or organ of the foreign State that is equivalent to the Department of Foreign Affairs.

(2) Where a document is to be served as mentioned in subsection (1), the person in whose favour the judgment was given shall give it, together with a request in accordance with Form 2 in the Schedule, to the Attorney General for transmission by the Department of Foreign Affairs to the department or organ of the foreign State that is equivalent to that Department.

(3) Where the document is delivered to the equivalent department or organ of the foreign State in the foreign State, service shall be taken to have been effected when it is so delivered.

(4) Where the document is delivered to some other person on behalf of and with the authority of the foreign State, service shall be taken to have been effected when it is so delivered.

(5) The time, if any, for applying to have the judgment set aside shall be at least 2 months after the date on which the document is delivered to or received on behalf of that department or organ of the foreign State.

(6) Where a judgment in default of appearance has been given by a court against a foreign State, the court may, on the application of the person in whose favour the judgment was given, permit, on such terms and conditions as it thinks fit, the judgment to be enforced in accordance with this Act against the foreign State before the expiration of the period mentioned in subsection (1).

29. Power to grant relief

(1) Subject to subsection (2), a court may make any order (including an order for interim or final relief) against a foreign State that it may otherwise lawfully make unless the order would be inconsistent with an immunity under this Act.

(2) A court may not make an order that a foreign State employ a person or re-inState a person in employment.

Part IV Enforcement

30. Immunity from execution

Except as provided by this Part, the property of a foreign State is not subject to any process or order (whether interim or final) of the courts of Australia for the satisfaction or enforcement of a judgment, order or arbitration award or, in Admiralty proceedings, for the arrest, detention or sale of the property.

31. Waiver of immunity from execution

(1) A foreign State may at any time by agreement waive the application of section 30 in relation to property, but it shall not be taken to have done so by reason only that it has submitted to the jurisdiction.

(2) The waiver may be subject to specified limitations.

(3) An agreement by a foreign State to waive its immunity under section 30 has effect to waive that immunity and the waiver may not be withdrawn except in accordance with the terms of the agreement.

that the rules of court or other laws (if any) in respect of service outside the jurisdiction of the court concerned have been complied with; and

(c) if English is not an official language of the foreign State:

(i) a translation of the initiating process into an official language of the foreign State; and

(ii) a certificate in that language, signed by the translator, setting out particulars of his or her qualifications as a translator and stating that the translation is an accurate translation of the initiating process.

(3) Where the process and documents are delivered to the equivalent department or organ of the foreign State in the foreign State, service shall be taken to have been effected when they are so delivered.

(4) Where the process and documents are delivered to some other person on behalf of and with the authority of the foreign State, service shall be taken to have been effected when they are so delivered.

(5) Subsections (1) to (4) (inclusive) do not exclude the operation of any rule of court or other law under which the leave of a court is required in relation to service of the initiating process outside the jurisdiction.

(6) Service of initiating process under this section shall be taken to have been effected outside the jurisdiction and in the foreign State concerned, wherever the service is actually effected.

(7) The time for entering an appearance begins to run at the expiration of 2 months after the date on which service of the initiating process was effected.

(8) This section does not apply to service of initiating process in a proceeding commenced as an action in rem.

25. Other service ineffective

Purported service of an initiating process upon a foreign State in Australia otherwise than as allowed or provided by section 23 or 24 is ineffective.

26. Waiver of objection to service

Where a foreign State enters an appearance in a proceeding without making an objection in relation to the service of the initiating process, the provisions of this Act in relation to that service shall be taken to have been complied with.

27. Judgment in default of appearance

(1) A judgment in default of appearance shall not be entered against a foreign State unless:

(a) it is proved that service of the initiating process was effected in accordance with this Act and that the time for appearance has expired; and

(b) the court is satisfied that, in the proceeding, the foreign State is not immune.

(2) A judgment in default of appearance shall not be entered against a separate entity of a foreign State unless the court is satisfied that, in the proceeding, the separate entity is not immune.

28. Enforcement of default judgments

(1) Subject to subsection (6), a judgment in default of appearance is not capable of being enforced against a foreign State until the expiration of 2 months after the date on which service of:

(a) a copy of the judgment, sealed with the seal of the court or, if there is no seal, certified by an officer of the court to be a true copy of the judgment; and

(4) The preceding provisions of this section do not apply in relation to the arrest, detention or sale of a ship or cargo.

(5) A reference in this section to a ship in use for commercial purposes or to a commercial cargo is a reference to a ship or a cargo that is commercial property as defined by subsection 32 (3).

19. Bills of exchange

Where:

(a) a bill of exchange has been drawn, made, issued or indorsed by a foreign State in connection with a transaction or event; and

(b) the foreign State would not be immune in a proceeding in so far as the proceeding concerns the transaction or event;

the foreign State is not immune in a proceeding in so far as the proceeding concerns the bill of exchange.

20. Taxes

A foreign State is not immune in a proceeding in so far as the proceeding concerns an obligation imposed on it by or under a provision of a law of Australia with respect to taxation, being a provision that is prescribed, or is included in a class of provisions that is prescribed, for the purposes of this section.

21. Related proceedings

Where, by virtue of the operation of the preceding provisions of this Part, a foreign State is not immune in a proceeding in so far as the proceeding concerns a matter, it is not immune in any other proceeding (including an appeal) that arises out of and relates to the first mentioned proceeding in so far as that other proceeding concerns that matter.

22. Application of Part to separate entities

The preceding provisions of this Part (other than subparagraph 11 (2) (a) (i), paragraph 16 (1) (a) and subsection 17 (3)) apply in relation to a separate entity of a foreign State as they apply in relation to the foreign State.

Part III Service and judgments

23. Service of initiating process by agreement

Service of initiating process on a foreign State or on a separate entity of a foreign State may be effected in accordance with an agreement (wherever made and whether made before or after the commencement of this Act) to which the State or entity is a party.

24. Service through the diplomatic channel

(1) Initiating process that is to be served on a foreign State may be delivered to the Attorney General for transmission by the Department of Foreign Affairs to the department or organ of the foreign State that is equivalent to that Department.

(2) The initiating process shall be accompanied by:

(a) a request in accordance with Form 1 in the Schedule;

(b) a statutory declaration of the plaintiff or applicant in the proceeding stating

(b) is incorporated or has been established under the law of Australia or is controlled from, or has its principal place of business in, Australia;

being a proceeding arising between the foreign State and the body or other members of the body or between the foreign State and one or more of the other partners.

(2) Where a provision included in:

(a) the constitution or other instrument establishing or regulating the body or partnership; or

(b) an agreement between the parties to the proceeding;

is inconsistent with subsection (1), that subsection has effect subject to that provision.

17. Arbitrations

(1) Where a foreign State is a party to an agreement to submit a dispute to arbitration, then, subject to any inconsistent provision in the agreement, the foreign State is not immune in a proceeding for the exercise of the supervisory jurisdiction of a court in respect of the arbitration, including a proceeding:

(a) by way of a case Stated for the opinion of a court;

(b) to determine a question as to the validity or operation of the agreement or as to the arbitration procedure; or

(c) to set aside the award.

(2) Where:

(a) apart from the operation of subparagraph 11 (2) (a) (ii), subsection 12 (4) or subsection 16 (2), a foreign State would not be immune in a proceeding concerning a transaction or event; and

(b) the foreign State is a party to an agreement to submit to arbitration a dispute about the transaction or event;

then, subject to any inconsistent provision in the agreement, the foreign State is not immune in a proceeding concerning the recognition as binding for any purpose, or for the enforcement, of an award made pursuant to the arbitration, wherever the award was made.

(3) Subsection (1) does not apply where the only parties to the agreement are any 2 or more of the following:

(a) a foreign State;

(b) the Commonwealth;

(c) an organisation the members of which are only foreign States or the Commonwealth and one or more foreign States.

18. Actions in rem

(1) A foreign State is not immune in a proceeding commenced as an action in rem against a ship concerning a claim in connection with the ship if, at the time when the cause of action arose, the ship was in use for commercial purposes.

(2) A foreign State is not immune in a proceeding commenced as an action in rem against a ship concerning a claim against another ship if:

(a) at the time when the proceeding was instituted, the ship that is the subject of the action in rem was in use for commercial purposes; and

(b) at the time when the cause of action arose, the other ship was in use for commercial purposes.

(3) A foreign State is not immune in a proceeding commenced as an action in rem against cargo that was, at the time when the cause of action arose, a commercial cargo.

(a) an Australian citizen; or

(b) a person resident in Australia whose continued presence in Australia is not subject to a limitation as to time imposed by or under a law of Australia.

13. Personal injury and damage to property

A foreign State is not immune in a proceeding in so far as the proceeding concerns:

(a) the death of, or personal injury to, a person; or

(b) loss of or damage to tangible property;

caused by an act or omission done or omitted to be done in Australia.

14. Ownership, possession and use of property etc.

(1) A foreign State is not immune in a proceeding in so far as the proceeding concerns:

(a) an interest of the State in, or the possession or use by the State of, immovable property in Australia; or

(b) an obligation of the State that arises out of its interest in, or its possession or use of, property of that kind.

(2) A foreign State is not immune in a proceeding in so far as the proceeding concerns an interest of the State in property that arose by way of gift made in Australia or by succession.

(3) A foreign State is not immune in a proceeding in so far as the proceeding concerns:

(a) bankruptcy, insolvency or the winding up of a body corporate; or

(b) the administration of a trust, of the estate of a deceased person or of the estate of a person of unsound mind.

15. Copyright, patents, trade marks etc.

(1) A foreign State is not immune in a proceeding in so far as the proceeding concerns:

(a) the ownership of a copyright or the ownership, or the registration or protection in Australia, of an invention, a design or a trade mark;

(b) an alleged infringement by the foreign State in Australia of copyright, a patent for an invention, a registered trade mark or a registered design; or

(c) the use in Australia of a trade name or a business name.

(2) Subsection (1) does not apply in relation to the importation into Australia, or the use in Australia, of property otherwise than in the course of or for the purposes of a commercial transaction as defined by section 11 (3).

16. Membership of bodies corporate etc.

(1) A foreign State is not immune in a proceeding in so far as the proceeding concerns its membership, or a right or obligation that relates to its membership, of a body corporate, an unincorporated body or a partnership that:

(a) has a member that is not a foreign State or the Commonwealth; and

(b) in so far as the proceeding concerns a payment in respect of a grant, a scholarship, a pension or a payment of a like kind.

(3) In this section, commercial transaction means a commercial, trading, business, professional or industrial or like transaction into which the foreign State has entered or a like activity in which the State has engaged and, without limiting the generality of the foregoing, includes:

(a) a contract for the supply of goods or services;

(b) an agreement for a loan or some other transaction for or in respect of the provision of finance; and

(c) a guarantee or indemnity in respect of a financial obligation; but does not include a contract of employment or a bill of exchange.

12. Contracts of employment

(1) A foreign State, as employer, is not immune in a proceeding in so far as the proceeding concerns the employment of a person under a contract of employment that was made in Australia or was to be performed wholly or partly in Australia.

(2) A reference in subsection (1) to a proceeding includes a reference to a proceeding concerning:

(a) a right or obligation conferred or imposed by a law of Australia on a person as employer or employee; or

(b) a payment the entitlement to which arises under a contract of employment.

(3) Where, at the time when the contract of employment was made, the person employed was:

(a) a national of the foreign State but not a permanent resident of Australia; or

(b) an habitual resident of the foreign State;

subsection (1) does not apply.

(4) Subsection (1) does not apply where:

(a) an inconsistent provision is included in the contract of employment; and

(b) a law of Australia does not avoid the operation of, or prohibit or render unlawful the inclusion of, the provision.

(5) Subsection (1) does not apply in relation to the employment of:

(a) a member of the diplomatic staff of a mission as defined by the Vienna Convention on Diplomatic Relations, being the Convention the English text of which is set out in the Schedule to the Diplomatic Privileges and Immunities Act 1967; or

(b) a consular officer as defined by the Vienna Convention on Consular Relations, being the Convention the English text of which is set out in the Schedule to the Consular Privileges and Immunities Act 1972.

(6) Subsection (1) does not apply in relation to the employment of:

(a) a member of the administrative and technical staff of a mission as defined by the Convention referred to in paragraph (5)(a); or

(b) a consular employee as defined by the Convention referred to in paragraph (5)(b);

unless the member or employee was, at the time when the contract of employment was made, a permanent resident of Australia.

(7) In this section, permanent resident of Australia means:

(4) Without limiting any other power of a court to dismiss, stay or otherwise decline to hear and determine a proceeding, the court may dismiss, stay or otherwise decline to hear and determine a proceeding if it is satisfied that, by reason of the nature of a limitation, condition or exclusion to which a submission is subject (not being a limitation, condition or exclusion in respect of remedies), it is appropriate to do so.

(5) An agreement by a foreign State to waive its immunity under this Part has effect to waive that immunity and the waiver may not be withdrawn except in accordance with the terms of the agreement.

(6) Subject to subsections (7), (8) and (9), a foreign State may submit to the jurisdiction in a proceeding by:

(a) instituting the proceeding; or

(b) intervening in, or taking a step as a party to, the proceeding.

(7) A foreign State shall not be taken to have submitted to the jurisdiction in a proceeding by reason only that:

(a) it has made an application for costs; or

(b) it has intervened, or has taken a step, in the proceeding for the purpose or in the course of asserting immunity.

(8) Where the foreign State is not a party to a proceeding, it shall not be taken to have submitted to the jurisdiction by reason only that it has intervened in the proceeding for the purpose or in the course of asserting an interest in property involved in or affected by the proceeding.

(9) Where:

(a) the intervention or step was taken by a person who did not know and could not reasonably have been expected to know of the immunity; and

(b) the immunity is asserted without unreasonable delay;

the foreign State shall not be taken to have submitted to the jurisdiction in the proceeding by reason only of that intervention or step.

(10) Where a foreign State has submitted to the jurisdiction in a proceeding, then, subject to the operation of subsection (3), it is not immune in relation to a claim made in the proceeding by some other party against it (whether by way of set off, counter claim or otherwise), being a claim that arises out of and relates to the transactions or events to which the proceeding relates.

(11) In addition to any other person who has authority to submit, on behalf of a foreign State, to the jurisdiction:

(a) the person for the time being performing the functions of the head of the State's diplomatic mission in Australia has that authority; and

(b) a person who has entered into a contract on behalf of and with the authority of the State has authority to submit in that contract, on behalf of the State, to the jurisdiction in respect of a proceeding arising out of the contract.

11. Commercial transactions

(1) A foreign State is not immune in a proceeding in so far as the proceeding concerns a commercial transaction.

(2) Subsection (1) does not apply:

(a) if all the parties to the proceeding:

(i) are foreign States or are the Commonwealth and one or more foreign States; or

(ii) have otherwise agreed in writing; or

5. Act to bind Crown

This Act binds the Crown in all its capacities.

6. Savings of other laws

This Act does not affect an immunity or privilege that is conferred by or under the Consular Privileges and Immunities Act 1972, the Defence (Visiting Forces) Act 1963, the Diplomatic Privileges and Immunities Act 1967 or any other Act.

7. Application

(1) Part II (other than section 10) does not apply in relation to a proceeding concerning:

(a) a contract or other agreement or a bill of exchange that was made or given;

(b) a transaction or event that occurred;

(c) an act done or omitted to have been done; or

(d) a right, liability or obligation that came into existence;

before the commencement of this Act.

(2) Section 10 does not apply in relation to a submission mentioned in that section that was made before the commencement of this Act.

(3) Part III and section 36 do not apply in relation to a proceeding instituted before the commencement of this Act.

(4) Part IV only applies where, by virtue of a provision of Part II, the foreign-State is not immune from the jurisdiction of the courts of Australia in the proceeding concerned.

8. Application to courts

In the application of this Act to a court, this Act has effect only in relation to the exercise or performance by the court of a judicial power or function or a power or function that is of a like kind.

Part II Immunity from Jurisdiction

9. General immunity from jurisdiction

Except as provided by or under this Act, a foreign State is immune from the jurisdiction of the courts of Australia in a proceeding.

10. Submission to jurisdiction

(1) A foreign State is not immune in a proceeding in which it has submitted to the jurisdiction in accordance with this section.

(2) A foreign State may submit to the jurisdiction at any time, whether by agreement or otherwise, but a foreign State shall not be taken to have so submitted by reason only that it is a party to an agreement the proper law of which is the law of Australia.

(3) A submission under subsection (2) may be subject to a specified limitation, condition or exclusion (whether in respect of remedies or otherwise).

and includes the principles and rules of the common law and of equity as so in force.

military property means:

(a) a ship of war, a Government yacht, a patrol vessel, a police or customs vessel, a hospital ship, a defence force supply ship or an auxiliary vessel, being a ship or vessel that, at the relevant time, is operated by the foreign State concerned (whether pursuant to requisition or under a charter by demise or otherwise); or

(b) property (not being a ship or vessel) that is:

(i) being used in connection with a military activity; or

(ii) under the control of a military authority or defence agency for military or defence purposes.

Minister for Foreign Affairs means the Minister who administers the Diplomatic Privileges and Immunities Act 1967.

proceeding means a proceeding in a court but does not include a prosecution for an offence or an appeal or other proceeding in the nature of an appeal in relation to such a prosecution.

property includes a chose in action.

separate entity, in relation to a foreign State, means a natural person (other than an Australian citizen), or a body corporate or corporation sole (other than a body corporate or corporation sole that has been established by or under a law of Australia), who or that:

(a) is an agency or instrumentality of the foreign State; and

(b) is not a department or organ of the executive government of the foreign State.

(2) For the purposes of the definition of separate entity in subsection (1), a natural person who is, or a body corporate or a corporation sole that is, an agency of more than one foreign State shall be taken to be a separate entity of each of the foreign States.

(3) Unless the contrary intention appears, a reference in this Act to a foreign State includes a reference to:

(a) a province, State, self governing territory or other political subdivision (by whatever name known) of a foreign State;

(b) the head of a foreign State, or of a political subdivision of a foreign State, in his or her public capacity; and

(c) the executive government or part of the executive government of a foreign State or of a political subdivision of a foreign State, including a department or organ of the executive government of a foreign State or subdivision;

but does not include a reference to a separate entity of a foreign State.

(4) A reference in this Act to a court of Australia includes a reference to a court that has jurisdiction in or for any part of Australia.

(5) A reference in this Act to a commercial purpose includes a reference to a trading, a business, a professional and an industrial purpose.

(6) A reference in this Act to the entering of appearance or to the entry of judgment in default of appearance includes a reference to any like procedure.

4. External Territories

This Act extends to each external Territory.

Foreign States Immunities Act, 1985 (Australia)

Part I Preliminary

1. Short title

This Act may be cited as the Foreign States Immunities Act 1985.

2. Commencement

The provisions of this Act shall come into operation on such day as is, or such respective days as are, fixed by Proclamation.

3. Interpretation

(1) In this Act, unless the contrary intention appears:

agreement means an agreement in writing and includes:

(a) a treaty or other international agreement in writing; and

(b) a contract or other agreement in writing.

Australia when used in a geographical sense, includes each of the external Territories.

bill of exchange includes a promissory note.

court includes a tribunal or other body (by whatever name called) that has functions, or exercises powers, that are judicial functions or powers or are of a kind similar to judicial functions or powers.

Department of Foreign Affairs means the Department administered by the Minister who administers the Diplomatic Privileges and Immunities Act 1967.

diplomatic property means property that, at the relevant time, is in use predominantly for the purpose of establishing or maintaining a diplomatic or consular mission, or a visiting mission, of a foreign State to Australia.

foreign State means a country the territory of which is outside Australia, being a country that is:

(a) an independent sovereign State; or

(b) a separate territory (whether or not it is self governing) that is not part of an independent sovereign State.

initiating process means an instrument (including a statement of claim, application, summons, writ, order or third party notice) by reference to which a person becomes a party to a proceeding.

law of Australia means:

(a) a law in force throughout Australia; or

(b) a law of or in force in a part of Australia;

is admissible in evidence as conclusive proof of any matter Stated in the certificate with respect to that question, without proof of the signature of the Minister of Foreign Affairs or other person or of that other person's authorization by the Minister of Foreign Affairs.

Idem

(2) A certificate issued by the Deputy Minister of Foreign Affairs, or on his behalf by a person designated by him pursuant to subsection 9 (2), with respect to service of an originating or other document on a foreign State in accordance with that subsection is admissible in evidence as conclusive proof of any matter Stated in the certificate with respect to that service, without proof of the signature of the Deputy Minister of Foreign Affairs or other person or of that other person's authorization by the Deputy Minister of Foreign Affairs.

Governor in Council may restrict immunity by order

15 The Governor in Council may, on the recommendation of the Minister of Foreign Affairs, by order restrict any immunity or privileges under this Act in relation to a foreign State where, in the opinion of the Governor in Council, the immunity or privileges exceed those accorded by the law of that State.

Inconsistency

16 If, in any proceeding or other matter to which a provision of this Act and a provision of the Extradition Act, the Visiting Forces Act or the Foreign Missions and International Organizations Act apply, there is a conflict between those provisions, the provision of this Act does not apply in the proceeding or other matter to the extent of the conflict.

Rules of court not affected

17 Except to the extent required to give effect to this Act, nothing in this Act shall be construed or applied so as to negate or affect any rules of a court, including rules of a court relating to service of a document out of the jurisdiction of the court.

Application

18 This Act does not apply to criminal proceedings or proceedings in the nature of criminal proceedings.

or the Minister of Foreign Affairs may, within the confines of his or her mandate, assist, to the extent that is reasonably practical, any judgment creditor in identifying and locating the following property, unless the Minister of Foreign Affairs believes that to do so would be injurious to Canada's international relations or either Minister believes that to do so would be injurious to Canada's other interests:

(a) in the case of the Minister of Finance, the financial assets of the foreign State that are held within Canadian jurisdiction; and

(b) in the case of the Minister of Foreign Affairs, the property of the foreign State that is situated in Canada.

Disclosure of information

(2) In exercising the power referred to in subsection (1), the Minister of Finance or the Minister of Foreign Affairs, as the case may be, may not disclose

(a) information that was produced in or for a government institution, without the authorization of the government institution; and

(b) information produced in circumstances other than those referred to in paragraph (a), without the authorization of the government institution that first received the information.

Definition of government institution

(3) In subsection (2), government institution means any department, branch, office, board, agency, commission, corporation or other body for the administration or affairs of which a minister is accountable to Parliament.

No fine for failure to produce

13 (1) No penalty or fine may be imposed by a court against a foreign State for any failure or refusal by the State to produce any document or other information in the course of proceedings before the court.

Exception

(2) Subsection (1) does not apply either to an agency of a foreign State or to a foreign State that is set out on the list referred to in subsection 6.1 (2) in respect of an action brought against that foreign State for its support of terrorism or its terrorist activity.

General

Certificate is conclusive evidence

14 (1) A certificate issued by the Minister of Foreign Affairs, or on his behalf by a person authorized by him, with respect to any of the following questions, namely,

(a) whether a country is a foreign State for the purposes of this Act,

(b) whether a particular area or territory of a foreign State is a political subdivision of that State, or

(c) whether a person or persons are to be regarded as the head or government of a foreign State or of a political subdivision of the foreign State,

Execution

12 (1) Subject to subsections (2) and (3), property of a foreign State that is located in Canada is immune from attachment and execution and, in the case of an action in rem, from arrest, detention, seizure and forfeiture except where

(a) the State has, either explicitly or by implication, waived its immunity from attachment, execution, arrest, detention, seizure or forfeiture, unless the foreign State has withdrawn the waiver of immunity in accordance with any term thereof that permits such withdrawal;

(b) the property is used or is intended to be used for a commercial activity or, if the foreign State is set out on the list referred to in subsection 6.1 (2), is used or is intended to be used by it to support terrorism or engage in terrorist activity;

(c) the execution relates to a judgment establishing rights in property that has been acquired by succession or gift or in immovable property located in Canada, or

(d) the foreign State is set out on the list referred to in subsection 6.1 (2) and the attachment or execution relates to a judgment rendered in an action brought against it for its support of terrorism or its terrorist activity and to property other than property that has cultural or historical value.

Property of an agency of a foreign State is not immune

(2) Subject to subsection (3), property of an agency of a foreign State is not immune from attachment and execution and, in the case of an action in rem, from arrest, detention, seizure and forfeiture, for the purpose of satisfying a judgment of a court in any proceedings in respect of which the agency is not immune from the jurisdiction of the court by reason of any provision of this Act.

Military property

(3) Property of a foreign State

(a) that is used or is intended to be used in connection with a military activity, and

(b) that is military in nature or is under the control of a military authority or defence agency

is immune from attachment and execution and, in the case of an action in rem, from arrest, detention, seizure and forfeiture.

Property of a foreign central bank immune

(4) Subject to subsection (5), property of a foreign central bank or monetary authority that is held for its own account and is not used or intended for a commercial activity is immune from attachment and execution.

Waiver of immunity

(5) The immunity conferred on property of a foreign central bank or monetary authority by subsection (4) does not apply where the bank, authority or its parent foreign government has explicitly waived the immunity, unless the bank, authority or government has withdrawn the waiver of immunity in accordance with any term thereof that permits such withdrawal.

Assistance for judgment creditors

12.1 (1) At the request of any party in whose favour a judgment is rendered against a foreign State in proceedings referred to in section 6.1, the Minister of Finance

Date of service

(5) Where service of an originating document is made in the manner provided in subsection (2), service of the document shall be deemed to have been made on the day that the Deputy Minister of Foreign Affairs or a person designated by him pursuant to subsection (2) certifies to the relevant court that the copy of the document has been transmitted to the foreign State.

Default judgment

10 (1) Where, in any proceedings in a court, service of an originating document has been made on a foreign State in accordance with subsection 9 (1), (3) or (4) and the State has failed to take, within the time limited therefor by the rules of the court or otherwise by law, the initial step required of a defendant or respondent in those proceedings in that court, no further step toward judgment may be taken in the proceedings except after the expiration of at least sixty days following the date of service of the originating document.

Idem

(2) Where judgment is signed against a foreign State in any proceedings in which the State has failed to take the initial step referred to in subsection (1), a certified copy of the judgment shall be served on the foreign State

(a) where service of the document that originated the proceedings was made on an agency of the foreign State, in such manner as is ordered by the court; or

(b) in any other case, in the manner specified in paragraph 9 (1)(c) as though the judgment were an originating document.

Idem

(3) Where, by reason of subsection (2), a certified copy of a judgment is required to be served in the manner specified in paragraph 9 (1) (c), subsections 9 (2) and (5) apply with such modifications as the circumstances require.

Application to set aside or revoke default judgment

(4) A foreign State may, within sixty days after service on it of a certified copy of a judgment under subsection (2), apply to have the judgment set aside or revoked.

No injunction, specific performance, etc., without consent

11 (1) Subject to subsection (3), no relief by way of an injunction, specific performance or the recovery of land or other property may be granted against a foreign State unless the State consents in writing to that relief and, where the State so consents, the relief granted shall not be greater than that consented to by the State.

Submission not consent

(2) Submission by a foreign State to the jurisdiction of a court is not consent for the purposes of subsection (1).

Exception

(3) This section does not apply either to an agency of a foreign State or to a foreign State that is set out on the list referred to in subsection 6.1 (2) in respect of an action brought against that foreign State for its support of terrorism or its terrorist activity.

Cargo

(2) A foreign State is not immune from the jurisdiction of a court in any proceedings that relate to

(a) an action in rem against any cargo owned by the State if, at the time the claim arose or the proceedings were commenced, the cargo and the ship carrying the cargo were being used or were intended for use in a commercial activity; or

(b) an action in personam for enforcing a claim in connection with any cargo owned by the State if, at the time the claim arose or the proceedings were commenced, the ship carrying the cargo was being used or was intended for use in a commercial activity.

Idem

(3) For the purposes of subsections (1) and (2), a ship or cargo owned by a foreign State includes any ship or cargo in the possession or control of the State and any ship or cargo in which the State claims an interest.

Property in Canada

8 A foreign State is not immune from the jurisdiction of a court in any proceedings that relate to an interest or, in the Province of Quebec, a right of the State in property that arises by way of succession, gift or *bona vacantia*.

Procedure and Relief

Service on a foreign State

9 (1) Service of an originating document on a foreign State, other than on an agency of the foreign State, may be made

(a) in any manner agreed on by the State;

(b) in accordance with any international Convention to which the State is a party; or

(c) in the manner provided in subsection (2) .

Idem

(2) For the purposes of paragraph (1) (c), anyone wishing to serve an originating document on a foreign State may deliver a copy of the document, in person or by registered mail, to the Deputy Minister of Foreign Affairs or a person designated by him for the purpose, who shall transmit it to the foreign State.

Service on an agency of a foreign State

(3) Service of an originating document on an agency of a foreign State may be made

(a) in any manner agreed on by the agency;

(b) in accordance with any international Convention applicable to the agency; or

(c) in accordance with any applicable rules of court.

Idem

(4) Where service on an agency of a foreign State cannot be made under subsection (3), a court may, by order, direct how service is to be made.

New application

(6) A foreign State set out on the list may not make another application under subsection (4), unless there has been a material change in its circumstances since the foreign State made its last application or the Minister of Foreign Affairs has completed the review under subsection (7).

Review of list

(7) Two years after the establishment of the list, and every two years after that, the Minister of Foreign Affairs must

(a) review the list in consultation with the Minister of Public Safety and Emergency Preparedness to determine whether there are still reasonable grounds, as set out in subsection (2), for a foreign State to be set out on the list and make a recommendation to the Governor in Council as to whether the foreign State should remain set out on the list; and

(b) review the list in consultation with the Minister of Public Safety and Emergency Preparedness to determine whether there are reasonable grounds, as set out in subsection (2), for a foreign State that is not set out on the list to be set out on the list and make a recommendation to the Governor in Council as to whether the foreign State should be set out on the list.

Effect of review

(8) The review does not affect the validity of the list.

Completion of review

(9) The Minister of Foreign Affairs must complete the review as soon as feasible, but in any case within 120 days, after its commencement. After completing the review, that Minister must without delay cause a notice to be published in the Canada Gazette that it has been completed.

Effect of removal from list on proceedings

(10) If proceedings for support of terrorism are commenced against a foreign State that is set out on the list, the subsequent removal of the foreign State from the list does not have the effect of restoring the State's immunity from the jurisdiction of a court in respect of those proceedings or any related appeal or enforcement proceedings.

Terrorist activity

(11) Where a court of competent jurisdiction has determined that a foreign State, set out on the list in subsection (2), has supported terrorism, that foreign State is also not immune from the jurisdiction of a court in proceedings against it that relate to terrorist activity by the State.

Maritime law

7 (1) A foreign State is not immune from the jurisdiction of a court in any proceedings that relate to

(a) an action in rem against a ship owned or operated by the State, or

(b) an action in personam for enforcing a claim in connection with a ship owned or operated by the State,

if, at the time the claim arose or the proceedings were commenced, the ship was being used or was intended for use in a commercial activity.

Third party proceedings and counter-claims

(4) A foreign State that initiates proceedings in a court or that intervenes or takes any step in proceedings before a court, other than an intervention or step to which paragraph (2) (c) does not apply, submits to the jurisdiction of the court in respect of any third party proceedings that arise, or counter-claim that arises, out of the subject-matter of the proceedings initiated by the State or in which the State has so intervened or taken a step.

Appeal and review

(5) Where, in any proceedings before a court, a foreign State submits to the jurisdiction of the court in accordance with subsection (2) or (4), that submission is deemed to be a submission by the State to the jurisdiction of such one or more courts by which those proceedings may, in whole or in part, subsequently be considered on appeal or in the exercise of supervisory jurisdiction.

Commercial activity

5 A foreign State is not immune from the jurisdiction of a court in any proceedings that relate to any commercial activity of the foreign State.

Death and property damage

6 A foreign State is not immune from the jurisdiction of a court in any proceedings that relate to

(a) any death or personal or bodily injury, or

(b) any damage to or loss of property

that occurs in Canada.

Support of terrorism

6.1 (1) A foreign State that is set out on the list referred to in subsection (2) is not immune from the jurisdiction of a court in proceedings against it for its support of terrorism on or after January 1, 1985.

List of foreign States

(2) The Governor in Council may, by order, establish a list on which the Governor in Council may, at any time, set out the name of a foreign State if, on the recommendation of the Minister of Foreign Affairs made after consulting with the Minister of Public Safety and Emergency Preparedness, the Governor in Council is satisfied that there are reasonable grounds to believe that the foreign State supported or supports terrorism.

Establishment of list

(3) The list must be established no later than six months after the day on which this section comes into force.

Application to be removed from list

(4) On application in writing by a foreign State, the Minister of Foreign Affairs must, after consulting with the Minister of Public Safety and Emergency Preparedness, decide whether there are reasonable grounds to recommend to the Governor in Council that the applicant no longer be set out on the list.

Notice of decision to applicant

(5) The Minister of Foreign Affairs must without delay give notice to the applicant of that Minister's decision respecting the application.

Meaning of supports terrorism

2.1 For the purposes of this Act, a foreign State supports terrorism if it commits, for the benefit of or otherwise in relation to a listed entity as defined in subsection 83.01 (1) of the Criminal Code, an act or omission that is, or had it been committed in Canada would be, punishable under any of sections 83.02 to 83.04 and 83.18 to 83.23 of the Criminal Code.

State Immunity

State immunity

3 (1) Except as provided by this Act, a foreign State is immune from the jurisdiction of any court in Canada.

Court to give effect to immunity

(2) In any proceedings before a court, the court shall give effect to the immunity conferred on a foreign State by subsection (1) notwithstanding that the State has failed to take any step in the proceedings.

Immunity waived

4 (1) A foreign State is not immune from the jurisdiction of a court if the State waives the immunity conferred by subsection 3 (1) by submitting to the jurisdiction of the court in accordance with subsection (2) or (4).

State submits to jurisdiction

(2) In any proceedings before a court, a foreign State submits to the jurisdiction of the court where it

(a) explicitly submits to the jurisdiction of the court by written agreement or otherwise either before or after the proceedings commence;

(b) initiates the proceedings in the court; or

(c) intervenes or takes any step in the proceedings before the court.

Exception

(3) Paragraph (2) (c) does not apply to

(a) any intervention or step taken by a foreign State in proceedings before a court for the purpose of claiming immunity from the jurisdiction of the court; or

(b) any step taken by a foreign State in ignorance of facts entitling it to immunity if those facts could not reasonably have been ascertained before the step was taken and immunity is claimed as soon as reasonably practicable after they are ascertained.

State Immunity Act, 1985 (Canada)

An Act to provide for State immunity in Canadian courts

Short Title

Short title
1 This Act may be cited as the State Immunity Act.

Interpretation

Definitions
2 In this Act,

agency of a foreign State means any legal entity that is an organ of the foreign State but that is separate from the foreign State;

commercial activity means any particular transaction, act or conduct or any regular course of conduct that by reason of its nature is of a commercial character;

foreign State includes

(a) any sovereign or other head of the foreign State or of any political subdivision of the foreign State while acting as such in a public capacity,

(b) any government of the foreign State or of any political subdivision of the foreign State, including any of its departments, and any agency of the foreign State, and

(c) any political subdivision of the foreign State;

political subdivision means a province, State or other like political subdivision of a foreign State that is a federal State.

terrorist activity in respect of a foreign State has the same meaning as in subsection 83.01 (1) of the Criminal Code, provided that a foreign State set out on the list referred to in subsection 6.1 (2) does the act or omission on or after January 1, 1985.

immunity or privilege conferred or granted by or under this Act, are sold or disposed of to a person who is not entitled to customs franchise privileges, the Controller of Customs and Excise may call upon the person selling or disposing of the goods or upon the person buying or receiving the goods to pay the duty thereon at the rate leviable at the date of the sale or disposal.

(2) For the purpose of determining the amount of duty payable on goods sold or disposed of after use, the Controller of Customs and Excise shall take into consideration the depreciation in value of such goods since their importation or removal from bond and shall, except in the case of motor vehicles, remit the duty if the sale or disposal is effected more than two years after the date of importation or removal from bond.

32. Evidence

If in any proceedings any question arises whether or not a person is entitled to the benefit of any privilege or immunity, or to exercise any power, under this Act, a certificate given by the Minister stating any fact relating to that question shall be conclusive evidence of that fact, and any certificate purporting to be signed by the Minister shall be presumed to have been signed by him until the contrary is proved.

33. Oaths and notarial acts

A diplomatic agent or consular officer of any State may, if authorized to do so under the laws of that State, administer oaths, take affidavits, and do notarial acts:

(a) required by any person for use in that State or under the laws thereof; or

(b) otherwise required by a national of that State but not for use in Malawi except under the laws of some other country.

(b) any recognized agency of such a government;

(c) any internationally recognized foundation or other body.

27. Modifications with respect to the United Nations Organization

In its application to the United Nations Organization established by Charter at San Francisco on 25th June, 1945, this Part has effect subject to the following modifications:

(a) any reference to the governing body or any committee of the organization shall be construed as referring to the General Assembly or any council or other organ of the United Nations Organization; and

(b) the powers conferred upon the Minister by section 24 (1) shall include power to confer upon the judges and registrars of the International Court set up under the Charter and on suitors to that Court and their agents, counsel and advocates, such immunities, privileges and facilities as may be required to give effect to any resolution of, or convention approved by, the General Assembly.

28. Reciprocal treatment

Notwithstanding anything in this Part, the Minister may decline to accord immunities and privileges to, and may withdraw immunities and privileges from, nationals or representatives of any State on the ground that such State is failing to accord corresponding immunities and privileges to citizens or representatives of Malaŵi.

Part VI GENERAL PROVISIONS

29. Restriction and extension of privileges, immunities or powers

(1) Where the immunities and privileges conferred by Part II in relation to a State—

(a) exceed or are less than those accorded by the law of that State in relation to Malaŵi; or

(b) are less than those required by any treaty, convention or other international agreement to which that State and Malaŵi are parties, the Minister may, by order, restrict or, as the case may be, extend those immunities and privileges to such extent as appears to him to be appropriate.

(2) Where the immunities, privileges or powers accorded in the territory of any State to a diplomatic mission or consular post of Malaŵi or to persons connected with that mission or post are less than those accorded by Part III or IV to the diplomatic mission or consular post of that State or to the persons connected therewith, the Minister may, by order, withdraw such of the immunities, privileges or powers accorded by Part III or IV from the diplomatic mission or consular post of that State or from persons connected therewith, as appears to him to be proper.

30. Admiralty jurisdiction of High Court

The High Court is declared to be a court of admiralty jurisdiction and shall, over the waters of Lake Malaŵi and other waters bordering partly upon Malaŵi and partly upon another State, have the same jurisdiction in respect of persons, matters or things thereon as the High Court in England has over the high seas and waters within its admiralty jurisdiction.

31. Special provisions relating to customs duty

(1) If goods which have been imported or taken out of bond without payment of customs duty by a person in pursuance of any diplomatic immunity or privilege or other

(ii) such number of officers of the organization as may be specified in the order, being the holders of such high offices in the organization as may be so specified; and

(iii) such persons employed on missions on behalf of the organization as may be so specified, to such extent as may be specified in the order, the immunities and privileges set out in Part II of the Fifth Schedule;

(c) confer upon such other classes of officers and servants of the organization as may be specified in the order, to such extent as may be so specified, the immunities and privileges set out in Part III of the Fifth Schedule, and Part IV of the Fifth Schedule shall have effect for the purpose of extending to the staffs of such representatives and members as are mentioned in subparagraph (i) of paragraph (b) and to the families of officers of the organization, any immunities and privileges conferred on the representatives, members or officers under that paragraph, except in so far as the operation of Part IV of that Schedule is excluded by the order conferring the immunities and privileges.

(2) An order under subsection (1) shall be so framed as to secure that there are not conferred upon any person any immunities or privileges greater in extent than those which, at the time of the making of the order, are required to be conferred on that person in order to give effect to any international agreement in that behalf, and that no immunity or privilege is conferred upon any person as the representative of the Government or as a member of the staff of such representative.

(3) The Minister may, by order, amend the Fourth Schedule.

25. Representatives of sovereign governments at international conferences

Where a conference is held in Malawi and is attended by representatives of the Government and the government or governments of one or more other States and it appears to the Minister that doubts may arise as to the extent to which the representatives of those States and members of their official staffs are entitled to diplomatic immunities and privileges, he may, by notice in the Gazette specify those persons and the Articles in the First Schedule which shall apply to them and, for the purposes of those Articles, every representative of a State who is named in the notice shall be deemed to be a head of mission and every member of his official staff named in the notice shall be deemed to be a member of the diplomatic staff.

26. External agencies which provide co-operation or co-assistance

(1) Where the Government has, whether before or after the commencement of this Act, entered into any agreement with an external agency under which, in return for co-operation or assistance in works executed in, or services rendered to, Malawi by such agency, the Government has agreed that such agency or person in its service should enjoy any immunities or privileges, the Minister may, by Order—

(a) declare that such agency is one to which this section applies;

(b) provide that, to such extent as may be specified in the Order, such agency shall have the immunities and privileges set out in Part I of the Fifth Schedule;

(c) confer upon such classes of officers and servants of such agency as may be specified in the Order, to such extent as may be so specified, the immunities and privileges set out in Part III of the Fifth Schedule, and for the purposes of any such Order references in the Fifth Schedule to the organization shall be construed as references to the external agency named in the Order.

(2) An Order under subsection (1) shall be so framed as to secure that there are not conferred on any person any immunities or privileges greater in extent than those which are required to be conferred on that person by the agreement concerned and that no immunity or privilege is conferred on any person who is a citizen of, or permanently resident in, Malawi.

(3) For the purposes of this section, "external agency" means—

(a) the government of a foreign State;

22. Agreements to accord immunities and privileges

(1) Where any agreement made, whether before or after the commencement of this Act, between Malawi and any other State provides for according to consular posts and persons connected with them immunities and privileges not accorded to them by this Act, the Minister may, by order, exercise with respect to the consular posts of that State and persons connected with them the powers specified in the Third Schedule so far as may be necessary to give effect to that Agreement.

(2) Where any agreement made, whether before or after the commencement of this Act, between Malawi and any other State provides for according to consular posts and persons connected with them some but not all of the immunities and privileges accorded to them by this Act, the Minister may, by order, provide for excluding with respect to consular posts of that State and persons connected with them any of the immunities and privileges which are not provided for by that agreement.

23. Commonwealth representatives

(1) The Minister may, by order, confer—

(a) on persons in the service of the government of a Commonwealth country who hold such offices or classes of offices which appear to the Minister to involve the performance of duties substantially corresponding to those which, in the case of foreign sovereign power, would be performed by a consular officer;

(b) on a person for the time being recognized by the Government as the chief representative of any State or province of a Commonwealth country (in this section referred to as a State representative);

(c) on members of the staff of any such person as is mentioned in paragraph (a) or (b), any immunities or privileges which are conferred by or may be conferred under this Part, and any such order may provide for extending, in relation to premises, official archives, communications, documents and personal property of persons on whom any immunities and privileges are or may be conferred under this subsection, and in relation to any fees and charges levied by them Articles 31, 32, 33, 35, 39 and 51 in the Second Schedule.

(2) An order under subsection (1) may exclude from any immunities and privileges conferred by it any persons who are permanently resident in Malawi, or who are citizens of Malawi, or any class of such persons.

(3) Notwithstanding anything in this section:

(a) a person for the time being recognized by the Government as the chief representative in Malawi of a Commonwealth country may waive any immunity conferred under this section on a person in the service of the government of the country which he represents;

(b) a State representative may waive any immunity conferred by subsection (1) on himself or a member of his staff.

PART V INTERNATIONAL ORGANIZATIONS, ETC.

24. Immunities and privileges of certain international organizations and persons connected therewith

(1) The Minister may, by order:

(a) provide that any organization specified in the Fourth Schedule (hereinafter referred to as the organization) shall, to such extent as may be specified in the order, have the immunities and privileges set out in Part I of the Fifth Schedule, and shall also have the legal capacities of a body corporate;

(b) confer upon:

(i) any persons who are representatives (whether of governments or not) on any organ of the organization or are members of any committee of the organization or of an organ thereof;

or any person for the time being performing his functions shall be deemed to be a waiver by that State.

(3) Articles 35, 36 and 40 shall be construed as granting any immunity or privilege which they require to be granted.

(4) The references in Articles 37 and 38 to the extent to which any immunities and privileges are admitted by the receiving State and to additional immunities and privileges which may be granted by the receiving State shall be construed as referring respectively to the extent to which any immunities or privileges are specified by the Minister by order and to any additional immunities and privileges which may be so specified.

(5) In its application to the immunity granted by paragraphs 2, 3 and 4 of Article 37 the expression "permanent resident" in Article 38 shall be deemed to extend to any individual other than one who is resident in Malawi solely for the purpose of performing the duties of his office for a mission.

PART IV   CONSULAR IMMUNITIES AND PRIVILEGES

21. Application of Convention on Consular Relations

(1) Subject to sections 22 (2) and 29 (2), the Articles set out in the Second Schedule (being Articles of the Vienna Convention on Consular Relations signed in 1963) have the force of law in Malawi and shall for that purpose be construed in accordance with subsections (2) to (9).

(2) The reference in paragraph 2 of Article 17 to any privileges and immunities accorded by customary international law or by international agreements shall be construed as a reference to any immunities and privileges conferred under Part V.

(3) The references in Article 44 to matters connected with the exercise of the functions of members of a consular post shall be construed as matters connected with the exercise of consular functions by consular officers or consular employees.

(4) For the purposes of Article 45 and that Article as applied by Article 58, a waiver shall be deemed to have been expressed by a State if it has been expressed by the head, or any person for the time being performing the functions of head, of the diplomatic mission of that State or, if there is no such mission, of the consular post concerned.

(5) Articles 50, 51, 52, 54, 62 and 67 shall be construed as granting any immunity or privilege which they require to be granted.

(6) The reference in Article 57 to the immunities and privileges provided in Chapter II shall be construed as references to those provided in section II of that Chapter.

(7) The reference in Article 70 to the rules of international law concerning diplomatic relations shall be construed as a reference to Part III of, and of the First Schedule to, this Act.

(8) The reference in Article 71 to additional immunities and privileges which may be granted by the receiving State or to immunities and privileges so far as these are granted by the receiving State shall be construed as referring to such immunities and privileges as may be specified by the Minister by order.

(9) In its application to the immunity granted by Article 49 the expression "permanent resident" in Article 71 shall be deemed to extend to any individual other than one who is resident in Malawi solely for the purpose of performing his duties for a consular post.

17. Heads of State

(1) Subject to this section and to any necessary modifications, Part III shall apply to—

(a) a sovereign or other head of State;

(b) members of his family forming part of his household; and

(c) his private servants, as it applies to the head of a diplomatic mission, to members of his family forming part of his household and to his private servants.

(2) The immunities and privileges conferred by virtue of subsection (1) (a) and (b) shall not be subject to the restrictions by reference to nationality or residence mentioned in Article 37 (1) or 38 in the First Schedule.

(3) This section applies to the sovereign or other head of any State on which immunities and privileges are conferred by the other relevant sections of this Part and is without prejudice to the application of those sections to any such sovereign or head of State in his public capacity.

18. Excluded matters

(1) This Part of the Act does not affect any immunity or privilege conferred by Part III or Part IV; and:

(a) section 6 does not apply to proceedings concerning the employment of the members of a mission within the meaning of Article 1 of the Convention in the First Schedule or of the members of a consular post within the meaning of Article 1 of the Convention in the Second Schedule:

(b) section 8 (1) does not apply to proceedings concerning a State's title to or its possession of property used for the purposes of diplomatic mission.

(2) This Part does not apply to criminal proceedings.

19. Evidence by certificate

A certificate by or on behalf of the Minister of External Affairs shall be conclusive evidence on any question—

(a) whether any country is a State for the purposes of this Part;

(b) whether any territory is a constituent part of a federal State for those same purposes;

(c) as to the person or persons to be regarded for the purposes of this Part as the head or government of a State;

(d) whether, and if so when, a document has been served or received as mentioned in section 14 (1) or (5) .

PART III DIPLOMATIC IMMUNITIES AND PRIVILEGES

20. Application of Convention on Diplomatic Relations

(1) Subject to section 29 (2) , the Articles set out in the First Schedule (being Articles of the Vienna Convention on Diplomatic Relations signed in 1961) have the force of law in Malaŵi and shall for that purpose be construed in accordance with subsections (2) to (5) .

(2) For the purposes of Article 32 a waiver by the head of the mission of any State

any manner to which the State has agreed and subsections (2) and (4) do not apply where service is effected in any such manner.

(7) This section shall not be construed as applying to proceedings against a State by way of counter-claim or to an action in rem, and subsection (1) shall not be construed as affecting any rules of court whereby leave is required for the service of process outside the jurisdiction

15. Other procedural privileges

(1) Subject to subsections (2) and (3):

(a) relief shall not be given against a State by way of injunction or order for specific performance or for the recovery of land or other property; and

(b) the property of a State shall not be subject to any process for the enforcement of a judgment or an arbitration award or, in an action in rem, for its arrest, detention or sale.

(2) Subsection (1) does not prevent the giving of any relief or the issue of any process with the written consent of the State concerned; and any such consent (which may be contained in a prior agreement) may be expressed so as to apply to a limited extent or generally; but a provision merely submitting to the jurisdiction of the courts is not to be regarded as a consent for the purposes of this subsection.

(3) Subsection (1) (b) shall not prevent the issue of any process in respect of property which is for the time being in use or intended for use for commercial purposes.

16. States entitled to immunities and privileges

(1) The immunities and privileges conferred by this Part apply to any foreign or Commonwealth State other than Malawi; and references to a State include references to—

(a) the sovereign or other head of that State in his public capacity;

(b) the government of that State; and

(c) any department of that government, but not to any entity (hereinafter referred to as a "separate entity") which is distinct from the executive organs of the government of the State and capable of suing or being sued.

(2) A separate entity is immune from the jurisdiction of the courts of Malawi if, and only if—

(a) the proceedings relate to anything done by it in the exercise of sovereign authority; and

(b) the circumstances are such that a State would have been so immune.

(3) If a separate entity (not being a State's central bank or other monetary authority) submits to the jurisdiction in respect of proceedings in the case of which it is entitled to immunity by virtue of subsection (2), section 15 shall apply to it in respect of those proceedings as if references to a State were references to that entity.

(4) Property of a State's central bank or other monetary authority shall not be regarded for the purposes of section 15 (3) as in use or intended for use for commercial purposes; and where any such bank or authority is a separate entity section 15 (1) and (2) shall apply to it as if references to a State were references to the bank or authority.

(5) This section applies to a territory forming a constituent part of a federal State as if such territory were a separate entity of that State.

may arise, to arbitration, the State is not immune as respects proceedings in the courts of Malawi which relate to the arbitration.

(2) This section has effect subject to any contrary provision in the arbitration agreement and does not apply to any arbitration agreement between States.

12. Proceedings against ships used for commercial purposes

(1) A State is not immune as respects—

(a) an action in rem against a ship belonging to that State; or

(b) an action in personam for enforcing a claim in connexion with such a ship, if, at the time when the cause of action arose, the ship was in use or intended for use for commercial purposes.

(2) A State is not immune as respects—

(a) an action in rem against a cargo belonging to that State if both the cargo and the ship carrying it were, at the time when the cause of action arose, in use or intended for use for commercial purposes; or

(b) an action in personam for enforcing a claim in connexion with such a cargo if the ship carrying it was then in use or intended for use for commercial purposes.

(3) References in this section to a ship or cargo belonging to a State include references to a ship or cargo in its possession or control or in which it claims an interest; and subject to subsection (2) subsection (1) applies to property other than a ship as it applies to a ship.

13. Duties and rates

A State is not immune as respects proceedings relating to its liability for—

(a) any duty of customs or excise; or

(b) rates in respect of premises occupied by it for commercial purposes.

14. Service of process and default judgments

(1) Any process or other document required to be served for instituting proceedings against a State shall be served by being transmitted through the Ministry of External Affairs to the Ministry of Foreign Affairs of that State and service shall be deemed to have been effected when the process or other document is received at that State's Ministry.

(2) Any time for entering an appearance (whether prescribed by rules of court or otherwise) shall begin to run two months after the date on which the process or document is received at the State's Ministry.

(3) A State which appears in proceedings cannot thereafter raise any objection on the ground that subsection (1) has not been complied with in the case of those proceedings.

(4) No judgment in default of appearance shall be given against a State except on proof that subsection (1) has been complied with and that the time for entering an appearance as extended by subsection (2) has expired.

(5) A copy of any judgment given against a State in default of appearance shall be transmitted through the Ministry of External Affairs to the Ministry of Foreign Affairs of that State and any time for applying to have the judgment set aside (whether prescribed by rules of court or otherwise) shall begin to run two months after the date on which the copy of the judgment is received at that State's Ministry.

(6) Subsection (1) does not prevent the service of a process or other document in

ment between the State and an individual if—

(a) the contract was entered into in Malawi of the work is to be performed wholly or partly in Malawi; and

(b) at the time when the contract was entered into the individual was a citizen of Malawi or was ordinarily resident in Malawi; and

(c) at the time when the proceedings are brought the individual is not a citizen of the State concerned.

(2) Subsection (1) does not apply if the parties to the contract have otherwise agreed in writing unless the law of Malawi requires the proceedings to be brought in Malawi.

7. Personal injuries and damage to property

A State is not immune as respects proceedings relating to—

(a) the death or injury of any person; or

(b) damage to or loss of tangible property, caused by an act or omission in Malawi.

8. Ownership, possession and use of property

A State is not immune as respects proceedings relating to—

(a) any interest of the State in, or its possession or use of immoveable property in Malawi;

(b) any obligation of the State arising out of its interest in, or its possession or use of, such property; or

(c) any interest of the State in moveable or immoveable property, being an interest arising by way of succession, gift or *bona vacantia*.

9. Patents, trade-marks, etc.

A State is not immune as respects proceedings relating to—

(a) any patent, trade-mark, design or plant breeder's right belonging to the State and registered or protected in Malawi or for which the State has applied in Malawi; or

(b) an alleged infringement by the State in Malawi of any patent, trade-mark, design, plant breeder's right or copyright; or

(c) the right to use a trade or business name in Malawi.

10. Membership of corporate bodies

(1) A State is not immune as respects proceedings relating to its membership of a body corporate, an unincorporated body or a partnership which—

(a) has members other than States; and

(b) is incorporated or constituted under the law of Malawi or is controlled from or has its principal place of business in Malawi, being proceedings arising between the State and the body or its other members or, as the case may be, between the State and the other partners.

(2) This section does not apply if provision to the contrary has been made by an agreement in writing between the parties to the dispute or by the constitution or other instrument establishing or regulating the body or partnership in question.

11. Arbitration

(1) Where a State has agreed in writing to submit a dispute which has arisen, or

(2) A court shall give effect to the immunity conferred by this section even though the State does not appear in the proceedings in question.

4. Submission to jurisdiction

(1) A State is not immune as respects proceedings in respect of which it has submitted to the jurisdiction of the courts of Malawi.

(2) A State may submit after the dispute giving rise to the proceedings has arisen or by a prior written agreement; but a provision in an agreement that it is to be governed by the law of Malawi is not to be regarded as a submission.

(3) A State is deemed to have submitted:

(a) if it has instituted the proceedings; or

(b) subject to subsection (4), if it has intervened or taken any step in the proceedings.

(4) Subsection 3 (b) does not apply to intervention or any step taken for the purpose only of—

(a) claiming immunity; or

(b) asserting an interest in property in circumstances such that the State would have been entitled to immunity if the proceedings had been brought against it.

(5) A submission in respect of any proceedings extends to any appeal but not to any counter-claim unless it arises out of the same legal relationship or facts as the claim.

(6) The head of a State's diplomatic mission in Malawi, or the person for the time being performing his functions, shall be deemed to have authority to submit on behalf of the State in respect of any proceedings; and any person who has entered into a contract on behalf of or with the authority of a State shall be deemed to have authority to submit on its behalf in proceedings arising out of contract.

5. Commercial transactions

(1) A State is not immune as respects proceedings relating to—

(a) a commercial transaction entered into by the State; or

(b) an obligation of the State which by virtue of a contract (whether a commercial transaction or not) falls to be performed wholly or partly in Malawi.

(2) Subsection (1) does not apply if the parties to the dispute are States or have otherwise agreed in writing.

(3) In subsection (1) "commercial transaction" means—

(a) any contract for the supply of goods and services;

(b) any loan or other transaction for the provision of finance and any guarantee or indemnity in respect of such transaction or of any other financial obligation; and

(c) any other transaction or activity of a commercial, industrial, financial, professional or other similar character into which a State enters or in which it engages otherwise than in the exercise of sovereign authority, but does not include a contract of employment between a State and an individual.

6. Contracts of employment

(1) A State is not immune as respects proceedings relating to a contract of employ-

Immunities And Privileges, 1984 (Malaŵi)

An Act to determine the extent of the immunity of foreign States from the jurisdiction of the courts of Malaŵi; to provide for diplomatic and consular privileges and immunities by giving effect to certain international conventions and otherwise and for privileges and immunities of international organizations; and for connected purposes.

[17th April 1984]

PART I PRELIMINARY

1. Short title

This Act may be cited as the Immunities and Privileges Act.

2. Interpretation

(1) In this Act—

"commercial purposes" means purposes of any commercial transaction as defined in section 5 (3);

"consular officer" means any person, including the head of a consular post, entrusted in that capacity with the exercise of consular functions and any person in the service of the government of a Commonwealth country performing any such functions;

"consular post" means any consulate-general, consulate, vice-consulate or consular agency;

"diplomatic agent" has the meaning assigned to it in Article 1 in the First Schedule.

(2) In the Articles set out in the First and Second Schedules—

"agent of the receiving State" or "authorities of the receiving State" shall be construed as including a police officer and any person exercising a power of entry into or upon premises under any written law;

"grave crime" shall be construed as meaning any offence which, on first conviction, is punishable with imprisonment for a term which may extend to five years or with a more severe sentence;

"national of the receiving State" shall be construed as meaning a citizen of Malaŵi.

PART II STATE IMMUNITY

3. General immunity from jurisdiction

(1) A State is immune from the jurisdiction of the courts of Malaŵi except as provided in this Part of this Act.

greement to which the Republic and the foreign state are parties, and any time prescribed by rules of court or otherwise for applying to have the judgment set aside shall begin to run tow months after the date on which the copy of the judgment is delivered to that ministry or made available to the foreign state, as the case may be. " .

5. Amendment of section 14 of Act 87 of 1981.

Section 14 of the principal Act is hereby amended by the substitution for paragraph (b) of subsection (1) of the following paragraph:

" (b) the property or any right or interest of a foreign state shall not be subject to any process—

(i) for its attachment in order to found or to confirm jurisdiction;

(ii) for the enforcement of a judgment or an arbitration award; or

(iii) in an action in rem, for its attachment or sale. " .

Other national legislation

6. Amendment of section 17 of Act 87 of 1981.

(a) by the substitution for the words preceding paragraph (a) of the following words:

"17. A certificate by or on behalf of the Minister of Foreign Affairs shall be conclusive evidence on any question—"; and

(b) by the substitution for paragraph (d) of the following paragraph:

" (d) whether, and if so when, any document has been delivered or made available as contemplated in section 13 (1) or (5) . " .

7. Short title and commencement.

This Act shall be called the Foreign States Immunities Act, 1988, and shall come into operation on a dete to be fixed by the State President by proclamation in the Gazette.

Foreign State Immunities Amendment Act
NO 48 OF 1985
ACT

To amend the Foreign States Immunities Act, 1981, so as to make it clear that the property of foreign state shall not be subject to attachment in order to found jurisdiction; and to provide for matters connected therewith.

1. Amends section 14 (1) of the Foreign States Immunities Act, No. 87 of 1981, by substituting paragraph (b).

2. Short title. —This Act shall be called the Foreign States Immunities Amendment Act, 1985.

Foreign State Immunities Amendment Act
No 5 OF 1988
ACT

To amend the Foreign States Immunities Act, 1981, so as to confirm the Immunity of foreign states from the jurisdiction of the courts of the Republic, and to remove certain ambiguities; and to provide for matters connected therewith.

1. Amendment of section 2 of Act 87 of 1981.

Section 2 of the Foreign States Immunities Act, 1981 (hereinafter refrred to as the principal Act) is hereby amended by the addition of the following subsection:

" (4) The exceptions to the immunity of foreign states from the jurisdiction of the courts of the Republic provided for in this Act shall not apply in disputes in which all the parties are sovereign states. ".

2. Amendment of section 9 of Act 87 of 1981.

Section 9 of the principal Act is hereby amended by the substitution for para-graph (a) of subsection (1) of the following paragraph.

" (a) has members that are not states; and".

3. Amendment of section 10 of Act 87 of 1981.

Section 10 of the principal Act is hereby amended by the substitution for paragraph (b) of subsection (2) of the following paragraph:

" (b) the parties to the arbitration agreement are states".

4. Amendment of section 13 of Act 87 of 1981.

(a) by the substitution for subsection (1) of the following subsection:

" (1) any process or other document required to be served for instituting proceedings against a foreign state shall be served by delivering it through the Department of Foreign Affairs of the Republic to the ministry of foreign affairs of the foreign state, or by making it available in any other manner to the foreign state in accordance with an agreement to which the Republic and that foreign state are parties, and service shall be deemed to have been effected when the process or other document is delivered to that ministry or made available to the foreign state, as the case may be. ",

(b) by the substitution for subsection (2) of the following subsection:

" (2) Any time prescribed by rules of court or otherwise for notice of intention to defend or oppose or entering an appearance shall begin to run tow months after the date on which the process or document is served as aforesaid" ; and

(c) by the substitution for subsection (5) of the following subsection:

" (5) A copy of any default judgment against a foreign state shall be delivered through the Department of Foreign Affairs of the Republic to the ministry of foreign affairs of the foreign state, or made available to the foreign state in accordance with an a-

(3) Subsection (1) (b) shall not prevent the issue of any process in respect of property which is for the time being in use or intended for use for commercial purposes.

15. Immunity of separate entities

(1) A separate entity shall be immune from the jurisdiction of the courts of the Republic only if:

(a) the proceedings relate to anything done by the separate entity in the exercise of sovereign authority; and

(b) the circumstances are such that a foreign State would have been so immune.

(2) If a separate entity, not being the central bank or other monetary authority of a foreign State, waives the immunity to which it is entitled by virtue of subsection (1) in respect of any proceedings, the provisions of section 14 shall apply to those proceedings as if references in those provisions to a foreign State were references to that separate entity.

(3) Property of the central bank or other monetary authority of a foreign State shall not be regarded for the purposes of subsection (3) of section 14 as in use or intended for use for commercial purposes, and where any such bank or authority is a separate entity the provisions of subsections (1) and (2) of that section shall apply to it as if references in those provisions to a foreign State were references to that bank or authority.

16. Restriction and extension of immunities and privileges

If it appears to the State President that the immunities and privileges conferred by this Act in relation to a particular foreign State:

(a) exceed or are less than those accorded by the law of that foreign State in relation to the Republic; or

(b) are less than those required by any treaty, convention or other international agreement to which that foreign State and the Republic are parties,

he may by proclamation in the Gazette restrict or, as the case may be, extend those immunities and privileges to such extent as appears to him to be appropriate.

17. Evidence by certificate

A certificate by or on behalf of the Minister of Foreign Affairs and Information shall be conclusive evidence on any question:

(a) whether any foreign country is a State for the purposes of this Act;

(b) whether any territory is a constituent part of a federal foreign State for the said purposes;

(c) as to the person or persons to be regarded for the said purposes as the head of State or government of a foreign State;

(d) whether, and if so when, any document has been served or received as contemplated in section 13 (1) or (5).

18. Short title and commencement

This Act shall be called the Foreign States Immunities Act, 1981, and shall come into operation on a date to be fixed by the State President by proclamation in the Gazette.

visions of subsection (2), subsection (1) shall apply to property other than a ship as it applies to a ship.

12. Taxes and duties

A foreign State shall not be immune from the jurisdiction of the courts of the Republic in proceedings relating to the foreign State's liability for:

(a) sales tax or any customs or excise duty; or

(b) rates in respect of premises used by it for commercial purposes.

13. Service of process and default judgments

(1) Any process or other document required to be served for instituting proceedings against a foreign State shall be served by being transmitted through the Department of Foreign Affairs and Information of the Republic to the ministry of foreign affairs of the foreign State, and service shall be deemed to have been effected when the process or other document is received at that ministry.

(2) Any time prescribed by rules of court or otherwise for notice of intention to defend or oppose or entering an appearance shall begin to run two months after the date on which the process or document is received as aforesaid.

(3) A foreign State which appears in proceedings cannot thereafter object that subsection (1) has not been complied with in the case of those proceedings.

(4) No judgment in default of appearance shall be given against a foreign State except on proof that subsection (1) has been complied with and that the time for notice of intention to defend or oppose or entering an appearance as extended by subsection (2) has expired.

(5) A copy of any default judgment against a foreign State shall be transmitted through the Department of Foreign Affairs and Information of the Republic to the ministry of foreign affairs of the foreign State, and any time prescribed by rules of court or otherwise for applying to have the judgment set aside shall begin to run two months after the date on which the copy of the judgment is received at that ministry.

(6) Subsection (1) shall not prevent the service of any process or other document in any manner to which the foreign State has agreed, and subsections (2) and (4) shall not apply where service is effected in any such manner.

(7) The preceding provisions of this section shall not be construed as applying to proceedings against a foreign State by way of counter-claim or to an action in rem, and subsection (1) shall not be construed as affecting any rules of court whereby leave is required for the service of process outside the jurisdiction of the court.

14. Other procedural privileges

(1) Subject to the provisions of subsections (2) and (3):

(a) relief shall not be given against a foreign State by way of interdict or order for specific performance or for the recovery of any movable or immovable property; and

(b) the property of a foreign State shall not be subject to any process:

(i) for its attachment in order to found jurisdiction;

(ii) for the enforcement of a judgment or an arbitration award; or

(iii) in an action in rem, for its attachment or sale.

(2) Subsection (1) shall not prevent the giving of any relief or the issue of any process with the written consent of the foreign State concerned, and any such consent, which may be contained in a prior agreement, may be expressed so as to apply to a limited extent or generally, but a mere waiver of a foreign State's immunity from the jurisdiction of the courts of the Republic shall not be regarded as a consent for the purposes of this subsection.

9. Membership of associations and other bodies

(1) A foreign State which is a member of an association or other body (whether a juristic person or not), or a partnership, which:

(a) has members that are not foreign States; and

(b) is incorporated or constituted under the law of the Republic or is controlled from the Republic or has its principal place of business in the Republic, shall not be immune from the jurisdiction of the courts of the Republic in proceedings which:

(i) relate to the foreign State's membership of the association, other body or partnership; and

(ii) arise between the foreign State and the association or other body or its other members, or as the case may be, between the foreign State and the other partners.

(2) Subsection (1) shall not apply if:

(a) in terms of an agreement in writing between the parties to the dispute; or

(b) in terms of the constitution or other instrument establishing or governing the association, other body or partnership in question,

the dispute is justiciable by the courts of a foreign State.

10. Arbitration

(1) A foreign State which has agreed in writing to submit a dispute which has arisen, or may arise, to arbitration, shall not be immune from the jurisdiction of the courts of the Republic in any proceedings which relate to the arbitration.

(2) Subsection (1) shall not apply if:

(a) the arbitration agreement provides that the proceedings shall be brought in the courts of a foreign State; or

(b) the parties to the arbitration agreement are foreign States.

11. Admiralty proceedings

(1) A foreign State shall not be immune from the admiralty jurisdiction of any court of the Republic in:

(a) an action in rem against a ship belonging to the foreign State; or

(b) an action in *personam* for enforcing a claim in connection with such a ship,

if, at the time when the cause of action arose, the ship was in use or intended for use for commercial purposes.

(2) A foreign State shall not be immune from the admiralty jurisdiction of any court of the Republic in:

(a) an action in rem against any cargo belonging to the foreign State if both the cargo and the ship carrying it were, at the time when the cause of action arose, in use or intended for use for commercial purposes; or

(b) an action in *personam* for enforcing a claim in connection with any such cargo if the ship carrying it was, at the time when the cause of action arose, in use or intended for use for commercial purposes.

(3) Any reference in this section to a ship or cargo belonging to a foreign State shall be construed as including a reference to a ship or cargo in the possession or control of a foreign State or in which a foreign State claims an interest, and, subject to the pro-

5. Contracts of employment

(1) A foreign State shall not be immune from the jurisdiction of the courts of the Republic in proceedings relating to a contract of employment between the foreign State and an individual if:

(a) the contract was entered into in the Republic or the work is to be performed wholly or partly in the Republic; and

(b) at the time when the contract was entered into the individual was a South African citizen or was ordinarily resident in the Republic; and

(c) at the time when the proceedings are brought the individual is not a citizen of the foreign State.

(2) Subsection (1) shall not apply if:

(a) the parties to the contract have agreed in writing that the dispute or any dispute relating to the contract shall be justiciable by the courts of a foreign State; or

(b) the proceedings relate to the employment of the head of a diplomatic mission or any member of the diplomatic mission or any member of the diplomatic, administrative, technical or service staff of the mission or to the employment of the head of a consular post or any member of the consular, labour, trade, administrative, technical or service staff of the post.

6. Personal injuries and damage to property

A foreign State shall not be immune from the jurisdiction of the courts of the Republic in proceedings relating to:

(a) the death or injury of any person; or

(b) damage to or loss of tangible property, caused by an act or ommission in the Republic.

7. Ownership, possession and use of property

(1) A foreign State shall not be immune from the jurisdiction of the courts of the Republic in proceedings relating to:

(a) any interest of the foreign State in, or its possession or use of, immovable property in the Republic;

(b) any obligation of the foreign State arising out of its interest in, or its possession or use of, such property; or

(c) any interest of the foreign State in movable or immovable property, being an interest arising by way of succession, gift or *bona vacantia*.

(2) Subsection (1) shall not apply to proceedings relating to a foreign State's title to, or its use or possession of, property used for a diplomatic mission or a consular post.

8. Patents, trade-marks, etc

A foreign State shall not be immune from the jurisdiction of the courts of the Republic in proceedings relating to:

(a) any patent, trade-mark, design or plant breeder's right belonging to the foreign State and registered or protected in the Republic or for which the foreign State has applied in the Republic; or

(b) an alleged infringement by the foreign State in the Republic of any patent, trade-mark, design, plant breeder's right or copyright; or

(c) the right to use a trade or business name in the Republic.

3. Waiver of immunity

(1) A foreign State shall not be immune from the jurisdiction of the courts of the Republic in proceedings in respect of which the foreign State has expressly waived its immunity or is in terms of subsection (3) deemed to have waived its immunity.

(2) Waiver of immunity may be effected after the dispute which gave rise to the proceedings has arisen or by prior written agreement, but a provision in an agreement that it is to be governed by the law of the Republic shall not be regarded as a waiver.

(3) A foreign State shall be deemed to have waived its immunity:

(a) if it has instituted the proceedings; or

(b) subject to the provisions of subsection (4), if it has intervened or taken any step in the proceedings.

(4) Subsection (3) (b) shall not apply to intervention or any step taken for the purpose only of:

(a) claiming immunity; or

(b) asserting an interest in property in circumstances such that the foreign State would have been entitled to immunity if the proceedings had been brought against it.

(5) A waiver in respect of any proceedings shall apply to any appeal and to any counter-claim arising out of the same legal relationship or facts as the claim.

(6) The head of a foreign State's diplomatic mission in the Republic, or the person for the time being performing his functions, shall be deemed to have authority to waive on behalf of the foreign State its immunity in respect of any proceedings, and any person who has entered into a contract on behalf of and with the authority of a foreign State shall be deemed to have authority to waive on behalf of the foreign State its immunity in respect of proceedings arising out of the contract.

4. Commercial transactions

(1) A foreign State shall not be immune from the jurisdiction of the courts of the Republic in proceedings relating to:

(a) a commercial transaction entered into by the foreign State; or

(b) an obligation of the foreign State which by virtue of a contract (whether a commercial transaction or not) falls to be performed wholly or partly in the Republic.

(2) Subsection (1) shall not apply if the parties to the dispute are foreign States or have agreed in writing that the dispute shall be justiciable by the courts of a foreign State.

(3) In subsection (1) "commercial transaction" means:

(a) any contract for the supply of services or goods;

(b) any loan or other transaction for the provision of finance and any guarantee or indemnity in respect of any such loan or other transaction or of any other financial obligation; and

(c) any other transaction or activity or a commercial, industrial, financial, professional or other similar character into which a foreign State enters or in which it engages otherwise than in the exercise of sovereign authority, but does not include a contract of employment between a foreign State and an individual.

Foreign States Immunities Act, 1981 (South Africa)

[ASSENTED TO 6 OCTOBER 1981] [DATE OF COMMENCEMENT: 20 NOVEMBER 1981]
(Afrikaans text signed by the State President)
as amended by
Foreign States Immunities Amendment Act 48 of 1985
also amended by
Foreign States Immunities Amendment Act 5 of 1988
[with effect from a date to be proclaimed-see PENDLEX]
ACT
To determine the extent of the immunity of foreign States from the jurisdiction of the courts of the Republic; and to provide for matters connected therewith.

1. Definitions

(1) In this Act, unless the context otherwise indicates—
"commercial purposes" means purposes of any commercial transaction as defined in section 4 (3);
"consular post" means a consulate-general, consulate, consular agency, trade office or labour office;
"Republic" includes the territorial waters of the Republic, as defined in section 2 of the Territorial Waters Act, 1963 (Act 87 of 1963);
"separate entity" means an entity referred to in subsection (2) (i).
(2) Any reference in this Act to a foreign State shall in relation to any particular foreign State be construed as including a reference to:
 (a) the head of State of that foreign State, in his capacity as such head of State;
 (b) the government of that foreign State; and
 (c) any department of that government, but not as including a reference to—
 (i) any entity which is distinct from the executive organs of the government of that foreign State and capable of suing or being sued; or
 (ii) any territory forming a constituent part of a federal foreign State.

2. General immunity from jurisdiction

(1) A foreign State shall be immune from the jurisdiction of the courts of the Republic except as provided in this Act or in any proclamation issued thereunder.
(2) A court shall give effect to the immunity conferred by this section even though the foreign State does not appear in the proceedings in question.
(3) The provisions of this Act shall not be construed as subjecting any foreign State to the criminal jurisdiction of the courts of the Republic.

16. Restriction and extension of immunities and privileges.

(1) If it appears to the Federal Government that the immunities and privileges conferred by this Ordinance in relation to any State:

(a) exceed those accorded by the law of that State in relation to Pakistan; or

(b) are less than those required by any treaty, conventional or other inter national agreement to which that State and Pakistan are parties,

the Federal Government may, by notification in the official Gazette provide for restricting or, as the case may be, extending those immunities and privileges to such extent as it may deem fit.

17. Savings, etc.

(1) This Ordinance does not affect any immunity or privilege conferred by the Diplomatic and Consular Privileges Act, 1972 (1X of 1972); and

(a) section 6 does not apply to proceedings concerning the employment of the members of a mission within the meaning of the Convention set out in the First Schedule to the said Act of 1972 or of the members of a consular post within the meaning of the Convention set out in the Second Schedule to that Act;

(b) sub-section (1) of section 7 does not apply to proceedings concerning a State's title to, or its possession of, property used for the purposes of a diplomatic mission.

(2) This Ordinance does not apply to

(a) proceedings relating to anything done by or in relation to the armed forces of a State while present in Pakistan;

(b) criminal proceedings; or

(c) proceedings relating to taxation other than those mentioned in section 12.

18. Proof as to certain matters.

A certificate under the hand of a Secretary to the Government of Pakistan shall be conclusive evidence on any question

(a) whether any country is a State for the purposes of this Ordinance, whether any territory is a constituent territory of a Federal State for those purposes or as to the person or persons to be regarded for those purposes as the head or government of a State; or

(b) whether, and if so when, a document has been served or received as mentioned in sub-section (1) or sub-section (5) of section 13.

19. Repeal.

Sections 86 and 87 of the Code of Civil Procedure, 1908 (Act V of 1908) are hereby repealed.

(b) the property of a State, not being property which is for the time being in use or intended for use for commercial purposes, shall not be subject to any process for the enforcement of a judgment or arbitration award or, in an action in rem, for its arrest, detention or sale.

(3) Sub-section (2) does not prevent the giving of any relief or the issue of any process with the written consent of the State concerned ; and any such consent, which may be contained in a prior agreement, may be expressed so as to apply to a limited extent or generally:

Provided that a provision merely submitting to the jurisdiction of the courts shall not be deemed to be a consent for the purposes of this sub-section.

(4) The head of a State's diplomatic mission in Pakistan, or the person for the time being performing his functions, shall be deemed to have authority to give on behalf of the State any such consent as is mentioned in sub-section (3) and, for the purposes of clause (b) of sub-section (2), his certificate that any property is not in use or intended for use by or on behalf of the State for commercial purposes shall be accepted as sufficient evidence of that fact unless the contrary is proved.

SUPPLEMENTARY PROVISIONS

15. States entitled to immunities and privileges.

(1) The immunities and privileges conferred by this Act apply to any foreign State; and references to State include references to

(a) the sovereign or other head of that State in his public capacity;

(b) the government of that State; and

(c) any department of that government ,

but not to any entity, hereinafter referred to as a "separate entity", which is distinct from the executive organs of the government of the State and capable of suing or being sued.

(2) A separate entity is immune from the jurisdiction of the courts of Pakistan if, and only if

(a) the proceedings relate to anything done by it in the exercise of sovereign authority; and

(b) the circumstances are such that a State would have been so immune.

(3) If a separate entity, not being a State's central bank or other monetary authority, submits to the jurisdiction in respect of proceedings in the case of which it is entitled to immunity by virtue of sub-section (2) of this section, the provisions of sub-sections (1) to (3) of section 14 shall apply to it in respect of those proceedings as if reference to a State were references to that entity.

(4) Property of a State's central bank or other monetary authority shall not be regarded for the purposes of sub-section (3) of section 14 as in use or intended for use for commercial purposes; and where any such bank or authority is a separate entity subsections (1) and (2) of that section shall apply to it as if references to a State were references to the bank or authority.

(5) Section 13 applies to proceedings against the constituent territories of a Federal State; and the Federal Government may, by notification in the official Gazette, provide for the other provisions of this Ordinance to apply to any such constituent territory specified in the notification as they apply to a State.

(6) Where the provisions of this Ordinance do not apply to a constituent territory by virtue of a notification under sub-section (5), the provisions of sub-sections (2) and (3) shall apply to it as if it were a separate entity.

(5) In the foregoing provisions references to a ship or cargo belonging to a State include references to a ship or cargo in its possession or control or in which it claims an interest; and, subject to sub-section (4), sub-section (2). applies to property other than a ship as it applies to a ship.

(6) Sections 5 and 6 do not apply to proceedings of the nature mentioned in sub-section (1) if the State in question is a party to the Brussels Convention and the claim relates to the operation of a ship owned or operated by that State, the carriage of cargo or passengers on any such ship or the carriage of cargo owned by that State on any other ship.

Explanation—In this section, "Brussels Convention" means the International Convention for the Unification of Certain Rules Concerning the Immunity of Stateowned Ships signed in Brussels on the tenth day of April 1926, and "ship" includes hovercraft.

12. Value added tax, customs duties, etc.

A State is not immune as respects proceedings relating to its liability for:

(a) value added tax, any duty of customs or excise or any agricultural levy; or

(b) rates in respect of premises occupied by it for commercial purposes.

PROCEDURE

13. Service of process and judgment in default of appearance.

(1) Any notice or other document required to be served for instituting proceedings against a State shall be served by being transmitted through the Ministry of Foreign Affairs or Pakistan to the Ministry of Foreign Affairs of the State and service shall be deemed to have been effected when the notice or document is received at the latter Ministry.

(2) Any proceedings in Court shall not commence earlier than two months after the date on which the notice or document is received as aforesaid.

(3) A State which appears in proceedings cannot thereafter object that sub-section (1) has not been complied with as respects those proceedings.

(4) No judgment in default of appearance shall be given against a State except on proof that sub-section (1) has been complied with and that the time for the commencement of proceedings specified in sub-section (2) has elapsed.

(5) A copy of any judgment given against a State in default of appearance shall be transmitted through the Ministry of Foreign Affairs of Pakistan to the Ministry of Foreign Affairs of the State and the time for applying to have the judgment set aside shall begin to run two months after the date on which the copy of the judgment is received at the latter Ministry.

(6) Sub-section (1) does not prevent the service of a notice or other document in any manner to which the State agreed and sub-sections (2) and (4) do dot apply where service is effected in any such manner.

(7) The preceding provisions of this section shall not be construed as applying to proceedings against the State by way of a counterclaim or to an action in rem.

14. Other procedural privileges.

(1) No penalty by way of committal to prison or fine shall be imposed in respect of any failure or refusal by or on behalf of a State to disclose or produce any document or information for the purposes of proceedings to which it is a party.

(2) Subject to sub-sections (3) and (4),

(a) relief shall not be given against a State by way of injunction or order for specific performance or for the recovery of land or other property; and

(b) an alleged infringement by the State in Pakistan of any patent, trade mark, design, plant breeders' rights or copyrights ; or

(c) the right to use a trade or business name in Pakistan.

9. Membership of bodies corporate, etc.

(1) A State is not immune as respects proceedings relating to its membership of a body corporate, an unincorporated body or a partnership which:

(a) has members other than States; and

(b) is incorporated or constituted under the law of Pakistan or is controlled from, or has its principal place of business in, Pakistan,

being proceedings arising between the State and the body or its other members or, as the case may be, between the State and the other partners.

(2) Sub-section (1) does not apply if provision to the contrary has been made by an agreement in writing between the parties to the dispute or by the constitution or other instrument establishing or regulating the body or partnership in question.

10. Arbitrations.

(1) Where a State has agreed in writing to submit a dispute which has arisen, or may arise, to arbitration, the State is not immune as respects proceedings in the courts of Pakistan which relate to the arbitration.

(2) Sub-section (1) has effect subject to the provisions of the arbitration agreement and does not apply to an arbitration agreement between States.

11. Ships used for commercial purposes.

(1) The succeeding provisions of this section apply to:

(a) Admiralty proceedings; and

(b) proceedings on any claim which could be made the subject of Admiralty proceedings.

(2) A State is not immune as respects—

(a) an action in rem against a ship belonging to it; or

(b) an action in *personam* for enforcing a claim in connection with such a ship;

if, at the time when the cause of action arose, the ship was in use or intended for use for commercial purposes.

(3) Where an action in rem is brought against a ship belonging to a State for enforcing a claim in connection with another ship belonging to that State, clause (a) of sub-section (2) does not apply as respects the first mentioned ship unless, at the time when the cause of action relating to the other ship arose, both ships were in use or intended for use for commercial purposes.

(4) A State is not immune as respects:

(a) an action in rem against a cargo belonging to that State if both the cargo and the ship carrying it were, at the time when the cause of action arose, in use or intended for use for commercial purposes; or

(b) an action in *personam* for enforcing a claim in connection with such a cargo if the ship carrying it was then in use or intended for use as aforesaid.

Explanation—In this sub-section, "proceedings relating to a contract of employment" includes proceedings between the parties to such a contract in respect of any statutory rights or duties to which they are entitled or subject as employer or employee.

(2) Subject to sub-sections (3) and (4), sub-section (1) does not apply if—

(a) at the time when the proceedings are brought the individual is a national of the State concerned; or

(b) at the time when the contract was made the individual was neither a citizen of Pakistan nor habitually resident in Pakistan; or

(c) the parties, to the contract have otherwise agreed in writing.

(3) Where the work is for an office, agency or establishment maintained by the State in Pakistan for commercial purposes, clauses (a) and (b) of sub-section (2) do not exclude the application of sub-section (1) unless the individual was, at the time when the contract was made, habitually resident in that State.

(4) Clause (c) of sub-section (2) does not exclude the application of sub-section (1) where the law of Pakistan requires the proceedings to be brought before a court in Pakistan.

7. Ownership, possession and use of property.

(1) A State is not immune as respects proceedings relating to:

(a) any interest of the State in, or its possession or use of, immovable property in Pakistan; or

(b) any obligation of the State arising out of its interest in, or its possession or use of, any such property.

(2) A State is not immune as respects proceedings relating to any interest of the State in movable or immovable property, being an interest arising by way of succession, gift or *bona vacantia*.

(3) The fact that a State has or claims an interest in any property shall not preclude any court from exercising in respect of such property any jurisdiction relating to the estates of deceased persons or persons of unsound mind or to insolvency, the winding up of companies or the administration of trusts.

(4) A court may entertain proceedings against a person other than a State notwithstanding that the proceedings relate to property:

(a) which is in the possession of a State; or

(b) in which a State claims an interest,

if the State would not have been immune had the proceedings been brought against it or, in a case referred to in clause (b), if the claim is neither admitted nor supported by prima facie evidence.

8. Patents, trade marks, etc.

A State is not immune as respects proceedings relating to:

(a) any patent, trade mark, design or plant breeders' rights belonging to State which are registered or protected in Pakistan or for which the State has applied in Pakistan;

(a) if it has instituted the proceedings; or

(b) subject to sub-section (4) it has intervened or taken any step in the proceedings.

(4) Clause (b) of sub-section (3) does not apply:

(a) to intervention or any step taken for the purpose only of:

(i) claiming immunity; or

(ii) asserting an interest in property in circumstances such that the State would have been entitled to immunity if the proceedings had been brought against it; or

(b) to any step taken by the State in ignorance of the facts entitling it to immunity if those facts could not reasonably have been ascertained and immunity is claimed as soon as reasonably practicable.

(5) A submission in respect of any proceedings extends to any appeal but not to any counter claim unless it arises out of the same legal relationship or facts as the claim.

(6) The head of a State's diplomatic mission in Pakistan, or the person for the time being performing his functions, shall be deemed to have authority to submit on behalf of the State in respect of any proceedings; and any person who has entered into a contract on behalf of and with the authority of a State shall be deemed to have authority to submit on its behalf in respect of proceedings arising out of the contract.

5. Commercial transactions and contracts to be performed in Pakistan.

(1) A State is not immune as respects proceedings relating to:

(a) a commercial transaction entered into by the State; or

(b) an obligation of the State which by virtue of a contract, which may or may not be a commercial transaction, falls to be performed wholly or partly in Pakistan.

(2) Sub-section (1) does not apply to a contract of employment between a State and an individual or if the parties to the dispute are States or have otherwise agreed in writing; and clause (b) of that sub-section does not apply if the contract, not being a commercial transaction, was made in the territory of the State concerned and the obligation in question is governed by its administrative law.

(3) In this section "commercial transaction" means:

(a) any contract for the supply of goods or services;

(b) any loan or other transaction for the provision of finance and any guarantee or indemnity in respect of any such transaction or of any other financial obligation; and

(c) any other transaction or activity, whether of a commercial, industrial, financial, professional or other similar character, into which a State enters or in which it engages otherwise than in the exercise of its sovereign authority.

6. Contracts of employment.

(1) A State is not immune as respects proceedings relating to a contract of employment between a State and an individual where the contract was made, or the work is to be wholly or partly performed in Pakistan.

The State Immunity Ordinance, 1981 (Pakistan)

ORDINANCE No. VI OF 1981

An Ordinance to amend and consolidate the law relating to the Immunity of States from the jurisdiction of courts.

WHEREAS it is expedient to amend and consolidate the law relating to the immunity of States from the jurisdiction of courts;

AND WHEREAS the President is satisfied that circumstances exist which render it necessary to take immediate action;

NOW, THEREFORE, in pursuance of the Proclamation of the fifth day of July, 1977, read with the Laws (Continuance in Force) Order, 1977 (C. M. L. A. Order No. 1 of 1977), and in exercise of all powers enabling him in that behalf, the President is pleased to make and promulgate the following Ordinance :

1. Short title, extent and commencement.

(1) This Ordinance may be called the State Immunity Ordinance, 1981.

(2) It extends to the whole of Pakistan.

(3) It shall come into force at once.

2. Interpretation.

In this Ordinance, "Court" includes any tribunal or body exercising judicial functions.

IMMUNITY FROM JURISDICTION

3. General immunity from jurisdiction.

(1) A State is immune from the jurisdiction of the courts of Pakistan except as hereinafter provided.

(2) A court shall give effect to the immunity conferred by sub-section (1) even if the State does not appear in the proceedings in question.

EXCEPTIONS FROM IMMUNITY

4. Submission to jurisdiction.

(1) A State is not immune as respects proceedings in respect of which it has submitted to jurisdiction.

(2) A State may submit to jurisdiction after the dispute giving rise to the proceedings has arisen or by a prior agreement; but a provision in any agreement that it is to be governed by the law of Pakistan shall not be deemed to be a submission.

Explanation—In this sub-section and in sub-section (3) of section 14, "agreement" includes a treaty, convention or other international agreement.

(3) A State shall be deemed to have submitted:

(b) are less than those required by any treaty, convention or other international agreement to which that State and Singapore are parties,

the President may, by order, provide for restricting or, as the case may be, extending those immunities and privileges to such extent as appears to the President to be appropriate.

18. Evidence by certificate

A certificate by or on behalf of the Minister for Foreign Affairs shall be conclusive evidence on any question —

(a) whether any country is a State for the purposes of Part 2, whether any territory is a constituent territory of a federal State for those purposes or as to the person or persons to be regarded for those purposes as the head or government of a State; and

(b) whether, and if so when, a document has been served or received as mentioned in section 14 (1) or (5).

19. Excluded matters

(1) Part 2 does not affect any immunity or privilege applicable in Singapore to diplomatic and consular agents, and section 8 (1) does not apply to proceedings concerning a State's title to or its possession of property used for the purposes of a diplomatic mission.

(2) Part 2 does not apply to —

(a) proceedings relating to anything done by or in relation to the armed forces of a State while present in Singapore and, in particular, has effect subject to the Visiting Forces Act (Cap. 344);

(b) criminal proceedings; and

(c) proceedings relating to taxation other than those mentioned in section 13.

(5) The head of a State's diplomatic mission in Singapore, or the person for the time being performing his functions, shall be deemed to have authority to give on behalf of the State any such consent as is mentioned in subsection (3) and, for the purposes of subsection (4), his certificate to the effect that any property is not in use or intended for use by or on behalf of the State for commercial purposes shall be accepted as sufficient evidence of that fact unless the contrary is proved.

PART 3 SUPPLEMENTARY PROVISIONS

16. States entitled to immunities and privileges

(1) The immunities and privileges conferred by Part 2 apply to any foreign or Commonwealth State other than Singapore; and references to a State include references to —

(a) the sovereign or other head of that State in his public capacity;

(b) the government of that State; and

(c) any department of that government,

but not to any entity (referred to in this section as a separate entity) which is distinct from the executive organs of the government of the State and capable of suing or being sued.

(2) A separate entity is immune from the jurisdiction of the courts in Singapore if, and only if —

(a) the proceedings relate to anything done by it in the exercise of sovereign authority; and

(b) the circumstances are such that a State would have been so immune.

(3) If a separate entity (not being a State's central bank or other monetary authority) submits to the jurisdiction in respect of proceedings in the case of which it is entitled to immunity by virtue of subsection (2), section 15 (1) to (4) shall apply to it in respect of those proceedings as if references to a State were references to that entity.

(4) Property of a State's central bank or other monetary authority shall not be regarded for the purposes of section 15 (4) as in use or intended for use for commercial purposes; and where any such bank or authority is a separate entity, section 15 (1), (2) and (3) shall apply to it as if references to a State were references to the bank or authority.

(5) Section 14 applies to proceedings against the constituent territories of a federal State; and the President may by order provide for the other provisions of this Part to apply to any such constituent territory specified in the order as they apply to a State.

(6) Where the provisions of Part 2 do not apply to a constituent territory by virtue of any such order, subsections (2) and (3) shall apply to it as if it were a separate entity.

17. Restriction and extension of immunities and privileges

If it appears to the President that the immunities and privileges conferred by Part 2 in relation to any State —

(a) exceed those accorded by the law of that State in relation to Singapore; or

Procedure

14. Service of process and judgments in default of appearance

(1) Any writ or other document required to be served for instituting proceedings against a State shall be served by being transmitted through the Ministry of Foreign Affairs, Singapore, to the ministry of foreign affairs of that State, and service shall be deemed to have been effected when the writ or document is received at that ministry.

(2) Any time for entering an appearance (whether prescribed by Rules of Court or otherwise) shall begin to run 2 months after the date on which the writ or document is so received.

(3) A State which appears in proceedings cannot thereafter object that subsection (1) has not been complied with in the case of those proceedings.

(4) No judgment in default of appearance shall be given against a State except on proof that subsection (1) has been complied with and that the time for entering an appearance as extended by subsection (2) has expired.

(5) A copy of any judgment given against a State in default of appearance shall be transmitted through the Ministry of Foreign Affairs, Singapore, to the ministry of foreign affairs of that State and any time for applying to have the judgment set aside (whether prescribed by Rules of Court or otherwise) shall begin to run 2 months after the date on which the copy of the judgment is received at that ministry.

(6) Subsection (1) does not prevent the service of a writ or other document in any manner to which the State has agreed and subsections (2) and (4) do not apply where service is effected in any such manner.

(7) This section shall not be construed as applying to proceedings against a State by way of counterclaim or to an action in rem; and subsection (1) shall not be construed as affecting any Rules of Court whereby leave is required for the service of process outside the jurisdiction.

15. Other procedural privileges

(1) No penalty by way of committal or fine shall be imposed in respect of any failure or refusal by or on behalf of a State to disclose or produce any document or other information for the purposes of proceedings to which it is a party.

(2) Subject to subsections (3) and (4) —

(a) relief shall not be given against a State by way of injunction or order for specific performance or for the recovery of land or other property; and

(b) the property of a State shall not be subject to any process for the enforcement of a judgment or an arbitration award or, in an action in rem, for its arrest, detention or sale.

(3) Subsection (2) does not prevent the giving of any relief or the issue of any process with the written consent of the State concerned; and any such consent (which may be contained in a prior agreement) may be expressed so as to apply to a limited extent or generally; but a provision merely submitting to the jurisdiction of the courts is not to be regarded as a consent for the purposes of this subsection.

(4) Subsection (2) (b) does not prevent the issue of any process in respect of property which is for the time being in use or intended for use for commercial purposes.

11. Arbitrations

(1) Where a State has agreed in writing to submit a dispute which has arisen, or may arise, to arbitration, the State is not immune as respects proceedings in the courts in Singapore which relate to the arbitration.

(2) This section has effect subject to any contrary provision in the arbitration agreement and does not apply to any arbitration agreement between States.

12. Ships used for commercial purposes

(1) This section applies to —

(a) Admiralty proceedings; and

(b) proceedings on any claim which could be made the subject of Admiralty proceedings.

(2) A State is not immune as respects —

(a) an action in rem against a ship belonging to that State; or

(b) an action in personam for enforcing a claim in connection with such a ship,

if, at the time when the cause of action arose, the ship was in use or intended for use for commercial purposes.

(3) Where an action in rem is brought against a ship belonging to a State for enforcing a claim in connection with another ship belonging to that State, subsection (2) (a) does not apply as respects the first mentioned ship unless, at the time when the cause of action relating to the other ship arose, both ships were in use or intended for use for commercial purposes.

(4) A State is not immune as respects —

(a) an action in rem against a cargo belonging to that State if both the cargo and the ship carrying it were, at the time when the cause of action arose, in use or intended for use for commercial purposes; or

(b) an action in personam for enforcing a claim in connection with such a cargo if the ship carrying it was then in use or intended for use for commercial purposes.

(5) In subsections (2), (3) and (4), references to a ship or cargo belonging to a State include references to a ship or cargo in its possession or control or in which it claims an interest; and, subject to subsection (4), subsection (2) applies to property other than a ship as it applies to a ship.

13. Customs duties, etc.

A State is not immune as respects proceedings relating to its liability for —

(a) any customs duty or excise duty;

(aa) any goods and services tax; or

(b) any tax in respect of premises occupied by it for commercial purposes.

(b) damage to or loss of tangible property,

caused by an act or omission in Singapore.

8. Ownership, possession and use of property

(1) A State is not immune as respects proceedings relating to —

(a) any interest of the State in, or its possession or use of, immovable property in Singapore; or

(b) any obligation of the State arising out of its interest in, or its possession or use of, any such property.

(2) A State is not immune as respects proceedings relating to any interest of the State in movable or immovable property, being an interest arising by way of succession, gift or *bona vacantia*.

(3) The fact that a State has or claims an interest in any property shall not preclude any court from exercising in respect of it any jurisdiction relating to the estates of deceased persons or mentally disordered persons or to insolvency, the winding up of companies or the administration of trusts.

(4) A court may entertain proceedings against a person other than a State notwithstanding that the proceedings relate to property —

(a) which is in the possession or control of a State; or

(b) in which a State claims an interest,

if the State would not have been immune had the proceedings been brought against it or, in a case within paragraph (b), if the claim is neither admitted nor supported by prima facie evidence.

9. Patents, trade marks, etc.

A State is not immune as respects proceedings relating to —

(a) any patent, trade mark or design belonging to the State and registered or protected in Singapore or for which the State has applied in Singapore;

(b) an alleged infringement by the State in Singapore of any patent, trade mark, design or copyright; or

(c) the right to use a trade or business name in Singapore.

10. Membership of bodies corporate, etc.

(1) A State is not immune as respects proceedings relating to its membership of a body corporate, an unincorporated body or a partnership which —

(a) has members other than States; and

(b) is incorporated or constituted under the law of Singapore or is controlled from or has its principal place of business in Singapore,

being proceedings arising between the State and the body or its other members or, as the case may be, between the State and the other partners.

(2) This section does not apply if provision to the contrary has been made by an agreement in writing between the parties to the dispute or by the constitution or other instrument establishing or regulating the body or partnership in question.

(a) a commercial transaction entered into by the State; or

(b) an obligation of the State which by virtue of a contract (whether a commercial transaction or not) falls to be performed wholly or partly in Singapore,

but this subsection does not apply to a contract of employment between a State and an individual.

(2) This section does not apply if the parties to the dispute are States or have otherwise agreed in writing; and subsection (1) (b) does not apply if the contract (not being a commercial transaction) was made in the territory of the State concerned and the obligation in question is governed by its administrative law.

(3) In this section, "commercial transaction" means —

(a) any contract for the supply of goods or services;

(b) any loan or other transaction for the provision of finance and any guarantee or indemnity in respect of any such transaction or of any other financial obligation; and

(c) any other transaction or activity (whether of a commercial, industrial, financial, professional or other similar character) into which a State enters or in which it engages otherwise than in the exercise of sovereign authority.

6. Contracts of employment

(1) A State is not immune as respects proceedings relating to a contract of employment between the State and an individual where the contract was made in Singapore or the work is to be wholly or partly performed in Singapore.

(2) Subject to subsections (3) and (4), this section does not apply if —

(a) at the time when the proceedings are brought the individual is a national of the State concerned;

(b) at the time when the contract was made the individual was neither a citizen of Singapore nor habitually resident in Singapore; or

(c) the parties to the contract have otherwise agreed in writing.

(3) Where the work is for an office, agency or establishment maintained by the State in Singapore for commercial purposes, subsection (2) (a) and (b) does not exclude the application of this section unless the individual was, at the time when the contract was made, habitually resident in that State.

(4) Subsection (2) (c) does not exclude the application of this section where the law of Singapore requires the proceedings to be brought before a court in Singapore.

(5) In this section, "proceedings relating to a contract of employment" includes proceedings between the parties to such a contract in respect of any statutory rights or duties to which they are entitled or subject as employer or employee.

7. Personal injuries and damage to property

A State is not immune as respects proceedings in respect of —

(a) death or personal injury; or

PART 2
PROCEEDINGS IN SINGAPORE BY OR AGAINST OTHER STATES

Immunity from jurisdiction
3. General immunity from jurisdiction

(1) A State is immune from the jurisdiction of the courts of Singapore except as provided in the following provisions of this Part.

(2) A court shall give effect to the immunity conferred by this section even though the State does not appear in the proceedings in question.

Exceptions from immunity
4. Submission to jurisdiction

(1) A State is not immune as respects proceedings in respect of which it has submitted to the jurisdiction of the courts of Singapore.

(2) A State may submit after the dispute giving rise to the proceedings has arisen or by a prior written agreement; but a provision in any agreement that it is to be governed by the law of Singapore is not to be regarded as a submission.

(3) A State is deemed to have submitted —

(a) if it has instituted the proceedings; or

(b) subject to subsections (4) and (5), if it has intervened or taken any step in the proceedings.

(4) Subsection (3) (b) does not apply to intervention or any step taken for the purpose only of —

(a) claiming immunity; or

(b) asserting an interest in property in circumstances such that the State would have been entitled to immunity if the proceedings had been brought against it.

(5) Subsection (3) (b) does not apply to any step taken by the State in ignorance of facts entitling it to immunity if those facts could not reasonably have been ascertained and immunity is claimed as soon as reasonably practicable.

(6) A submission in respect of any proceedings extends to any appeal but not to any counterclaim unless it arises out of the same legal relationship or facts as the claim.

(7) The head of a State's diplomatic mission in Singapore, or the person for the time being performing his functions, shall be deemed to have authority to submit on behalf of the State in respect of any proceedings; and any person who has entered into a contract on behalf of and with the authority of a State shall be deemed to have authority to submit on its behalf in respect of proceedings arising out of the contract.

5. Commercial transactions and contracts to be performed in Singapore

(1) A State is not immune as respects proceedings relating to —

State Immunity Act, 1979 (Singapore)

(CHAPTER 313)

(Original Enactment: Act 19 of 1979)

REVISED EDITION 2014

(31st December 2014)

An Act to make provision with respect to proceedings in Singapore by or against other States, and for purposes connected therewith. [26th October 1979]

PART 1   PRELIMINARY

1. Short title and application

(1) This Act may be cited as the State Immunity Act.

(2) Subject to subsection (3), Part 2 does not apply to proceedings in respect of matters that occurred before the commencement of this Act and, in particular —

(a) sections 4 (2) and 15 (3) do not apply to any prior agreement; and

(b) sections 5, 6 and 11 do not apply to any transaction, contract or arbitration agreement, entered into before that date.

(3) Section 14 applies to any proceedings instituted after the commencement of this Act.

2. Interpretation

(1) In this Act —

"commercial purposes" means purposes of such transactions or activities as are mentioned in section 5 (3);

"court" includes any tribunal or body exercising judicial functions;

"ship" includes hovercraft.

(2) In this Act —

(a) references to an agreement in sections 4 (2) and 15 (3) include references to a treaty, convention or other international agreement; and

(b) references to entry of appearance and judgments in default of appearance include references to any corresponding procedures.

(2) Section 13 of the Administration of Justice (Miscellaneous Provisions) Act 1938 and section 7 of the Law Reform (Miscellaneous Provisions) (Scotland) Act 1940 (which become unnecessary in consequence of Part I of this Act) are hereby repealed.

(3) Subject to subsection (4) below, Parts I and II of this Act do not apply to proceedings in respect of matters that occurred before the date of the coming into force of this Act and, in particular—

(a) sections 2 (2) and 13 (3) do not apply to any prior agreement, and

(b) sections 3, 4 and 9 do not apply to any transaction, contract or arbitration agreement,

entered into before that date.

(4) Section 12 above applies to any proceedings instituted after the coming into force of this Act.

(5) This Act shall come into force on such date as may be specified by an order made by the Lord Chancellor by statutory instrument.

(6) This Act extends to Northern Ireland.

(7) Her Majesty may by Order in Council extend any of the provisions of this Act, with or without modification, to any dependent territory.

(4) Except as respects value added tax and duties of customs or excise, this section does not affect any question whether a person is exempt from, or immune as respects proceedings relating to, taxation.

(5) This section applies to the sovereign or other head of any State on which immunities and privileges are conferred by Part I of this Act and is without prejudice to the application of that Part to any such sovereign or head of State in his public capacity.

21. Evidence by certificate.

A certificate by or on behalf of the Secretary of State shall be conclusive evidence on any question—

(a) whether any country is a State for the purposes of Part I of this Act, whether any territory is a constituent territory of a federal State for those purposes or as to the person or persons to be regarded for those purposes as the head or government of a State;

(b) whether a State is a party to the Brussels Convention mentioned in Part I of this Act;

(c) whether a State is a party to the European Convention on State Immunity, whether it has made a declaration under Article 24 of that Convention or as to the territories in respect of which the United Kingdom or any other State is a party;

(d) whether, and if so when, a document has been served or received as mentioned in section 12 (1) or (5) above.

22. General interpretation.

(1) In this Act "court" includes any tribunal or body exercising judicial functions; and references to the courts or law of the United Kingdom include references to the courts or law of any part of the United Kingdom.

(2) In this Act references to entry of appearance and judgments in default of appearance include references to any corresponding procedures.

(3) In this Act "the European Convention on State Immunity" means the Convention of that name signed in Basle on 16th May 1972.

(4) In this Act "dependent territory" means—

(a) any of the Channel Islands;

(b) the Isle of Man;

(c) any colony other than one for whose external relations a country other than the United Kingdom is responsible; or

(d) any country or territory outside Her Majesty's dominions in which Her Majesty has jurisdiction in right of the government of the United Kingdom.

(5) Any power conferred by this Act to make an Order in Council includes power to vary or revoke a previous Order.

23. Short title, repeals, commencement and extent.

(1) This Act may be cited as the State Immunity Act 1978.

(b) if the result of the judgment is inconsistent with the result of another judgment given in proceedings between the same parties and—

(i) the other judgment is by a court in the United Kingdom and either those proceedings were the first to be instituted or the judgment of that court was given before the first-mentioned judgment became final within the meaning of subsection (1) (b) of section 18 above; or

(ii) the other judgment is by a court in another State party to the Convention and that section has already become applicable to it.

(3) Where the judgment was given against the United Kingdom in proceedings in respect of which the United Kingdom was not entitled to immunity by virtue of a provision corresponding to section 6 (2) above, a court need not give effect to section 18 above in respect of the judgment if the court that gave the judgment—

(a) would not have had jurisdiction in the matter if it had applied rules of jurisdiction corresponding to those applicable to such matters in the United Kingdom; or

(b) applied a law other than that indicated by the United Kingdom rules of private international law and would have reached a different conclusion if it had applied the law so indicated.

(4) In subsection (2) above references to a court in the United Kingdom include references to a court in any dependent territory in respect of which the United Kingdom is a party to the Convention, and references to a court in another State party to the Convention include references to a court in any territory in respect of which it is a party.

Part III Miscellaneous and Supplementary

20. Heads of State.

(1) Subject to the provisions of this section and to any necessary modifications, the Diplomatic Privileges Act 1964 shall apply to—

(a) a sovereign or other head of State;

(b) members of his family forming part of his household; and

(c) his private servants,

as it applies to the head of a diplomatic mission, to members of his family forming part of his household and to his private servants.

(2) The immunities and privileges conferred by virtue of subsection (1) (a) and (b) above shall not be subject to the restrictions by reference to nationality or residence mentioned in Article 37 (1) or 38 in Schedule 1 to the said Act of 1964.

(3) Subject to any direction to the contrary by the Secretary of State, a person on whom immunities and privileges are conferred by virtue of subsection (1) above shall be entitled to the exemption conferred by section 8 (3) of the Immigration Act 1971.

(4) In sections 3 (1), 4 (1), 5 and 16 (2) above references to the United Kingdom include references to its territorial waters and any area designated under section 1 (7) of the Continental Shelf Act 1964.

(5) In relation to Scotland in this Part of this Act "action in rem" means such an action only in relation to Admiralty proceedings.

Part II Judgments against United Kingdom in Convention States

18. Recognition of judgments against United Kingdom.

(1) This section applies to any judgment given against the United Kingdom by a court in another State party to the European Convention on State immunity, being a judgment—

(a) given in proceedings in which the United Kingdom was not entitled to immunity by virtue of provisions corresponding to those of sections 2 to 11 above; and

(b) which is final, that is to say, which is not or is no longer subject to appeal or, if given in default of appearance, liable to be set aside.

(2) Subject to section 19 below, a judgment to which this section applies shall be recognised in any court in the United Kingdom as conclusive between the parties thereto in all proceedings founded on the same cause of action and may be relied on by way of defence or counter-claim in such proceedings.

(3) Subsection (2) above (but not section 19 below) shall have effect also in relation to any settlement entered into by the United Kingdom before a court in another State party to the Convention which under the law of that State is treated as equivalent to a judgment.

(4) In this section references to a court in a State party to the Convention include references to a court in any territory in respect of which it is a party.

19. Exceptions to recognition.

(1) A court need not give effect to section 18 above in the case of a judgment—

(a) if to do so would be manifestly contrary to public policy or if any party to the proceedings in which the judgment was given had no adequate opportunity to present his case; or

(b) if the judgment was given without provisions corresponding to those of section 12 above having been complied with and the United Kingdom has not entered an appearance or applied to have the judgment set aside.

(2) A court need not give effect to section 18 above in the case of a judgment—

(a) if proceedings between the same parties, based on the same facts and having the same purpose—

(i) are pending before a court in the United Kingdom and were the first to be instituted; or

(ii) are pending before a court in another State party to the Convention, were the first to be instituted and may result in a judgment to which that section will apply; or

15. Restriction and extension of immunities and privileges.

(1) If it appears to Her Majesty that the immunities and privileges conferred by this Part of this Act in relation to any State—

(a) exceed those accorded by the law of that State in relation to the United Kingdom; or

(b) are less than those required by any treaty, convention or other international agreement to which that State and the United Kingdom are parties,

Her Majesty may by Order in Council provide for restricting or, as the case may be, extending those immunities and privileges to such extent as appears to Her Majesty to be appropriate.

(2) Any statutory instrument containing an Order under this section shall be subject to annulment in pursuance of a resolution of either House of Parliament.

16. Excluded matters.

(1) This Part of this Act does not affect any immunity or privilege conferred by the Diplomatic Privileges Act 1964 or the Consular Relations Act 1968; and—

(a) section 4 above does not apply to proceedings concerning the employment of the members of a mission within the meaning of the Convention scheduled to the said Act of 1964 or of the members of a consular post within the meaning of the Convention scheduled to the said Act of 1968;

(b) section 6 (1) above does not apply to proceedings concerning a State's title to or its possession of property used for the purposes of a diplomatic mission.

(2) This Part of this Act does not apply to proceedings relating to anything done by or in relation to the armed forces of a State while present in the United Kingdom and, in particular, has effect subject to the Visiting Forces Act 1952.

(3) This Part of this Act does not apply to proceedings to which section 17 (6) of the Nuclear Installations Act 1965 applies.

(4) This Part of this Act does not apply to criminal proceedings.

(5) This Part of this Act does not apply to any proceedings relating to taxation other than those mentioned in section 11 above.

17. Interpretation of Part I.

(1) In this Part of this Act—

"the Brussels Convention" means the International Convention for the Unification of Certain Rules Concerning the Immunity of State-owned Ships signed in Brussels on 10th April 1926;

"commercial purposes" means purposes of such transactions or activities as are mentioned in section 3 (3) above;

"ship" includes hovercraft.

(2) In sections 2 (2) and 13 (3) above references to an agreement include references to a treaty, convention or other international agreement.

(3) For the purposes of sections 3 to 8 above the territory of the United Kingdom shall be deemed to include any dependent territory in respect of which the United Kingdom is a party to the European Convention on State Immunity.

(b) for paragraph (b) of subsection (2) above there shall be substituted the following paragraph—

" (b) the property of a State shall not be subject to any diligence for enforcing a judgment or order of a court or a decree arbitral or, in an action in rem, to arrestment or sale. "; and

(c) any reference to "process" shall be construed as a reference to "diligence", any reference to "the issue of any process" as a reference to "the doing of diligence" and the reference in subsection (4)(b) above to "an arbitration award" as a reference to "a decree arbitral".

Supplementary provisions
14. States entitled to immunities and privileges.

(1) The immunities and privileges conferred by this Part of this Act apply to any foreign or commonwealth State other than the United Kingdom; and references to a State include references to—

(a) the sovereign or other head of that State in his public capacity;

(b) the government of that State; and

(c) any department of that government,

but not to any entity (hereafter referred to as a "separate entity") which is distinct from the executive organs of the government of the State and capable of suing or being sued.

(2) A separate entity is immune from the jurisdiction of the courts of the United Kingdom if, and only if—

(a) the proceedings relate to anything done by it in the exercise of sovereign authority; and

(b) the circumstances are such that a State (or, in the case of proceedings to which section 10 above applies, a State which is not a party to the Brussels Convention) would have been so immune.

(3) If a separate entity (not being a State's central bank or other monetary authority) submits to the jurisdiction in respect of proceedings in the case of which it is entitled to immunity by virtue of subsection (2) above, subsections (1) to (4) of section 13 above shall apply to it in respect of those proceedings as if references to a State were references to that entity.

(4) Property of a State's central bank or other monetary authority shall not be regarded for the purposes of subsection (4) of section 13 above as in use or intended for use for commercial purposes; and where any such bank or authority is a separate entity subsections (1) to (3) of that section shall apply to it as if references to a State were references to the bank or authority.

(5) Section 12 above applies to proceedings against the constituent territories of a federal State; and Her Majesty may by Order in Council provide for the other provisions of this Part of this Act to apply to any such constituent territory specified in the Order as they apply to a State.

(6) Where the provisions of this Part of this Act do not apply to a constituent territory by virtue of any such Order subsections (2) and (3) above shall apply to it as if it were a separate entity.

(5) A copy of any judgment given against a State in default of appearance shall be transmitted through the Foreign and Commonwealth Office to the Ministry of Foreign Affairs of that State and any time for applying to have the judgment set aside (whether prescribed by rules of court or otherwise) shall begin to run two months after the date on which the copy of the judgment is received at the Ministry.

(6) Subsection (1) above does not prevent the service of a writ or other document in any manner to which the State has agreed and subsections (2) and (4) above do not apply where service is effected in any such manner.

(7) This section shall not be construed as applying to proceedings against a State by way of counter-claim or to an action in rem; and subsection (1) above shall not be construed as affecting any rules of court whereby leave is required for the service of process outside the jurisdiction.

13. Other procedural privileges.

(1) No penalty by way of committal or fine shall be imposed in respect of any failure or refusal by or on behalf of a State to disclose or produce any document or other information for the purposes of proceedings to which it is a party.

(2) Subject to subsections (3) and (4) below—

(a) relief shall not be given against a State by way of injunction or order for specific performance or for the recovery of land or other property; and

(b) the property of a State shall not be subject to any process for the enforcement of a judgment or arbitration award or, in an action in rem, for its arrest, detention or sale.

(3) Subsection (2) above does not prevent the giving of any relief or the issue of any process with the written consent of the State concerned; and any such consent (which may be contained in a prior agreement) may be expressed so as to apply to a limited extent or generally; but a provision merely submitting to the jurisdiction of the courts is not to be regarded as a consent for the purposes of this subsection.

(4) Subsection (2)(b) above does not prevent the issue of any process in respect of property which is for the time being in use or intended for use for commercial purposes; but, in a case not falling within section 10 above, this subsection applies to property of a State party to the European Convention on State Immunity only if—

(a) the process is for enforcing a judgment which is final within the meaning of section 18 (1) (b) below and the State has made a declaration under Article 24 of the Convention; or

(b) the process is for enforcing an arbitration award.

(5) The head of a State's diplomatic mission in the United Kingdom, or the person for the time being performing his functions, shall be deemed to have authority to give on behalf of the State any such consent as is mentioned in subsection (3) above and, for the purposes of subsection (4) above, his certificate to the effect that any property is not in use or intended for use by or on behalf of the State for commercial purposes shall be accepted as sufficient evidence of that fact unless the contrary is proved.

(6) In the application of this section to Scotland—

(a) the reference to "injunction" shall be construed as a reference to "interdict";

(b) an action in personam for enforcing a claim in connection with such a ship,

if, at the time when the cause of action arose, the ship was in use or intended for use for commercial purposes.

(3) Where an action in rem is brought against a ship belonging to a State for enforcing a claim in connection with another ship belonging to that State, subsection (2) (a) above does not apply as respects the first-mentioned ship unless, at the time when the cause of action relating to the other ship arose, both ships were in use or intended for use for commercial purposes.

(4) A State is not immune as respects—

(a) an action in rem against a cargo belonging to that State if both the cargo and the ship carrying it were, at the time when the cause of action arose, in use or intended for use for commercial purposes; or

(b) an action in personam for enforcing a claim in connection with such a cargo if the ship carrying it was then in use or intended for use as aforesaid.

(5) In the foregoing provisions references to a ship or cargo belonging to a State include references to a ship or cargo in its possession or control or in which it claims an interest; and, subject to subsection (4) above, subsection (2) above applies to property other than a ship as it applies to a ship.

(6) Sections 3 to 5 above do not apply to proceedings of the kind described in subsection (1) above if the State in question is a party to the Brussels Convention and the claim relates to the operation of a ship owned or operated by that State, the carriage of cargo or passengers on any such ship or the carriage of cargo owned by that State on any other ship.

11. Value added tax, customs duties etc.

A State is not immune as respects proceedings relating to its liability for—

(a) value added tax, any duty of customs or excise or any agricultural levy; or

(b) rates in respect of premises occupied by it for commercial purposes.

Procedure

12. Service of process and judgments in default of appearance.

(1) Any writ or other document required to be served for instituting proceedings against a State shall be served by being transmitted through the Foreign and Commonwealth Office to the Ministry of Foreign Affairs of the State and service shall be deemed to have been effected when the writ or document is received at the Ministry.

(2) Any time for entering an appearance (whether prescribed by rules of court or otherwise) shall begin to run two months after the date on which the writ or document is received as aforesaid.

(3) A State which appears in proceedings cannot thereafter object that subsection (1) above has not been complied with in the case of those proceedings.

(4) No judgment in default of appearance shall be given against a State except on proof that subsection (1) above has been complied with and that the time for entering an appearance as extended by subsection (2) above has expired.

(a) which is in the possession or control of a State; or

(b) in which a State claims an interest,

if the State would not have been immune had the proceedings been brought against it or, in a case within paragraph (b) above, if the claim is neither admitted nor supported by *prima facie* evidence.

7. Patents, trade-marks etc.

A State is not immune as respects proceedings relating to—

(a) any patent, trade-mark, design or plant breeders' rights belonging to the State and registered or protected in the United Kingdom or for which the State has applied in the United Kingdom;

(b) an alleged infringement by the State in the United Kingdom of any patent, trade-mark, design, plant breeders' rights or copyright; or

(c) the right to use a trade or business name in the United Kingdom.

8. Membership of bodies corporate etc.

(1) A State is not immune as respects proceedings relating to its membership of a body corporate, an unincorporated body or a partnership which—

(a) has members other than States; and

(b) is incorporated or constituted under the law of the United Kingdom or is controlled from or has its principal place of business in the United Kingdom,

being proceedings arising between the State and the body or its other members or, as the case may be, between the State and the other partners.

(2) This section does not apply if provision to the contrary has been made by an agreement in writing between the parties to the dispute or by the constitution or other instrument establishing or regulating the body or partnership in question.

9. Arbitrations.

(1) Where a State has agreed in writing to submit a dispute which has arisen, or may arise, to arbitration, the State is not immune as respects proceedings in the courts of the United Kingdom which relate to the arbitration.

(2) This section has effect subject to any contrary provision in the arbitration agreement and does not apply to any arbitration agreement between States.

10. Ships used for commercial purposes.

(1) This section applies to—

(a) Admiralty proceedings; and

(b) proceedings on any claim which could be made the subject of Admiralty proceedings.

(2) A State is not immune as respects—

(a) an action in rem against a ship belonging to that State; or

(a) at the time when the proceedings are brought the individual is a national of the State concerned; or

(b) at the time when the contract was made the individual was neither a national of the United Kingdom nor habitually resident there; or

(c) the parties to the contract have otherwise agreed in writing.

(3) Where the work is for an office, agency or establishment maintained by the State in the United Kingdom for commercial purposes, subsection (2) (a) and (b) above do not exclude the application of this section unless the individual was, at the time when the contract was made, habitually resident in that State.

(4) Subsection (2)(c) above does not exclude the application of this section where the law of the United Kingdom requires the proceedings to be brought before a court of the United Kingdom.

(5) In subsection (2)(b) above "national of the United Kingdom" means—

(a) a British citizen, a British Dependent Territories citizen, a British National Overseas or a British Overseas citizen; or

(b) a person who under the British Nationality Act 1981 is a British subject; or

(c) a British protected person (within the meaning of that Act).

(6) In this section "proceedings relating to a contract of employment" includes proceedings between the parties to such a contract in respect of any statutory rights or duties to which they are entitled or subject as employer or employee.

5. Personal injuries and damage to property.

A State is not immune as respects proceedings in respect of—

(a) death or personal injury; or

(b) damage to or loss of tangible property,

caused by an act or omission in the United Kingdom.

6. Ownership, possession and use of property.

(1) A State is not immune as respects proceedings relating to—

(a) any interest of the State in, or its possession or use of, immovable property in the United Kingdom; or

(b) any obligation of the State arising out of its interest in, or its possession or use of, any such property.

(2) A State is not immune as respects proceedings relating to any interest of the State in movable or immovable property, being an interest arising by way of succession, gift or *bona vacantia*.

(3) The fact that a State has or claims an interest in any property shall not preclude any court from exercising in respect of it any jurisdiction relating to the estates of deceased persons or persons of unsound mind or to insolvency, the winding up of companies or the administration of trusts.

(4) A court may entertain proceedings against a person other than a State notwithstanding that the proceedings relate to property—

(a) claiming immunity; or

(b) asserting an interest in property in circumstances such that the State would have been entitled to immunity if the proceedings had been brought against it.

(5) Subsection (3) (b) above does not apply to any step taken by the State in ignorance of facts entitling it to immunity if those facts could not reasonably have been ascertained and immunity is claimed as soon as reasonably practicable.

(6) A submission in respect of any proceedings extends to any appeal but not to any counter-claim unless it arises out of the same legal relationship or facts as the claim.

(7) The head of a State's diplomatic mission in the United Kingdom, or the person for the time being performing his functions, shall be deemed to have authority to submit on behalf of the State in respect of any proceedings; and any person who has entered into a contract on behalf of and with the authority of a State shall be deemed to have authority to submit on its behalf in respect of proceedings arising out of the contract.

3. Commercial transactions and contracts to be performed in United Kingdom.

(1) A State is not immune as respects proceedings relating to—

(a) a commercial transaction entered into by the State; or

(b) an obligation of the State which by virtue of a contract (whether a commercial transaction or not) falls to be performed wholly or partly in the United Kingdom.

(2) This section does not apply if the parties to the dispute are States or have otherwise agreed in writing; and subsection (1) (b) above does not apply if the contract (not being a commercial transaction) was made in the territory of the State concerned and the obligation in question is governed by its administrative law.

(3) In this section "commercial transaction" means—

(a) any contract for the supply of goods or services;

(b) any loan or other transaction for the provision of finance and any guarantee or indemnity in respect of any such transaction or of any other financial obligation; and

(c) any other transaction or activity (whether of a commercial, industrial, financial, professional or other similar character) into which a State enters or in which it engages otherwise than in the exercise of sovereign authority;

but neither paragraph of subsection (1) above applies to a contract of employment between a State and an individual.

4. Contracts of employment.

(1) A State is not immune as respects proceedings relating to a contract of employment between the State and an individual where the contract was made in the United Kingdom or the work is to be wholly or partly performed there.

(2) Subject to subsections (3) and (4) below, this section does not apply if—

State Immunity Act, 1978
(United Kingdom)

An Act to make new provision with respect to proceedings in the United Kingdom by or against other States; to provide for the effect of judgments given against the United Kingdom in the courts of States parties to the European Convention on State Immunity; to make new provision with respect to the immunities and privileges of heads of State; and for connected purposes.

[20th July 1978]

Part I Proceedings in United Kingdom by or against Other States

Immunity from jurisdiction

1. General immunity from jurisdiction.

(1) A State is immune from the jurisdiction of the courts of the United Kingdom except as provided in the following provisions of this Part of this Act.

(2) A court shall give effect to the immunity conferred by this section even though the State does not appear in the proceedings in question.

Exceptions from immunity

2. Submission to jurisdiction.

(1) A State is not immune as respects proceedings in respect of which it has submitted to the jurisdiction of the courts of the United Kingdom.

(2) A State may submit after the dispute giving rise to the proceedings has arisen or by a prior written agreement; but a provision in any agreement that it is to be governed by the law of the United Kingdom is not to be regarded as a submission.

(3) A State is deemed to have submitted—

(a) if it has instituted the proceedings; or

(b) subject to subsections (4) and (5) below, if it has intervened or taken any step in the proceedings.

(4) Subsection (3) (b) above does not apply to intervention or any step taken for the purpose only of—

§ 1611-Certain types of property immune from execution

(a) Notwithstanding the provisions of section 1610 of this chapter, the property of those organizations designated by the President as being entitled to enjoy the privileges, exemptions, and immunities provided by the International Organizations Immunities Act shall not be subject to attachment or any other judicial process impeding the disbursement of funds to, or on the order of, a foreign State as the result of an action brought in the courts of the United States or of the States.

(b) Notwithstanding the provisions of section 1610 of this chapter, the property of a foreign State shall be immune from attachment and from execution, if—

(1) the property is that of a foreign central bank or monetary authority held for its own account, unless such bank or authority, or its parent foreign government, has explicitly waived its immunity from attachment in aid of execution, or from execution, notwithstanding any withdrawal of the waiver which the bank, authority or government may purport to effect except in accordance with the terms of the waiver; or

(2) the property is, or is intended to be, used in connection with a military activity and

(A) is of a military character, or

(B) is under the control of a military authority or defense agency.

(c) Notwithstanding the provisions of section 1610 of this chapter, the property of a foreign State shall be immune from attachment and from execution in an action brought under section 302 of the Cuban Liberty and Democratic Solidarity (LIBERTAD) Act of 1996 to the extent that the property is a facility or installation used by an accredited diplomatic mission for official purposes.

(2)

(A) At the request of any party in whose favor a judgment has been issued with respect to a claim for which the foreign State is not immune under section 1605 (a)(7) (as in effect before the enactment of section 1605A) or section 1605A, the Secretary of the Treasury and the Secretary of State should make every effort to fully, promptly, and effectively assist any judgment creditor or any court that has issued any such judgment in identifying, locating, and executing against the property of that foreign State or any agency or instrumentality of such State.

(B) In providing such assistance, the Secretaries—

(i) may provide such information to the court under seal; and

(ii) should make every effort to provide the information in a manner sufficient to allow the court to direct the United States Marshall's office to promptly and effectively execute against that property.

(3) Waiver. —

The President may waive any provision of paragraph (1) in the interest of national security.

(g) Property in Certain Actions. —

(1) In general. —Subject to paragraph (3), the property of a foreign State against which a judgment is entered under section 1605A, and the property of an agency or instrumentality of such a State, including property that is a separate juridical entity or is an interest held directly or indirectly in a separate juridical entity, is subject to attachment in aid of execution, and execution, upon that judgment as provided in this section, regardless of—

(A) the level of economic control over the property by the government of the foreign State;

(B) whether the profits of the property go to that government;

(C) the degree to which officials of that government manage the property or otherwise control its daily affairs;

(D) whether that government is the sole beneficiary in interest of the property; or

(E) whether establishing the property as a separate entity would entitle the foreign State to benefits in United States courts while avoiding its obligations.

(2) United States sovereign immunity inapplicable. —

Any property of a foreign State, or agency or instrumentality of a foreign State, to which paragraph (1) applies shall not be immune from attachment in aid of execution, or execution, upon a judgment entered under section 1605A because the property is regulated by the United States Government by reason of action taken against that foreign State under the Trading With the Enemy Act or the International Emergency Economic Powers Act.

(3) Third-party joint property holders. —

Nothing in this subsection shall be construed to supersede the authority of a court to prevent appropriately the impairment of an interest held by a person who is not liable in the action giving rise to a judgment in property subject to attachment in aid of execution, or execution, upon such judgment.

cordance with the terms of the waiver, or

(2) the judgment relates to a claim for which the agency or instrumentality is not immune by virtue of section 1605 (a) (2), (3), or (5) or 1605 (b) of this chapter, regardless of whether the property is or was involved in the act upon which the claim is based, or

(3) the judgment relates to a claim for which the agency or instrumentality is not immune by virtue of section 1605A of this chapter or section 1605 (a)(7) of this chapter (as such section was in effect on January 27, 2008), regardless of whether the property is or was involved in the act upon which the claim is based.

(c) No attachment or execution referred to in subsections (a) and (b) of this section shall be permitted until the court has ordered such attachment and execution after having determined that a reasonable period of time has elapsed following the entry of judgment and the giving of any notice required under section 1608 (e) of this chapter.

(d) The property of a foreign State, as defined in section 1603 (a) of this chapter, used for a commercial activity in the United States, shall not be immune from attachment prior to the entry of judgment in any action brought in a court of the United States or of a State, or prior to the elapse of the period of time provided in subsection (c) of this section, if—

(1) the foreign State has explicitly waived its immunity from attachment prior to judgment, notwithstanding any withdrawal of the waiver the foreign State may purport to effect except in accordance with the terms of the waiver, and

(2) the purpose of the attachment is to secure satisfaction of a judgment that has been or may ultimately be entered against the foreign State, and not to obtain jurisdiction.

(e) The vessels of a foreign State shall not be immune from arrest in rem, interlocutory sale, and execution in actions brought to foreclose a preferred mortgage as provided in section 1605 (d).

(f)

(1)

(A) Notwithstanding any other provision of law, including but not limited to section 208 (f) of the Foreign Missions Act (22 U. S. C. 4308 (f)), and except as provided in subparagraph (B), any property with respect to which financial transactions are prohibited or regulated pursuant to section 5 (b) of the Trading with the Enemy Act (50 U. S. C. App. 5 (b)), section 620 (a) of the Foreign Assistance Act of 1961 (22 U. S. C. 2370 (a)), sections 202 and 203 of the International Emergency Economic Powers Act (50 U. S. C. 1701 – 1702), or any other proclamation, order, regulation, or license issued pursuant thereto, shall be subject to execution or attachment in aid of execution of any judgment relating to a claim for which a foreign State (including any agency or instrumentality or such State) claiming such property is not immune under section 1605 (a)(7) (as in effect before the enactment of section 1605A) or section 1605A.

(B) Subparagraph (A) shall not apply if, at the time the property is expropriated or seized by the foreign State, the property has been held in title by a natural person or, if held in trust, has been held for the benefit of a natural person or persons.

§ 1609-Immunity from attachment and execution of property of a foreign State

Subject to existing international agreements to which the United States is a party at the time of enactment of this Act the property in the United States of a foreign State shall be immune from attachment arrest and execution except as provided in sections 1610 and 1611 of this chapter.

§ 1610-Exceptions to the immunity from attachment or execution

(a) The property in the United States of a foreign State, as defined in section 1603 (a) of this chapter, used for a commercial activity in the United States, shall not be immune from attachment in aid of execution, or from execution, upon a judgment entered by a court of the United States or of a State after the effective date of this Act, if—

(1) the foreign State has waived its immunity from attachment in aid of execution or from execution either explicitly or by implication, notwithstanding any withdrawal of the waiver the foreign State may purport to effect except in accordance with the terms of the waiver, or

(2) the property is or was used for the commercial activity upon which the claim is based, or

(3) the execution relates to a judgment establishing rights in property which has been taken in violation of international law or which has been exchanged for property taken in violation of international law, or

(4) the execution relates to a judgment establishing rights in property—

(A) which is acquired by succession or gift, or

(B) which is immovable and situated in the United States: Provided, That such property is not used for purposes of maintaining a diplomatic or consular mission or the residence of the Chief of such mission, or

(5) the property consists of any contractual obligation or any proceeds from such a contractual obligation to indemnify or hold harmless the foreign State or its employees under a policy of automobile or other liability or casualty insurance covering the claim which merged into the judgment, or

(6) the judgment is based on an order confirming an arbitral award rendered against the foreign State, provided that attachment in aid of execution, or execution, would not be inconsistent with any provision in the arbitral agreement, or

(7) the judgment relates to a claim for which the foreign State is not immune under section 1605A or section 1605 (a) (7) (as such section was in effect on January 27, 2008), regardless of whether the property is or was involved with the act upon which the claim is based.

(b) In addition to subsection (a), any property in the United States of an agency or instrumentality of a foreign State engaged in commercial activity in the United States shall not be immune from attachment in aid of execution, or from execution, upon a judgment entered by a court of the United States or of a State after the effective date of this Act, if—

(1) the agency or instrumentality has waived its immunity from attachment in aid of execution or from execution either explicitly or implicitly, notwithstanding any withdrawal of the waiver the agency or instrumentality may purport to effect except in ac-

a signed receipt, to be addressed and dispatched by the clerk of the court to the Secretary of State in Washington, District of Columbia, to the attention of the Director of Special Consular Services—and the Secretary shall transmit one copy of the papers through diplomatic channels to the foreign State and shall send to the clerk of the court a certified copy of the diplomatic note indicating when the papers were transmitted.

As used in this subsection, a "notice of suit" shall mean a notice addressed to a foreign State and in a form prescribed by the Secretary of State by regulation.

(b) Service in the courts of the United States and of the States shall be made upon an agency or instrumentality of a foreign State:

(1) by delivery of a copy of the summons and complaint in accordance with any special arrangement for service between the plaintiff and the agency or instrumentality; or

(2) if no special arrangement exists, by delivery of a copy of the summons and complaint either to an officer, a managing or general agent, or to any other agent authorized by appointment or by law to receive service of process in the United States; or in accordance with an applicable international convention on service of judicial documents; or

(3) if service cannot be made under paragraphs (1) or (2), and if reasonably calculated to give actual notice, by delivery of a copy of the summons and complaint, together with a translation of each into the official language of the foreign State—

(A) as directed by an authority of the foreign State or political subdivision in response to a letter rogatory or request or

(B) by any form of mail requiring a signed receipt, to be addressed and dispatched by the clerk of the court to the agency or instrumentality to be served, or

(C) as directed by order of the court consistent with the law of the place where service is to be made.

(c) Service shall be deemed to have been made—

(1) in the case of service under subsection (a) (4), as of the date of transmittal indicated in the certified copy of the diplomatic note; and

(2) in any other case under this section, as of the date of receipt indicated in the certification, signed and returned postal receipt, or other proof of service applicable to the method of service employed.

(d) In any action brought in a court of the United States or of a State, a foreign State, a political subdivision thereof, or an agency or instrumentality of a foreign State shall serve an answer or other responsive pleading to the complaint within sixty days after service has been made under this section.

(e) No judgment by default shall be entered by a court of the United States or of a State against a foreign State, a political subdivision thereof, or an agency or instrumentality of a foreign State, unless the claimant establishes his claim or right to relief by evidence satisfactory to the court. A copy of any such default judgment shall be sent to the foreign State or political subdivision in the manner prescribed for service in this section.

§ 1606-Extent of liability

As to any claim for relief with respect to which a foreign State is not entitled to immunity under section 1605 or 1607 of this chapter, the foreign State shall be liable in the same manner and to the same extent as a private individual under like circumstances; but a foreign State except for an agency or instrumentality thereof shall not be liable for punitive damages; if, however, in any case wherein death was caused, the law of the place where the action or omission occurred provides, or has been construed to provide, for damages only punitive in nature, the foreign State shall be liable for actual or compensatory damages measured by the pecuniary injuries resulting from such death which were incurred by the persons for whose benefit the action was brought.

§ 1607-Counterclaims

In any action brought by a foreign State, or in which a foreign State intervenes, in a court of the United States or of a State, the foreign State shall not be accorded immunity with respect to any counterclaim—

(a) for which a foreign State would not be entitled to immunity under section 1605 or 1605A of this chapter had such claim been brought in a separate action against the foreign State; or

(b) arising out of the transaction or occurrence that is the subject matter of the claim of the foreign State; or

(c) to the extent that the counterclaim does not seek relief exceeding in amount or differing in kind from that sought by the foreign State.

(Amended Pub. L. 110-181, div. A, title X, § 1083 (b) (2), Jan. 28, 2008, 122 Stat. 341.)

§ 1608-Service; time to answer; default

(a) Service in the courts of the United States and of the States shall be made upon a foreign State or political subdivision of a foreign State:

(1) by delivery of a copy of the summons and complaint in accordance with any special arrangement for service between the plaintiff and the foreign State or political subdivision; or

(2) if no special arrangement exists, by delivery of a copy of the summons and complaint in accordance with an applicable international convention on service of judicial documents; or

(3) if service cannot be made under paragraphs (1) or (2), by sending a copy of the summons and complaint and a notice of suit, together with a translation of each into the official language of the foreign State, by any form of mail requiring a signed receipt, to be addressed and dispatched by the clerk of the court to the head of the ministry of foreign affairs of the foreign State concerned; or

(4) if service cannot be made within 30 days under paragraph (3), by sending two copies of the summons and complaint and a notice of suit, together with a translation of each into the official language of the foreign State, by any form of mail requiring

(2) the term "hostage taking" has the meaning given that term in Article 1 of the International Convention Against the Taking of Hostages;

(3) the term "material support or resources" has the meaning given that term in-section 2339A of title 18;

(4) the term "armed forces" has the meaning given that term in section 101 of title 10;

(5) the term "national of the United States" has the meaning given that term in section 101 (a) (22) of the Immigration and Nationality Act (8 U. S. C. 1101 (a) (22));

(6) the term "State sponsor of terrorism" means a country the government of which the Secretary of State has determined, for purposes of section 6 (j) of the Export Administration Act of 1979 (50 U. S. C. App. 2405 (j)), section 620A of the Foreign Assistance Act of 1961 (22 U. S. C. 2371), section 40 of the Arms Export Control Act (22 U. S. C. 2780), or any other provision of law, is a government that has repeatedly provided support for acts of international terrorism; and

(7) the terms "torture" and "extrajudicial killing" have the meaning given those terms in section 3 of the Torture Victim Protection Act of 1991 (28 U. S. C. 1350 note).

§ 1605B-Responsibility of foreign States for international terrorism against the United States

(a) Definition. —In this section, the term "international terrorism" —

(1) has the meaning given the term in section 2331 of title 18, United States Code; and

(2) does not include any act of war (as defined in that section).

(b) Responsibility of Foreign States. —A foreign State shall not be immune from the jurisdiction of the courts of the United States in any case in which money damages are sought against a foreign State for physical injury to person or property or death occurring in the United States and caused by—

(1) an act of international terrorism in the United States; and

(2) a tortious act or acts of the foreign State, or of any official, employee, or agent of that foreign State while acting within the scope of his or her office, employment, or agency, regardless where the tortious act or acts of the foreign State occurred.

(c) Claims by Nationals of the United States. —

Notwithstanding section 2337 (2) of title 18, a national of the United States may bring a claim against a foreign State in accordance with section 2333 of that title if the foreign State would not be immune under subsection (b).

(d) Rule of Construction. —

A foreign State shall not be subject to the jurisdiction of the courts of the United States under subsection (b) on the basis of an omission or a tortious act or acts that constitute mere negligence.

(d) Additional Damages. —

After an action has been brought under subsection (c), actions may also be brought for reasonably foreseeable property loss, whether insured or uninsured, third party liability, and loss claims under life and property insurance policies, by reason of the same acts on which the action under subsection (c) is based.

(e) Special Masters. —

(1) In general. —

The courts of the United States may appoint special masters to hear damage claims brought under this section.

(2) Transfer of funds. —

The Attorney General shall transfer, from funds available for the program under section 1404C of the Victims of Crime Act of 1984 (42 U. S. C. 10603c), to the Administrator of the United States district court in which any case is pending which has been brought or maintained under this section such funds as may be required to cover the costs of special masters appointed under paragraph (1). Any amount paid in compensation to any such special master shall constitute an item of court costs.

(f) Appeal. —

In an action brought under this section, appeals from orders not conclusively ending the litigation may only be taken pursuant to section 1292 (b) of this title.

(g) Property Disposition. —

(1) In general. —In every action filed in a United States district court in which jurisdiction is alleged under this section, the filing of a notice of pending action pursuant to this section, to which is attached a copy of the complaint filed in the action, shall have the effect of establishing a lien of lis pendens upon any real property or tangible personal property that is—

(A) subject to attachment in aid of execution, or execution, under section 1610;

(B) located within that judicial district; and

(C) titled in the name of any defendant, or titled in the name of any entity controlled by any defendant if such notice contains a statement listing such controlled entity.

(2) Notice. —

A notice of pending action pursuant to this section shall be filed by the clerk of the district court in the same manner as any pending action and shall be indexed by listing as defendants all named defendants and all entities listed as controlled by any defendant.

(3) Enforceability. —

Liens established by reason of this subsection shall be enforceable as provided in chapter 111 of this title.

(h) Definitions. —For purposes of this section—

(1) the term "aircraft sabotage" has the meaning given that term in Article 1 of the Convention for the Suppression of Unlawful Acts Against the Safety of Civil Aviation;

ed action under section 1605 (a) (7) (as in effect before the enactment of this section) or section 589 of the Foreign Operations, Export Financing, and Related Programs Appropriations Act, 1997 (as contained in section 101 (c) of division A of Public Law 104 - 208) was filed;

(ii) the claimant or the victim was, at the time the act described in paragraph (1) occurred—

(Ⅰ) a national of the United States;

(Ⅱ) a member of the armed forces; or

(Ⅲ) otherwise an employee of the Government of the United States, or of an individual performing a contract awarded by the United States Government, acting within the scope of the employee's employment; and

(iii) in a case in which the act occurred in the foreign State against which the claim has been brought, the claimant has afforded the foreign State a reasonable opportunity to arbitrate the claim in accordance with the accepted international rules of arbitration; or

(B) the act described in paragraph (1) is related to Case Number 1: 00CV03110 (EGS) in the United States District Court for the District of Columbia.

(b) Limitations. —An action may be brought or maintained under this section if the action is commenced, or a related action was commenced under section 1605 (a) (7) (before the date of the enactment of this section) or section 589 of the Foreign Operations, Export Financing, and Related Programs Appropriations Act, 1997 (as contained in section 101 (c) of division A of Public Law 104 -208) not later than the latter of—

(1) 10 years after April 24, 1996; or

(2) 10 years after the date on which the cause of action arose.

(c) Private Right of Action. —A foreign State that is or was a State sponsor of terrorism as described in subsection (a) (2) (A) (i), and any official, employee, or agent of that foreign State while acting within the scope of his or her office, employment, or agency, shall be liable to—

(1) a national of the United States,

(2) a member of the armed forces,

(3) an employee of the Government of the United States, or of an individual performing a contract awarded by the United States Government, acting within the scope of the employee's employment, or

(4) the legal representative of a person described in paragraph (1), (2), or (3), for personal injury or death caused by acts described in subsection (a) (1) of that foreign State, or of an official, employee, or agent of that foreign State, for which the courts of the United States may maintain jurisdiction under this section for money damages. In any such action, damages may include economic damages, solatium, pain and suffering, and punitive damages. In any such action, a foreign State shall be vicariously liable for the acts of its officials, employees, or agents.

(ⅲ) the taking occurred after 1900;

(ⅳ) the court determines that the activity associated with the exhibition or display is commercial activity, as that term is defined in section 1603 (d); and

(ⅴ) a determination under clause (ⅳ) is necessary for the court to exercise jurisdiction over the foreign State under subsection (a) (3) .

(3) Definitions. —For purposes of this subsection—

(A) the term "work" means a work of art or other object of cultural significance;

(B) the term "covered government" means—

(ⅰ) the Government of Germany during the covered period;

(ⅱ) any government in any area in Europe that was occupied by the military forces of the Government of Germany during the covered period;

(ⅲ) any government in Europe that was established with the assistance or cooperation of the Government of Germany during the covered period; and

(ⅳ) any government in Europe that was an ally of the Government of Germany during the covered period; and

(C) the term "covered period" means the period beginning on January 30, 1933, and ending on May 8, 1945.

§ 1605A-Terrorism exception to the jurisdictional immunity of a foreign State

(a) In General. —

(1) No immunity. —

A foreign State shall not be immune from the jurisdiction of courts of the United States or of the States in any case not otherwise covered by this chapter in which money damages are sought against a foreign State for personal injury or death that was caused by an act of torture, extrajudicial killing, aircraft sabotage, hostage taking, or the provision of material support or resources for such an act if such act or provision of material support or resources is engaged in by an official, employee, or agent of such foreign State while acting within the scope of his or her office, employment, or agency.

(2) Claim heard. —The court shall hear a claim under this section if—

(A)

(ⅰ)

(Ⅰ) the foreign State was designated as a State sponsor of terrorism at the time the act described in paragraph (1) occurred, or was so designated as a result of such act, and, subject to subclause (Ⅱ), either remains so designated when the claim is filed under this section or was so designated within the 6-month period before the claim is filed under this section; or

(Ⅱ) in the case of an action that is refiled under this section by reason of section 1083 (c) (2) (A) of the National Defense Authorization Act for Fiscal Year 2008 or is filed under this section by reason of section 1083 (c) (3) of that Act, the foreign State was designated as a State sponsor of terrorism when the original action or the relat-

(4) Bar on motions to dismiss. —

A stay of discovery under this subsection shall constitute a bar to the granting of a motion to dismiss under rules 12 (b)(6) and 56 of the Federal Rules of Civil Procedure.

(5) Construction. —

Nothing in this subsection shall prevent the United States from seeking protective orders or asserting privileges ordinarily available to the United States.

(h) Jurisdictional Immunity for Certain Art Exhibition Activities. —

(1) In general. —If—

(A) a work is imported into the United States from any foreign State pursuant to an agreement that provides for the temporary exhibition or display of such work entered into between a foreign State that is the owner or custodian of such work and the United States or one or more cultural or educational institutions within the United States;

(B) the President, or the President's designee, has determined, in accordance with subsection (a) of Public Law 89 - 259 (22 U. S. C. 2459 (a)), that such work is of cultural significance and the temporary exhibition or display of such work is in the national interest; and

(C) the notice thereof has been published in accordance with subsection (a) of Public Law 89 - 259 (22 U. S. C. 2459 (a)), any activity in the United States of such foreign State, or of any carrier, that is associated with the temporary exhibition or display of such work shall not be considered to be commercial activity by such foreign State for purposes of subsection (a) (3).

(2) Exceptions. —

(A) Nazi-era claims. —Paragraph (1) shall not apply in any case asserting jurisdiction under subsection (a) (3) in which rights in property taken in violation of international law are in issue within the meaning of that subsection and—

(i) the property at issue is the work described in paragraph (1);

(ii) the action is based upon a claim that such work was taken in connection with the acts of a covered government during the covered period;

(iii) the court determines that the activity associated with the exhibition or display is commercial activity, as that term is defined in section 1603 (d); and

(iv) a determination under clause (iii) is necessary for the court to exercise jurisdiction over the foreign State under subsection (a) (3).

(B) Other culturally significant works. —In addition to cases exempted under subparagraph (A), paragraph (1) shall not apply in any case asserting jurisdiction under subsection (a) (3) in which rights in property taken in violation of international law are in issue within the meaning of that subsection and—

(i) the property at issue is the work described in paragraph (1);

(ii) the action is based upon a claim that such work was taken in connection with the acts of a foreign government as part of a systematic campaign of coercive confiscation or misappropriation of works from members of a targeted and vulnerable group;

(d) A foreign State shall not be immune from the jurisdiction of the courts of the United States in any action brought to foreclose a preferred mortgage, as defined in section 31301 of title 46. Such action shall be brought, heard, and determined in accordance with the provisions of chapter 313 of title 46 and in accordance with the principles of law and rules of practice of suits in rem, whenever it appears that had the vessel been privately owned and possessed a suit in rem might have been maintained.

[(e),(f) Repealed. Pub. L. 110 - 181, div. A, title X, § 1083(b)(1)(B),Jan. 28, 2008, 122 Stat. 341.]

(g) Limitation on Discovery. —

(1) In general. —

(A) Subject to paragraph (2), if an action is filed that would otherwise be barred by section 1604, but for section 1605A or section 1605B, the court, upon request of the Attorney General, shall stay any request, demand, or order for discovery on the United States that the Attorney General certifies would significantly interfere with a criminal investigation or prosecution, or a national security operation, related to the incident that gave rise to the cause of action, until such time as the Attorney General advises the court that such request, demand, or order will no longer so interfere.

(B) A stay under this paragraph shall be in effect during the 12-month period beginning on the date on which the court issues the order to stay discovery. The court shall renew the order to stay discovery for additional 12-month periods upon motion by the United States if the Attorney General certifies that discovery would significantly interfere with a criminal investigation or prosecution, or a national security operation, related to the incident that gave rise to the cause of action.

(2) Sunset. —

(A) Subject to subparagraph (B), no stay shall be granted or continued in effect under paragraph (1) after the date that is 10 years after the date on which the incident that gave rise to the cause of action occurred.

(B) After the period referred to in subparagraph (A), the court, upon request of the Attorney General, may stay any request, demand, or order for discovery on the United States that the court finds a substantial likelihood would—

(i) create a serious threat of death or serious bodily injury to any person;

(ii) adversely affect the ability of the United States to work in cooperation with foreign and international law enforcement agencies in investigating violations of United States law; or

(iii) obstruct the criminal case related to the incident that gave rise to the cause of action or undermine the potential for a conviction in such case.

(3) Evaluation of evidence. —

The court's evaluation of any request for a stay under this subsection filed by the Attorney General shall be conducted *ex parte* and in camera.

(B) any claim arising out of malicious prosecution, abuse of process, libel, slander, misrepresentation, deceit, or interference with contract rights; or

(6) in which the action is brought, either to enforce an agreement made by the foreign State with or for the benefit of a private party to submit to arbitration all or any differences which have arisen or which may arise between the parties with respect to a defined legal relationship, whether contractual or not, concerning a subject matter capable of settlement by arbitration under the laws of the United States, or to confirm an award made pursuant to such an agreement to arbitrate, if (A) the arbitration takes place or is intended to take place in the United States, (B) the agreement or award is or may be governed by a treaty or other international agreement in force for the United States calling for the recognition and enforcement of arbitral awards, (C) the underlying claim, save for the agreement to arbitrate, could have been brought in a United States court under this section or section 1607, or (D) paragraph (1) of this subsection is otherwise applicable.

(b) A foreign State shall not be immune from the jurisdiction of the courts of the United States in any case in which a suit in admiralty is brought to enforce a maritime lien against a vessel or cargo of the foreign State, which maritime lien is based upon a commercial activity of the foreign State: Provided, That—

(1) notice of the suit is given by delivery of a copy of the summons and of the complaint to the person, or his agent, having possession of the vessel or cargo against which the maritime lien is asserted; and if the vessel or cargo is arrested pursuant to process obtained on behalf of the party bringing the suit, the service of process of arrest shall be deemed to constitute valid delivery of such notice, but the party bringing the suit shall be liable for any damages sustained by the foreign State as a result of the arrest if the party bringing the suit had actual or constructive knowledge that the vessel or cargo of a foreign State was involved; and

(2) notice to the foreign State of the commencement of suit as provided in section 1608 of this title is initiated within ten days either of the delivery of notice as provided in paragraph (1) of this subsection or, in the case of a party who was unaware that the vessel or cargo of a foreign State was involved, of the date such party determined the existence of the foreign State's interest.

(c) Whenever notice is delivered under subsection (b) (1), the suit to enforce a maritime lien shall thereafter proceed and shall be heard and determined according to the principles of law and rules of practice of suits in rem whenever it appears that, had the vessel been privately owned and possessed, a suit in rem might have been maintained. A decree against the foreign State may include costs of the suit and, if the decree is for a money judgment, interest as ordered by the court, except that the court may not award judgment against the foreign State in an amount greater than the value of the vessel or cargo upon which the maritime lien arose. Such value shall be determined as of the time notice is served under subsection (b) (1). Decrees shall be subject to appeal and revision as provided in other cases of admiralty and maritime jurisdiction. Nothing shall preclude the plaintiff in any proper case from seeking relief in *personam* in the same action brought to enforce a maritime lien as provided in this section.

(c) The "United States" includes all territory and waters, continental or insular, subject to the jurisdiction of the United States.

(d) A "commercial activity" means either a regular course of commercial conduct or a particular commercial transaction or act. The commercial character of an activity shall be determined by reference to the nature of the course of conduct or particular transaction or act, rather than by reference to its purpose.

(e) A "commercial activity carried on in the United States by a foreign State" means commercial activity carried on by such State and having substantial contact with the United States.

§ 1604-Immunity of a foreign State from jurisdiction

Subject to existing international agreements to which the United States is a party at the time of enactment of this Act a foreign State shall be immune from the jurisdiction of the courts of the United States and of the States except as provided in sections 1605 to 1607 of this chapter.

§ 1605-General exceptions to the jurisdictional immunity of a foreign State

(a) A foreign State shall not be immune from the jurisdiction of courts of the United States or of the States in any case—

(1) in which the foreign State has waived its immunity either explicitly or by implication, notwithstanding any withdrawal of the waiver which the foreign State may purport to effect except in accordance with the terms of the waiver;

(2) in which the action is based upon a commercial activity carried on in the United States by the foreign State; or upon an act performed in the United States in connection with a commercial activity of the foreign State elsewhere; or upon an act outside the territory of the United States in connection with a commercial activity of the foreign State elsewhere and that act causes a direct effect in the United States;

(3) in which rights in property taken in violation of international law are in issue and that property or any property exchanged for such property is present in the United States in connection with a commercial activity carried on in the United States by the foreign State; or that property or any property exchanged for such property is owned or operated by an agency or instrumentality of the foreign State and that agency or instrumentality is engaged in a commercial activity in the United States;

(4) in which rights in property in the United States acquired by succession or gift or rights in immovable property situated in the United States are in issue;

(5) not otherwise encompassed in paragraph (2) above, in which money damages are sought against a foreign State for personal injury or death, or damage to or loss of property, occurring in the United States and caused by the tortious act or omission of that foreign State or of any official or employee of that foreign State while acting within the scope of his office or employment; except this paragraph shall not apply to—

(A) any claim based upon the exercise or performance or the failure to exercise or perform a discretionary function regardless of whether the discretion be abused, or

§ 1391- Venue generally

...

(f) Civil Actions Against a Foreign State. —A civil action against a foreign State as defined in section 1603 (a) of this title may be brought—

(1) in any judicial district in which a substantial part of the events or omissions giving rise to the claim occurred, or a substantial part of property that is the subject of the action is situated;

(2) in any judicial district in which the vessel or cargo of a foreign State is situated, if the claim is asserted under section 1605 (b) of this title;

(3) in any judicial district in which the agency or instrumentality is licensed to do business or is doing business, if the action is brought against an agency or instrumentality of a foreign State as defined in section 1603 (b) of this title; or

(4) in the United States District Court for the District of Columbia if the action is brought against a foreign State or political subdivision thereof.

...

Chapter 97-JURISDICTIONAL IMMUNITIES OF FOREIGN STATES

§ 1602-Findings and declaration of purpose

The Congress finds that the determination by United States courts of the claims of foreign States to immunity from the jurisdiction of such courts would serve the interests of justice and would protect the rights of both foreign States and litigants in United States courts. Under international law, States are not immune from the jurisdiction of foreign courts insofar as their commercial activities are concerned, and their commercial property may be levied upon for the satisfaction of judgments rendered against them in connection with their commercial activities. Claims of foreign States to immunity should henceforth be decided by courts of the United States and of the States in conformity with the principles set forth in this chapter.

§ 1603-Definitions

For purposes of this chapter—

(a) A "foreign State", except as used in section 1608 of this title, includes a political subdivision of a foreign State or an agency or instrumentality of a foreign State as defined in subsection (b).

(b) An "agency or instrumentality of a foreign State" means any entity—

(1) which is a separate legal person, corporate or otherwise, and

(2) which is an organ of a foreign State or political subdivision thereof, or a majority of whose shares or other ownership interest is owned by a foreign State or political subdivision thereof, and

(3) which is neither a citizen of a State of the United States as defined in section 1332 (c) and (e) of this title, nor created under the laws of any third country.

Foreign Sovereign Immunities Act, 1976
(United States)

U. S. Code: Title 28-JUDICIARY AND JUDICIAL PROCEDURE
Part IV-JURISDICTION AND VENUE

Chapter 85-DISTRICT COURTS; JURISDICTION

§ 1330-Actions against foreign States

(a) The district courts shall have original jurisdiction without regard to amount in controversy of any nonjury civil action against a foreign State as defined in section 1603 (a) of this title as to any claim for relief in personam with respect to which the foreign State is not entitled to immunity either under sections 1605 - 1607 of this title or under any applicable international agreement.

(b) Personal jurisdiction over a foreign State shall exist as to every claim for relief over which the district courts have jurisdiction under subsection (a) where service has been made under section 1608 of this title.

(c) For purposes of subsection (b), an appearance by a foreign State does not confer personal jurisdiction with respect to any claim for relief not arising out of any transaction or occurrence enumerated in sections 1605 - 1607 of this title.

§ 1332-Diversity of citizenship; amount in controversy; costs

(a) The district courts shall have original jurisdiction of all civil actions where the matter in controversy exceeds the sum or value of $75,000, exclusive of interest and costs, and is between—

...

(2) citizens of a State and citizens or subjects of a foreign State, except that the district courts shall not have original jurisdiction under this subsection of an action between citizens of a State and citizens or subjects of a foreign State who are lawfully admitted for permanent residence in the United States and are domiciled in the same State;

(3) citizens of different States and in which citizens or subjects of a foreign State are additional parties; and

(4) a foreign State, defined in section 1603 (a) of this title, as plaintiff and citizens of a State or of different States.

...

Part I
National Legislation

Law on Jurisdictional Immunities of Foreign State and Property

of Foreign State in the Russian Federation, 2015 (Russia)   **125**

Part II International Conventions   **131**

European Convention on State Immunity and Additional Protocol, 1972   **133**

United Nations Convention on Jurisdictional Immunities of States

and Their Property, 2004   **149**

Part III Other International Instruments   **161**

Draft Articles on Jurisdictional Immunities of States

and Their Property, 1991 (ILC)   **163**

Contemporary Problems Concerning the Immunity of States in

Relation to Questions of Jurisdiction and Enforcement, 1991 (IDI)   **171**

Resolution on the Immunity from Jurisdiction of the State and

of Persons Who Act on Behalf of the State in Case of International

Crimes, 2009 (IDI)   **175**

Declaration on Jurisdictional Immunities of State Owned Cultural

Property, 2013 (Council of Europe)   **177**

Contents

Part I　National Legislation	**001**
Foreign Sovereign Immunities Act, 1976 (United States)	003
State Immunity Act, 1978 (United Kingdom)	019
State Immunity Act, 1979 (Singapore)	031
The State Immunity Ordinance, 1981 (Pakistan)	039
Foreign States Immunities Act, 1981 (South Africa)	046
Immunities And Privileges, 1984 (Malaŵi)	054
State Immunity Act, 1985 (Canada)	065
Foreign States Immunities Act, 1985 (Australia)	074
Inmunidad Jurisdiccional De Los Estados Extranjeros Ante Los Tribunales Argentinos, 1995 (Argentina)	088
Law on Judicial Immunity from Compulsory Measures Concerning the Property of Foreign Central Banks, 2005 (China)	090
Foreign States Immunity Law, 2008 (Israel)	091
Act on the Civil Jurisdiction of Japan with Respect to a Foreign State, 2009 (Japan)	096
Organic Law on Privileges and Immunities of Foreign States etc. , 2015 (Spain)	103

A COLLECTION OF NATIONAL LEGISLATION AND INTERNATIONAL LEGAL INSTRUMENTS ON STATE IMMUNITY